Democracy
in Poland

Democracy in Poland

Second Edition

Marjorie Castle
and
Ray Taras

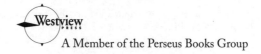

A Member of the Perseus Books Group

Copyright © 2002 by Westview Press, A Member of the Perseus Books Group

Westview Press books are available at special discounts for bulk purchases in the United States by corporations, institutions, and other organizations. For more information, please contact the Special Markets Department at The Perseus Books Group, 11 Cambridge Center, Cambridge MA 02142, or call (617) 252-5298.

Published in 2002 in the United States of America by Westview Press, 5500 Central Avenue, Boulder, Colorado 80301–2877, and in the United Kingdom by Westview Press, 12 Hid's Copse Road, Cumnor Hill, Oxford OX2 9JJ

Find us on the World Wide Web at www.westviewpress.com

A CIP catalog record for this book is available from the Library of Congress.

ISBN 0-8133-3995-2 (hc) ; 0-8133-3935-9 (pbk.)

The paper used in this publication meets the requirements of the American National Standard for Permanence of Paper for Printed Library Materials Z39.48–1984.

10   9   8   7   6   5   4   3   2   1

Contents

List of Tables and Figures

Tables

Figures

List of Acronyms

AK	Home Army (Armia Krajowa)
AWS	Solidarity Electoral Action (Akcja Wyborcza Solidarność)
AWSP	Solidarity Electoral Action—Right (Akcja Wyborcza Solidarność—Prawica)
BBWR	Nonparty Bloc for Reform (Bezpartyjny Blok Wspierania Reform)
CBOS	Center for Public Opinion Research (Centrum Badania Opinii Społecznej)
ChDIIIRP	Christian Democracy of the Third Republic (Chrześcijańska Demokracja III Rzeczypospolitej)
Ind.	Independent
GL	People's Guard (Gwardia Ludowa)
KdP	Coalition for Poland (Koalicja dla Polski)
KLD	Liberal Democratic Congress (Kongres Liberalno-Demokratyczny)
KO	Citizens' Committees (Komitety Obywatelskie)
KOR	Workers' Defense Committee (Komitet Obrony Robotników)
KPN	Confederation for an Independent Poland (Konfederacja Polski Niepodległej)
LPR	League of Polish Families (Liga Polskich Rodzin)
OBOP	Public Opinion Survey Center (Ośrodek Badania Opinii Publicznej)
OPZZ	National Trade Union Accord (Ogólnopolskie Porozumienie Związków Zawodowych)
PC	Center Accord (Porozumienie Centrum)
PiS	Law and Justice (Prawo i Sprawiedliwość)
PKWN	Polish Committee of National Liberation (Polski Komitet Wyzwolenia Narodowego)
PL	Peasant Accord (Porozumienie Ludowe)

PO	Civic Platform (Platforma Obywatelska)
PP	Polish Accord (Porozumienie Polski)
PPPP	Polish Beer Lovers' Party (Polska Partia Przyjaciół Piwa)
PPR	Polish Workers' Party (Polska Partia Robotnicza)
PPS	Polish Socialist Party (Polska Partia Socjalistyczna)
PRL	People's Republic of Poland (Polska Rzeczpospolita Ludowa)
PSL	Polish Peasant Party (Polskie Stronnictwo Ludowe)
PZPR	Polish United Workers Party (Polska Zjednoczona Partia Robotnicza)
RdR	Movement for the Republic (Ruch dla Rzeczypospolitej)
ROAD	Citizens' Movement for Democratic Action (Ruch Obywatelski Akcja Demokratyczna)
ROP	Movement for Poland's Reconstruction (Ruch Odrodzenia Polski)
ROPCiO	Committee for the Defense of Human and Civil Rights (Ruch Obrony Praw Człowieka i Obywatela)
S	Solidarity (Solidarność)
SD	Democratic Party (Stronnictwo Demokratyczne)
SDKPiL	Social Democratic Party of the Kingdom of Poland and Lithuania (Socjaldemokracja Królestwa Polskiego i Litwy)
SdRP	Social Democracy of the Republic of Poland (Socjaldemokracja Rzeczypospolitej Polskiej)
SLD	Alliance of the Democratic Left (Sojusz Lewicy Demokratycznej)
SO	Self-Defense (Samoobrona)
UD	Democratic Union (Unia Demokratyczna)
UP	Union of Labor (Unia Pracy)
UPR	Union of Political Realism (Unia Polityki Realnej)
UW	Union of Freedom (Unia Wolności)
WAK	Catholic Electoral Action (Wyborcza Akcja Katolicka)
ZChN	Christian National Union (Zjednoczenie Chrześcijańsko Narodowe)
ZSL	United Peasant Party (Zjednoczone Stronnictwo Ludowe)

Acknowledgments

The list of colleagues, friends, and family who have helped each of us make sense of the complexities of Polish politics is too long to enumerate here. Conversations with and advice from Mirosława Grabowska, Tadeusz Szawiel, and Jane Curry have been invaluable. Others who have helped shape our understanding of these phenomena include Ryszard and Marysia Holzer, Tomek and Beata Wróblewski, Krzysztof Jasiewicz, Radosław Markowski, Stanisław Gebethner, Wojciech Maziarski, Maciej Słomczyński, Regina Kacprzyk, and Joanna Szczęsna. Over the years Philippe Schmitter has been a source of intellectual inspiration. Piotr Pawlikowski has always been available for checking the nuance of an idiom, searching his memory for a long-lost name, or providing encouragement.

We would like to express gratitude to the Polish–U.S. Fulbright Commission and the Collegium Civitas for providing support that allowed one of the authors to spend the spring of 2001 in Warsaw researching this book. The University of Utah supported a research visit to Poland for the 2000 presidential elections. We are grateful to our project editor at Westview, Katharine Chandler, for her conscientious attention to this book. Our copyeditor, John Thomas, offered comments that were both constructive and witty, adding to the ease of the production process.

We also thank Krzysztof and Gabriela for their patience and forbearance. They were an inspiration to us both.

Introduction: Understanding a Functioning Democracy

The Contemporary Landscape of Poland

Not everyone is aware that Poland is one of the largest countries in Europe. In terms of size, its surface area—which is roughly hexagonal—of 120,700 square miles is slightly larger than Italy but somewhat smaller than today's Germany. Its population of close to 40 million is greater than that of other Central European states such as the Czech Republic, Slovakia, Hungary, Croatia, or Slovenia, as well as that of the three Baltic states put together.[1] Four of its cities have populations of close to one million or higher: the capital, Warsaw; the industrial centers of Katowice and Łódź; and the historic former capital, Cracow. The country is divided into 16 provinces (*wojewódstwo*), 308 counties (*powiat*) and county towns, and 2,489 rural districts (*gmina*). Poland's urban population has increased from 34 percent of the total population in 1946 to 62 percent in 2000.[2]

Much of the country lies in the great central lowlands of Europe, which are intersected by the Vistula River, which flows approximately from south to north. Poland has no real natural borders in the west or east, though the Oder and Neisse Rivers provide a general demarcation line between Germany and Poland, and the Bug River and Pripet marshlands roughly delimit the eastern frontier. The Baltic Sea to the north gives Poland an extended coastline and a number of seaports, the largest being Gdańsk and Szczecin. The Carpathian mountain range to the south sets Poland off from the Czech Republic, with which it shares its longest border today. Going clockwise, Poland's seven neighbors since the emergence of new states in the region in the early 1990s are the Russian Federation (specifically, the Kaliningrad region), Lithuania, Belarus, Ukraine, Slovakia, the Czech Republic, and Germany.

In 1995 close to 7 percent of the population aged 15 and over had gone to college; over half had gone to secondary or technical schools; one-third had finished only primary school; and 6 percent had not completed elementary school. However, the number of college graduates more than doubled between 1995 and 2000 as more private institutions—many with less rigorous academic standards—were opened.

In 1999 the average life expectancy for a female was 77.5 years and for a male 68.8 years. Close to one-fifth of the population was under 15, making Poland a more youthful society than, for example, France or Germany. Polish society was exceptional in its ethnic and religious homogeneity: 98 percent were ethnic Poles and 96 percent were Catholic. The largest minorities were Germans and Ukrainians.

The Gross Domestic Product (GDP) per capita in Poland in 1999 was $6,800. Since that year the value of the *złoty*, the Polish currency unit, has ranged from four to four-and-a-half to the dollar. Currency stabilization is owed in part to the emergence of a dynamic private sector. In 1999 it employed nearly three times as many people as the public sector. By contrast, in 1990 the numbers of workers in each were nearly equal, and of course under communism almost everyone worked for a state enterprise. What has not changed dramatically since 1989 is the proportion of Poles working on the land—just over one in four in 1999. The proportion of Poles employed in the industrial sector was nearly the same (27 percent). The expanding service sector accounted for the remaining 46 percent of the labor force.

Women made up 48 percent of the workforce and on average earned less than men in 1999; in no occupation did females earn as much as males, with the gap ranging from just 20 *złoty* per month for office clerks to over 1,100 *złoty* for legislators, top officials, and managers. The average monthly salary in 1999 was 1,700 *złoty*. Wages in the public sector (1,830 *złoty*) were higher than in the risk-filled private one (1,580 *złoty*). The best-paid employees in the state sector were coal miners (3,000 *złoty*); they earned the same amount as the highest-paid group in the private sector, financial analysts. Among the poorest-paid workers were those in agriculture, fisheries, catering, and health care (making between 1,200 and 1,500 *złoty*). With well over 10 percent of the labor force unemployed throughout most of the 1990s, any job was a relief for many living in depressed regions. While women consistently suffered from a higher unemployment rate than men, this disparity reached unprecedented proportions in 1999, when 13 percent of men but 18 percent of women were without a job.

The country's major mineral resources have been coal, copper, lead, sulfur, and natural gas. Its largest industries are chemical and petrochemical, food processing, metallurgy, and shipbuilding. Livestock farming includes pigs, cattle, and poultry, and crops include cereals, potatoes, and sugar beets. Following the transition to a market economy in the 1990s, commerce, trade, and finance have become important sectors.

The Study of Polish Democracy

Poland was a communist-party-ruled authoritarian state from shortly after the end of World War II to the summer of 1989, when a noncommunist government was formed after legislative elections. Today it is a democratic state and is bordered by countries with a mix of governments: in the West by a consolidated German democracy, in the south by consolidating democracies in the Czech and Slovak Republics, and in the east and north by large quasi-democratic states, Ukraine and Russia. Two other eastern neighbors offer a study in contrasts: Lithuania has made rapid democratic progress since shaking off Soviet rule, while Belarus has remained mired in Soviet-type authoritarianism.

Scholarly writing about politics in Central and Eastern Europe in recent years has been concerned with the protracted *transition* from communism to democracy and capitalism. The historic changes that took place in the region in 1989 have justifiably inspired extensive research aimed at explaining why the Soviet bloc suddenly crumbled and parliamentary democracy quickly found many supporters.

In contrast, this book examines the democratic processes in Poland at the start of a new century. The focus is on what the country has achieved since 1989. To be sure, it is important at the outset to consider the shaping of Poland over the centuries, and especially during the tumultuous twentieth century, which on three occasions gave Poles hope for the geopolitical space necessary to chart an independent and democratic course, but on two occasions (the outbreak of World War II and the Soviet conquest at its end) just as quickly dashed them. It is essential here to analyze Poland's communist period, four decades that can still evoke both disdain and nostalgia. The historic events of 1989—taking the country from roundtable negotiations in February between communist rulers and the dissidents they jailed, to enactment by parliament in late December of shock economic therapy that produced a functioning free market in a matter of years—need examination.

But what we want to learn about most is what Polish democracy is all about today. Who are the principal political players? What are the rules and outcomes of the democratic games? How does Polish society pick and choose between political actors, and on what basis? What are the arenas in which democracy is played out? What are the policy challenges that Poland needs to meet in order to become a full partner in Europe?

The Study of Democracy

Many factors have been identified as crucial to the making of democracy.[3] In his study of the most recent wave of democratization, the political scientist Samuel Huntington compiles a lengthy, though not exhaustive, list of factors that scholars have singled out as promoting democratization:

- a high overall level of economic wealth;
- relatively equal distribution of income and/or wealth;
- a market economy;
- economic development and social modernization;
- a feudal aristocracy at some point in the history of a society;
- the absence of feudalism in the society;
- a strong bourgeoisie ("no bourgeoisie, no democracy," in Barrington Moore's succinct formulation);
- a strong middle class;
- high levels of literacy and education;
- an instrumental rather than consumatory culture;
- Protestantism;
- social pluralism and strong intermediate groups;
- the development of political contestation before the expansion of political participation;
- democratic authority structures within social groups, particularly those closely connected to politics;
- low levels of civil violence;
- low levels of political polarization and extremism;
- political leaders committed to democracy;
- experience as a British colony;
- traditions of toleration and compromise;
- occupation by a pro-democratic foreign power;
- influence of a pro-democratic foreign power;
- an elite desire to emulate democratic nations;
- traditions of respect for law and individual rights;

- communal (ethnic, racial, religious) homogeneity;
- communal (ethnic, racial, religious) heterogeneity;
- consensus on political and social values; and
- absence of consensus on political and social values.[4]

A number of conclusions can be drawn from this checklist. First, contending theories of democratization are occasionally contradictory; some rest on the presence of certain factors, for example, ethnic homogeneity, and others on the absence of these same factors. Further, as Huntington points out, although virtually all factors offer plausible explanations for democratization, each is likely to be relevant to only a few cases. Thus, being Protestant, being a British colony, and not experiencing feudalism severely limit the number of states we can examine that may or may not have been pushed toward democracy as a result of such factors. Some explanatory factors are themselves in need of explanation. For example, the existence of pro-democratic elites inevitably raises the subject of the causes for such elite orientation. Some variables seem to be as much the outcome as the cause of democracy, such as low levels of civil violence or respect for individual rights.

The list overlooks a few powerful explanatory frameworks. Marxist theories highlight capitalist exploitation and deep structures of power in the modern state as sources of a democratic impulse; even today, their arguments cannot be dismissed out of hand. Post-Marxist theories look to metaclass forms of domination and the postmaterialist demand for direct participation as factors that can effect democratic breakthroughs. The Zapatista movement that emerged in southern Mexico in January 1994 is an example: It is not a classic revolutionary organization but a nonclass movement pressing for the empowerment of Indian groups and the democratization of regional and national politics. Was there really no connection between the rise of the Zapatistas and the end of one-party rule in Mexico in 2000?

Postmodernist explanations can provide new items for the checklist of factors triggering democratization. They explore new forms of empowerment that can replace conventional representational structures that, they contend, depict an outside world that does not exist. A search for new understandings of political self-determination and freedom, identities and consciousness raising, popular control and direct democracy is designed to reassert the primacy of the subject, and of human agency generally, in politics. Thus postmodernism would stress the interconnectedness, for example, of the democratization thrust and feminists' search for truth and identity.

Are there any single-factor theories of democratization that are plausible? Late-twentieth-century history seems to have substantiated classical economist Adam Smith's stress on the intimate relationship between liberty and commerce.[5] Max Weber employed somewhat different logic—arguing that capitalism promoted democracy mainly by separating political from economic power—in reaching a similar conclusion.[6] In the same spirit, Barrington Moore was close to formulating an iron law for democratization theorists when he asserted that there can be no democracy without a bourgeoisie.[7] None of these writers would have overstated their findings, however, and they would undoubtedly have qualified their propositions by noting that the existence of commerce or independent economic power or an entrepreneurial middle class constituted a necessary if insufficient condition of democracy.

Even after the most recent wave of democratic transitions, scholars are still debating what configuration of institutions is most likely to consolidate democracy. Nevertheless, late-transiting states stand to benefit from historical experience; certain institutional formulae have been developed for crafting democracy, and democratic transition management is now being conducted with greater confidence. Political scientist Adam Przeworski has described what it takes for a democratic system to be sturdy: "Democracy is consolidated," he has written, "when it becomes self-enforcing, that is, when all the relevant political forces find it best to continue to submit their interests and values to the uncertain interplay of institutions."[8] There are many related tests of consolidated democracy—nearly all of which Poland can pass.[9] Technical criteria of democratic consolidation, such as holding at least two successive elections, providing for the alternation of parties in power, the renewal of government at regular intervals, and the replacement of at least one government by the opposition, have all been met in Poland. Likewise the processual aspect—bargaining and compromise between groups about power and policy—has characterized Poland's politics from 1989 to the present.

Writing of the study of regime change, Philippe Schmitter and Terry Karl underscore the importance of detachment from the minutiae of transition:

The one thing that *cannot* be done is to take refuge in *empirie*—in the diligent collection of facts without any guidance from theories and models. Given the sheer volume of data, not to mention their frequently contradictory referents, without some sense of priorities and categories for classification no analyst is likely to be able to make much sense of what is going on.[10]

Their advice is for scholars to spend more effort on conceptualization than on diligent data gathering. This book, we hope, combines the two, using theoretical questions to guide our selection and presentation of data.

In the late eighteenth century, Alexis de Tocqueville set a problematic for himself, which he outlined in Chapter 9 of *Democracy in America*. Entitled "The Main Causes Tending to Maintain a Democratic Republic in the United States," he proposed three general categories of causes: "The first is the peculiar and accidental situation in which Providence has placed the Americans. Their laws are the second. Their habits and mores are the third."[11] For contemporary Poland as much as for eighteenth-century America, geopolitics, institutions, and political culture count in assessing prospects for democratic consolidation. But this is where the similarity ends. Democracy in twenty-first-century Poland is hardly comparable to American democracy forged in a much earlier era. Poland is not a continental power that claims a manifest destiny. And politics is infinitely more complex in the twenty-first century.

The structure of this book follows from our purposes. The first three chapters present various aspects of the historical legacies shaping Polish politics today. First we present the varied historical traditions and patterns that shaped the Polish nation up to the close of World War II. Then we examine the communist system itself—its political, geopolitical, and economic logics, as well as the political culture and structures that it produced. Our review of past legacies concludes with an analysis of a relatively short period of time that has left a lasting imprint on Polish institutions and political life, the transition from communist rule.

The fourth through seventh chapters address our primary concern, Polish politics today. Given the youth of Poland's current democracy we start not with democratic institutions but with political players. As parties scholar Herbert Kitschelt has observed, in young democracies the rules of the game are still endogenous to the competition, still amenable to alteration by actors seeking advantage.[12] Thus we look first at political party elites, parties themselves, and the other groups that play political roles. Here in the fourth chapter we find that the fundamental feature of the Polish political scene is a historical-cultural cleavage (that is, a cleavage based on relationships to the past and to religion), which deeply divides elites.

As we move on to society, the "played upon," in the following chapter we continue our focus on cleavages, the lines that divide Poles in their public lives as voters and sometime protestors. The sixth chapter presents the existing political and economic arenas and shows how they still are—as Kitschelt argues—the products of contemporary politics just as much as they themselves shape political games. Finally, we examine four major policy challenges that these actors, operating within these political institutions, must confront.

The study of Poland's democratic system is, we feel, an exciting and important undertaking. If, as some experts feel, Poland more than any other country in the region really represents the postcommunist future, we need to be attentive to what has made it successful, as well as be aware of what pitfalls lie ahead.

1

Historic Discontinuities: Shaping Poland's Political Traditions

What others say about a particular nation can offer insights that self-narration may lack. How has Poland's history been viewed by its largest neighbor? Early in the nineteenth century, the Russian poet Alexander Pushkin remarked that the history of Poland was and ought to be a disaster. In 1939, Russia's Foreign Minister, Vyacheslav Molotov, contemptuously referred to Poland as the bastard offspring of the Versailles Treaty. Both observations came at times when Poland had been dismantled as an independent state. After Pushkin's death, Poland was not to reappear on the map of Europe until 1918. After the nonaggression pact that Molotov signed with Hitler, which included a protocol to carve up Poland, the country disappeared as an independent state from the political map of Europe until the Soviet-imposed communist regime was toppled in 1989. But as if to remind Poles that their future was still not secure, nationalist firebrand Vladimir Zhirinovsky exhorted Russians in the mid-1990s to reclaim Poland, together with Finland and Alaska, for Moscow.

A nation's history does not end when it has lost statehood and independence. Historical grievances often serve as powerful forces for national mobilization long after the events in question have passed. The cynical eighteenth-century partitions of Poland, like the forcible mid-twentieth-century incorporation of Poland into the Soviet political bloc, have remained points of reference for many Poles and color their world outlook.

Relations with Russia over the last two centuries have deeply affected Poland's political development. But the nation's efforts at establishing constitutional rule, checking the power of its leaders, modernizing its social and economic structures, and securing its borders also need to be examined if we are to make sense of the democratic political system that came to replace communism. This chapter considers the importance of the many other regimes—monarchies, republics, and foreign occupations—experienced by Poland before the communists came to power.

Beginnings: Dynastic Poland

Even though a vernacular language is by itself not the only or even most important criterion for nationhood, it can serve as a crucial marker of national identity. Polish belongs to the western group of Slavic languages that includes Czech and Slovak. Poles form part of an even wider Slavic world that encompasses an eastern linguistic group—Russian, Belarus, and Ukrainian—and a southern one—Serbian, Croatian, Slovene, and Bulgarian. Much historical evidence suggests that the original home of all the Slavs was territory that came to be ruled by Polish kings around the fourteenth century.

The ancestors of the Poles were drawn from such different ethnographic groups as the Polanie (literally, "dwellers of the plain"), Pomeranians ("coast dwellers"), Mazovians, and Silesians. The conditions initially promoting the physical security of these tribes simultaneously served to retard the establishment of a unified state. As one eminent Polish historian observed, "Dwelling in the center of the Slav world, removed from the routes of the great migrations and even from the great trade routes, the tribes which were to form the Polish nation only experienced later the grave difficulties and dangers that beset their neighbors."[1] When the Germanic threat became serious, the various tribes submitted to the leadership of the Polanie and this name was soon employed to designate all of these groups. Their relative security as well as geographic dispersion delayed the founding of a Polish state until the second half of the tenth century—about a century after Slavic states had emerged in Carinthia (in what is now Austria), Moravia, Kievan Rus, and Bulgaria.

Polish history is generally dated from 966, the year Mieszko I of the Piast dynasty converted to Christianity and became the nation's first king. External relations during Mieszko's twenty-six-year reign—he died in 992—prefigured later Polish history. His conversion was designed to strengthen Poland's alliance with Bohemia in the face of a Germanic threat, yet it was a Rus invasion in 981 that stripped the country of much of its lands. Mieszko then turned to the Apostolic See for protection and obtained its recognition of Poland as an independent church province and separate kingdom. But it was his son Bolesław Chrobry (967–1025) who did most to consolidate Piast rule over the Polish tribes, symbolized by his coronation on Easter Day 1025. Poland's first chronicler, Gallus Anonymus, described Bolesław as "the father of these lands, defender, lord."[2]

The last ruler of the Piast dynasty was Kazimierz the Great (1310–1370), who ushered in Poland's Golden Age. His achievements included the establishment of Central Europe's second university in Cracow in 1364 (after the one in Prague in 1348), the first codification of Polish law, the promotion of trade and commerce between Polish cities, the settlement of previously uninhabited regions, increased protection for oppressed peoples (such as Jews fleeing persecution in Western Europe and peasants threatened with famine), the construction of fortified castles along Polish borders, and the creation of a permanent force of mercenaries to defend these borders. Kazimierz also challenged the Order of the Teutonic Knights at the height of its power and concluded a favorable peace treaty restoring Pomerania to Poland and giving the country access to the Baltic Sea. There is an apt saying that Kazimierz inherited a Poland built of wood and bequeathed to posterity a Poland made of stone.

After his death the crown of the Piasts was offered to the Hungarian dynasty. It was bestowed upon a twelve-year-old Hungarian princess, Jadwiga, who was then given in marriage to the favorite of the Polish nobility, Jagiełło, Grand Duke of Lithuania. This union profoundly shaped the subsequent political development of the Polish state. The resulting Polish–Lithuanian political union transformed the ethnically homogeneous state of the Piasts into a multinational one, and established expansive new frontiers that extended from the Baltic to the Black Sea. Large populations of Ukrainians and Belorussians were incorporated into the state. The structure of power within the new kingdom also dramatically changed. Jagiełło had been chosen by the nobility, and from then on the Polish throne was to be subject to elective confirmation by this class. In 1386 Jagiełło was formally elected king, baptized into Catholicism, married to the initially disconsolate Jadwiga, and given an elaborate coronation ceremony. The dynastic transfer consummated in that year produced, then, enormous territorial, ethnic, and structural shifts in the Polish state. It also made possible one of the most glorious military victories in Polish and Lithuanian history—the final defeat of the Teutonic Order at the battle of Grunwald in 1410.

In the second half of the fifteenth century, Poland's internal politics shifted toward a type of democracy exercised by and for the nobility. At this time regional assemblies (*sejmiki*) began to assert influence in central affairs, thereby increasing gentry encroachment on the power of the wealthy magnates. Although the nobility, or *szlachta*, had generally accepted the legal equality of everyone in its ranks regardless of individual wealth or power, this did not preclude political conflict between groups within this class. By 1493 the Sejm (or national parliament) had been divided into an upper chamber, or Senate, consisting of bishops and high-ranking magnates, and a lower Chamber of Deputies representing the lesser gentry. This latter group made up close to 10 percent of the total population and thereby represented the largest enfranchised class in all of Europe; only 2 percent of Russia's population and 1 percent of France's were enfranchised at this time. The Chamber of Deputies also included token representation for the burgher class, drawn exclusively from the capital, Cracow. Conflict between the two chambers and the strata they represented became a distinguishing feature of Polish politics.

The Polish nobility was a remarkably heterogeneous class at this time. As a historian noted, "In it were the great lords, holders of the highest positions in the state, owners of substantial landed estates, possessors of considerable wealth. . . . At the other end of the spectrum were the poor gentry, descendants of medieval knights, warriors or courtiers, entitled to noble rank and privileges but frequently possessing little or no land."[3] Members of the first group, the magnates, disposed of exceptional power as a result of wealth and office. Accordingly, they "acted as the focus of political activity, as the center around which factions formed; they were the bridges between the central government and the provincial nobility. . . . In many spheres of activity they simply replaced the functions of the royal court and the central government."[4] Not surprisingly, the monarch often sought out the lower nobility as allies to check the power of the magnates, but the royal pursuit of *absolutum dominium* was irreconcilable with the self-interest of the *szlachta*.

As its power was increasing, this ruling gentry became conscious of Poland's role as *antemurale christianitatis*—Roman Catholicism's eastern-most bulwark. Over the next centuries, this Polish version of manifest destiny, or mission, came to be given a secular, political interpretation as well. Poland was viewed as the outpost of European civilization beyond which Russian and Asiatic culture began. As a country at the crossroads of Western and Eastern civilizations, it had to deal with threats both from the Teutonic Order and from the Mongols, Tatars, and Turks to the east. A philosophy emerged that became known as Sarmatianism. This name was derived from the ancient tribe that had lived on the banks of the Dniester River seven centuries before Christ. Jan Długosz, a historian of Poland writing in the fifteenth century, gave credence to this myth by recounting how the inhabitants of proto-Slavonic lands had conquered local tribes and thus emerged as the ruling elite. The Sarmatian ideology claimed a special mission for Poland—a shield protecting Christianity from paganism. The crowning glory of this historic mission took place in 1683 when King Jan Sobieski defeated the Turkish armies outside of Vienna, thereby saving Christian Europe from Islam.

The gentry in the Commonwealth of Poland invoked its supposed Sarmatian origins to justify its assuming all the obligations associated with Poland's manifest destiny. In the first place the Sarmatian was a heroic knight and defender of the faith and the fatherland. In addition, the myth of the *szlachta*'s common ancestry contributed to the integration of otherwise diverse ranks of the nobility and made other differentiating factors such as language spoken, religion practiced, or wealth accumulated less important. Furthermore, the Sarmatian myth promoted cultural homogeneity within the Commonwealth and led to widespread Polonization of the gentry of Lithuania and Ruthenia (Ukraine).

Two largely unintended consequences followed from the Sarmatian myth. First, Polish burghers and peasants were not treated as integral parts of the nation because their ancestry was considered non-Sarmatian and therefore different. As with Athenian democracy, the exclusion of certain people from the community and the denial of their political rights were not seen as in contradiction with the notion of democracy. So long as all noblemen enjoyed equal privileges and responsibilities, the crucial test of *szlachta* democracy was passed. But *not* utilizing common ethnicity as the basis for nationhood was eventually to produce mixed foci of identity, divided loyalties, and political tensions within the Polish state.

The second by-product of Sarmatianism was, paradoxically, the "'easternization' of Polish national consciousness," as the historian Andrzej Walicki has contended. Collaboration between the Polish elite and the Polonized elites of Lithuania and Ukraine was pursued at the expense of contacts with the West. Moreover, according to Walicki,

> The Sarmatian ideology developed the concept of a cultural uniqueness of "Sarmatia," its fundamental difference from everything Western. The

traditional view of Poland as the "bulwark of Christianity" ceased to be identical with perceiving Poland as a part and parcel of the West. On the contrary: the ideologists of Sarmatianism constantly warned their compatriots against Western royalism and moral corruption.[5]

Whereas republicanism seemed to locate Poland squarely in the Western European tradition, Sarmatianism pulled the country in the opposite direction, toward the east. These countervailing tendencies have affected Polish politics up to the present. That is why admission into the European Union would mark a historical *caesura*: Poland would, probably irreversibly, turn its back on the Sarmatian myth.

Given Poland's renewed ambitions since the 1990s to become an integral part of Europe, the controversy over Sarmatianism has intensified. A leading historian, Janusz Tazbir, asked rhetorically how long the West expected Poles to serve as the eastern bulwark of Western civilization. He questioned whether Western Europe had ever treated Poland as a full-fledged European country.[6] He noted that in the fifteenth and sixteenth centuries Polish kings readily waged wars against the Turks, and in the seventeenth century Poland drove back invasions launched by Turks and Tatars. Yet the only recognition of these historic exploits by an ungrateful Western Europe was peripheral status that provided little satisfaction to Polish leaders. Similarly, up to the eighteenth century the *szlachta* had been convinced that Europe would never permit Poland to be divided. In fact, of course, Europe both permitted and confirmed Poland's dismemberment. A skepticism about Western Europe's real commitment to Poland's security has represented a legacy of that distant period.

Democratic Breakthrough:
The Republican Commonwealth

Poland was an intact kingdom until the partitioning that began in the late eighteenth century. At first blush monarchy would seem to be incompatible with the idea of republican government. But the king's power was severely restricted by the gentry and in some ways he was limited to functions not unlike those performed by a modern ceremonial head of state. The Polish nobility was convinced of the superiority of its representative, republican-style system and the country became identified with *szlachta* democracy rather than monarchy. And despite the *antemurale christianitatis* idea, this nascent democratic order also limited the influence of the Catholic Church in state matters. As one scholar put it, "*Szlachta* democracy of the federalist republic of nobles frustrated both centralized absolutism and the identification of church and state. Early modern Poland became a haven for dissenting faiths fleeing generalized religious warfare in Europe."[7]

When compared with some of the absolutist, monarchical, and theocratic systems found elsewhere in Europe at the time, Poland's political system seemed exceptional indeed. The Latin term *res publica* (in Polish, *rzeczpospolita*) was used by nobles to suggest this political system's direct descent from the Roman Republic, much in the way that Thomas Jefferson associated fledgling American democracy with Roman origins.

If political power was not concentrated in the hands of any individual or office, did Polish political culture of the period reflect both a relatively liberal and democratic ethos? The sixteenth-century Reformation in Poland, even though encompassing only a small minority of the population, nudged the country toward increased liberalism, seeming naturally to complement the country's developing democratic features. Formal steps toward greater tolerance were taken when, first, legal recognition was extended to Protestantism in 1555 and then, second, the Confederation of Warsaw proclaimed the principles of religious toleration and religious equality in 1573. The supposed stranglehold of the Catholic Church on politics was never as complete as has been commonly assumed.

The sixteenth century also marked the Golden Age of Polish culture, which was contemporaneous with the Polish Renaissance. The country's capital, Cracow, and its royal court, seated in nearby Wawel Castle, became a cosmopolitan center for the arts—this at a time when Ivan the Terrible ruled Russia. This was the age of the astronomer Nicolaus Copernicus, the lyric poet Jan Kochanowski, and the prose writer regarded as the father of Polish literature, Mikołaj Rey.

But even as Polish political society was becoming more liberal, conflict with despotically ruled Russia appeared to be inevitable. The Polish–Lithuanian kingdom had been anchored in a union personified by the king, but more tangible and durable foundations were needed to fend off Muscovite ambitions in the Baltic region. In 1569 the Union of Lublin sought to institutionalize the relationship by requiring that the parliaments of Poland and Lithuania meet jointly to enact legislation. The site of the meetings was to be Warsaw, a town roughly equidistant from the two capitals, Cracow and Vilnius. A short time later, in 1596, Warsaw officially became the new capital of the kingdom.

The Union of Lublin proved to be of exceptional significance when Zygmunt II died in 1572 without leaving an heir, thereby putting an end to the Jagiellon dynasty. The gentry assembled to select a successor and decided to adopt a radical new principle, "one nobleman, one vote," as the method for electing the Polish monarch. This device became the political cornerstone of the post-Jagiellonian Republican Commonwealth; a more accurate term was democratic kingdom. Power was now formally vested in the *szlachta*.

Accordingly, in 1573, some 50,000 members representing all ranks of the nobility convened in Warsaw to elect a king. They chose a Frenchman, Henri de Valois, who proved to be not a wise choice. Within a year he had become disillusioned with *szlachta* democracy, which from his perspective produced little but strife, and he fled to France, where after the sudden death of his brother a more secure throne awaited him. In 1575 another convocation had to be held, and after a bitter dispute over rival candidates the *szlachta* again looked to Hungary and again was not disappointed. The Transylvanian prince Stefan Batory was chosen, and though he ruled Poland for just over a decade, he became legendary for his exploits in wars with Russia. Under Batory's rule the Commonwealth's eastern territories were more secure than ever before or after.

Heartened by victories over Russia, the rulers of the Commonwealth hatched elaborate schemes designed to extend Polish influence into the tsarist court itself. The figure of False Dimitri, an obscure Russian who had arrived in Poland with claims to the throne of Muscovy, served as a convenient pretext for king Zygmunt III Vasa, crowned as Batory's successor in 1587, to mount a campaign against Russia. Zygmunt wanted to incorporate Russia into the Polish Commonwealth and convert its heathen people to Catholicism. His early successes were as impressive as they were short-lived: In 1610 Polish armies captured Smolensk and briefly held Moscow.

The Polish king's power in Russia seemed boundless when he had his son Władysław chosen as tsar. But this arrangement proved untenable, as was a fallback one. "False Dimitri" was named tsar and his Polish wife, Marina Mniszech, became tsarina. But they occupied their thrones in the Kremlin for all of ten days! Shortly after, the Polish garrison was driven out of Moscow, and in 1613 the Russian boyars chose Mikhail Romanov to lead the country out of its Time of Troubles. The Romanov dynasty ruled over an ever-expanding Russian empire until 1917, but it is valuable to remember that it was the threat from Poland that had indirectly brought them to the throne. It is hard to believe that at the beginning of the seventeenth century the balance of power between Poland and Russia was just the reverse of what it was to become later on.

By the mid-seventeenth century the Republican Commonwealth was more expansive than ever, thereby also making it more vulnerable to the enemies surrounding it. To make matters worse, Poland's ruling elite was more ethnically homogeneous than it had been under the Jagiellonian state. This served to buoy separatist tendencies among non-Polish nations. The country fell prey to the perils of imperial overstretch: It had overextended its rule and lacked the economic and military capacity to keep order in the multiethnic state.

A deteriorating military balance of power was directly responsible for ending Poland's great power status, but the country's political structure contributed immensely to its instability and the Commonwealth's eventual collapse. On the one hand, constitutional laws incorporating the ideas of liberty, equality, and government based on the consent of a significant part of the nation enshrined the important principle of the rule of law—*non Rex sed lex regnat* ("no King but law reigns"). The reason for this was that the gentry's interests were best served by a system that asserted libertarian, republican values. On the other hand, such loose political arrangements, though arguably ahead of their time, contributed to a general breakdown of authority and to a popular belief that Poland was governed by unrule (*Polska nierządem stoi*). Indeed, foreign adversaries skillfully used the argument that Poland was ungovernable to justify its dismemberment.

The procedure for electing kings, whether to confirm them in office as under the Jagiellon dynasty or to choose them from a slate of candidates as after 1572, produced intrigues and infighting. The system compelled the monarch to earn power and prestige rather than to assume them ex officio. Another destabilizing mechanism was the *pacta conventa*, which identified the king's personal obligations to the country in the key areas of foreign policy and finance. Even before his coronation he had to pledge that he would abide by the terms set by the lower chamber. The related Henrician Articles, promulgated by Henri de Valois in 1573, further obliged the monarch to convene the Sejm regularly and obtain the advice of its permanent council at all times. Failure to comply with the articles freed the gentry from its oath of allegiance and officially sanctioned opposition to the king (*de non praestanda obedientia*). As if these were not sufficient controls on royal power, already in 1430 the king had been obliged to recognize the principle of *neminem captivabimus nisi iure victum*, which granted all noblemen personal immunity from arrest until a court could pass sentence and prohibited the confiscation of their land without a court order. As a result, the monarch faced daunting legal obstacles when trying to undermine political opponents.

A number of other institutional arrangements undergirded *szlachta* democracy. At the beginning of the sixteenth century the Sejm passed the *incompatibilitas* act, which prohibited an individual from holding more than one high state office at a time. Moreover, lands formally belonging to the crown were to be managed by the Sejm, not the king. Already in 1505 the famous principle of *nihil novi* found expression in Polish jurisprudence; it meant that "nothing new" in the way of legislation could be enacted by the king unless it received the consent of both chambers. Finally, the sixteenth-century execution-of-law movement insisted that high state officials be held accountable to the gentry, an early form of transparency. This elaborate checks-and-balances system limiting the prerogatives of the monarch made the Polish state both more democratic and more prone to anarchy than any European state of the time.

These were not all the procedures and principles that undermined the viability of the Commonwealth. The institution of *confederatio* was first employed at the beginning of the fourteenth century but possibly may have had even more distant origins. It sanctioned the mobilization of groups of citizens, specifically nobles and burghers, for the redress of grievances. A group could also declare itself a confederation in order to advance its special interests; all that was required was a majority vote among those attending the assembly. In sum, "confederation was a legal procedure. It was undertaken in the name of the common good, by citizens acting in defense of the law, and conscious of its protection."[8] But by 1606 confederation had grown into something more, called *rokosz*, "a legalized insurrection whereby the nation in arms could even impeach the king."[9] In that year Zygmunt III Vasa, a monarch brought from Sweden and accustomed to much broader royal authority than the Polish nobility allowed, was threatened with deportation for failing to pay adequate attention to the wishes of the gentry. Although this episode— which produced bloodshed between royalist forces and rebels—came to be considered a regrettable misunderstanding, fear of absolute government had become so acute among the nobility that it led to the enshrinement of the most famous principle of the Polish Commonwealth, the *liberum veto*.

The crucial feature of this mechanism was the prerogative of any member of the Sejm to veto a proposed act. For a while resort to *liberum veto* was unnecessary because agreements were carefully worked out prior to Sejm sessions in order to secure unanimity. In 1580, however, the power of the Sejm to impose taxation was quashed when a disgruntled representative invoked this principle. Worse was to come: In 1652 all legislation enacted during a session of the Sejm was nullified when one nobleman cast a veto. Six years later the *liberum veto* was employed before the session had even begun, thereby paralyzing the actions of central government. Under August III (1733–1763) recourse to the principle had become so absurd that only one session of the Sejm was able to pass any legislation at all. As one historian reconstructed the *szlachta*'s reasoning in support of this principle, "The *liberum veto* would defend the sovereignty of the individual. God and Europe would defend that of the *Rzecz-pospolita*."[10] As we shall see, this reasoning proved flawed.

The sheer number of procedures designed as checks on autocracy inevitably engendered the opposite—political chaos and disorder. Some strata of the nobility began to interpret the principles of *de non praestanda obedientia*, *rokosz*, and *liberum veto* in conjunction. Taken together, they seemed to spell *liberum conspiro*—"the right to conspire against authority." The so-called Golden Freedom of the Polish nobility was increasingly perceived by leaders of other countries, in particular the Russian tsars, as a way to make the Polish Republic weak, disorganized, and divided. Members of the Polish nobility were played off against each other, a number of prominent nobles came to serve the interests of the Romanovs, and inherent anti-centralist tendencies in the system of government were exacerbated. Although the Polish state had devised an ingenious system of checks and balances meant to preserve the democracy of the gentry, this system also generated self-destructive tendencies that, when artfully exploited by its foes, were to spell the end of an independent Poland.

Reform and Breakdown:
The Destruction of the Commonwealth

While the institutional arrangements of the Commonwealth aggravated internal instability, it was a series of armed insurrections and invasions that led directly to the collapse of the state. The revolt of the Ukrainian Cossacks in 1648 triggered what is known as the "Deluge." In quick succession, Tatars, Turks, Russians, and Swedes went to war against Poland. The Swedish army swiftly overran the country and only the miraculous, last-ditch defense of the monastery at Częstochowa in 1655—attributed by devout Poles to the intercession of the Blessed Virgin whose icon, the Black Madonna, is kept there—turned the tide of war. Collaboration by some Polish magnates with foreign armies also produced a short but bitter civil war in 1665–1666.

The last of the Vasa kings, Jan Kazimierz, recognized the urgency of reform of the political system. He moved toward centralizing power and emancipating the serfs, but the nobility blocked these projects. In this period the Sarmatian myth was rekindled; once again the *szlachta* identified itself as the descendants of the ancient Sarmatians and invoked a kind of divine right of the nobility to govern. Jan Kazimierz's designs were thwarted and, like his French predecessor of a century earlier, the embattled monarch abdicated and left for France.

Jan Sobieski, the vanquisher of the Turks at Vienna in 1683, for a time halted the erosion of the Republic, but he nevertheless failed to recast the monarchy into the stronger, dynastic form that at this juncture might have served Poland better. He was bogged down in foreign wars for seventeen years and, paradoxically, his successes ultimately promoted the resurgence of the Habsburg empire more than they did that of his own country. Moreover, his lack of interest in the eastern borderlands cost Poland dearly. As the historian Norman Davies has written, "In 1686, at the whim of one wayward ambassador, the entire Ukraine, provisionally assigned to Muscovy since the truce of 1667, was needlessly abandoned. This one step . . . marked the transformation of little Muscovy into 'great Russia' and tipped the scales of power in Eastern Europe in Moscow's favor."[11]

The Saxon kings who reigned between 1697 and 1763 were generally absent from and uninterested in the country and this accelerated the process of political degeneration. The Saxon period was marked by dual elections, rival candidacies, and even dethronements and further weakened Poland's place in Europe. Even as unprecedented peace reigned in the country, Poland was becoming a pawn in the strategy of the Northern System—the coalition made up of Catherine the Great of Russia and Frederick II of Prussia.

In looking for reasons for Poland's collapse, we should not overlook social and ethnic factors in addition to political ones. Approximately 7 percent of the Polish population in 1791 was made up of burghers. Together with the clergy, who accounted for another 0.5 percent, they enjoyed considerable autonomy from the nobility and possessed legal status protected by royal charters, but played little part in central government (with the inevitable exception of the bishops). Moreover, though a few wealthy burghers could buy their way into *szlachta* ranks, social mobility between the estates—from peasant to burgher to nobleman—was negligible in the seventeenth and eighteenth centuries. In addition, peasant rebellions, particularly among the Cossacks, occurred early in the seventeenth century and should have served as a warning about spreading discontent among the rural population. But *szlachta* democracy stubbornly refused to alter the rigid system of social stratification right up to the death throes of the Republic.

The ethnic makeup of Poland also contributed to the erosion of national unity. Although the gentry in Lithuania and Ukraine was almost completely Polonized by the late eighteenth century, about half of the peasantry remained non-Polish, consisting of Ukrainians, Belorussians, and Lithuanians. Many towns that had been almost exclusively Polish until the sixteenth century now became ethnically mixed following an influx of German burghers, Dutch Mennonites, Silesian Protestants, and Jewish and Armenian merchants. Large Jewish communities located in urban areas (in addition to rural shtetls) were particularly distinctive in this period. Seeking a haven from the persecution they were suffering in much of Western Europe, Jews migrated in increasing numbers to Polish towns and their proportion of the urban population grew from approximately 10 percent in the early sixteenth century to as high as 80 percent in certain towns in eastern Poland by the eighteenth century. Given such change in social and ethnic structures, it is not surprising that the survival of the Polish state, identified as it had been almost exclusively with the *szlachta*, came under challenge.

Poland's last king was Stanisław August Poniatowski (1764–1795), whose reign corresponded with tsarist Russia's protectorate over Poland. It was Poniatowski's misfortune to preside over the series of partitions that eliminated the Polish state from the European map. Historians disagree whether he was merely a "creature"—in addition to being a lover— of Catherine the Great or an independent and patriotic leader. From the outset of his reign, he had to contend not only with the powerful Russian empress and with Frederick of Prussia but with his own incorrigible *szlachta*. The Sejm of 1767–1768 demonstrated its intransigence, for example, when it reaffirmed that the Polish state was based on five "eternal and invariable" principles: (1) the free election of kings, (2) the principle of *liberum veto*, (3) the nobility's right to renounce allegiance to the king, (4) the nobility's exclusive right to hold office, and (5) the nobility's dominion over the peasantry.[12] Unfortunately, within a few decades it became clear that neither these principles nor the state they governed were eternal and invariable.

Some of these principles were put into practice one last time when the Confederation of Bar rose up against the Polish king. Although quickly crushed with the help of outside Russian troops in 1771, the confederation had extraordinary political significance. It represented a final attempt by the *szlachta* to safeguard its privileged status. More importantly, it reflected the first stirrings of modern Polish nationalism. The uprising by the confederation revealed the military genius of Kazimierz Pułaski, who was to become an important figure in the American Revolutionary War. It also served as the pretext for the first partition undertaken by Russia, Prussia, and Austria of what was now dismissively termed the Republic of Anarchy. Finally, the confederation elicited a mixed assessment from French political philosopher Jean-Jacques Rousseau, who was commissioned to report on the country. In *The Government of Poland*, he reached this understated conclusion: "It is hard to understand how a state so oddly constituted can have survived for so long." But sensing imminent disaster for the Republic, Rousseau urged: "Establish the republic in the Poles' own hearts, so that it will live on in them despite anything your oppressors may do."[13] This was precisely what Poles had to do for the next century and a half.

The specific plans for annexing various parts of Poland were drawn up by Frederick II as early as 1768, but it was only in 1772 that a formal treaty specifying the lands to be partitioned was concluded. A year later, under duress, Poniatowski and the Sejm formally consented to the partition. The ostensible reason for the first partition was given in the preamble to the treaty:

> In the Name of the Most Holy Trinity! The spirit of faction, the troubles and internecine war which had shaken the Kingdom of Poland for so many years, and the Anarchy which acquires new strength every day . . . give just apprehension for expecting the total decomposition of the state. . . . At the same time, the Powers neighboring on the Republic are burdened with rights and claims which are as ancient as they are legitimate.[14]

The more the government of what remained of Poland tried to reform the country over the next two decades, the more determined were the partitioning powers to have done with Poland as quickly and completely as possible. Soon after the partition, the Sejm established the first Ministry of Education in Europe—the Commission of National Education. The Four-Year Sejm from 1788 to 1792 introduced unprecedented taxes on revenue from land and on ecclesiastical property. Local government was modernized and a standing army was established. The famous constitution of May 3, 1791, inspired by the emancipatory ideas of the French Revolution, granted burghers access to public office and representation in the Sejm. And although serfdom was not abolished, peasants were now extended "the protection of the law and the government." Poland was transformed from a nation of the gentry to a nation of proprietors and protected peasants.

Reformed in this way, Poland might have been able to foil the ambitions of the partitioning powers. The anarchy and decomposition of the state, cited in 1772 as justification for partition, would undoubtedly have been checked by the remarkable constitutional document of May 3. Fearing a revitalized Poland, Russian military forces confronted the new Polish standing army within a year. The threat of full-scale war led to several Polish magnates signing an act of confederation at Targowica in 1792. This disreputable confederation condemned the May 3 constitution and asked Russian troops to help put down what was viewed as rebellion. Poniatowski cast his lot in with the Targowica confederation. Although perhaps intended only as a political maneuver justified in terms of *raison d'état*, Poniatowski's action was to go down in Polish history as treason.

The second partition concluded between Russia and Prussia in 1793 reduced Poland to a rump state. Tadeusz Kościuszko's national insurrection of 1794 foundered and led to bloody reprisals by Russian troops. The spiral of dismemberment continued when the third partition was signed by Russia, Prussia, and Austria in October 1795. All remaining Polish lands were divided up, the king was forced to abdicate, and, by agreement of the three powers, the name Poland was supposed to disappear from international law forever.

Resistance: The Struggle for Independence

For the next 125 years, the Polish nation was able to survive where the Polish state had not. Still, national survival was by no means a certainty under the partitions.[15] In the lands occupied by Prussia and, to a lesser extent, Austria, a cultural Germanization process was pursued. By contrast, the Polish population living in lands ruled over by the tsarist empire was subjected to sporadic violent repression. Poles organized to resist the occupying powers: "Six times during the years between 1793 and 1864 the Poles rose up to fight for independence and social change. The uprisings disrupted economic development and destroyed hundreds of thousands of the most patriotic families whose properties were confiscated by the partitioning powers."[16]

Certain institutional vestiges of the dismembered Polish state were still discernible in the nineteenth century. So long as Napoleon's armies posed a threat to the partitioning powers, Poles felt that a national resurrection was possible. The Duchy of Warsaw, which Napoleon carved out from Prussian-occupied lands, seemed a partial realization of these hopes. But the French emperor's attitude toward his Polish supporters was cynical at best. He used them to buttress his forces in Lombardy, Spain, and even distant Haiti, engaged them in fighting Austria, and marshaled them for his disastrous campaign against Russia in 1812. Napoleon took a Polish mistress, Maria Walewska, who sought favors from him on behalf of her compatriots. Yet he made no firm commitment to help Poles in their struggle for independence and his defeats at Borodino and Waterloo put an end to even the Duchy of Warsaw's existence. At the Congress of Vienna in 1815, Polish territories were redistributed for a fifth time, among Austria, Prussia, and Russia. One insignificant concession to Polish nationhood was the creation of a rump state, the Congress Kingdom of Poland, with Tsar Alexander I as its king.

Congress Poland symbolized both the expansion of the Russian empire westward and the implicit acknowledgment by the tsar of the Poles' right to limited autonomy. Polish anger over both of these developments was expressed in a large-scale uprising launched in late November 1830 but crushed by Russian forces by September 1831. A period of bitter repression and forced Russification followed. The Congress constitution was abolished by Tsar Nicholas, state lands were confiscated and deeds transferred to Russian generals and government officials, and the cultural vanguard of Polish society was driven into exile.

But the nationalist movement had not been completely destroyed by repression and the emigration that accompanied it. In quick succession other insurrections flared up. In 1846 there was an uprising in Austrian-occupied Galicia, but Habsburg leaders played on the ingrained conservatism of the local peasantry and persuaded it to massacre much of the Cracow nobility that had issued the call to arms. Two years later, during the "springtime of nations," revolts were staged in various parts of Poland, extending from Poznań in the west to Lwów in the east. Remarking on these events, Prince Metternich, the Austrian chancellor, reached this embittered conclusion:

> Polonism is only a formula, the sound of a word underneath which hides a revolution in its most glaring form; it is not a small part of a revolution, but revolution itself. Polonism does not declare war on the monarchies which possess Polish territory, it declares war on all existing institutions and pro-

claims the destruction of all the common foundations which form the basis of society.

Poles were stereotyped as conspirators, revolutionaries, anarchists, and even barbarians, inhabiting "swamps, woods and marshes on which wolves and bears swarm in packs and endanger the roads."[17]

In January 1863, Polish insurgents launched one more desperate attack on Russian garrisons in their country. In May a national government was established that received moral backing from Western European states such as France, England, the Vatican, and even Austria. Unfortunately, the Polish leadership was fragmented into rival factions. The "reds," or radicals, stressed the indispensability of insurrection to attain independence and the centrality of a peasant revolt to such an insurrection. By contrast, the "whites," led by members of the nobility, sought, initially at least, to reach an accommodation with Russia. Even setting aside internal differences, the uprising was doomed without outside help. By October 1863 it had been brutally suppressed and a number of its leaders hanged. In 1864 Congress Poland was abolished and its territory incorporated into Russia as one of its provinces. The reign of terror instigated by Russian officials was designed to eradicate Polish nationalism once and for all.

Sensing advantages for Germany in Russian repression, Bismarck instituted his own *Kulturkampf* in Prussian-occupied lands. It, too, sought to eliminate all manifestations of Polish language and culture. But in stark contrast, following Austria's 1867 *Ausgleich* (compromise) with Hungary, the Austrian government granted virtual autonomy to Galicia in southern Poland. The differentiated treatment meted out by the partitioning powers left enduring marks on Poland's regional political cultures.

The series of nineteenth-century insurrections left the Poles exhausted and forlorn. Following an analogy drawn by their national poet Adam Mickiewicz, many now believed that Poland, like Christ, was destined to suffer in order to redeem the sins of other nations so that they, too, would become worthy of liberty. In the second half of the nineteenth century Poles came to believe that this cross should be borne heroically and stoically. Catholic messianism helped reinforce the identity of a people under threat. On the other hand, the role of the church hierarchy has to be treated with circumspection. One historian pointed out that "the fusion of the Polish national and Catholic identities took place even in the face of reactionary Vatican policies that consistently supported the conservative monarchies and condemned the Polish risings."[18] The emergence late in the nineteenth century of Catholic social doctrine expressing a concern for the plight of workers and peasants exploited by ruthless capitalists gave the church a renewed appeal notwithstanding the policies of the Vatican. Poles learned to distinguish between Catholic faith and ecclesiastical politics.

Disillusionment with romantic nationalism coupled with the beginnings of industrialization led to a shift in the value system espoused by intellectuals toward the end of the nineteenth century. The new intellectual currency was positivism—the belief that reason and intelligence determine the pace and direction of progress. A corollary of positivism was "organic work"—a spirit of industriousness intended to raise the social, economic, and cultural level of the nation and, in this way, make Poland strong again.

Exhaustion with the insurrectionary tradition combined with continued dour life under the partitions led many Poles to work at developing their own civil society separate from alien state structures. In general, civil society signifies living in a collective entity that exists independently from the state. One sociologist emphasized that "the sense of a shared public is constitutive of civil society." But, further, "civil society is, most essentially, that realm where the concrete person—that particular individual, subject to his or her own wants, caprices, and physical necessities—seeks the attainment of these 'selfish' aims. It is that arena where the 'burgher' as private person seeks to fulfill his or her own interests."[19] The notion of civil society had particular relevance to Poland: "Poland never had an autonomous State in modern times. The idea of civil society thus provided the only ideological alternative to foreign domination."[20] Late nineteenth-century positivism was a manifestation of Poles' efforts to forge a civil society that fused the individual's private and public spheres while remaining outside the reach of alien state structures. The task of constructing an independent civil society was resumed almost a century later, when Poles found no other way to confront externally imposed communist rule.

Political Traditions: Polonia Reconstituta

At the turn of the twentieth century, industrial development led in Poland, as in many other European nations, to the rise of mass political movements, in particular those of the left. In 1893 the Polish Socialist Party (PPS) was secretly formed; it emphasized the primacy of national independence over proletarian internationalism. The PPS argued that public ownership of the means of production could be achieved only if national oppression was lifted and capitalism allowed to run its course. This would lead, in turn, to the eventual overthrow of the capitalist order by socialist forces. PPS leaders such as Józef Piłsudski were reluctant to subordinate the Polish socialist movement to a Russian one, which would have transposed Poland's inferior status to the socialist movement. Another party of the left, the Social Democratic Party of the Kingdom of Poland and Lithuania (SDKPiL), founded in 1894, was more internationalist in orientation. Its best-known leader, Rosa Luxemburg, held that the struggle for national independence was anachronistic. In the case of Poland, regaining independence would only produce an impoverished capitalist state unprepared for a socialist revolution.

Thus, in various forms, social democracy established itself as a vital political current in pre-independence Poland. It could already draw on a rich leftist tradition going back to the 1870s when the Marxist-influenced Proletariat party had been formed. The Polish cause was also at the center of debates of the Second Socialist International that met regularly in the last decades of the nineteenth century. Regardless how illegitimate the communist takeover of Poland was after World War II, the left had been playing an important role in the country's politics for many decades.

The right also enjoyed a long-standing political tradition. A movement known as National Democracy (ND or "Endecja") was formed in 1887. Led by Roman Dmowski, it was extremely nationalist. It did not advocate the establishment of Polish independence by any means possible but, rather, stressed the need to give a homogeneous, exclusively Polish character to a new state. For Dmowski, Poland's past failures were precisely the result of its religious toleration, ethnic equality, and humanist tradition. In particular, the sizable Jewish and Ukrainian minorities had allegedly weakened the social fabric of Poland and made it an "effeminate nation." Minorities had to be fully assimilated if a strong Polish nation was to come into being. Dmowski remained equivocal about the desirability of national independence but underscored the tactical importance of collaborating with the Russian autocracy, an argument that he justified by invoking Neo-Slavism. The Endecja tradition has always caused controversy on the Polish right, with many nationalist, Catholic, and anti-Russian leaders expressing strong reservations about Dmowski's overall program. Perhaps more than the socialist movement, then, Poland's right has undergone many ideological changes over the past century.

To summarize, on the eve of World War I political leaders envisaged very different programs and alliances that could lead to the reemergence of a strong Poland. Dmowski's scenario assumed that only a pro-Russian policy could provide the opportunity for statehood. Luxemburg's belief was that a Europe-wide socialist conflagration would liberate Poland from economic and national oppression. Piłsudski's conception was predicated on the total collapse of the Russian empire. The fortunes of war were to prove the latter's views correct.

But Piłsudski was not one to let history run its course. Five days after the war began he led a company of riflemen—a precursor of his famous legions—against Russian troops. His decisiveness and determination in this military engagement meshed well with popular anti-Russian sentiments and went a long way toward making him the obvious candidate to become independent Poland's first strongman.[21]

During the war years offers were made by the various combatants to enlist Poland on their side. As Davies noted, "In 1914–16, the Tsar, the Kaiser, and the Emperor-King proposed mounting degrees of autonomy. By 1917, the President of the United States, the Provisional government in Petrograd, and even the leader of the Bolsheviks declared themselves in favor of Polish independence. In 1918, they were copied by France, Italy, Japan, and, last of all, Great Britain."[22] But the reemergence of a Polish state was ultimately contingent on the outcome of the war, in particular on the weakening of the partitioning powers. The Bolshevik Revolution of October 1917 represented a step in this direction. Russia withdrew from the war, signed an unfavorable peace treaty with Germany, and annulled tsarist partition agreements. The approaching collapse of the central powers, in turn, presaged a weakened Germany and a collapse of the Habsburg empire.

On January 8, 1918, President Woodrow Wilson put forward his general plan for peace in the Fourteen Points. The thirteenth point foresaw a "united, independent and autonomous Poland with free unrestricted access to the sea" and situated on "territories inhabited by an indubitably Polish population." On November 7 of that year, just prior to the armistice, a provisional government was set up. Four days later Piłsudski officially became head of state as well as supreme commander of the army. The Polish state had finally been reconstituted.

The interwar Second Polish Republic did not emerge, therefore, in the manner envisaged by nineteenth-century romantic or positivist theorists or by most socialist thinkers. Instead, a fortuitous combination of external actors and events provided propitious conditions for reclaiming Polish statehood.

The formative years of the interwar republic also did not generate universal enthusiasm among Poles, contrary to what might be expected given the 150-year interval since the first partition. The constitutional system was modeled on the French Third Republic and reproduced all of its shortcomings: a weak president, a powerful legislature, a profusion of political parties (in 1925 there were ninety-two registered parties and thirty-two actually represented in the Sejm), and rapid turnover of governments. The premier of the first national government was Ignacy Paderewski, more famous as a concert pianist than as a founding father of the Second Republic. Its first president, Gabriel Narutowicz, was assassinated in 1922, two days after being sworn in. No Polish king had suffered such a fate.

The first elections, held in January 1919, demonstrated deep political divisions between Poles who had lived under the different partitioning powers. In the former Kingdom of Poland the right-wing National Democrats scored a clear victory. In Galicia the centrist Piast faction of the Polish Peasant Party (PSL), led by the indomitable self-educated peasant Wincenty Witos, was the winner. Witos was a charismatic agrarian radical who served three times as premier in the interwar years and almost single-handedly put the Polish peasant movement at the center of national politics. The 1922 elections proved to be the last genuinely free elections of the interwar republic, for Piłsudski's coup in May 1926 put an end to just eight years of fledgling democracy.

Poland's international politics were no less conflictual at this time. Between 1918 and 1921 the country became embroiled in six conflicts, all brought on by border disputes. The Poles took on the Ukrainians regarding eastern Galicia; on two occasions the Germans threatened Poland concerning Poznania and Silesia, where national uprisings had broken out; the Lithuanians wanted the return of their capital, Vilnius; the Czechs disputed the border in the Cieszyn region; and, most menacingly, Soviet leaders questioned Poland's right to the territories of western Ukraine.

In the "forgotten war" between Poland and Russia of 1920–1921, Piłsudski's troops (which were not allied with the White Armies fighting the Bolsheviks) captured Kiev in May 1920. A Russian counteroffensive drove them back to Warsaw by August and Lenin set up a Provisional Polish Revolutionary Committee headed by Polish communist Julian Marchlewski. Throughout this war Lenin made it clear that his objective was to create a "red" Poland, not to annex lands to Russia as the tsars had done. Ultimately his hopes were frustrated by Piłsudski's military genius. In the "miracle on the Vistula," the Polish commander turned the imminent capture of Warsaw into a rout of the Russian army, advanced eastward rapidly, and contemplated striking at Moscow itself. In the end he negotiated a favorable peace treaty with the Bolsheviks that was signed in Riga in March 1921. By this treaty Poland was awarded more land than the British intermediary, Foreign Secretary Lord Curzon, had proposed in July 1920. In addition to Piłsudski, another key figure in Poland's victory over the Bolsheviks in 1920 was Witos, who rallied the countryside against the Russian invaders.

To be sure, the Ribbentrop–Molotov pact, concluded in August 1939 on the eve of World War II, more than offset Russia's 1920–1921 losses. The pact's secret protocol gave the Soviet Union all of eastern Poland, that is, western Ukraine and parts of Belarus. Soviet Foreign Minister Molotov asserted that this was the fate that the illegitimate offspring of the Versailles Treaty deserved.

Interwar Poland turned out to be ethnically more heterogeneous than U.S. President Wilson had anticipated. In 1921 about 70 percent of the population was ethnically Polish and the rest minorities. The latter included approximately 5–6 million Ukrainians, 3 million Jews, 1.5 million Belorussians, and more than 1 million Germans. Deprived of statehood for so long, the new leaders of independent Poland were more concerned with asserting their national interests than with ensuring the rights of minorities. Thus, although anti-Semitism never became official government policy, neither was it opposed with much energy by Piłsudski's governments. Furthermore, as far as another minority group in the country—the Lithuanians—was concerned, General Lucjan Żeligowski's capture of Vilnius in October 1920 and the incorporation of the entire region around it into Poland two years later smacked of Polish imperialism. Clearly, the Second Republic's policies toward minorities were not a model of multinationalism. It was this flawed legacy that in their own ways both the postwar communist regime and the Third Republic, established after the democratic breakthrough in 1989, tried to disassociate themselves from.

Poland's interwar class structure was another shortcoming that the independent state had to wrestle with. Compared to Western European societies it was backward and archaic. The peasantry comprised the largest single class—in the early 1920s, approximately three-quarters of the population were engaged in agriculture—but it was generally impoverished. Also on the land was the landed aristocracy, which included those with extraordinary wealth and prestige, those whose estates were rapidly shrinking, and those whose politics were, paradoxically, of the radical left. Although the size and political influence of this latter group were very limited, some of its members became prominent leaders. Thus "socially Piłsudski was a typical representative of the revolutionary intelligentsia of noble origin, he was hated by the nationalistically-oriented bourgeoisie as a leftist but loved by his soldiers, who originated from all social classes."[23] Another son of the surviving interwar landed nobility—Wojciech Jaruzelski—went on to make his mark in politics in the communist period.

In contrast to the nobility, the working class was expanding, growing from 22 percent to 25 percent of the population in the 1920s alone and increasing in political visibility, though not enough yet to make a difference. Located in industrial centers like Łódź and Warsaw, it began to organize strikes and demonstrations that often involved political as well as economic demands. By contrast the bourgeoisie, or capitalist class, accounted for a minuscule 2 percent of the population and constituted only a small sector of the middle class, but its political clout was disproportionately strong.

Arguably the most important group in interwar Poland was the middle class, broadly defined. Together with its small capitalist sector and the intelligentsia, or well-educated white-collar workers, it accounted for about 11 percent of the population. One writer drew attention to Polish interwar society's unusual makeup when compared to the United States:

> In the 1920s and 1930s the typical representative of the American middle class would have been a small businessman, someone with at best a high school education but making a good income. In contrast, the typical member of the Polish (or East European) intelligentsia would have been a government employee, probably no more than a glorified clerk, possessed of a university education and perhaps an advanced degree, but making a very small salary and with little hope of ever having any financial independence.[24]

Of special importance was the distinctive status enjoyed by the intelligentsia. This status was an outgrowth of historical conditions: "The growth of the intelligentsia is attributable in part to the efforts of the imperial courts in Moscow, Berlin, and Vienna to 'denobilize' the Polish nobility."[25] Even though it ranked high in prestige, the intelligentsia lacked the commercial and entrepreneurial skills needed to trigger socioeconomic change, which middle classes elsewhere were able to engineer.

Without a critical mass capable of exhibiting risk taking, dynamism, and innovation, Poland was to fall farther behind other European countries in economic development.

Even if the country faced various problems associated with a transition to modernization, it was the political system that failed it most. Parliamentary government was difficult to establish under conditions of inconclusive elections and vacillating party coalitions between 1922 and 1926. Piłsudski finally lost patience and launched a coup in May 1926. The new regime strengthened the power of the executive—Piłsudski was even prevailed upon to become premier for several years—but for the most part his dictatorship was camouflaged in parliamentary guise. Parliamentary support was drummed up by forming a Nonparty Bloc for Cooperation with the Government (BBWR) in 1928. The common convention under a parliamentary system of a cabinet emerging from an elected legislature was reversed; Piłsudski's cronies in large part determined the shape of parliament. Increasingly rigged elections, harassment and even internment of opposition officials, and more widespread censorship brought the regime into disrepute. The irony was that an anti-corruption program stood at the heart of Piłsudski's misnamed *sanacja* ("purification") regime.

When Piłsudski died in 1935, a colonels' regime, buttressed by a realigned parliamentary group calling itself the Camp of National Unity, was set up.[26] Its major failure was in foreign policy, although in some ways it was only following the course on which Piłsudski had put the country. He had resisted overtures to align Poland with one of its great neighbors, Russia or Germany, even after nonaggression pacts were concluded with each in 1932 and 1934, respectively. Piłsudski had seemed blithely unconcerned by the rise of the Nazis in Germany and described them as "nothing but windbags." Poland's foreign minister from 1932 to 1939, Colonel Józef Beck, had greater illusions. Great-power status for his country would be attained, he imagined, through the creation of a Third Europe that included the small Central European states—under the leadership of Poland, of course. Even after the 1938 Munich Agreement dismembered Czechoslovakia, the Polish government appeared oblivious to external threats and did little to prepare for the impending European war.[27]

The Ribbentrop–Molotov pact was concluded by the Third Reich and the Soviet Union on August 23, 1939, and a provisional partition line for Poland was agreed upon. Nine days later the Germans invaded Poland, and the Russians followed on September 17, claiming their spoils. Polish resistance on both fronts was quickly crushed. Although partition was nothing new to Poland, World War II posed a threat to the very existence of the Polish nation.

The war proved a holocaust for Polish Jews, 3 million (or 90 percent) of whom were killed. Some 3 million ethnic Poles also lost their lives, only a small proportion (10 percent) of them as military casualties. Total battle deaths were about 660,000, approximating the number suffered by British and U.S. forces combined. Civilian populations were transported to extermination camps in Auschwitz–Birkenau (where 4 million people, mostly Jews from various countries of Eastern Europe, were slaughtered), Treblinka, and Majdanek. Summary mass killing took place on city streets and in small villages throughout the country, and many died of starvation and in labor camps in Poland and the Reich. The Nazis found very few willing collaborators in the country nor did they particularly search for them. The Poles under occupation offered valiant resistance unmatched by almost any other nation. It took a month of bitter fighting for the German forces to liquidate the Jewish ghetto of Warsaw in April–May 1943. Close to 60,000 Polish Jews were killed in the uneven struggle. In the sixty-three days of fighting between August and October 1944 that marked the Warsaw uprising, nearly 200,000 Poles lost their lives. The 800,000 survivors were removed from the capital, many to labor camps in Germany, and the city was methodically razed to the ground.

In sum, 20 percent of Poland's prewar population, or more than 6 million people, were killed between 1939 and 1945. This marked the highest attrition rate of any nation in the war. Only 50,000 Polish Jews survived the holocaust. On a few occasions Poles took part in the killing of Jews, such as in the notorious massacre of over a thousand Jews in Jedwabne in July 1941.[28] On the other hand, more Poles than members of any other single nation are memorialized at Jerusalem's Yad Vashem Holocaust Memorial as "Righteous Among the Nations," that is, Gentiles who risked their lives to save Jews.

Hitler's genocidal policies in Poland became known to the world. By contrast, the tragic consequences of Russian occupation of eastern Poland were shrouded in secrecy. If we accept the conclusion reached by historian Jan Gross, Soviet wartime occupation of the eastern part of the interwar republic may have been worse than Nazi administration of the remainder of Poland. The Soviets sent over 1.2 million Polish citizens into forcible exile compared to the forced resettlement of 2.5 million Poles by the Germans. However, 13 million Polish citizens were under Soviet jurisdiction compared with 23 million under Nazi administration. Furthermore, of those deported by the Germans about 1.5 million were transferred from western Poland, which was formally annexed into the Reich, to central Poland, which was administered as a *Generalgubernat*. Soviet deportation points, on the other hand, were remote and inhospitable: Siberia, Kazakhstan, and other parts of Asiatic Russia.

Moreover, up to the time that the Nazis began the systematic extermination of Jews in Poland in the late fall of 1941, Soviet mass executions matched German atrocities. The story of the 15,000 Polish officers executed by Stalin's security forces, the NKVD, in 1940, many in the forest of Katyn, is well documented.[29] But a further 100,000 Soviet-held prisoners may have been killed by the NKVD in June–July 1941 during the evacuation of prisons. By contrast, Germans executed some 120,000 people in the first two years of their occupation of Poland. On the basis of a rough comparison of Nazi and Soviet occupations, Gross concluded that "if we measure the victimization of Polish citizens in terms of loss of life, of sufferings inflicted by forced resettlement, and of material losses through confiscation and fiscal measures, the Soviet actions, relatively speaking, would prove far more injurious than those of the Nazis."[30] Although eastern Poland was characterized by great ethnic diversity— Ukrainians, Belorussians, and Jews outnumbered Poles—"all nationalities were victimized during the Sovietization of the Western Ukraine and Western Belorussia."[31]

The atrocities committed by foreign occupying powers made Poles overlook some of the differences that had divided them in the interwar years. One historian asserted that "Poles were perhaps more united under foreign occupation than they were under governments of their own election."[32] Yet some of the political divisions that were to trouble the communist regime could already be discerned in the wartime resistance movements. By 1942 two separate resistance organizations had emerged, the larger linked to the London government in exile, the smaller to the Soviet Union. The Home Army (Armia Krajowa, AK) numbered some 200,000 by 1944 and was united behind General Władysław Sikorski until his death in 1943. After that, the AK was split into two groups. The first, represented by the new premier and PSL leader Stanisław Mikołajczyk, sought accommodation with the USSR; the second, linked to the commander in chief of Polish forces, Kazimierz Sosnkowski, was virulently anti-Soviet. Yet a third approach emerged later when resistance leaders in Warsaw, such as Tadeusz Bór-Komorowski, argued that Poles should fight the Germans militarily but had to fight the communists politically. These divisions within the AK proved fatal when the ill-conceived Warsaw uprising was launched in August 1944. It was not co-ordinated beforehand with either the Western Allies or the Soviet Union, or even with the London government in exile. The only forces in a posi-tion to offer assistance to the besieged insurrectionists were Red Army troops, who made only a feeble attempt to help.

In spite of these political divisions, the Polish resistance movement was arguably the most effective of any established in a Nazi-occupied coun-try.[33] Some 150,000 Germans, including top SS officials, were killed in Poland. Well-planned attacks on particularly brutal Nazi leaders and elaborate ambushes of military transports, payroll vehicles, trains, and the like became commonplace as the occupation continued.

The other resistance force, the People's Guard (Gwardia Ludowa, GL), had a membership of at most 50,000 in 1944. This communist military organization was less divided than the pro-Western resistance and quickly saw the advantages of working closely with Moscow. With Stalin's approval a political wing, the Polish Workers' Party (PPR), was created in January 1942. It formed the core of a provisional government, the Polish Committee of National Liberation (PKWN), that was set up in July 1944 to rival the London one. On January 5, 1945, the USSR offi-cially recognized this government, and twelve days later the Red Army entered Warsaw. Poland's political fate for the next forty-four years was effectively sealed by these last two developments.

Political realists have argued that no solution other than an unequal al-liance with the USSR was possible for Poland. Western sensitivity to Russia's interests had already become discernible during wartime since maintaining the alliance against Hitler was an overriding imperative. Al-ready at the Anglo-American conference held in Québec City in August 1943, the foreign ministers of these two countries cryptically expressed readiness "to contemplate a substantial measure of satisfaction on what we understand Soviet territorial claims to be."[34] Satisfying these claims signified acceptance of the Curzon Line, first proposed in 1920 to end the Polish–Russian war, as the border between Poland and the USSR. It would have transferred western Ukraine and Belorussia from Polish to Soviet jurisdiction. Another consequential decision for Poland stemming from the Québec meeting was the joint Anglo-American decision not to assist the Home Army in its struggle against German occupation.

In Teheran, Iran, in November 1943, Churchill, Roosevelt, and Stalin duly affirmed the Curzon Line as Poland's eastern border. Loss of terri-tory to Russia was to be partially compensated by obtaining German lands; the Oder and Neisse Rivers were to serve as Poland's postwar western frontier. In this way, "like soldiers taking two steps 'left close,'" as Churchill put it, Poland was transposed 250 miles westward. With German forces driven out of Poland by spring 1945, the British prime minister reaffirmed Polish absorption of the western territories: "By taking over and holding firmly the present German territories up to the Oder, they [the Poles] will be rendering a service to Europe as a whole." Churchill recognized that, as a result, Germany would effectively be divided into five zones of occupation.[35]

After the Teheran meeting, the Polish Peasant Party head Mikołajczyk spurned an offer to serve as premier of the provisional government. He rejected the Curzon Line as a way to demarcate the country's eastern border and he also opposed the distribution of ministerial portfolios in the proposed government—fourteen PKWN members and only four London members. Churchill retorted that he was not prepared "to wreck the peace of Europe because of quarrels between Poles."[36] But the bargaining power of the government-in-exile was whittled away as the Red Army marched into Warsaw in January 1945 and pushed forward to other Polish cities. At the Yalta Conference held the following month, Britain, the United States, and the Soviet Union reached an agreement on an interim government of national unity for Poland. It would be composed of representatives from the two Polish governments and Churchill was persuaded that the "free and unfettered elections" called for by the Yalta accord would be enough to entice Mikołajczyk to return to Poland and take an active part in governing the country.[37] When he did return in June 1945, the composition of the provisional government was even more stacked against his party than previously. Moreover, instead of being offered the premiership, he now had to be satisfied with the posts of vice-premier and minister of agriculture. A month after Mikołajczyk's acceptance of these secondary positions, the United States and Britain extended diplomatic recognition to the new government.

The last year of the war had provided a new generation of Poles with a refresher course in history. Once again Poles were taught that insurrections (such as the Warsaw uprising) did not lead to national independence. Agreements concluded among the great powers most often determined how independent Poland could be. A corollary of this was that the will of the Western powers to preserve the country's independence was of utmost importance to deciding its fate. Could Poland escape the vise that geopolitics had imposed on it? Could it survive politically if abandoned by the West? For the next four decades of communist rule, few Poles ventured optimistic answers to these questions.

2

The Communist Era: The System and Its Crises

Peacetime meant an end to the horrific devastation Poland had suffered during World War II, but it did not bring with it the possibility of self-determination. The Yalta agreement made the country dependent on the good faith of longtime Soviet dictator Stalin, whose record already included the policy of forced collectivization in the 1930s that killed millions of peasants, a contrived famine in Ukraine at the beginning of that decade in which at least another million people perished, the great purges of 1936–1938 that eliminated most of the top leaders in the communist party and the Red Army, and the forced deportation of entire nations, especially from the north Caucasus, which were suspected of pro-German sympathies. Brutal Soviet occupation of eastern Poland during World War II, the Katyn massacre of Polish officers in 1941, the hostility to the Home Army's resistance movement and cynical passivity during the Warsaw uprising in 1944, and the territorial and political coups in the last year of the war that reduced Poland in size and placed it under a pro-Soviet government were indications of Stalin's imperialist attitude to Poland. The only consolation for Poles was that at least their country was not incorporated into the USSR as were Lithuania, Latvia, and Estonia.

It may be surprising, then, that Poland was able to weather the worst years of Stalinization and held on to a limited degree of autonomy until the Soviet dictator died in 1953. After that a Polish road to socialism crystallized that, while not altogether freeing the country from Soviet interference, gave its citizens cause for hope. Let us examine how between 1945 and 1989 Polish political traditions bent Soviet-style communism into a distinctive shape, then disposed of it altogether in 1989.

Much of Polish politics in the 1990s and after is comprehensible only in the context of the preceding forty-odd years of communist rule. The most remarkable development was, arguably, that the communist leadership itself, accustomed to playing a political game based on elite in-fighting and winning Soviet favor, was the political group that most quickly adapted to the dictates of democracy. Against all expectations the reformed communist party was therefore able to establish itself as the party of government in the Third Republic. By contrast, the Polish right, effectively put out of existence under communism, was slow to regroup after 1989. Once its standard-bearer, Lech Wałęsa, lost credibility, the weakness of the center and right was revealed. Much of this can be explained by what occurred in the communist period.

The Soviet Model and Its Polish Variant

From the very beginning the Bolshevik seizure of power in Russia in 1917 posed a direct threat to Poland. But it was only with the Red Army's liberation of the country from German occupation in 1944 and 1945 that Poland became a Soviet satellite. Western armies were never in a position—nor wanted to put themselves in a position—to beat the Red Army to Warsaw and most other Eastern European capitals, so an iron curtain descended on Europe at war's end.

Between 1944 and 1948 Stalin carried out a step-by-step program of reshaping Poland on the Soviet model, skillfully exploiting Polish hopes that full-scale Sovietization could be avoided while discreetly (and sometimes not so discreetly) implementing the communist program. As we saw in the first chapter, a representative of Poland's government-in-exile in London, the Polish Peasant Party (PSL) leader Stanisław Mikołajczyk, was persuaded to take part in a communist-dominated coalition government. Very quickly he recognized that the influence of the London Poles would be negligible compared with that of Polish communists and he resigned and left the country in 1948.

On the left of the political spectrum, the Polish Socialist Party (PPS) had had a long tradition of promoting a democratic road to socialism, and for a while after the war it seemed destined to play a pivotal role in the formation of a noncapitalist political order. Polish communists were themselves divided between those stressing the distinctive national conditions prevailing in the country and those advocating implementation of the Soviet model in its entirety. Some communists were eager to work together with the PPS in bringing socialism to Poland; others would simply do whatever Stalin ordered. In 1948 Stalin ordered that the Polish communist party swallow up the PPS. The result was the formation of the Polish United Workers' Party (PZPR), in practice a hegemonic communist party modeled on its Soviet counterpart.

If the character of Poland's postwar regime was not fully clear at the time the Red Army marched across the country in 1945, it became transparent with the PZPR's creation in 1948. Historians still ask whether Poland was inevitably earmarked for Sovietization. The overriding consensus is that after the Yalta meeting Poland was at the mercy of Stalin. In February 1945 the Soviet leader had played host to U.S. President Franklin D. Roosevelt and British Prime Minister Winston Churchill. The three had come up with a plan for Poland's future that anticipated free elections among "democratic and anti-Nazi parties" that would be based on "universal suffrage and secret ballot." While in theory the call for the pro-communist Polish provisional government to be "reorganized on a broader democratic basis" seemed like sound politics, in practice it represented Roosevelt and Churchill's acquiescence to a bogus body Stalin had created.

But did Stalin really have a communist blueprint ready? One historian was not sure: "It is difficult to decide whether Stalin and the Polish communists never intended to allow free elections in Poland."[1] And by the end of 1945 some signs suggested that the orthodox Stalinist model would not be forced upon all of Eastern Europe. Soviet troops had liberated neighboring Czechoslovakia but had then departed for home. Competitive parliamentary elections in Hungary had led to a defeat for the communist party. Yugoslavia had charted a national road to socialism that Stalin had been unable to halt. The Comintern—the Communist International set up after the Bolshevik Revolution to dictate Soviet policy to communists throughout the world—had not been reestablished. To be sure, a conference in Szklarska Poręba, Poland, in 1947 created the Cominform but it had been marked by unprecedented dissension among Soviet and East European communist leaders about the desirability and scope of a new communist international. Polish communist head Władysław Gomułka was particularly outspoken about this organization.

Arguably, the regime that was poised to rule Poland at war's end could to a limited degree have been pluralist, democratic, and nationalist. It might have accepted a private sector within a centrally planned economy.

What were the factors that sidetracked Poland from a moderate, measured developmental path?

Of all of these expectations about a diluted Stalinist system for Poland, it was easiest to forecast that political pluralism would be unacceptable. The elections called for by the Yalta and Potsdam accords were never likely to be wholly free. Marxist-Leninist ideology posited a proletarian dictatorship that would ensure the liquidation of the capitalist class. Accordingly, one political organization was all that workers needed to protect their interests. Communist hegemony also followed from the fact that from Stalin to Chernenko, Soviet leaders were of one mind concerning the threat posed by any form of pluralism, whether it be autonomy for trade unions, the existence of dissident organizations, or the prospects of a full-fledged multiparty system. When threatened by the emergence of pluralism in a satellite state, Soviet leaders did not shy away from staging palace coups, using covert measures, or sending in tanks to eliminate independent political forces. Such paranoia on the part of Kremlin rulers, fearing that communism was unpopular and needed to be propped up by force, seems justified in hindsight. When Gorbachev failed to crack down on pluralist tendencies in his empire, it quickly crumbled.

To be sure, some semblance of pluralism was approved for Poland. Given the role played by Catholicism in the everyday lives of Poles, communist leaders sought to elicit the support of church groups. Two Catholic groups, Znak and Pax, were even provided with representation in the Sejm. But after the events of the 1956 Polish October failed to secure genuine political competition, it became clear that communism and pluralism were mutually exclusive. In that year, workers protested about deteriorating living standards and the self-styled national communist, Gomułka, returned to power. He hinted at greater political liberalization, but by the 1960s had adopted the same neo-Stalinist methods of which he had been a victim after the war—this created among Poles an enduring cynicism about "well-intentioned" communists. In short, the Polish People's Republic, proclaimed in 1948, was structurally incapable of accepting political pluralism.

Within the ruling PZPR, democratic processes were also suppressed and the public face of the party invariably presented a show of unanimity. But that only led to intense behind-the-scenes factional fighting pitting liberal against hard-line communists and nationalist against Muscovite communists. Because these struggles were played out behind closed doors and the broader public was not allowed to pass judgment on contesting policy programs and rival leaders, factional conflicts were often ruthless.

In 1948 the Stalinist leader Bolesław Bierut was a supporter of Gomułka one day but on the next accused him of a serious rightist-nationalist deviation—cause for Gomułka's subsequent expulsion from the party, imprisonment, and torture. In 1970, Gomułka's opponents in the party set him up for another fall from grace by having him announce food-price increases two weeks before Christmas, thereby triggering massive demonstrations in coastal cities. Edward Gierek was kept around just long enough to sign accords with Solidarity leaders in August 1980, making it possible for his party opponents to unite and accuse him *both* of allowing a counterrevolutionary organization to come into being *and* of not recognizing popular discontent early enough. Without open democracy in the communist party, all of society was affected by intrigues hatched by rival communist factions.

Poland's communists have been accused of having betrayed the country's national interests during their years in power. The argument is made that Bierut, Gomułka, Gierek, and Wojciech Jaruzelski served as mere surrogates of Soviet leaders. There is little question that Soviet-type policies pursued by Polish leaders were mostly alien to Polish society. Nevertheless, like Mickiewicz's famous character Konrad Wallenrod, some Polish communists were persuaded that cooperation with Moscow could be used to advance the national interest. Few Polish communists were ever complete pawns of the Kremlin. But Soviet sabotage, threats, and blackmail were often enough to assure compliance by the top Polish leadership with its dictates.

The International Environment

International systems theory holds that under bipolarity, when two great powers dominate world politics, small and medium powers have little room for maneuver. They must join the alliance system of one or the other hegemon. By contrast, under multipolarity—such as in the interwar period—a medium-sized power like Poland could shift fluidly from one alliance system to another. Setting aside all other factors, then, just the international politics of the Cold War period forced Poland into political and economic dependency on the USSR, its superpower neighbor.

From its creation in July 1944, the very legitimacy of a communist-ruled Polish state and the international acceptance of the revised postwar boundaries were of concern to the communist leadership. If the country had been the bastard child of Versailles during the interwar period, how much truer it was to claim that postwar communist Poland was the illegitimate offspring of the Yalta agreement. Indeed, whereas the Yalta accord was repeatedly invoked by Western powers in the first two decades after the war to criticize the undemocratic nature of the Polish regime, by the 1970s it was communist leaders who invoked Yalta to criticize Western meddling in the region. Yalta had become a euphemism for Realpolitik and mutually recognized spheres of influence.

With regard to the country's borders, Poland's western, or "recovered," territories were recognized as Polish by the Federal Republic of Germany only in 1970. Throughout the lifetime of the People's Republic, Polish touchiness about the border question played into the hands of the Soviet Union and contributed to its satellite status. The loss to the USSR of eastern agricultural lands inhabited largely by non-Poles was not offset by acquisition of the Silesian industrial and coal basins and the Pomeranian coast in the west. If Poland lost net territory but gained net resources in this exchange, it also inherited tensions with West Germany, a vital player in Europe's postwar reconstruction.

Poland's foreign policy objective was the same as the Soviet objective: full integration into the various institutions created by the Soviet Union. The most important of these was the Warsaw Pact, a military alliance set up in 1955. In 1967 Poland and other East European states had to follow Soviet cues and condemn "Israeli Zionist imperialism" following the Six-Day War in the Middle East. A year later Poland was required to provide "fraternal assistance" to Czechoslovakia by joining in the Warsaw Pact invasion of that country. Poland regularly had to express its solidarity with national liberation fronts emerging in what for Poles were exotic Third World nations and to extend diplomatic and material support to socialist dictators who had seized power.

Another Soviet-created intergovernmental organization was the Council for Mutual Economic Assistance (CMEA), an East European version of the European Common Market. Poland's role in the Council's general division of labor was to specialize in certain sectors (for example, cosmetics and textiles) while renouncing the development of others (for example, optical products and pharmaceuticals). Such arrangements inhibited Poland's overall economic growth.

Of overriding salience to Polish rulers from Bierut to Jaruzelski was that all departures from the *prevailing* Soviet model (whether that of Stalin or Brezhnev) required negotiation and, ultimately, approval from Moscow. French political scientist Hélène Carrère d'Encausse referred evocatively to "the shadow of the Kremlin" that hung over East European leaders."[2] This reality shaped what was possible in People's Poland, and it was this reality that had to be changed if, as the popular song of the 1981 Solidarity period had it, Poland was really to become Poland. Thus, the postwar experience could be reduced to "the paradox of a communist state presiding over a nation that is in the Soviet orbit of power and yet not of it."[3]

But even the Soviet bloc was not hermetically sealed. Changes in the international system had an impact on the bloc as a whole and on its individual members in particular. One general theory of democratization, elaborated by political scientist Francis Fukuyama, claimed that "there is a fundamental process at work that dictates a common evolutionary pattern for *all* human societies—in short, something like a Universal History of mankind in the direction of liberal democracy."[4] A universal force based on the imperatives of science pushed human societies toward convergence. The end point for these societies was liberal democracy. A corollary of Fukuyama's thesis was that communist systems had become anachronistic and therefore untenable.

Another general theory of democratization developed by a political scientist, Samuel Huntington, pointed to 1974 as the year in which several southern Europe states achieved democratic breakthroughs. By 1990 democratic regimes had replaced authoritarian ones in some thirty countries around the world. Instead of highlighting a universal source of this change as Fukuyama did, Huntington stresses the different starting points these states had. Some had alternated between democratic and authoritarian governments (for example, Argentina and Brazil), others were making their second try at democracy (Poland was cited as an example), others had resumed democratic practices after an interruption (Chile), some were making a direct transition (Romania), while a few were the product of decolonization (Papua New Guinea). Huntington identified Eastern Europe as the region in which the most dramatic "snowballing," or demonstration effect, took place. Changes in the lead country—for him it was Poland—"helped stimulate demands for comparable changes in neighboring and culturally similar countries."[5]

The changing relationship between the superpowers was a source of these political changes. Other outside actors such as international regimes contributed further to democratization. An important example was the 1975 Helsinki Agreement concluded by thirty-five European and North American states. It pledged signatories to respect human rights and fundamental freedoms and ultimately had a significant impact on opening up Soviet bloc societies. In the 1970s the European Community (EC), the precursor of the European Union (EU), was supportive of

TABLE 2.1 Indicators of Economic and Social Change, 1946–1999

	1946	*1950*	*1960*	*1970*	*1980*	*1990*	*1999*
Economy							
Per capita gross domestic product ($)	n.d.	271	564	955	1,676[a]		
					4,276	4,099	8,651
Urban population (%)	33.9	36.8	48.3	52.3	58.8	61.8	61.8
Workforce outside of agriculture (%)	n.d.	46.4	56.7	65.7	70.3	73.2	74.3
Electricity production (kW-h)	244	380	987	1,984	3,426	3,577	3,677
Unemployed (000s)	—	—	—	—	—	1,126	2,350
Doctors (per 10,000)	3.2	3.7	9.6	14.2	17.8	21.4	22.6
Education							
Students in primary schools (000s)	3,291	3,303	4,875	5,343	4,265	5,287	3,958
High School graduates (000s)	16	112	85	266	466	424	554
College graduates (000s)	4	15	21	47	84	52	215
Communication and Transport							
Radio subscribers (000s)	475	1,464	5,268	5,658	8,666	10,944	9,461
Television subscribers (000s)	—	—	426	4,215	7,954	9,919	9,187
Cars (per 1,000 people)	1	2	4	15	67	138	240

Source: Główny Urząd Statystyczny, *Rocznik Statystyczny.* Warsaw: GUS, yearbooks from 1950 to 2000.
[a]Net material product (NMM) per capita before 1980; NMM and GDP for 1980; GDP after 1980.

democratization. As a model of successful integration and economic growth, its influence increased, providing tangible incentives for democratization in Poland and the rest of the bloc. The Vatican, too, played a pivotal role in democratizing Catholic societies: "Rome delegitimated authoritarian regimes in Catholic countries."[6] Already in the 1970s the Catholic Church had become a force for democratic change in Latin America, and after John Paul II's accession in 1978 it was able to effect similar change in the Catholic countries of Eastern Europe.

Huntington also established a correlation between economic development and democratization. Three-quarters of countries that were nondemocratic in 1974 and had per capita GNPs of between $1,000 and $3,000 in 1976 had democratized significantly by 1989. With a per capita GNP of over $2,000, Poland was already high in the "transition zone" in the mid–1970s. This analysis identifies yet another factor triggering change: "The combination of substantial levels of economic development and short-term economic crisis or failure was the economic formula most favorable to the transition from authoritarian to democratic government."[7] Data from Table 2.1 on per capita gross domestic product clearly indicate how steady growth between 1950 and 1980 gave way to regression between 1980 and 1990.

An analysis of the impact of the international environment on undermining communist regimes must include the international political economy. In an increasingly interdependent world, a regime's capacity to maintain growth was affected by external international processes and actors. Global economic cycles of recession or boom, expansion in world trade, and increasing aid from international organizations, foreign governments, and commercial banks could leave one country behind and push another one ahead in terms of economic development. Between 1971 and 1980 the Gierek administration secured close to $40 billion in credits from nonsocialist countries, thereby making Poland's economy very dependent on capitalist markets and also more vulnerable to economic cycles in the West. Poland's objective in obtaining Western investment, licenses, technology, and consumer goods on credit was to generate export-led growth. But a combination of factors—many but not all of the communist regime's own making—made this strategy backfire. Deteriorating terms of trade for Poland's agricultural and energy (coal) products were exacerbated by a rising interest burden fueled by double-digit inflation in Western nations. Thus, although foreign capital flooded Poland for a time, trade with the West did not take off. By the 1980s Poland's external indebtedness, its inability to purchase Western goods, and the economic sanctions imposed on it following martial law hamstrung economic growth. Even the Soviet Union was no longer a secure trade partner. Increases in the price of Soviet energy imports and cutbacks in Soviet deliveries forced Poland to look to the hard-currency energy markets of the Middle East. In short, the international political and economic trends of the 1980s conspired to throttle communism.

Socialist Socioeconomic Development

If socialist democracy, the slogan promulgated by communist parties in Eastern Europe, was an oxymoron, what can be said of the centrally planned economy that accompanied the installation of a communist regime? The first fact we must remember is that East European economies had lagged considerably behind their Western counterparts even before communist systems were established. In tracing Eastern Europe's backwardness, political scientist Andrew Janos estimated that around 1800 the ratio of the aggregate national product per capita between Eastern and Western Europe was on the order of 80:100. By 1910, the per capita income gap between six East European and six West Euro-

pean nations had widened to about 48:100. Averaging out the 1926–1934
period produced a further deterioration in the ratio, to 37:100 (for Poland
35:100).

Janos's calculations for the level of economic development in the communist period up to 1980 led to the conclusion that "whatever method-
ological assumptions we make, Communist economies were drifting
downward from the relative position their countries had held in the world
economy prior to the Second World War."[8] The 1980 per capita income
ratio stood at 33:100. For Poland it was 34:100, that is, almost unchanged
from the 1926–1934 period. The Polish economy seemed, therefore, to be
holding its own under communism, at least until 1980. The economic
crisis of the 1980s devastated Eastern Europe, and the hardship of economic transformation in 1990–1992 reduced gross domestic product
(GDP) by about 26 percent (for Poland 18 percent). Janos's estimate for
the end of 1992 was a 25:100 ratio, a historic low, between Eastern and
Western Europe. He concluded: "The sad fact is that Eastern Europe has
never been more economically backward or underdeveloped compared to
the West than it is today."[9]

With all its rhetoric of economic development and modernization, why
did the communist system not produce better results for Poland? To answer this we need to consider a devastating critique of central planning
advanced by the Austrian economist Friedrich Hayek. In his view, socialism was flawed at a philosophical level: The assumptions that Marxist
economists made about human morality and motivation were off the
mark. Human cooperation was promoted by capitalism and individualism, not by planning and collectivism.[10]

Hayek addressed the often-cited proposition that cooperation is better
than competition: "Cooperation, like solidarity, presupposes a large measure of agreement on ends as well as on methods employed in their pursuit." Although feasible in a small group, cooperation is less probable in
an extended order. Further, cooperation cannot by itself ensure effective
coordination of efforts undertaken under unpredictable conditions, as in
the economy. By contrast, Hayek described competition as "a procedure
of discovery . . . that led man unwittingly to respond to novel situations;
and through further competition, not through agreement, we gradually
increase our efficiency."[11]

The Hayekian critique of planning and a state-controlled economy began with the proposition that "the whole idea of 'central control' is confused. There is not, and never could be, a single directing mind at
work."[12] Central planners were dependent on the quality of reporting

from the production frontiers and this reporting was usually shoddy and incomplete. In addition, the centralized system of allocation of resources was flawed in several ways. Hayek believed that the totality of resources is simply not knowable. Further, under socialism it was impossible to place value on resources. Managers were given incentives to skew reporting. They overstated shortages of inputs in order to be allocated greater inputs in the future and understated the amount of outputs to prevent production targets from being raised subsequently. It was a perfectly rational choice, then, for managers to understate any surplus of inputs, labor, and plant capacity.

Above all, central planning was incapable of performing the task assigned to it—coordinating production across many sectors of the economy. For Hayek the free market was above all an information-gathering institution. By contrast, central planning generated inaccurate and belated information about changes in scarcity values. Accordingly "'macroeconomic' knowledge of aggregate quantities available of different things is neither available nor needed, nor would it even be useful."[13] Not least of the problems caused by a command economy was that anything that might disrupt the production cycle, such as technological innovation or research and feasibility studies, was discouraged.

Finally, central planners operated under political directives more constraining than economic ones and therefore took many myopic policy decisions, for example, promoting growth of heavy industry at the expense of light industry, the consumer sector, and agriculture. Together with incompetent and corrupt management, capricious wage policies, a retail price system having no connection with market values, an alienated, unproductive workforce, inefficient use of raw materials, and environmental degradation, central planning produced a deteriorating quality of life for much of society.

The economic failings of socialism were the unavoidable consequence of entrusting the making of economic policy to unelected and unaccountable party apparatchiks. Whether an earlier shift toward a mixed economy—which a first wave of Polish reform economists had urged—could have prevented economic disaster was questionable, given the Hayekian critique.[14]

Was Poland's centrally planned economy a disaster, then? One of its characteristics was that it lurched from one set of priorities to another. After the war the first task, mapped out in the 1947–1949 three-year plan, was to rebuild the country's infrastructure. To accomplish this, the country's largest factories were nationalized in line with socialist ideology.

By contrast, the struggle to eradicate the private retail sector continued into the early 1950s and, to some degree, was never completed.

The 1950–1955 six-year plan gave overriding priority to rapid industrialization. When Gomułka took power in 1956 he insisted on the virtue of austerity and neglect of the consumer sector remained government policy. In the 1970s, the Gierek administration promoted the opposite policy. A rapid growth of a second economy—the black market—was permitted and it provided a genuine if expensive free market in consumer goods. In turn, Jaruzelski's martial-law regime sought legitimacy by enacting laws against speculators (as black marketeers were euphemistically termed). Jaruzelski was still strongman when Poland turned to a free market in the late 1980s.

Despite the ultimate economic failures that were attributable to the communist system, the modernization of social and economic life was undeniable. The proportion of the labor force employed in the agricultural sector was halved, from 54 percent in 1950 to 27 percent in 1990. If we consider that, according to the last prewar census carried out in 1931, some 73 percent of the population was rural with 60 percent making their livelihood from agriculture, the transformation of economic life appears even more dramatic. Communists could point to other positive results. Between 1950 and 1990 the percentage of women making up the workforce grew from 31 percent to 47 percent. The number of college graduates increased from 3,900 in 1946 to 52,300 in 1990.[15] By that year both the industrial and service sectors employed about 36 percent of the active workforce. But, while reflecting impressive growth, Poland's service sector remained about half the size of its counterparts in advanced Western states, where about 70 percent of the labor force was employed.

The ideological rationale for the command economy was that social justice could be achieved only if the communist state micromanaged economic affairs. The communist goal of an egalitarian society was never approached in postwar Poland, but it is generally true that in its first twenty years the regime provided increased opportunities for lower social groups to become upwardly mobile. Peasants were recruited into the labor force to become unskilled, semiskilled, or peasant-workers who commuted from farmland to factory. Even if peasants stayed on the farm, that farm belonged to them: Stalin's collectivization policy had been resisted by Gomułka in 1948 and it was not forcefully pursued by any of his successors.

In the 1950s blue-collar workers moved up the social ladder to administrative and management posts. Three decades later they also formed part of the economic elite. In 1983 coalface miners became the best-paid occupational group in Poland, earning 50 percent more than factory directors, three times more than doctors, and five times more than teachers.[16] In terms of general social prestige, only the intelligentsia ranked ahead of skilled workers. Private employers and white-collar workers followed.

Communist leaders took care to extend socio-occupational mobility to women. They were increasingly recruited into lower-level administrative positions previously closed to them, as well as into more traditionally feminized occupational sectors such as light industry, health care, and the education system. Though central planners expanded day care facilities for working mothers, the burden of housework continued to fall on women. Furthermore, they had little chance of advancing into directorial positions even in feminized occupations such as medicine and textiles.

Until 1956 top political and economic appointments had been made on the basis of individuals' class backgrounds and party credentials rather than formal qualifications. Central government ministries were filled with cadres drawn from the working class and, to a lesser extent, the peasantry. By contrast, people of white-collar or intelligentsia background faced discrimination in getting into university, securing administrative positions, and obtaining professional advancement. The inefficiency, incompetence, and corruption of the Polish communist system owed much to this wave of party-sponsored *awans społeczny* (social promotion). Communist leaders' notion of affirmative action permitted many poorly prepared persons to be catapulted into positions of political and economic responsibility.

Gierek's slogan in the early 1970s of filling the right job with the right person was intended to be a corrective to the misguided personnel policy of the past. But he was responsible for the growth of a new social pathology, the entrenchment and expansion of the infamous "new class" of communist officialdom. Also referred to as the *nomenklatura*, it sought to perpetuate its status by passing on privileges to its children. It raised the entry costs for recruits into this class by exacting bribes and political and economic servility. This engendered a "new new class" of *arrivistes* who were usually not party members but were connected to the *nomenklatura* through social and economic networks. In this way Gierek's administration represented the pinnacle of an extensive patron–client nexus.

Do longitudinal aggregate data corroborate the evolution of Poland over time into an upwardly mobile, better-off society? Table 2.1 reports how much change occurred in the following areas: gross domestic product per capita, percent of the workforce employed outside the agricultural sector, urbanization, educational attainment (number of students enrolled in primary, secondary, and higher education), and media diffusion (number of radio and television subscribers). The data draw our attention to an increasingly better-educated and better-informed population in the communist period. The falloff in the number of high school and college graduates in the 1980s was largely the result of demographic factors. A more curious phenomenon was the drop in newspaper and magazine sales by the end of the 1980s. On the one hand, it could be associated with the precipitous decline in people's disposable income. On the other hand, similar declines were recorded in other cultural arenas such as book buying, movie going, and attendance at concerts and theaters. The ways in which people made use of free time began to change in the last years of communist rule.

When we look at indicators not included in Table 2.1, the achievements of the communist regime are mixed. Real income nearly tripled between 1955 and 1981, the peak year. But it fell by one-third from 1981 to 1990—perhaps the clearest reason why the communist leadership turned to the "shadow" Solidarity leadership and asked it to share responsibility for economic policy. Material living standards improved between 1946 and 1990 as evidenced by the quadrupling of meat consumption— historically a reliable indicator of living standards. But again the period from 1982 to 1988 reveals the impoverishment of people in all social groups, and above all in the ranks of unskilled workers and peasants.

In relative terms the centrally planned economy did not advance Poland's prosperity and modernization to the fullest. It expanded the telephone system nearly twentyfold between 1946 and 1990, but that was a hollow success when it still left Poland close to the bottom of the list of European countries in the size of its telephone grid. Similarly, the number of car owners increased from 23,000 in 1946 to 5.3 million in 1990— interestingly, continuing to rise steadily even in the recession years of the 1980s, which tells us something about consumer preferences. But the majority of the cars on the road were small Polish Fiats, only marginally better than the notorious East German Trabant and far below the quality of West European cars.

As we have indicated, economic stagnation hit Poland hard in the 1980s. What the Marxists had said of the crises of capitalism proved to be an accurate description of the communist economy: It tended to deteriorate more frequently and more profoundly over time. Economic decline affected social classes in different ways. Whereas all of Polish soci-

ety suffered *absolute* deprivation, the greatest *relative* deprivation was experienced by peasants and unskilled workers, and the least by professionals and private entrepreneurs. In fact the number of professional house-
holds ranked as wealthy actually increased.[17] Thus the shift away from a
socioeconomic structure favoring workers and peasants and the economic
comeback of professional and entrepreneurial groups predated the fall of
communism. By the late 1980s the rising expectations of these latter
groups helped raise the pressure for systemic change.

Political Culture

The study of political culture focuses on the attitudes, values, and knowledge of citizens as they relate to political issues. From the beginning of
communist rule, the regime's prescriptive political culture, heavily influenced by the writings of Marx and Lenin, clashed with the existing political culture of Polish society. More generally, the utopian thrust of communist ideology appeared to be at odds with human nature. As writer
George Steiner put it, "Communism means taking the errata out of history. Out of man."[18] Out of Poland's political culture, too, we could add.
Traditional Polish suspicions of the empire to the east made even the
most attractive ideology in Russian hands a hard sell.

Communism required a political culture at once compliant and engagé:
Citizens were expected to take an active part in the construction of the
socialist order while, at the same time, never meaningfully participating
in the political process. In a sense, communist leaders were never sure
whether a parochial (uninformed), subject (deferential), or participant
(assertive) political culture was preferable, given the enormous transformative task at hand. In the end a subject political culture was to be created even while ideology advocated a participatory one.

The communist regime did not inherit a normative tabula rasa. As we
have seen, over the centuries Polish culture had developed individualistic,
anti-authoritarian traditions. Only on rare occasions in history did Poles
give their unconditional obedience to rulers, foreign-born or not. The
communist regime learned that it would be difficult to overcome society's
distrust of government, an orientation nurtured over centuries. The existing value system was, therefore, an obstacle to building a new order and
the cyclical revolts against communist rulers were the consequence. But
other dimensions of the value system posited by Marxism and the one internalized by Poles collided. The atheist world outlook espoused by communism was alien to a nation whose historians had been describing it as

the *antemurale christianitatis*. The supposed superiority of class solidarity over patriotism left Poles cold. For Marx, work would ideally have an intrinsic value as an expression of human emancipation and self-fulfillment. In a nation like Poland, which had sometimes been stereotyped as lacking a work ethic altogether, such an outlook was unlikely to take root quickly.

Notwithstanding these conditions, communist leaders were convinced that Polish political culture was amenable to transformation. Few of them doubted that the macrolevel political and economic changes they had engineered had gained popular support. They interpreted literacy and educational campaigns as successful political socialization work. Although party theoreticians occasionally reported on shortcomings in political socialization, it was generally not regarded as a serious problem. The modus vivendi achieved with the only institution possessing a viable competing ideology, the Catholic Church, reassured party ideologues that anticommunist attitudes had been neutralized. PZPR leaders read much into membership figures, such as the 3 million Poles who belonged to the party in 1980. Another 500,000 had joined the obedient satellite peasant party, the United Peasant Party (ZSL). Millions of Poles were registered in communist-organized trade unions and professional associations and in women's, student, and youth movements. The numbers were impressive enough for the authorities to convince themselves that the system enjoyed participatory support.

Public opinion research provided a more complicated picture. Munich-based Radio Free Europe took surveys of Polish citizens visiting the West in the late 1950s, the 1960s, and the early 1970s. As unrepresentative as these samples were, results suggested that the communist system/socialism/the party first secretary received mixed evaluations. On the other hand, the majority of respondents in the early 1970s said they would have voted for the communist party and, next, for a social democratic party if Poland had free elections.[19] In free elections held three decades later a plurality of Poles did in fact vote for a social democratic party (the former communists).

The first reliable surveys carried out in Poland date from the 1980s. They indicated limited public support for the communist party and the socialist project. Findings of the *Polacy* surveys pointed to at most 25 percent of the population acknowledging pro-regime attitudes.[20] Beginning in 1981, another series of polls asked the public about its degree of confidence in various institutions—official (the government, the communist party) and unofficial (Solidarity, the church). The PZPR always ranked as one of the least-trusted institutions. Even a 1988 study of persons employed in large Warsaw enterprises—seemingly a communist stronghold—recorded a minuscule 7 percent of respondents asserting confidence in the party, "probably less than the total number of party members in those enterprises!"[21] A government-sponsored survey of young people asked the question: "Is it worthwhile to continue socialism in our country?" In 1986, 60 percent of respondents answered no and 29 percent yes.[22]

Public perceptions of conflict also revealed growing hostility toward the political system. A comparative survey of oppositional consciousness in 1984 and 1988 found that "the great majority of those who perceive conflict define it as between the authorities and society."[23] Why Poles were obedient to a political system they did not like was the subject of a different survey. In 1984 the most commonly perceived sources of obedience were fear of repression, the demands of everyday life, and acceptance of the legality of the authorities. All three of these were, in the researchers' view, disconnected from trust in political institutions and therefore "one can consider authority as legal without trusting any of its main institutions."[24] Developing the logic further, the authors of the study claimed that "an important element of legitimacy in real socialism is the fact that it remained in power. This legality is not a condition of obedience, but rather obedience a condition of legality."[25]

Examining causes of disobedience, the same 1984 survey found that by far the most common reason identified by respondents was lack of trust in the authorities stemming from unfulfilled promises (51 percent). The authorities' incompetence and pursuit of their own interests (16 percent), their undemocratic and repressive nature (6 percent), and the national character of Poles (7 percent) ranked well behind.[26] In general, then, respondents cited pragmatic reasons tied to regime performance rather than ideological ones grounded in a worldview such as liberalism for obeying or disobeying political authority.

It seems wrong, then, to depict the entire communist period as a titanic struggle between intransigent communist rulers and opposition freedom fighters. Psychologist Janusz Reykowski argued that such an interpretation was ahistorical because it presumed that "over decades the same forces were fighting for the same issues."[27] His own survey data "put into question the widely accepted notion that the entire Polish society (or at least its overwhelming majority) espoused the same sociopolitical values, was inimical toward the system over the entire forty-five-year period, and just waited for a convenient opportunity to topple it."[28]

One of the main sources of pride for communist leaders was the rise in egalitarian attitudes in the first decades of socialism. There was growing public acknowledgment of the advantages of the welfare state and of state ownership of the larger factories rather than ownership by unscrupulous local or foreign capitalists. The principle of "to each according to his work" also seemed to be embraced by large sections of Polish society. Yet in this respect, too, the communist rulers' world began to crumble in the 1980s as the public's adherence to egalitarian attitudes began to wane. One Poland specialist asserted that "Poles exhibit a dramatic move away from egalitarianism during the 1980s." The clearest evidence came from surveys in the *Polacy* series, where, he summarized, "from 1980 to 1988 there is a dramatic decline in those 'decisively' favoring limiting the highest earnings (from 70.6 percent to 27.5 percent)."[29] Another Polish political scientist went farther and pointed to the "slow but steady shift in societal preferences from 'equality' . . . to 'freedom'—an acceptance of various forms of economic, social and political activity and the differing consequences of that activity."[30] The changed preferences were reflected in survey data on public confidence in political institutions and political leaders (Table 2.2). Those representing equality—the communist institutions—fell from grace, whereas those symbolizing freedom—such as Solidarity—regained stature. The Catholic Church was the single most trusted institution, but by the time of the democratic breakthrough in the summer of 1989, Solidarity and its newly created government had joined it as the most trusted institutions.

Over the years the leading specialist on egalitarian attitudes in Poland has been Lena Kolarska-Bobińska. She invoked the classic distinction between equality of opportunity and equality of benefits (or outcomes) to argue that in Poland's communist system egalitarian attitudes primarily reflected support for greater opportunities, not the leveling of differences. Even support for equality of benefits played a very specific psychological function: "The principle of equal benefits . . . does not reflect a widely preferred model of social order. Instead, it is a mechanism guaranteeing protection of interests of those groups which do not participate in the governing system, groups which cannot influence the distribution of desired goods."[31] Put another way, communist leaders may have found reassurance in survey results pointing to widespread support for egalitarianism in Polish society. Yet, paradoxically, these egalitarian attitudes were actually targeted *against* them since society embraced egalitarianism as a defense mechanism that could normatively restrain an inordinate buildup of privilege and benefits by the ruling elite. Egalitarian demands were an expression of concern over privilege.

Defining egalitarians as those who supported both ceilings on earnings and full employment and inegalitarians as those who supported neither,

TABLE 2.2 Coefficients of Confidence in Selected Political Leaders and
Institutions, 1984–1990

Leader or Institution	1984	1985	1987	Spring 1988	Spring 1989	Fall 1989	Summer 1990
Jaruzelski	0.21	0.51	0.39	0.39	-0.01	0.25	-0.09
Wałęsa	0.04	-0.03	-0.09	-0.01	0.68	0.67	0.49
Church	0.65	0.72	0.65	0.74	0.66	0.58	0.59
Sejm	0.31	0.49	0.45	0.37	0.13	0.58	0.45
Army	0.39	0.46	0.42	0.44	0.19	0.16	0.41
Government	0.17	0.39	0.26	0.26	-0.12	0.61	0.47
PZPR	-0.08	0.12	-0.08	-0.17	-0.48	-0.76	—
Solidarity	-0.52	-0.55	-0.23	-0.46	0.58	0.61	0.45

Note: Variation in the coefficients of confidence is from -1 to +1.
Source: Krzysztof Jasiewicz, "Polish Elections of 1990," in Walter D. Connor and Piotr
Ploszajski (eds.), *The Polish Road from Socialism.* Armonk, N.Y.: M.E. Sharpe, 1992,
pp. 184–185.

Kolarska-Bobińska concluded that by 1990 about 40 percent of Poles
were egalitarian and just over 10 percent were inegalitarian; half the population exhibited mixed attitudes.[32] Predictably, socio-occupational dis-
tinctions more greatly accounted for attitudinal differences by the end of
the decade than at the beginning, with professionals and technicians wel-
coming merit-based inequalities and unskilled workers more than ever
supporting a full-employment policy.

Finally, popular attitudes about international politics can also tell us
about value change in Polish society. The list of countries that are ad-
mired or feared, considered to offer assistance or to pose a threat, reveals the degree to which Poles accept or reject such "myths" as Sarmatianism (manifest destiny in the Slavic world), geopolitical reality (the
notion of two natural enemies as neighbors), and the common European heritage (traditional friendship with France, Britain, and other
Western states).

Polish respondents' perceptions of other nations underwent consider-
able change in ranking between 1975 and December 1989. In this period
Americans went from fifth to first place in terms of the confidence of
Poles; they effectively exchanged places with Russians over these years.
The greatest single change, however, was in Poles' confidence in Ger-
mans; placing twenty-first in 1975 and maintaining this rank in 1987,

Germans were ranked fourth in 1989 (after Americans, Italians, and Hungarians).[33]

A different data set tells us more about the likes and dislikes of Poles. In 1991, 68 percent of respondents said that they liked Americans. The next best-liked nations were, in descending order, French (61 percent), Italians (59 percent), English (50 percent), and Hungarians (44 percent). The most disliked nations were Gypsies (47 percent), Ukrainians (38 percent), Arabs (32 percent), and Russians (32 percent). Attitudes toward Jews were mixed, with 17 percent sympathetic and 19 percent hostile. This survey's author correlated preferences expressed with reasons given for them and concluded that "the wealth of a nation, Catholicism, and wartime allies exerted the strongest relative influence on Poles' likes."[34]

A survey question closely related to attitudes toward other nations asked which countries posed potential threats to Polish independence. Half of the respondents in 1980 identified the USSR as the most serious threat, with the Federal Republic of Germany a distant second with 15 percent. Despite many years of communist propaganda discrediting them, then, capitalist countries, including NATO and the United States, were seen as threatening by only 10 percent of respondents. To be sure, in 1990, on the eve of its unification, Germany was most often named as threatening (by 41 percent) and the USSR/Russia was down to 21 percent.[35] But as we shall see in Chapter 7, by 2000 Poles' perceptions of international politics were strongly pro-West European while suspicions of Vladimir Putin's Russia had risen.

Political attitudes were clearly very different at the time communism collapsed from what they had been several decades earlier. Attitudinal support for the socialist system had peaked in the early 1970s and declined thereafter. Apart from a few ambiguous areas, political culture had not been transformed in the way that the communist regime had hoped. Instead it had become the regime's adversary.

Political Structure and Ruling Coalitions

The organizational framework of the Polish communist regime followed the Soviet model. Its most distinctive feature was the idea of separation of powers—not, as we might anticipate, of the executive and legislative branches as in Western states, but of the communist party and the institutions of government. The PZPR was to formulate overall policy for the country; the government's job was to implement that policy. The slogan launched in the 1970s—the party directs and the government governs—

may not have resolved the many ambiguities stemming from the existence of two massive parallel institutions, but it captured the general division of labor between the two. As the source of policymaking, the communist party was concerned above all with politics. As the implementer of the party's policies, the government performed primarily administrative functions. And if the head of the communist party was the most powerful politician in the country, the government head, or prime minister, was in many ways the country's economic overlord.

This organizational structure served, of course, as a façade for arbitrary rule by the communist elite. For starters the attention paid to the legal system was a charade. As one Polish sociologist noted, "This is exactly the essence of the revolutionary doctrine and practice of Communism: to create an order in which any arbitrary decision by authority is legal, while any reference made to law that runs contrary to the authorities' wish is illegal."[36] Thus communist authorities always acted within the law, the opposition invariably outside of it.

Every four years elections were held and all adult Polish citizens were expected to vote. But they were presented with a list of candidates approved earlier by the PZPR. The majority of candidates were drawn from PZPR ranks, which had swelled as the party took a more liberal approach to the ideological and class background of prospective members. But candidates for parliament also included members of two satellite parties of the PZPR—the United Peasant Party and the Democratic Party (SD). A minority also belonged to approved Catholic lay groups, Pax and Znak, and some were officially "independent" candidates who had earned the trust of the PZPR.

Ostensibly, as under the Westminster model, cabinet government was created from the ranks of the Sejm and was answerable to it. In People's Poland the government was called the Council of Ministers and was headed by the prime minister. Only in the periods 1952–1954 (Bierut) and 1981–1985 (Jaruzelski) were the prime ministers simultaneously the leaders of the PZPR. Prime ministers were always high-ranking party officials and at times may have disagreed with the party head, but they were never invested with the power of the latter. Poland also had a head of state, formally called president of the Council of State. Although this was not really a presidency, in his bid to make Poland resemble a Western democracy Jaruzelski appointed himself to this position in 1985 and raised its stature. Giving increased political significance to the presidency was to become a central issue in the transition to democracy in 1989.

If one asked the basic question—Who governs?—in communist Poland, the answer was not a governmental institution but the executive body of the PZPR—the Politburo—and its head, the first secretary. The Politburo consisted of the twelve or so most powerful men in the country (only one woman ever served on the Politburo in the communist period), and the party head presided over its weekly meetings. From the Stalinist period on, the most important matters of state were discussed and decided upon within this body, giving communist rule in Poland an oligarchical rather than dictatorial character.

Even authoritarian systems require a measure of coalition-building, that is, the process by which leaders secure support for their position and policies from their closest associates (who also may become their most serious rivals). In order to stay in power, Polish communist party heads were often forced into coalitions of expediency rather than choice. For example, Kremlin prompting during wartime led Bierut to join forces with the nativist Gomułka in 1944. He was then compelled to purge him from the coalition in 1948 when Sovietization began. Crucial to Bierut's tenure as party leader were close working relationships with the security and defense establishments, both controlled by Soviet officials appointed to Polish posts.

When Gomułka returned to power in 1956 the ruling coalition he established excluded party officials linked to liberal and hard-line factions. But a decade later, Mieczysław Moczar, an important ally who had headed the security apparatus and held himself up as a Polish patriot, turned on Gomułka. Within a few years he was out of power as his coalition unraveled and technocrats like Gierek also defected.

Gierek's ascendancy to the top party post at the end of 1970 was based on a looser, less disciplined coalition. He wanted to make the PZPR a catch-all institution and opened up the party to anyone interested in joining it—Catholics, Marxist heretics, the ideologically indifferent, careerists. Gierek saw himself as an "imperial party secretary," more imperious than authoritarian. The result was that a number of challenges to his leadership came from his inner circle. His prime minister, Piotr Jaroszewicz, had close connections in the Kremlin, had lived in Moscow, and spoke Russian well, contrasting with the more "Westernized" Gierek, a Silesian who as a child had been baptized, had worked as a coal miner in Belgium, and now was a hunting partner of the president of France and a guest of the Vatican. Other ambitious politicians in the PZPR were no longer afraid to challenge the first secretary's authority. The ruling coalition of the 1970s was, then, a more precariously divided group than earlier ones, and cracks within the Politburo appeared at the same time that the political opposition began to organize. The coexistence of a shaky ruling coalition and a more determined opposition provided Solidarity with the opportunity to organize in 1980. Several days after Solidarity was legalized, Gierek's loose coalition disintegrated and he was removed as party head.

After a brief, indecisive period under Stanisław Kania, who was unable to forge a consensus around what the PZPR should do about Solidarity, in 1981 General Jaruzelski was brought in at the head of a coalition of defense and security officials, together with a few key reformist leaders who had become convinced that Solidarity was leading the country toward disaster. In theory Jaruzelski adopted a "clipping of wings" policy that resembled Gomułka's in 1956: Party liberals and conservatives were purged from top party posts in equal numbers. But Jaruzelski presided over a shifting coalition that reflected growing uncertainty about the regime's future, especially after Gorbachev took power in Moscow in 1985. If in the early 1980s under martial law Jaruzelski's coalition hinged on support from hard-liners and military officials, by the late 1980s, ironically, his coalition became dependent on support from party reformers. They supplied Jaruzelski with the political resources needed to approach the Solidarity opposition and set up roundtable talks.

The parallel government–party structures and the intricate processes of coalition-building were replicated in People's Poland at all levels of administration, from the province to town and rural districts. The system bred many problems: duplication of functions by state and party officials, unclear divisions of responsibility between them, cumulation of posts by leaders, at times intense rivalry between incumbents of party and government positions, and their general incompetence, corruption, irresponsibility, and lack of accountability to the public. A persuasive case can be made that communism's collapse was occasioned in large part by an overinstitutionalization of politics and an underinstitutionalization of power and authority. There were simply too many overlapping official structures, while power was defined informally.

In the end, however, it was the regime's performance that brought the system down. It seems self-evident that had it not been for rapid economic decline, the communists would never have consented to a transfer of power to the political opposition. Notwithstanding the many sophistic and metaphysical interpretations of the communist collapse—moral bankruptcy, psychological loss of nerve, creation of a civil society—in the end society judged the regime by its performance and decided to have done with it. Marx had been correct that, in the last instance, economic factors determined the political superstructure.

Popular Mobilization Against Communist Rule

The political behavior of citizens under communism underwent change in tandem with regime performance. Political behavior was affected by social cleavages and mass alignments that, in turn, stemmed from a transformed social structure. The size, salience, and resources of the principal social groups were determined by their changed place in the social hierarchy. Groups disaffected by social change were the ones most likely to take collective action. From the mid-1970s in Poland, more and more disaffected groups became involved in protests. One of their common objectives was to create a civil society free from the influence of the communist party-state.

In Poland protests against communist rule had a cyclical nature. They were sufficiently large scale and threatening to the regime that communist rulers resorted to force to quash them. Up to 1948 irregular and scattered "forest detachments" of partisans that had fought in World War II carried out a struggle against the Soviet-imposed regime but proved no match for Polish troops and security forces operating under Soviet command. In June 1956, workers at one of the country's largest factories, in Poznań, demanded bread and freedom. They were shot at and strike leaders were imprisoned, but the momentum they created led to mass rallies in Warsaw in October of that year, which brought Gomułka back to power. In March 1968, students in Warsaw, like students in many other parts of the world that year, protested against their government. Many were beaten up, student leaders were imprisoned, and professors who were Jewish were identified as mentors of the protesting students and many of them were expelled from Poland.

Just over two years later shipyard workers in Gdańsk staged violent protests against an increase in food prices. The regime used deadly force to suppress them: More than 40 workers were killed in the December 1970 uprising. But the events allowed Gierek to seize power. When factory workers in Radom and Ursus (outside Warsaw) downed tools in 1976 to protest food prices, Gierek was more cautious in ordering force to be used against them: It was limited to beatings and imprisonment of strike leaders. The protest actions from which the communist regime never recovered were the nationwide strikes organized in the summer of

1980 after shipyard workers in Gdańsk demanded higher wages and registration of an independent trade union, Solidarity. After considerable delay and negotiations, the authorities gave in to these demands. But wildcat strikes in 1981 that Solidarity leaders could not control, coupled with the threat of a Soviet invasion, convinced General Jaruzelski to impose martial law in December 1981.

For the rest of the 1980s an underground resistance organization survived and put the legitimacy of the martial law regime into question. When industrial strife spread across the country again in the summer of 1988, communist leaders realized that there was no "final solution" available to prop up the discredited system. They therefore turned to Solidarity leaders as potential partners in government and convened roundtable talks in 1989.

Though public protests against the communist system were cyclical in nature, the main actors involved and the mass alignments they established differed. Let us examine the groups and movements that formed the basis for popular mobilization.

Catholic Mobilization

Political mobilization encompassed diverse social groups and required years of spadework to become effective. From its inception, the backbone of resistance to the communist regime was the Catholic Church. The primate of the church, Cardinal Stefan Wyszyński, was even imprisoned from September 1953 to October 1956 during the last gasp of Polish Stalinism. While some Catholic lay groups like Pax and Znak were willing in varying degrees to work within the system, it was Wyszyński with whom successive communist leaders had to contend. His prison notebooks from the 1950s reveal a clear understanding of the logic of communist rule.[37] By the time of the Great Novena in 1966, celebrating the millennium of Christianity in Poland, the primate had become an outspoken critic of the Gomułka regime. Though he agreed to a modus vivendi with Gierek, Gomułka's pragmatic successor, in the 1970s, embryonic dissident groups such as independent trade unions and the Workers' Defense Committee were not disappointed when they turned to the church for shelter.

Meanwhile lay Catholic groups whittled away at Marxist influence. "The rational arguments of Catholics contrasted with the Marxist belief in a religion of humanity where will rather than reason was supposed to change the world."[38] In the late 1960s "the image of the Church as a symbol of national self-identification grew as Gomułka's popularity declined."[39] Whereas Wyszyński invoked nationalist symbols, lay groups appealed to reason and intellect, thereby establishing dialogue with liberal Marxists in the PZPR and strengthening their influence within it.

Cardinal Wyszyński died in May 1981, shortly after participating in two historic events: the election of fellow Polish Cardinal Karol Wojtyła to the throne of St. Peter in 1978 and the legalization of the Solidarity movement in August–September 1980. In referring to Wyszyński as "Primate of the Millennium"—arguably the greatest Polish church figure in ten centuries—Pope John Paul II acknowledged his debt to Wyszyński as he began to steer a subtle course designed to weaken the will of communist rulers and ultimately shame them.[40] Two American political scientists contend that "if one does not organize society morally, one is unlikely to succeed in organizing it materially."[41] It was the Polish Catholic Church that, over the decades, consistently challenged the moral basis of communist rule.

When General Jaruzelski declared martial law in December 1981 so as to destroy the Solidarity trade union, Wyszyński's successor, Cardinal Józef Glemp, sought to prevent bloodshed by appealing for national reconciliation. In return for its moderate stance the episcopate was given permission by the state to embark upon an unprecedented expansion of church building in the 1980s. This was the start of a decline in the church's prestige that carried over to the democratic system. On the other hand, many radical parish priests decried martial law from the pulpit, harbored underground leaders on the run, raised funds to support underground publications, and distributed food and clothes to families whose breadwinners had been interned. The best known was Father Jerzy Popiełuszko from a Warsaw parish. One writer summarized the activity of radical priests this way: "By recreating sacramentally . . . the collective effervescence of the original experience of Solidarity, they were helping to maintain alive the movement as well as its norms and values."[42] When Popiełuszko was murdered by agents of the security police in October 1984, the Catholic faithful turned him into a political martyr.

As we shall see in the next chapter, the church played an important part in communism's endgame. Even with a less effective leadership, its status as the repository and guardian of Polish national culture made it a pivotal institution in regime transition.

Workers' Mobilization

Apart from Catholic groups, the other principal type of political organization not controlled by the party was that of workers. The political centrality of the industrial working class resulted from two countervailing processes: its rapid growth in the first two decades of communism and the blocked avenues for its further upward mobility by the mid-1970s.

The conflict of interests among, on the one hand, skilled workers, professionals, and the intelligentsia and, on the other hand, the *nomenklatura*—party officials and the party-appointed managerial class—was becoming more and more evident. Whereas the resources common to the first groups were their skills and qualifications, those held by the *nomenklatura* were connections. Of the workers, professionals, and intelligentsia, the workers played the paramount role of agents of change in People's Poland: They protested in Poznań in 1956, in Gdańsk in 1970, in Radom and Ursus in 1976, and, finally, nationwide in the summer of 1980. They brought down party leaders and finally succeeded in creating a nationwide organization, the Solidarity trade union, not under the control of the PZPR. Not surprisingly, a comparative Polish–French study conducted in the spring of 1989 found that "Polish workers perceive themselves as the main actors of change more often than other groups and more often than French workers."[43]

Long-standing worker activism triggered the birth of the Solidarity movement, but it was undergirded by a consensus crystallizing across all groups in society about the terminal crisis of communism. In an open-ended question in the *Polacy 1984* survey, 81 percent of respondents asserted that dishonesty and theft by those in power were causes of the crisis. These specific complaints gave way in time to the more general criticism that the authorities were not concerned with the interests of ordinary people or that channels of interest articulation were blocked. As particularist grievances were replaced by universalist grievances, the pressure for change built.

A considerable literature on the origins and evolution of Solidarity has emerged. One of the principal controversies is whether the trade union remained an *ouvrieriste* or purely worker-led movement or whether it was taken over by dissident intellectuals.[44] To be sure, both social groups saw reason to collaborate within a single movement in order to challenge the hegemony of the communist party. The transformation of Polish society produced by Solidarity in 1980–1981 was so profound and sweeping that it made the events of 1989 possible.

By the time its membership had reached nearly 10 million in 1981, Solidarity was a broad social movement that included in its ranks workers and white-collar employees, intellectuals and entrepreneurs, Catholics and communists. David Ost made the important point that "the experience of autonomous public activity was in and of itself a major goal of the movement."[45] It proved to be a critical experiment in political alignment and mobilization that charted the path for the democratic breakthrough later in the decade.

The internal organization of Solidarity had to respond to the broadening of the movement, the idiosyncratic preferences of its former electrician leader, Lech Wałęsa, as well as to the functional imperatives confronting any organization. Ost conceptualized its response as "organizational ambiguity" and "decisive indecisiveness." Solidarity's survival depended on such a paradoxical strategy and its organizational ambiguity was intentional. Many instances of ambiguity in Solidarity and by Wałęsa himself can be identified. Doublespeak punctuated the transcript of the Gdańsk meeting that established Solidarity: Wałęsa concluded that "here in Gdańsk there is a central power except it is not a central body."[46] Earlier he had asserted "everyone can adopt our [Gdańsk] statute," but just as quickly he conceded that chapters could "re-do it any way they like."[47] He continued, "We aren't going to be building chapels in our unions," but added, "As long as I am here, a cross will always be on the wall and a representative of the Primate will be with us."[48] In the summer of 1981 he endorsed strike action on his visits to troubled regions, but once back in Gdańsk he made efforts to stop them.

How much of this inconsistency was really strategic and how much due to Wałęsa's own irresoluteness, vacillation, susceptibility to the influence of his entourage, and response to government actions is difficult to say. But we can agree with Ost that Solidarity's survival ability was enhanced by its inconsistencies: "Only an ambiguous authority structure, where the union could appear sometimes to control a unified national movement, and at other times to have control over no one at all, had a chance of allowing Solidarity to succeed."[49]

In considering ambiguity as an organizational weapon, we have to ask why it sputtered when martial law was declared in December 1981. For Ost, Solidarity's ambiguity broke down as an effective strategy by July 1981, when the communist authorities embarked on the equally ingenious policy of doing nothing.[50] Why Solidarity was weakened when the authorities did nothing but was destroyed when the authorities did something—impose martial law—is a logical dilemma left unresolved by his analysis. If, however, ambiguity had been intentionally cultivated, it would indeed explain why Solidarity could survive first under the conspiratorial conditions created by martial law and second during the period of disillusionment of the mid-1980s when societal support for the movement dwindled. In both periods it made Solidarity an elusive target.

Whatever the case, it was clear that the basis of Solidarity's challenge to the political authorities lay in its legitimating formula. As two political scientists argued, "its own internal functioning exemplified a principle of legitimate political authority that contradicted the party-state's primary rationale of legitimacy."[51] The conflict between the independent trade-union movement and the regime could, accordingly, be viewed as one between two forms of rationality. Solidarity's was based on redefining political rules and procedures in Poland, the regime's on the substantive claim of guaranteeing welfarism and delivering material goods to society, in line with the society of plenty that communist ideology promised.

Solidarity calculated that it was more realistic, initially, to change the form of governance at the local level than to overhaul the central political system. The establishment of self-government in all spheres of society could lead to a self-governing republic, an objective contained in the program adopted at its first congress. Solidarity's own organization was to be exemplary in this regard: "Its principle of democratic, territorially-based organization, which penetrated the party, formed the core of its challenge to the legitimacy of the party-state based on substantive rationality. The organizational weapon was indeed one of Solidarity's strongest."[52] Polish sociologist Jadwiga Staniszkis believed, then, that this revolutionary form of self-government would have proved a "self-limiting revolution" because these self-governing organizations were not interested in taking over or sharing government responsibility.[53] That, of course, was just the contrary of what was to happen in 1989.

Another Polish writer, Jacek Kurczewski, exposed other contradictions in Solidarity's strategy. It aimed to unify society but instead polarized it by forcing citizens to take a stand on its goals. It wanted to civilize the political system (for example, by relaxing censorship laws) but ended up barbarizing the adversary. It pursued political power but found it a burden as rival camps sought to gain control of it. It stood for political egalitarianism vis-à-vis the communist party but promoted inegalitarianism in its own economic policies. Finally, it wanted to institutionalize the social revolution it had launched, but institutions invariably displace idealistic goals.[54]

Solidarity's governance of itself was a crucial aspect of its general politics. The new, highly skilled working class and the traditional one combined to provide a model of democratic activity consistent with its espoused social democratic ideology. Some argue that workers' innate common sense formed a sturdier base for alternative government than the intellectual contortions of some Solidarity experts. Roman Laba asserts that it was precisely the worker roots of Solidarity that gave the movement its nobility.[55]

During 1980–1981 Solidarity faced various efforts by the communist authorities to split and weaken the movement. By undermining Solidarity's ability to develop working relationships with six major political actors and exaggerating the likelihood of collaboration with a seventh, the regime could cast doubt on Solidarity's claim to embody the real interests of Polish society. The inability of Solidarity chiefs to find trustworthy partners was to destroy its alliance-building strategy. These are the institutional relationships that, for many different reasons, Solidarity was unable to cement:

1. Solidarity could not depend on maintaining a lasting working relationship with the *communist party*. Although some leaders like Kania, Jaruzelski, and reputed liberal Mieczysław Rakowski appeared trustworthy, the party always seemed a hairbreadth away from being taken over by hard-liners, as the sinister Bydgoszcz affair of March 1981 (when security agents beat up local Solidarity activists) suggested. The rulers were well served by this depiction of the party: Solidarity could never be sure that negotiations with it would prove useful or durable.
2. Solidarity could not count on the *government* as a reliable partner in negotiations. When even a minister as supposedly well-disposed toward the union as Rakowski walked out on talks with Wałęsa in August 1981, cooperation with the government seemed bound to prove ephemeral, unpredictable, or irrelevant. Solidarity leaders were kept guessing whether the August accords reached with the government meant anything.
3. The *Soviet Union* was the wild card in the political events, which Polish communists stressed they could not control. The senile Brezhnev, his aging Politburo, and his World War II–era generals

were impatient with the Polish communist party's tolerance of Solidarity. If a few Solidarity activists launched bravado verbal attacks on the USSR, it served only to heighten tension with the neighboring superpower. The pre-Gorbachev USSR was an implausible partner for Solidarity.

4. Rival *trade unions* enjoying communist support were strengthened in order to challenge Solidarity. Branch unions representing an entire industry, for example, metallurgy, appealed to workers to desert the all-purpose Solidarity union and join them. To complicate matters for Solidarity, some union chapters previously part of the communist structure applied to join Solidarity and it was not always clear whether they were acting in good faith. Even rural Solidarity, set up in 1981 as a farmers' organization, was suspect because of its better rapport with the authorities.

5. The actions of the *Catholic Church* did not inspire full confidence. First Cardinal Wyszyński, then Cardinal Glemp expressed only lukewarm support for the free trade-union movement. The ecclesiastical hierarchy was self-interested, its primary constituency was the countryside, and it was unwilling to risk its privileged position to defend a workers' movement.

6. Some *social groups* were not proving to be reliable supporters of Solidarity. In the summer of 1981 large numbers of Poles of different social backgrounds—doctors and carpenters, technicians and peasants—were leaving the Poland of Solidarity for the refugee camps of Austria. By the fall some groups had grown sufficiently disenchanted with Solidarity that they ceased to participate in demonstrations and strikes called by the movement's leadership.

7. It was the seventh institutional relationship that directly undermined Solidarity. To believe the communist regime, Solidarity *could* trust the Polish *army*. Military goodwill missions in the fall of 1981 to the countryside (to distribute fertilizers, repair tractors, and harvest crops) and to the cities (to fix potholes, bring order to lines in front of stores, and root out corrupt practices) were intended to demonstrate that the army was on the side of society. Official opinion polls reflected its growing popularity: The army was perceived to be equally intolerant of the government's and Solidarity's mishandling of politics. The army was presented as the one institution capable of putting right the ills of Polish society, that is, as naturally sharing Solidarity's cause but being more efficient at advancing it.

It was the military, of course, that imposed and enforced martial law, and it was Jaruzelski's military regime that by the fall of 1982 had declared Solidarity illegal. Even now that archival material on the period has been opened up, there is very little evidence that Solidarity leaders appreciated the danger of trusting the military. Instead, during 1981 they seemed to be fixated by the first two relationships identified, with the party and with the government. To be sure, Wałęsa and his colleagues had good reason to be suspicious of the intentions of Kania, his Politburo, and the communist government. If Solidarity was characterized by organizational ambiguity, the communist regime was distinguished by normative ambiguity: Some leaders seemed genuine in establishing a partnership with the social movement whereas others were little more than surrogates of the Kremlin. But even if the regime was to some degree successful in misrepresenting Solidarity's institutional allies, the movement irreversibly changed social consciousness, in particular, imbuing society with a sense of political efficacy. This was the groundwork for the realignment in Polish politics that occurred at the end of the 1980s.

Mobilization of Dissident Intellectuals

We have described how Poland's transformed social structure contributed to the rise of Solidarity and how Solidarity turned into a broad-based social movement whose strengths and weaknesses were determined by mass alignments. The *issues* of common concern to social groups also shaped the pattern of mass alignments. The belief, for example, that without the participation and input of average citizens the communist authorities would continue to mismanage the economy played a direct role in the rise of Solidarity. The role of intellectuals in defining a political agenda was instrumental to the emergence of Solidarity.

Although Solidarity was the culmination of organized opposition to the regime, the creation of the Workers' Defense Committee (KOR) a few years earlier, in 1976, was crucial in a number of ways. First, its membership included many well-known dissidents who had served an apprenticeship in the opposition: Jacek Kuroń, Jan Józef Lipski, Adam Michnik, and Karol Modzelewski. Second, it quickly proved to be more than a mere group of intellectuals theorizing about politics; it helped provide tangible support for workers and their families in Radom and Ursus who had been persecuted for their role in the 1976 protests. When interfactory strike committees were set up in the summer of 1980, the KOR became a critical channel for communication across the country. Third, its establishment gave other groups the confidence to organize. Within three years, a Helsinki agreement-oriented Committee for the Defense of Human and Civil Rights (ROPCiO), a "Flying University" presenting lectures to students by dissidents, a nationalist right-wing Confederation for an Independent Poland (KPN), and a Solidarity precursor—the Free Trade Unions of the Coast, which included Wałęsa in its leadership—had come into being. Fourth, the program and strategy developed by the KOR proved to be very effective in the context of the late 1970s. Its call for the construction of a civil society that would expand in numbers as well as scope of action and its forging of ties with Catholic groups became extremely successful.[56] Although the KOR's leadership recognized the limits of the group's usefulness and disbanded in 1981, its individual members went on to play key roles during the roundtable talks in 1989 and in the politics of the Third Republic.

British journalist Neil Ascherson introduced the term "forum politics" to describe the political opposition in the late communist period. Although "forum" was not a term used in the Polish oppositional context, its counterpart in other socialist states (such as the Civic Forum in Czechoslovakia) often preferred the word to "movement," "association," or "league." What was common to opposition dissident movements in these countries was that their core group consisted of intellectuals. Occasionally workers were included, but even then the character of forum politics was primarily intellectual. Ascherson listed the shared characteristics of forum politics, of which the KOR was a prime example: (1) an emphasis on human rights, (2) use of nonviolent methods, (3) the vision of a self-managing civil society functioning independently of the state, (4) the belief that such a civil society could be constructed even before the communist system was replaced, (5) stress on the importance of cross-national activity in the development of civil society, (6) advocacy of social liberalism, thereby distinguishing forum politics from positions held by the Catholic Church, (7) the frequent Marxist pedigree of practitioners, who were either the offspring of communists or had themselves been critical Marxists, and (8) third-way ideals that made forum politics skeptical of Western capitalist models as well as opposed to state socialist ones.[57]

It is debatable how directly forum politics contributed to the collapse of communism. Certainly without strikes by workers and union organization, the weapons of intellectual dissidents were limited. Nevertheless, Ascherson contended that "the Forum people were to lead the revolutionary movements of 1989 throughout central and north-eastern Europe, and to form the first post-revolutionary governments."[58] In Poland, former KOR members played a major role at the roundtable talks discussed in the following chapter.

In sum, group alignments had a profound effect on politics in 1970s Poland. Through trial and error, the repeated efforts to unify Catholic, worker, and intellectual movements ultimately proved successful. They gave birth to Solidarity and, by the late 1980s, to a new political system.

Impasse

Writers striving to explain the crisis of communism have identified numerous factors as sources of popular dissatisfaction and political mobilization against the regime. The list—by no means exhaustive—includes: (1) regime performance, (2) relative deprivation and rising expectations, (3) cultural transformations and changing value systems, (4) shifting social cleavages and political alignments, and (5) rising participatory demands stimulated by the emergence of new groups with new resources and new agendas. These factors combined can account for the sudden breakdown of an authoritarian system that had a record of employing force whenever its survival was threatened.

In this chapter we have traced the evolution of mass alignments and the mobilization of opposition forces that were the product of a transformed, less agrarian social structure. Cleavages based on ethnicity or religion, which in many other societies have hamstrung democratic mobilization, were virtually absent in Poland. Economic cleavages based on class differences can often hamper unified collective action. Yet in Poland a class alliance—rather than schism—between workers and intellectuals proved crucial to creating a democratic breakthrough. In terms of both political attitudes and behavior, then, the operative distinction in communist Poland was primarily between rulers and ruled, the regime and civil society, authoritarians and liberals. The next chapter describes what happened when these two forces were pulled toward each other.

3

Regime Change and Democratization

By the late 1980s the ruling coalition, led by the communist party, and the Polish opposition had reached a stalemate. Neither side could achieve its goals without the cooperation of the other. The ruling party had found itself unable to reform the economy on its own; it needed the legitimacy that the opposition could lend it, legitimacy both in the eyes of Polish society and in the eyes of international lenders. The opposition had their independent trade union, Solidarity, but this union was still illegal and relatively weak, and by itself could provide no solution to Poland's serious economic problems; it certainly was not capable of wresting power from the communist party, with its army and its police, in a direct confrontation. They needed each other in order to get anywhere, so in February 1989 they sat down to the bargaining table.

Two months later they signed a settlement that included arrangements for immediate June elections and several constitutional changes, including a new Senate and a new presidency. The election was played out largely according to the agreed upon rules, which were intended to prevent any risk of an immediate transfer of power. The new state institutions were set up according to these rules. Nevertheless, a few months later, by September 1989, Poland was being governed by a prime minister from the Solidarity opposition, presiding over a largely noncommunist government.

Regime change in Poland took place more swiftly than any political actors expected. A pact intended to control the pace and scope of the transition had been concluded; yet in less than half a year the political landscape was altered beyond the imaginings of the pact-crafters. This chapter analyzes the dynamics and implications of this sudden transformation.

Of course the futures of both institutions and actors are affected by much more than the transition itself. Preexisting factors—from the experiences of individuals, to commonly shared attitudes, to institutions relatively unaffected by the change—will also shape the new system; such key elements for Poland were discussed in the previous chapters. But times of regime change—political transitions—are crucial junctures in politics, both for shaping institutional trajectories and for the fortunes of political players. While particular institutions are rarely in their final form at the close of a regime transition, transitional choices, deals, and their unexpected consequences create institutional facts that limit possibilities in the following years. Similarly, the unpredictable, rapidly changing, even chaotic games of transition (qualitatively different from the games of "normal politics," within stable institutional arenas) leave political actors in particular positions, of relative strength or weakness, on the newly created playing fields. While players may of course improve their lot according to the rules of the new games, their own trajectories will be affected by this starting point.

In the following pages we examine the players, their resources and issue preferences, and their actions and responses to others' actions, in order both to make this sudden and dramatic regime change comprehensible and to present its possible implications for later outcomes.

The Players of Transition

We concentrate in this analysis on elite actors—individuals, informal groups, and organizational leaderships. This is not to say that larger groups in society—social classes and mass movements, in particular—played no role in these events. But their active role came at a few key moments, such as workers prompting the elite's recognition of stalemate through their strikes in the spring and summer of 1988, workers again putting pressure on the elite negotiators with further strikes and protest actions during the talks, and Polish voters making their preferences clear at the polls on June 4 and 18, 1989. The dynamics and indeed the outcome of the regime change are better understood through analysis of key elite political players, who often of course derived both their resources and their constraints from these larger social groups.

The Communist Party

By 1988 it was clear to insiders (party leaders), outsiders (Solidarity leaders), and external brokers (Gorbachev) alike that the resources of Poland's political opposition had been accruing as it built an independent civil society. The communist leadership felt under pressure to redistribute rewards and values in a manner more reflective of society's preferences. As economic crisis deepened, certain political actors—primarily party reformers—stressed the need to establish larger coalitions in order to secure a broader mandate and to diffuse responsibility for state policy (in 1981 Solidarity was accused of being unwilling to shoulder even partial responsibility). Furthermore, the position of the communist political class had turned into a free fall. As sociologist Jadwiga Staniszkis wrote, members of this political class had become "dependent on the state, unaccustomed to expressing their own position (that in the past did not need justification), and caught in the trap of their own calls for 'reforms.'"[1]

In December 1988 an extraordinary meeting was held in Paris that brought together for the first time some of the communist bloc's leading dissidents. Among them was Wałęsa, making his first foreign trip in many years. According to the recollections of one of Solidarity's main leaders, Bronisław Geremek, "For me the year 1989 began really in Paris, in mid-December 1988. There would be no perestroika, no Gorbachev, if not for Poland's Solidarity. In the ensuing months the list of facts which would never have occurred increased dramatically."[2]

Solidarity's brief existence in 1980–1981, with its then pro forma commitment to the socialist system, had another important consequence for the Polish communist party. As Geremek put it: "It took away the party's own legitimacy, which was based on the assumption that it served the national interest and represented it in Moscow. Though it did not wish to recognize it, the suspicion arose, especially in 1989, that the party might in fact be the representative of the Soviet Union's interests in its own country, not the other way around."[3]

What were the pivotal events that led to the party leadership's conversion to the cause of reform in the late 1980s and to the system's total destruction in 1989? According to one Politburo member, the national referendum called by Jaruzelski in the fall of 1987 to seek approval of a package of political and economic reforms was understood by the party leadership as a pathbreaking step toward the Polish road to socialism so often talked about in the past.[4] In order to obtain public approval of proposed price increases (price rises announced suddenly in both 1970 and 1976 had triggered antigovernment demonstrations), the referendum asked whether voters supported accelerated economic reform even if it might cause temporary hardship. In referring to the referendum, sociologist Jacek Kurczewski correctly observed that "to vague questions one gets vague answers. To an absurd question one gets an answer which is absurd."[5]

Nevertheless, the fact that a referendum was held at all pried open additional political space, as the Politburo had intended, and augured a series of party initiatives. Strikes organized by activists of the still illegal Solidarity movement in May 1988 did not immediately produce any significant political concessions. The symbolic politics pursued by party leaders in postcrisis situations, especially creating a game of musical chairs for political leaders (about which the public had become blasé), this time involved the replacement of the prime minister. Zbigniew Messner, who had presided over limited economic reform, was dumped in favor of the communist party's consummate politician, Mieczysław Rakowski. On the surface, a party liberal was succeeding an unimaginative technocrat. In reality, Alfred Miodowicz, head of the proregime trade unions and regarded as a hard-liner, had been influential in having Messner removed, thereby casting doubt on whether political liberalization was indeed the desired outcome of the change.[6]

In July 1988 Gorbachev visited Poland and embraced the cause of reform, declaring that Poles had the right to determine their own political destiny. Without this personal endorsement from the Kremlin leader it is doubtful whether Jaruzelski could have gone ahead with plans for talks between the ruling party and political dissidents. The urgency of breaking out of a cycle of crises was heightened when Solidarity staged a second wave of strikes in August, but the strikes were only the most dramatic sign of crisis. The government-run polling agency found that the percentage of respondents agreeing that the general economic condition of the country was poor had risen from 64 percent at the end of summer in 1987 to 85 percent at the end of summer in 1988. More ominous for the authorities, the proportion of respondents agreeing that the *political* situation was bad had nearly doubled, increasing from 21 percent to 41 percent over the same period. According to a Public Opinion Survey Center report, "The communist party (PZPR) was rapidly losing what remained of its authority: early in 1988 the non-approvers outnumbered the supporters. Starting from 1988, the net support for PZPR was expressed in negative numbers only."[7]

As traditionally happened in crisis situations, the party convened its Central Committee on August 26. On the same day, Interior Minister Czesław Kiszczak appeared on television officially to announce the desirability of roundtable talks with representatives of various social and occupational milieux: "I stipulate no preconditions regarding the subject of the talks nor regarding the composition of participants."[8] A round of "talks about talks" began in August 1988 between Politburo member Józef Czyrek and Solidarity leader Andrzej Stelmachowski. It was quickly followed by an informal meeting between Kiszczak, Wałęsa, and their teams of advisers on September 16. Held in Magdalenka, the venue for future full-blown roundtable negotiations, this meeting explored the viability of roundtable negotiations and the scope for compromise between party and opposition positions. The last of these informal Magdalenka talks before the formal roundtable began was held on January 27, 1989.

The first tangible public result of Kiszczak's offer was the appearance on state-owned television of Wałęsa on November 30, 1988, in a debate with the fiery Miodowicz. Wałęsa scored a debating victory, and soon afterward he received a passport to travel to the extraordinary Paris meeting, held December 10–11, where he confirmed his still unblemished international prestige as a Nobel Peace Prize laureate. A week later, on December 18, Solidarity held a major meeting in Warsaw that established the Citizens' Committee advising the Solidarity leader. This proved an important juncture in the late organizational development of Solidarity.

The Eighth Plenum seemed to embrace liberalization but at the same time provided discouraging signs about the likelihood of political change. In this respect it scarcely differed from many preceding Central Committee sessions at times of crisis. It condemned efforts at political destabilization undertaken by the opposition while accepting Kiszczak's initiative for immediate roundtable talks with opposition members. But a more obvious caesura in the formulation of party policy on liberalization was the first session of the Central Committee's Tenth Plenum, held shortly after the Paris conference, in late December 1988 and mid-January 1989. In terms of personnel changes the meeting marked the departure of party conservatives such as General Józef Baryła and their replacement with liberals such as Janusz Reykowski.

In substantive terms, it is significant that the first section of the Politburo's theses on party reform was titled "The Polish Road to Socialism Today." According to this document, "In many areas of systemic transformations, Polish approaches are pioneering and blazing new paths." Even the experience of the Stalinist era had shown that "Poland was not a place where distortions occurred on such a scale as are revealed today in other countries. The PZPR also carried out in public the quickest and deepest accounting with them." In addition, the Tenth Plenum theses asserted that "socialism on Polish land grew on national soil." Furthermore, the party considered itself nothing less than "the critical inheritors of the entire history of the Polish nation and state" and believed that it had sustained Poland by "defending her national interests, the sovereignty of the country, and the durability of the alliance system originating in the Yalta–Potsdam framework of territorial–political order on our continent."[9]

The PZPR was proclaiming, then, that it was the least evil of regional communist parties, that it had largely been faithful to Polish national interests, and that, where unpopular international alliances had been forged, they reflected the Realpolitik sanctioned by the West both in wartime and during the Cold War. A scant year after the sophistic theses of the Tenth Plenum had been advanced, the PZPR ceased to exist. To be sure, the theses did refer to a modern type of socialism that in future would fuse a socialist democratic state and a civil society, but they did not entirely abandon the idea of the party's leading role in society or the internal party principle of democratic centralism. Whether sufficient room remained for negotiating constructively with Solidarity seemed doubtful.

On January 16, 1989, however, the Plenum's second session came out squarely in favor of political and trade-union pluralism. This occurred only after heated debate and a divisive vote: 143 members supporting pluralism, 32 against, 14 abstaining. The feasibility of roundtable talks, in abeyance for four months, now became real. Conceding the need to legalize Solidarity, the party sought to steer the required changes. Rakowski made reference to a new, less dominant role for the party in society. His conception was intended to form part of the Tenth Plenum theses but, significantly, it was defeated by diehard communist hard-liners. Still, he expressed confidence that as prime minister he had bailed the party out of a crisis: "When I was nominated to be prime minister and started with our early reform program, all the opinion polls predicted our victory" in free elections.[10]

The first of Jaruzelski's threats to resign his posts—as party leader, president of the Council of State, and commander in chief—forced the Plenum to give his leadership and its policy of dialogue a vote of confidence: It was endorsed unanimously, with four abstentions.[11] That Jaruzelski had persuaded his closest associates—Prime Minister

Rakowski, Defense Minister Florian Siwicki, and Interior Minister Kiszczak—to threaten to resign, too, made his case unassailable. If, however, any one of these leaders had not gone along with Jaruzelski, had allied himself with the Central Committee conservatives, or had put himself forward as an alternative to Jaruzelski, the final vote at the Tenth Plenum in favor of dialogue might have been different. Although it is difficult to estimate what proportion of the party rank and file supported liberalization, one calculation is that 50–70 percent of party members backed Jaruzelski's initiative.[12]

Shortly thereafter, party notables gathered one final time before the roundtable talks to theorize about the future character of Polish socialism. The party's third national theoretical-ideological conference was held on February 2–4 and, as in the case of the first two, provided no new ideological directions. Symbolically, this final confirmation of the PZPR's theoretical sterility was followed two days later, on February 6, by the beginning of the roundtable between the governing coalition and opposition forces. The talks ran till April 5, 1989, and for the first time since the late 1940s effectively displaced the Central Committee as the most important locus of political decisionmaking.

On May 5, the broader party leadership reconstituted itself, this time as the Second National Conference of Delegates to the Tenth Congress.[13] The electoral platform that the party intended to use to contest the competitive elections the following month was the most notable product of this meeting. The party resolved to undertake a major overhaul of party statutes and suggestively noted that the PZPR could not continue as the party it had been since 1948.[14]

To summarize, a series of events seemingly engineered by party leaders appeared to spin out of control for them and weakened their political capabilities. Following the 1987 referendum verdict on economic reform, the Wałęsa–Miodowicz television debate that embarrassed the authorities, and the industrial strife in the summer of 1988, the Jaruzelski administration could continue to perceive the Solidarity movement as a political competitor, but it could have no doubt about the political consciousness of most of the key sectors of society—industrial workers and intellectuals—and their resolve to bring about change. By the time the Tenth Plenum opened in December 1988, the party was in disarray. A sizable minority of Central Committee members refused to acquiesce to any declaration espousing political and trade-union pluralism; for them even the re-legalization of Solidarity was too bitter a pill to swallow. Others, the party paternalists, believed that the party would do itself credit by

charting change and leading the country to democracy; Rakowski represented this viewpoint. Finally, the three generals, Jaruzelski, Kiszczak,
and Siwicki, the leaders who were best-informed and probably most
alarmed about the state of Polish society, urged genuine compromise,
which they treated as a goal in itself.

Party–Solidarity Interaction

The opposition's strategy preceding the roundtable talks was to stress its
utility to the authorities in crisis management. It refrained from threatening to mobilize and organize popular upheaval—at least not immediately.
The unproven electoral record of the opposition made reformist party
leaders (though as "reformists" they had retained pivotal positions in the
martial-law period) additionally tempted to secure Solidarity's co-
responsibility at perceived low risk to the party. Survey data available to
party leaders at the time suggested that the party could expect to gain no
less than 25–30 percent of the vote and Solidarity 20 percent, with the remainder of the electorate uncommitted.[15]

Authorities and opposition shared certain fears: impending economic
disaster accompanied by a return to the social anarchy of late 1981, when
not even Wałęsa could rein in the wildcat strikes throughout the country.
They also shared the same generalized vision with regard to getting out
of this impasse: the urgency of profound structural economic change going beyond that attempted by the Messner government of the mid-1980s
and the interconnectedness of economic and political reform. By 1988
Jaruzelski needed a partner more influential and dynamic than the embattled reformist wing of his party. One survey found that his approval
rating had dropped from 71 percent in 1985 to 44 percent in 1989. In this
same four-year period Wałęsa's rating had shot up, from 45 to 85 percent.[16] Clearly, Wałęsa was the most politically attractive partner that
Jaruzelski could hope for.

The opposition, in its turn, saw its immediate goal of political liberalization—and in particular the legalization of Solidarity—as being in the
hands of the communists, and was willing to pay some kind of price for
this goal. The extent to which compromise and a satisfying strategy characterized the opposition at this stage depended on its perceptions of the
authorities' resources. Although in objective terms these remained pre-
ponderant, many opposition activists sensed a loss of will and a crisis of
confidence within the party leadership, evidenced in its concession to
hold Poland's first referendum since 1946 in November 1987. In terms of

substance, it was hard to object to the referendum, but because it was pro-posed by the communists, Solidarity called for a boycott. It was the first public test of will between incumbent and opposition camps since martial law had put an end to political contestation. The turnout for the referen-dum was 67 percent—far from the 98 percent claimed by the communists in pre-1980 elections, about the same as in elections held in the 1980s, but far from the low level intended by the boycott call. About two-thirds of those who voted backed the reform package. Here, too, both govern-ment and opposition could claim victory. Although a substantial majority of the electorate turned out at the ballot box and voted for the govern-ment proposal, the proposal failed on the technicality that a simple ma-jority of all those eligible to vote had not been obtained.

The party leadership's go-ahead for the televised Wałęsa–Miodowicz debate was less a sign of liberalization than evidence of weakness. But the memory of martial law still haunted the dissidents, and they had learned from the mistake of overconfidence committed by Solidarity at that time. Further, the impressive resources they had marshaled by 1988, which could be lost as suddenly as in December 1981, inclined the opposition to enter into dialogue.

Both party reformers and opposition moderates increasingly defined their identity in terms of serving as the primary agents of change. The al-ternative of confrontation was unrealistic for both sides. Over fifteen years the authorities had done everything in their power, short of a return to the Stalinist police state, to eliminate the opposition; there was noth-ing left to be tried to reach that objective now. As for the Solidarity-led opposition, it had discovered the limits of self-organizing society, with its underground "second-circulation" press, books, theater, and postage stamps—this would never pull in more than a fraction of society. As they saw it, neither ignoring the communist state nor confronting it offered a solution to the deepening economic problems facing Poland.

The Solidarity Opposition

How were the liberalization moves originally limited to party bodies and orchestrated by the Jaruzelski leadership perceived by the Solidarity lead-ers? To what extent were Solidarity leaders aware of the growing schisms within the PZPR that would help them calculate their own political strength when the course of political liberalization still seemed reversible? As Geremek summarized the political situation after the summer of 1988 strikes, although the authorities believed Solidarity to be an unpredictable partner, "the Party wanted legitimacy for its authority, which it could obtain only from a stronger partner that had general societal support."[17] The appointment of Rakowski as prime minister in mid-October was viewed as a bad sign; it seemed to put an end to hopes for the quick legalization of Solidarity, given Rakowski's role in breaking off talks with Wałęsa in August 1981 and his triumphalist speech justifying Solidarity's dissolution on his visit to the Lenin shipyards in 1982. Rakowski reasoned that, because of his close personal contacts with a number of Western European leaders, he could obtain economic assistance to see Poland through its economic crisis while having to accept only limited political liberalization that would keep Solidarity out of the political process. In addition, Miodowicz's uncompromising position on union pluralism caused the first round of "talks about talks" to founder. The Czyrek–Stelmachowski and Kiszczak–Wałęsa meetings in August and September 1988, where the roundtable idea was first put forward, were in danger of going nowhere.

According to Geremek, Rakowski's unsuccessful trip to Austria and West Germany, together with "the dramatic debates and simulated games regarding economic perspectives that were held in the Central Committee, from which a frightening picture emerged," produced self-doubt within the PZPR. Party authorities began to think in new terms: "Let us do things as we did in 1945; let us return to the situation before mistakes began to be made. Poland is again in ruins. Let us create an opposition party on the PSL [Mikołajczyk] model. This time let that party not make the mistake of turning its back on us, and we won't repeat the mistake of destroying the opposition."[18] The implied sense of magnanimity on the part of the party seemed out of keeping with its imminent irrelevance.

The roundtable talks were, at the time, justifiably viewed by the opposition as a potential trap. Rakowski had submitted to the Central Committee a declaration of the "Rakowski doctrine": Bring the opposition into the orbit of the authorities where it could be kept from accumulating political capital, corrupt it, divide it, and compromise its leading figures. Moreover, as we have noted, the party remained divided about talks with the opposition, and only the threat of resignation by Jaruzelski and his chief ministers forced it to accept the idea.

Roundtable Procedures

Without Jaruzelski's approval there would have been no roundtable talks in the spring of 1989. How, then, did he see his role in the overture to the political opposition? One telling remark attributed to him was: "Please remember that only General de Gaulle was capable of getting France out of Algeria." Geremek concluded: "This was a portentous statement, because it meant that only General Jaruzelski could get the PZPR out of Poland."[19] Although Jaruzelski was pivotal in the democratic transition, a number of other communist leaders—day-to-day participants of the roundtable talks—seem to have been committed to the success of the negotiations. Among these were, in Solidarity's perception, Kiszczak and Stanisław Ciosek.

It was Kiszczak who presided over the opening ceremony of the roundtable on February 6 in the Palace of the Council of Ministers in Warsaw. There was nothing in the constitution that anticipated a forum that, in effect, proved to be an unelected constituent assembly. Then again, the communist party had ruled the country for thirty years before it was thought expedient to enshrine the PZPR's leading role in the constitution. The constitutionality of the martial-law decree and the military council that ruled Poland for the next year were also debatable. Regime transitions such as France's change from the Fourth to the Fifth Republic are grounded more in the constitutional deficiencies of the previous regime than in existing constitutional provisions.

The roundtable had two sides and three major subtables. The "coalition–government side" included representatives not only of the communist leadership, but also of the satellite parties (the ZSL and the SD) and several small Catholic organizations long allied with the communists (the regime-allied trade-union federation, the National Trade Union Accord or OPZZ, at its own insistence officially constituted a distinct entity). The cavalier treatment accorded to representatives of the ZSL and the SD during the roundtable talks by communist party leaders was to boomerang only months later when the issue of forming a new coalition government arose.

The "opposition–Solidarity" side was represented by a delegation from the ad hoc Citizens' Committee of the Chairman of Solidarity. The Catholic episcopate was not officially a side. Declaring its neutrality, it sent representatives to mediate and facilitate discussions; for example, a bishop and two priests were delegated by the secretariat of the episcopate to the Magdalenka sessions. But participants in the talks concurred that when impasses arose church representatives invariably backed the positions advocated by Solidarity.[20] Party trust in the nonpolitical nature of the church proved overoptimistic both during the negotiations and in the electoral campaign that followed.

The subtables of the talks included one on socioeconomic policy, another on trade-union pluralism, and a third on political reform. These subtables in turn often created working groups to consider specific topics such as wage indexation, workers' self-management, and local government reform. Over six hundred participants had provided input into the roundtable negotiations by the time the talks adjourned two months later. Clearly, the actors and issues involved in the political-reform subtable were most important in determining the transition and the new rules of the game. Narrowing the crux of the negotiation process further, the private talks between top party and Solidarity leaders at a villa in Magdalenka (the site of Wałęsa's earlier meetings with Kiszczak in 1988) were of the utmost importance in arriving at a negotiated transition. Although tentative agreements reached in private had to be approved at the official political-reform subtable, the result of the test of wills between the high-powered delegations attending Magdalenka invariably stood. Wałęsa, for example, participated only in the negotiations conducted with the authorities in Magdalenka (as well as the ceremonial opening and closing sessions of the roundtable). Jaruzelski did not directly participate in talks but was provided with a running account by Kiszczak by telephone. In addition, he had his own special staff to address roundtable issues, separate from the staffs assembled by government negotiators Kiszczak, Czyrek, and Ireneusz Sekuła (a deputy premier and labor minister who went on to become one of the most prominent ex-communist entrepreneurs until his violent death in mysterious circumstances). This led at times to serious problems in coordinating the authorities' policy positions.

The secretive nature of the discussions at Magdalenka caused some observers to think that a tacit deal was being worked out between the two elite groups. For example, it was regularly alleged over the next few years that in exchange for extricating itself from politics, the ruling communist class was to have free rein in appropriating for itself the economic assets previously owned by the state. This idea became known as *uwłaszczenie,* "appropriation." But for the most belligerent anti-communist forces it was the political ties between communists and Solidarity that aroused the most suspicion, providing a convenient explanation for inadequate change in the following years. Suspicions about it were captured by the definition of Magdalenka as "a place where during roundtable talks open communists (Kiszczak, Jaruzelski, Ciosek) reached an understanding with their own agents (see exposure of agents) and crypto-communists

(Michnik, Kuroń, Geremek) in order to hold onto power, rob Poland, and cheat true Poles and patriots (Morawiecki, Jurczyk, Gwiazda)."[21]

Roundtable Bargaining

Readiness to make good on commitments affects the making of commitments, and this was clearly in evidence at the roundtable. The general character of the roundtable discussions was pragmatic, which surprised both sides given their perceptions of each other up to that time. As Geremek recalled them:

> In none of the negotiations did General Kiszczak ever invoke ideological arguments. He never referred to the ideology of the communist movement. They all used pragmatic arguments almost exclusively. The first was the question of power. . . . The second essential argument was Poland's place in the communist system. This concerned both relations within the bloc of real socialism and dependence on the Soviet Union—our place in the Soviet empire.[22]

Geremek indicated how Solidarity negotiators exploited this weakness: "We contended that the Polish leadership was not keeping up with Gorbachev and his reforms."[23] Nevertheless, the party's trump card was its mythical monopoly on good relations with the Soviets.

Expectations about the final outcome differed dramatically from what actually came to pass by summer's end 1989. Both party and Solidarity leaders assumed that they would remain government and opposition for some time to come. There might be limited power sharing, negotiators speculated, but no full power transfer. The diffidence of Solidarity was evidenced in the fact that its negotiating team brought up defense policy only once throughout the bargaining, proposing a 20 percent cut in military and security apparatus budgets. It was enough for the authorities to point to data showing recent decreases in funding for these two institutions for Solidarity to drop the subject.

Early in the talks, party representatives persisted in asking the opposition, "Do you really want socialism, or do you want to overthrow it?" This negotiating tactic was designed to persuade Solidarity representatives that only by agreeing to be co-opted and serve in a communist-majority government could the charge of seeking to overthrow the regime be deflected. Co-optation would, of course, have done little to change the underlying principles of the system, because political competition would have been put aside. In addressing whether Solidarity supported or opposed socialism, Tadeusz Mazowiecki, an editor and Catholic intellectual, inquired: "You talk about socialism, but tell us exactly what socialism you're referring to—Swedish socialism or Pol Pot's socialism?"[24] One Solidarity answer was, "Let's say that we are for socialism; later we'll decide what it means."[25] Geremek saw the issue not in terms of what type of socialism was preferable but in terms of "the need to disarm the party." He added, "Instead of legitimating the system we wanted to jump-start the process of democratization." The essential difference for Geremek was between liberalization as proposed by Rakowski and democratization: "Liberalization has been tried many times and leads nowhere. Its essence is to restore homeostasis to the system."[26]

Generally, the party leadership was more divided than its stated commitment to succeed at roundtable talks suggested. In particular, "The lack of a clear political identity of the reformist group dominant in the PZPR power structure made its consolidation more difficult and weakened its chances in conflicts with conservative elements."[27]

At a meeting of the heads of the working groups for the roundtable on March 17, 1989, Ciosek provided the most alarming assessment of the threat posed by party hard-liners to a successful agreement to the talks. It came in the form of a reply to Michnik's expressed concern about the "rush that the government side is imposing" on the talks and his suggestion that "waiting might be better than a false start." Ciosek's view was that "the machine has been started, and halting it would be a great problem." Furthermore, the quick tempo was necessitated by fear that Politburo members opposed to the contract would gain the upper hand if agreement was not reached soon: "Our will is weakening, I say this openly. It is not that we are opposed to an agreement but that over time we are becoming ever weaker," Ciosek reported. "After a twelve-hour, very difficult discussion, the Politburo agreed that, yes, we are entering into this contract." But referring to "aggressive" comments made by Jerzy Urban, the government's spokesman, and a hard-line article published in *Trybuna Ludu* by a veteran party journalist, Ciosek admitted that "what characterizes our [the government coalition's] dialogue is not chaos but political struggle. This struggle is taking place within the governing party." As a result, Ciosek asserted, "I've been telling you that there isn't just one 'red spider.' There is a plurality of 'red spiders.'"[28]

Invoking the potential militancy of party conservatives as a reason for speeding the talks along was sound bargaining strategy for the authorities. But it had a disadvantage as well, for it became clear to Solidarity delegates at the roundtable that the PZPR was to some degree split and therefore vulnerable. At the same time, in pressing its advantage Solidarity also had to know when to stop, for it never assumed that party disunity would necessarily lead to the crumbling of the entire communist regime. The more cautious and moderate Solidarity leaders, such as Geremek and Mazowiecki, were taken by surprise, then, at the speed of the party's demise in the second half of 1989. They were subsequently criticized for not having been more uncompromising at the roundtable.

At the center of negotiations was the issue of how Solidarity was to be represented in politics. Having failed to co-opt it into the government, the party proposed successive formulae to get it into the legislature. At the start of talks, the opposition preferred to concentrate on its main goal, the legalization of the Solidarity trade union and similar organizations, but saw participation in elections as the necessary price to pay.

Even before the formal roundtable began, it seemed likely that the authorities would be willing to offer Solidarity 30–40 percent of the seats in the Sejm. But this bloc was to be *allocated* to Solidarity, and no direct contests between the party and the opposition were foreseen. Further, both regime and opposition would support a common platform that of necessity consisted of generalities and platitudes.

For Solidarity's leaders, such an arrangement would turn the organization into a satellite party resembling the ZSL or the SD. It also resonated of a private extraconstitutional agreement rather than a formal, legal provision. Consequently, they quickly rejected this proposal. As Lech Kaczyński put it to regime negotiators, "Keep your controlling packet and give the rest not to us but to society."[29] Better that 30 percent of the seats be freely contested, Solidarity reasoned, than that 40 percent be allocated to it without a political fight. Coupled with this requirement was Solidarity's insistence that such a "contract Sejm" be a one-off venture—that future elections be fully democratic. When regime negotiators were reminded that public opinion overwhelmingly favored free elections, the "allocated, uncontested seats" proposal was dropped.[30] Thirty-five percent of the seats would be open to all nonparty candidates, while 65 percent would be allocated to the incumbent governing coalition—including not just the PZPR, but also its satellite parties and allied organizations.

After not getting its way on a number of issues, the strategic bargaining of the communist camp seemed to slip away from it. Not only was there going to be a competitive dimension to the elections, it was going to be regulated by a first-past-the-post majoritarian system of voting in contested constituencies. If regime negotiators had insisted on a proportional representation system, they would not have suffered such a humiliating loss in the election contest with Solidarity. In addition, the regime should have paid more attention to the nature of the ballot itself. Requiring voters to affirm their preferences by marking a cross by a candidate's name (like in most Western democracies) would have avoided the havoc wreaked on the regime's national list, where voters were able, with one stroke of the pen, to cross off the names of all communist candidates.[31]

The communists continued to fool themselves by insisting on the idea of "nonconfrontational" elections, however. They proposed a joint national list of candidates that would reflect the same proportion of seats allotted to each side as in the single-member constituencies. The idea of a joint ticket that would blur political differences between government and opposition was rejected by Solidarity. It recommended instead that the national list consist exclusively of candidates nominated by the party, in this way allowing it to secure for itself the legislative majority that both sides agreed was nonnegotiable.

Having agreed to participate in elections, Solidarity's bargaining strategy shifted to acceptance of the political reality of continued communist rule—locked in through the national list—while maximally exposing the charade of such rule. Many observers believe that, more than the Solidarity sweep of seats in contested Sejm elections in June 1989, it was the unexpected (even for Solidarity) defeat of most candidates on the party's unopposed national list that thwarted the communists' plans for remaining in power. The debacle of the communists on the list had international implications as well: It presaged the defeat of older-generation communists throughout much of the Soviet bloc in 1989.

In addition to efforts to incorporate Solidarity into a party-dominated coalition through a contract Sejm, regime negotiators proposed the restoration of the presidency that had been abolished in 1952. The assumption was that the president could serve as a stabilizing force and as a symbol of continuity in the transition period. The party's obvious candidate was Jaruzelski, and even much of Solidarity recognized the advantages of having the long-serving Polish leader preside over a protracted transition. Even after the June electoral defeat of the communists, Michnik acknowledged this political desideratum in the formula he proposed on July 4: "your president, our prime minister." Just as at the roundtable, so too with regard to this formula, charges were made of collaboration between two powerful elites.

Notwithstanding such open efforts to share spoils and thereby to stabilize the transition, disagreement between the two sides arose over the regime's position that the president should be elected by the Sejm, in which the party would continue to hold a majority, and that the term of office should be a lengthy seven years. More contentious than who would occupy the presidency were the powers to be conferred upon it. The ruling coalition proposed extensive powers that would have created a presidential system. Presidentialism would then compensate for whatever influence the communists lost in a partially freely elected Sejm.

The opposition accepted the principle that a communist president could provide the regime with the safeguards it needed in a transition period. In particular, the opposition acknowledged that the presidency should be given responsibility for defense and foreign policy. But it could not accept the full package of a powerful president (which Wałęsa must have rued having opposed once he took office; see Chapter 6), a Sejm elected noncompetitively, and a joint national list.

In order to break the political standoff over the regime package, Kiszczak threw in another new idea based on a former institution—the reestablishment of the second chamber, the Senate, abolished after the spurious results of a referendum held in 1948. Kiszczak expected that senators would be appointed by the president rather than elected, though the president would first consult with all parties represented in the Sejm.[32] The initial proposal for a return to an upper house provided Solidarity with no new or added incentive to accept the enlarged package. After deadlock on the issue, party negotiator Aleksander Kwaśniewski suddenly suggested that the senate might be transformed into a freely elected body.[33] The possibility of such a senate, in which Solidarity could flex its political muscle, laid the basis for compromise. No better evidence that roundtable negotiations were taking on a momentum of their own and leading in unanticipated directions is available than Kwaśniewski's apparently spontaneous suggestion. Several days later, after Jaruzelski had considered the implications of this twist, the proposal was formally put to Solidarity.

Since it was not envisaged that this upper chamber would have much power (even though it would elect the president in joint session with the 460-seat Sejm) and since the original formula of electing two senators from each of forty-nine provinces overrepresented rural Poland, where the party seemed stronger than Solidarity, the risks for the regime seemed worth taking. For Solidarity, completely free elections—even to a largely ceremonial chamber—symbolized a dramatic break with the practices of the communist regime. When Solidarity was able to extract from the regime a general commitment to make the next elections fully democratic—the final roundtable resolution pledged that "the sides will do everything to ensure that the composition of the next parliament will be determined completely by the will of the voters"[34]—the basis for the roundtable agreement had been secured.

Difficult negotiating lay ahead as the party, for a moment, seemed to back away from Senate elections and then suggested a national list for the Senate and sought to expand the president's decree powers. These eleventh-hour revisions were beaten back but other technicalities remained to be worked out. One was an eventual agreement to hold a second, runoff round for Sejm and Senate elections whenever the leading candidate failed to obtain 50 percent of the vote in the first round. As Solidarity had hoped, only the party would present a national list of candidates. No provisions were made for a second round here, because even Solidarity anticipated that since the party candidates were running unopposed they would secure the necessary 50 percent of votes cast. This proved to be shortsighted when the national-list candidates went down to defeat.

Another outstanding issue was how the Sejm could override a veto cast by the president or the Senate. A compromise was worked out whereby either a presidential or a Senate veto of Sejm legislation could be overturned by a two-thirds majority of the Sejm. This meant that if the party and Solidarity were to sweep all the representation set aside for them, the party bloc of 65 percent of the Sejm would be insufficient to overturn a Solidarity-dominated Senate veto. Conversely, a communist president could veto a bill and find it improbable that it would be overturned by the minority Solidarity group in the Sejm.

One issue that was left unresolved by the roundtable was the independence of the judiciary. The communist delegation refused to give up party control over the appointment of judges while Solidarity insisted that judges should not belong to a political party. The communist negotiators held out for a state procuracy independent of all other bodies, and the opposition demanded the subordination of this notorious communist-era institution to the Ministry of Justice. In the end, the protocol of the roundtable agreement simply reported the positions of the two sides and did not recommend a solution.[35] This again furnishes incontrovertible evidence that communist negotiators expected key elements of their system to survive the roundtable pact.

The most important institutional outcomes of the negotiated transition were, therefore, a contract Sejm with a built-in 65 percent party-controlled majority, a national list of unopposed party candidates that was to make up part of this majority, a Senate elected freely, and a president elected jointly by the National Assembly–Sejm and Senate in joint session. After all the careful calculations, expectations, and perceptions of the adversaries on both sides, it seemed unlikely that such a checks-and-balances pact could produce a lopsided victory for either side. The meticulously crafted pact was intended to ensure that the transition proceeded at a pace that posed no risks to either the old or the new elite. Shortly after it was signed on April 5, a national survey suggested a different reading of the agreement by the public. Fifty-nine percent of respondents believed that the opposition had gained support through the roundtable process, only 3 percent said the party was the beneficiary, and a surprisingly small 18 percent thought that both sides had increased their support.[36] These first impressions were a foretaste of the election results to come.

The June 1989 Elections

The semifree elections agreed upon at the roundtable left the two principal protagonists with little time to prepare full-fledged electoral campaigns. The communist party had never participated in competitive elections, and no part of the Solidarity opposition was legal as late as April 1989. Indeed, in the elections themselves, Solidarity candidates were listed as belonging to Citizens' Committees (KO) rather than to a formal party. Even after the elections, Solidarity deputies were organized into a Citizens' Parliamentary Club rather than a formal party. To support the electoral campaign of this semiorganized political group, Adam Michnik assembled a staff of journalists who had worked for the underground *Tygodnik Mazowsze* ("The Mazowsze Weekly"), Solidarity's Warsaw newspaper, and began publishing a daily, *Gazeta Wyborcza* ("The Election Gazette") in May. Introducing KO candidates and their platforms was the initial raison d'être for what was soon to become one of Poland's most widely read dailies.

The uncharted waters affected opinion pollsters as well. According to a Public Opinion Survey Center (OBOP) report, "There were no typical pre-election polls in Poland in 1989. CBOS and OBOP [the two major polling organizations] made an attempt to find out about the pre-election mood of the people, but the final surveys were conducted three weeks

TABLE 3.1 Voting Intentions of the Electorate, April–May 1989 (in percent)

Poll and Date[a]	Government Coalition	Solidarity Opposition	Undecided
CBOS			
April 10	15	38	47 [b]
May 17	14	34	52 [c]
OBOP			
May 2	25	45	30
May16	23	57	20
May 23	24	55	21

[a] CBOS, Center for Public Opinion Research; OBOP, Public Opinion Survey Center.

[b] The political attitudes of the "undecided" included 8 percent who supported the party, 27 percent Solidarity, and 13 percent neither.

[c] The political attitudes of the "undecided" included 11 percent who supported the party, 28 percent Solidarity, and 13 percent neither.

Source: Piotr Kwiatkowski, "Opinion Research and the Fall of Communism: Poland 1981 1990," *International Journal of Public Opinion Research,* 4, no. 4 (Winter 1992), 370.

prior to the election."[37] Still, these polls did test regional variations, voter interest, and knowledge about individual candidates in some detail.[38] What became clear from the survey results was that the communist party was facing defeat. Although these results were not published at the time and therefore could not have influenced voters, they all pointed to Solidarity enjoying at least two-to-one stronger support than the communist coalition (Table 3.1).

As we have seen, at the time of the roundtable negotiations some advisers to the communist leadership calculated that the party might obtain at least a quarter of the votes cast. It might even win a majority of the openly contested seats to the Senate, since, as we have seen, Senate constituencies overrepresented rural areas and Solidarity's strength lay primarily in the cities. But the results of an opinion poll carried out in mid-May for a French polling organization already indicated that only in about ten provinces was the party in a position to win even one of the two senatorial seats, which meant at best a total of just ten seats in the upper chamber. These provinces were largely agrarian, located in central (Wielkopolska) and north-central Poland.[39]

The final results produced, as expected, a Solidarity sweep of the 35 percent of Sejm seats allocated to nonparty candidates. But almost none of the seats set aside for the government coalition were filled in the first round—only three candidates (all party members backed by Solidarity) managed to win the over 50 percent of the vote required to avoid a second round. In terms of the popular vote distribution, earlier party forecasts proved accurate. The government coalition received just over a quarter of all valid votes cast (26.8 percent) and Solidarity got 69.9 percent (the remainder going to independents).

Turnout for the first round was 62.7 percent of eligible voters—less than anticipated given the historic nature of these elections, and the one important setback that Solidarity suffered. A number of reasons can be advanced for the sizable number of nonvoters. Possibly these elections lacked authenticity for voters who saw them as worked out by two establishment parties—the communists and Solidarity. The same suspicions aroused by the talks in Magdalenka—"elites talking to elites," in Staniszkis's encapsulation of the attitude of the populist faction in Solidarity[40]—were now spreading as Poles contemplated whether voting had in fact become meaningful. In addition, registered voters had no way of knowing how "historic" this election was to be. That the party would still control 65 percent of Sejm seats no matter what happened at the polls was a deterrent to voting for many.

In examining the impact of the perception of "two establishments" on voter abstention, Jasiewicz disaggregated nonvoters into three categories: the 23 percent who did not see the importance of politics to their own personal situation, the 10 percent who were unable to get to their polling places even though they wanted to, and the 5 percent who staged a politically motivated boycott.[41] Whatever the exact causes, the relatively low turnout was one of the few results of the elections that heartened the ruling communists. They could continue to question whether Solidarity had really been given a popular mandate to govern.

One particular surprise was Solidarity's capture of all but one of the Senate seats. The one exception was an atypical candidate—a former party member turned private entrepreneur who had run an expensive electoral campaign. The breakdown of the popular vote for the Senate was 20.4 percent for the government and 65.0 percent for Solidarity (again, the remainder going to independents).[42] Significantly, Solidarity had sufficient support even in the most rural Polish provinces to elect its slate, defying the party's calculations.

Solidarity's stubborn refusal to provide candidates for a national list proved to have been a stroke of genius. About 35 percent of voters crossed out the names of *all* the candidates on the uncontested national list. Only two party-backed candidates won the necessary 50 percent majority to avoid participating in a second round. Virtually the entire top party leadership, then, was humiliated by this result (as a presidential aspirant, Jaruzelski did not run for parliament), but there was no provision for a second round to fill these seats. So legal improvisation was needed to replace the communist-allocated seats on the national list with new seats carved out of existing constituencies and to be filled in the second-round runoffs.

The communist leadership felt that the role played by the church in the elections had been insidious. Although the church hierarchy had appealed for national accord and, ostensibly, acted as impartial mediator during the electoral campaign, its support at the grassroots level was crucial to Solidarity's success. The vast majority of Citizens' Committees had begun their operations in parish halls, and some never left until after the election results were in. Except for Solidarity campaign materials produced in its national headquarters, flyers and leaflets for local candidates were printed using church-owned presses. Most important, priests were active in many different ways in support of KO candidates. One writer identified thirteen methods employed by the clergy in localities to ensure Solidarity victories, from organizing candidate meetings with voters, protecting Solidarity posters from defacement or removal, and warning KOs of unfavorable publicity to using religious occasions (Mass, Corpus Christi processions) to urge voter support. Election day was a Sunday. It was not uncommon for priests to lead prayers for a Solidarity victory.[43] That the communist party, which had reneged on promises for democracy throughout Poland's postwar history, should have been surprised by the partisan activism of the church in the 1989 elections is not without irony.

The election results had a domino effect on other provisions of the roundtable agreement. Recognizing public anger at his imposition of martial law in 1981, Jaruzelski announced that he would not be a candidate for the revamped presidency. The careful arithmetic of the round-table negotiators turned out to be for naught, with many new Sejm deputies in both ZSL- and SD-designated seats prepared to join Solidarity's representatives to vote against him. But in July Solidarity leaders still planned to bide their time and remain in the ranks of the opposition. When Wałęsa made clear that he did not intend to stand for the presidency, Jaruzelski reversed his earlier decision and, on July 19, was elected by a bare majority in the two houses—270 to 233, with 34 abstentions. Strategic voting by the KO parliamentary bloc was intended to allow him to assume the presidency, but only at the pleasure of Solidarity.

The last issue to be resolved in the summer of 1989 was the formation of a government. Since the communist bloc had been technically assured of a working majority in the contract Sejm, everyone had assumed that a prime minister would be chosen from its ranks. And indeed, on August 2, Jaruzelski nominated Kiszczak, the congenial head of the party's round-table negotiating team, to the post. But this would have left both major offices in the hands of leaders of the communist party (not to say the chief architects of martial law). Solidarity therefore opposed Kiszczak's candidature. With the surprise defection of the two satellite parties (the ZSL and the SD) from the government camp, Wałęsa announced on August 17 that the Citizens' Parliamentary Club was prepared to form a coalition government with these two small parties. That same day, acting Prime Minister Kiszczak gave up trying to form a communist government. The next day Wałęsa and the leaders of the ZSL and the SD, Roman Malinowski and Jerzy Jóźwiak, went to the Belvedere Palace, the residence of the president, formally to present him with the coalition-government proposal.

In line with Michnik's July 4 proposal "your president, our prime minister," on August 24 Mazowiecki—editor of the famous Solidarity opposition newspaper of 1980, *Tygodnik Solidarność* ("Solidarity Weekly")— was appointed prime minister. With all but the hard-line communists accepting the new political reality, Mazowiecki was given a vote of confidence by the Sejm (378 to 4, with 41 abstentions). On September 12 he submitted his cabinet nominees to the Sejm for approval. Eleven of the twenty-three ministerial posts were taken by Solidarity, only four were given to the PZPR, and the rest went to the ZSL, the SD, and an independent. Although communist ministers were to hold on to the pivotal defense and security portfolios, Mazowiecki's cabinet became the first noncommunist government in Eastern Europe since Stalin. The Sejm vote approving his cabinet now had no opposition: 420 to 0, with 13 abstentions. Few if any participants at the roundtable talks of a few months earlier could have foreseen this course of events or this outcome.

After the June Elections: The End of the Communist Party?

Even with electoral defeat, party notables felt that the negotiated transition provided the political safeguards that would allow a communist-based government to continue to rule. Prime Minister Rakowski's speech in the Sejm to the parliamentary clubs of the PZPR's satellite parties, the SD and the ZSL, the night after the June election was intended to scare the coalition partners into voting for Kiszczak as prime minister. Gere-mek described the intent of the speech: "Rakowski equated the departure of the small clubs from the PZPR-led coalition with the outbreak of civil war. Reject Kiszczak tomorrow and the day after tomorrow there will be martial law."[44] By August 14, however, Kiszczak had not been able to form a government but no civil war appeared imminent.

Following the electoral cataclysm of the PZPR, the Thirteenth Plenum was summoned on June 30 and then adjourned to July 28–29. Since Jaruzelski had accepted the office of president, Rakowski replaced him as party leader. The Central Committee called for a party congress to decide the future of the PZPR. The Fourteenth Plenum convened on August 19 and was confronted with the defection of the two satellite par-ties to Solidarity. Consistent with its communist ethos, the Plenum con-demned the ingratitude that these parties had shown the PZPR for hav-ing secured them parliamentary seats at all.[45] As Mazowiecki was officially being designated prime minister that day, the Plenum declared that history would hold the satellite parties responsible for the dismem-berment of the "social coalition."

Seemingly dismissing the electoral verdict passed on it, the Plenum in-sisted that the party should be represented in the new government in terms of its "political and state potential."[46] The next day Party Secretary Leszek Miller launched the slogan "your government, our program." On October 10 Rakowski flew to Moscow to present his assessment of the political situation to Kremlin leaders. All of these efforts were aimed at preventing the disappearance of the PZPR from the Polish political land-scape.

At the Central Committee's Fifteenth Plenum on September 18, it was reported that 72 percent of party respondents favored radical change in the party. Two weeks later, on October 3, the second session of the plenum committed the PZPR to holding the Eleventh Congress in Janu-ary, democratizing its methods of selecting delegates and electing leader-ship, and changing the party's name, program, and structures.[47] The Politburo report to the Central Committee still cautioned, in characteris-tically ambiguous and pompous terms, that "the road to such a [trans-formed] party cannot be just a linear continuation, but neither should it produce self-destruction of the party—building a new one on the ruins of the old."[48]

Political clumsiness continued to plague the communist leadership. When opportunities to curry favor with the public presented themselves, it often seemed unable to take advantage—perhaps a reflex from decades of ignoring popular sentiment, perhaps a sign of hard-line retrenchment within the party. For example, on the day Mazowiecki was named to form a noncommunist government, PZPR leaders received a letter from the Romanian communist party condemning the Polish party's tolerance and referring obliquely to Soviet invasions of Warsaw Pact countries. But the PZPR leadership did not rebuff the criticism and the suspicion arose that hard-liners had effectively stymied such a response. Only months earlier, the Chinese communist party had cracked down on democracy support-ers in Tiananmen Square, and a recourse to force by disaffected elements in the security apparatus—a Polish version of the August 1991 putsch in the USSR—could not totally be excluded.

In contrast to the PZPR, Gorbachev refused even to meet with the Romanian emissary carrying the letter of complaint about the alleged Polish betrayal—a fact that became quickly known in Warsaw.[49] A Polish Politburo hard-liner lamented the fact that Soviet support for the use of force as a conflict-resolution method had disappeared: "All our contacts to date have been severed. There are new people there [in Moscow] now who do not understand our arguments. Up to now we have been talking with a group of people we have known for years. They understood our in-terests, we understood theirs. Now the situation has changed. They are pragmatists, and we have no access to them." Geremek concluded from this that "by 1989 each group within the power structure could articulate its views, and there was no longer an arbiter who could say which position was correct. Until then it was Moscow that had been saying this."[50]

By December 1989 circumstances had changed so drastically that can-didates for the leadership of the communist successor party were lining up to meet with Wałęsa so as to broaden their popular support. These in-cluded not only his preferred candidate, Tadeusz Fiszbach, but also Rakowski and Miller. The last Central Committee Plenum of the PZPR was the Seventeenth, held on January 6, 1990. Although this meeting was ostensibly intended to ratify documents to be considered by the congress and to carry out a survey for a proposed new name for the party, a one-time Politburo member recalled that it was "very dramatic" and engaged in a "very probing discussion." He added that, "fortunately, the dominant view was that Polish matters were matters for Poland and it was necessary to continue on the road of reform."[51]

The PZPR's last congress began on January 27, 1990, and quickly fin-ished the business of dissolving the party. Over the next three days a new party—Social Democracy of the Polish Republic (SdRP)—was estab-lished that inherited the PZPR's real estate and financial assets. As the

SdRP and later as the Alliance of the Democratic Left (SLD), this party would go on to establish itself as the party of government in the Third Republic. True, in 1990 it looked as if the post-communist left would be divided and therefore weak. Eighty-nine Congress delegates (including twenty-five Sejm deputies) decided to establish a separate party—the Polish Social Democratic Union (PUS)—with Fiszbach as leader. Both parties expressed a commitment to freedom, equality, social justice, parliamentary democracy, and serving Poland's national interests, but from the very start the SdRP was more pragmatic and the Union more idealistic in its commitment to the socialist project. Yet a third post-communist party was formed in March 1990—the Union of Communists of the Polish Republic "Proletariat" (an allusion to the country's first communist movement in the late nineteenth century). Within a few years neither of these last two parties would lead an independent existence, leaving the PZPR legacy in the hands of the SdRP.

Jaruzelski and Change in the Power Structure

Ideological conflict within the PZPR was not the sole axis along which the party disintegrated. A revealing case of institutional confrontation between the traditional party power base, the Central Committee, and an emerging one within the new parliamentary system, the PZPR Parliamentary Club (or Caucus), can be discerned in the last six months of the party's existence. Jaruzelski's part in favoring the parliamentary group was crucial in the demise of the Central Committee and with it, effectively, of the Leninist party.

The "party-savers" who had been so noisy at the August Fourteenth Plenum were suffering from a major disadvantage: Jaruzelski was no longer with them organizationally, nor probably ideologically either. His distancing himself from the PZPR affected the composition of the Mazowiecki government. Initially the party wanted to obtain the posts of deputy premier, television committee head, six ministerial portfolios (finance, communications, transport, foreign affairs, defense, and internal affairs), and the secretaries and undersecretaries of state in all ministries. But Jaruzelski's acceptance of a new coalition government and his own institutional power base as president rather than party leader made him less dependent on the party apparatus. Moreover, the PZPR Parliamentary Club consisted primarily of managers and party bureaucrats, not blue-collar workers, thereby eliminating "class conflict" from the newly elected Sejm.[52]

The first president in the new regime left his former party colleagues to define new roles for themselves. PZPR members who were Sejm deputies now had to challenge representatives of the Solidarity bloc in parliament. This entailed a changed relationship between the PZPR parliamentary deputies and the party bodies. Given that the most determined resistance to reform had come from the Central Committee, Jaruzelski quickly saw the advantages of siding with PZPR deputies in the Sejm. These deputies themselves were intent on increasing their independence and, in so doing, gaining the stature within the party organization that their counterparts in the noncommunist parties enjoyed. In this respect, Carl Linden's "second antagonistic axis" of Leninist systems[53]—the friction between party and state that played so important a role in the Gierek–Piotr Jaroszewicz competition in the mid-1970s—was now actively fostered by Jaruzelski so as to outflank the conservative party apparatus.

An important step in diluting the authority of the Central Committee was the convening of the first—in Jaruzelski's term, "historic"—joint plenum of the Central Committee and the Parliamentary Caucus on June 30, 1989. It was at this meeting that Jaruzelski officially proposed Kiszczak as candidate for the presidency. Explaining his own unwillingness at that time to stand, he recognized that he was more often perceived as the instigator of martial law than as a proponent of the "reform line." As with martial law, Jaruzelski invoked overriding reasons of state: "If on the road to an agreement and to unifying all social forces an obstacle emerged, even if the obstacle were to be Wojciech Jaruzelski, there would be only one possible solution."[54] He underscored that the new president had to be recognized as a reformer but also as a leader who would "keep his head high." Obviously referring to himself, Jaruzelski remarked that an inappropriate candidate for the office of president would be a person who would be "the object of some kind of charitable gesture."[55]

Despite the overwhelming electoral defeat suffered by the party, Jaruzelski still contextualized political change within the framework of Polish socialism. He interpreted the roundtable agreement as intended to bring about "unity of action in the most important matters serving Poland, the real Poland, a Poland whose construction of socialism develops on the road to democratic reforms that are a great historical experiment, offer us a great opportunity, put us in the avant-garde of the reformist processes occurring in the socialist world."[56]

A number of Sejm deputies of the PZPR criticized the Central Committee during the joint session, in particular for failing to persuade Jaruzelski to accept the presidency. They contended that in spite of momentous changes taking place around them, the Central Committee remained disproportionately influential. One speaker caught the irony of the joint session: "Here I heard that we are meeting for the first time, and, in effect, already our roads are just about going separate ways."[57] Another irony, apparently lost in the Caucus–Central Committee showdown, was that governing in late June 1989 was already out of the hands of party groups, however constituted. This was clearly illustrated in Prime Minister Rakowski's late arrival at the joint meeting to report that the cabinet had just frozen prices and wages.

The final irony that emerged from this joint meeting was purely symbolic in nature. At the end of the session Jaruzelski informed the deputies' group that it was the custom at the end of a Central Committee Plenum to sing the Internationale. "I am counting on you deputies—party members—to join in." As power was being transferred from the party administration to party parliamentarians, the party chief was not sure that the latter were well versed in the party ethos or even that they could be counted on to take it up.

The Parliamentary Caucus

The emergence of the Parliamentary Club, with its membership of 173 beleaguered and electorally tainted deputies, did signal the decline of the party ethos and of the Internationale, sung for the last time when the demise of the PZPR was made official.[58] It also pointed to a commitment to a democratic form of socialism. The success of the SdRP in subsequent parliamentary elections can be traced to the decisive action of the Caucus in reorganizing the PZPR power structure in the second half of 1989. This was achieved quietly, in the shadow of Mazowiecki's groundbreaking government. It required further prodding, and a meeting between the presidium of the Parliamentary Club and the Politburo of the Central Committee, held on September 16, 1989, was pivotal.

Sejm Deputy Józef Oleksy (later to become marshal of the Sejm and then prime minister) presented a lengthy report on the objectives of the Caucus. Acknowledging that "only the Eleventh Congress can ultimately delineate the role of the parliamentary fraction in relation to the party and its leadership," he was clear about how the balance of power had to shift: "We have to be aware that today the vast majority of issues that the party wishes to adopt—impose and regulate—for the state has to pass through the Parliamentary Club. In such a context the Club has to be seen in a new light, very different from that of the past unfavorable, bad practice."[59] Oleksy complained that hardly had the Caucus been formed but "immediately opinions began to circulate about the 'maverick' or 'destructive' work of the Club, about efforts at secession and lack of consciousness and political 'maturity' with regard to the Central Committee." At the heart of such criticisms, he added, lay "the desire to ensure that the Club remained entirely at the disposal of the party leadership."[60] The Club received little help from the entrenched party bureaucracy and, indeed, was portrayed in the party press as a rebellious faction. Yet it was now the most important means the party had left of influencing matters of state.

The party's official position on the newly formed Mazowiecki government was to lend it support qua legal government of the Polish state, not qua the government of Solidarity. PZPR deputies were unclear about whether party support was to be unconditional, and what the party's policy was on changes in property relations, privatization, trade unions, constitutional reform, subsidies, unemployment, the market, and the overhaul of the Ministries of Defense and Internal Affairs. The Central Committee provided them with no guidelines. Not surprisingly, if party representatives in the Sejm appeared cautious, unsure of themselves, and less adversarial, it was due in part to the fact that the PZPR bureaucracy had deserted them. Oleksy thus expressed concern about "the degree of ideological and psychological 'desertion' of party members" and the impact this might have on the creation of a strong leftist party.[61] He also admitted to disappointment that the term "socialism" had all but disappeared from their political lexicon and continued to be employed only by party chief Jaruzelski.

An October 1989 Politburo resolution made one last attempt to instill the PZPR with an explicitly socialist program: "The Central Committee of the PZPR, in creating for its deputies the necessary conditions to carry out the mandate of a deputy, expects from them a thorough internalization of the program, policy, and resolutions of the party; these ought to be the source of inspiration for deputies' activities, the goal being implementing them in the Sejm."[62] The obligations of Sejm deputies to the party were also made clear: They were to brief Central Committee departments about bills tabled before the Sejm, including supplying minutes of Sejm and Senate sessions. The revised PZPR statutes did not clarify whether deputies would have much influence in the selection of the PZPR leadership. As a result, there was little in the 1989 changes to suggest that the PZPR would operate like other political parties, with its leaders emerging from the parliamentary group.

The communist equivalent of a backbench rebellion became evident in the hostile reaction of the Parliamentary Caucus to the leadership's initiatives. In January 1990 it issued an appeal to choose reformists as delegates to the upcoming Eleventh Congress. It urged the election of delegates "who were not afraid to attack conservatives, the old order, the old routine, the trepidation before profound changes." Specifically, "the PZPR Parliamentary Caucus believes that newly elected delegates should themselves immediately plan the Congress," breaking with the tradition that a specially constituted Central Committee commission would prepare the draft program. Not that it made much difference at this point, but the Caucus's practical concern with overhauling the procedures used to plan party congresses was designed to construct a "credible, modern leftist party" on the ruins of the PZPR.[63]

In the week preceding the Eleventh Congress, the Caucus issued a further policy statement regarding the future of the PZPR. Again, the group's focus was on securing autonomy for itself vis-à-vis the party bureaucracy. The Caucus "recognized the right of delegates to take the final decisions regarding the future of the party." Ensuring the "organizational unity and practical cohesiveness" of the Caucus was therefore seen as "a political value in itself." The call for the PZPR's dissolution was linked to the explicit notion of forging a different Polish road to socialism: "We support the creation of a completely new, pluralist leftist party whose program will reflect the will and aspirations of progressive forces of the Polish nation."[64]

The unexpected confrontation between the two PZPR organizations was perhaps best illustrated in the selection of a leader to head the successor party. Rakowski had actively canvassed support for election throughout the fall of 1989, using Plenum meetings and the party press to advance his position. But the chairman of the PZPR Parliamentary Club and onetime ideological secretary, Marian Orzechowski, questioned Rakowski's credentials to lead a new party and implied that his election would change the party in "symbols and emblems only."[65]

Implications of the Polish Transition

Institutional consequences of this transition process will be examined further in Chapter 6. Although the presidency did have a prior history in Poland, and indeed restoration of the presidency had been one of the programmatic goals of the communist-satellite Democratic Party, it is uncertain that this office would have been established if not part of the roundtable agreement. Certainly we can conclude that the ambivalent powers of the presidency, with contradictions still not cleared up after several years of constitutional revision, derive directly from the particular role that both the regime and the opposition in 1989 expected the president to play. The restoration of the Senate was another accidental by-product of the negotiated transition, but as we shall see this institution has been of little consequence.

Potentially more consequential was the delay in full democratization of Poland's institutions. While this did not preserve communist power, it did have important implications for consolidation and institutional legitimacy. Most striking in this regard is the year in which the "contract" Sejm coexisted with a democratically elected president.

A pacted and peaceful transition may be expected to heal historical wounds and reduce the intensity of conflict-caused cleavages. In Spain, for example, the transitional pact symbolized reconciliation among the opposing parties. Pacting and compromise became virtues. But the Spanish pact was a conscious compromise; the mistakes of the Polish transition, with its unexpected outcomes, led to so many recriminations between and within the opposing sides that compromise itself was discredited. It appears that the peaceful transition process did little to weaken the deep cleavage between former communists and former anticommunists.

In fact, the Polish roundtable may have created or at least strengthened an additional division—one within the former opposition camp. After 1989 and indeed into the new millennium, this has been articulated as a division between those who participated in the roundtable process and consider it to have been valuable for Poland and those who reject its compromises, ascribe present problems to the pact's flaws, and even see it as a conscious betrayal of the true interests of the Polish nation. As we shall see in the next chapter, one more cause for backbiting and division was hardly what the former opposition camp needed.

Certainly the communist camp had equal reason for mutual recriminations, given the apparent power position that its leaders had bargained away in 1989. Why did bitterness and criticism not make it difficult for the former communists to operate as a unified and effective political force? Any answer must be speculative, but we may find a plausible one, paradoxically, in the failure of the communists to assure firm and fast institutional guarantees for themselves. Their vulnerability meant that the only effective protection could be found in unity and mutual support—in maintaining and strengthening political organizations to represent their

interests. This, together with the shock treatment of their 1989 humilia-
tion and the fact that the first Solidarity government–which was initially
uncertain of the limits it faced and constrained by a feeling of obligation
to their fellow signators of the pact—did not directly challenge the party's
rights to its own organizational assets, left them in a surprisingly advan-
tageous position as the democratic game began. In fact, as the following
chapter discusses, the former communist party would stage an impressive
comeback, becoming by far the most effective political party in the democratic electoral game.

An interesting contrast here is the position of the Catholic Church as
democratic politics began. The church appeared to be triumphant—we
have seen how in the years leading up to the roundtable, in the negotiations themselves, and in the system-changing elections the hierarchy and
especially parish priests consistently backed the forces of change. When
change came, when communist rule ended and the political system democratized, the church could fairly claim a considerable share of the
credit. It seemed likely that the church would now play an even greater
role in politics and policy in newly democratic Poland. But just like the
other political players, the Catholic Church would have to adapt its tactics and resources to the new political arena.

4

The Political Players:
Elites, Parties, and Other Actors in
the Third Republic

Who are the players of Poland's new democratic games? During the four decades plus of People's Poland, politics had been viewed either as a war of "them versus us" ("them" understood to be the communists, "us" as the Polish people, a subset that somehow did not include Polish communists) or as a game of factional politics and personal ambitions among the communist elite. Both perspectives were valuable, and indeed, as the preceding chapter shows, a combination of the two is particularly powerful for understanding the collapse of the communist system. But in the Third Republic, these perspectives are anachronistic. Instead we need an approach based on the crucial characteristics and defining differences of the most important political players in the postcommunist democracy.

In order to identify these players, we first examine the patterns of winners and losers in the electoral contests for control of the state and state policy from 1990 through 2001. Then we look more closely at political elites and the parties they lead, at interest groups, and at those other crucial actors in Polish democratic politics—the Catholic Church and the mass media.

Winners and Losers in the
New Democratic Games, 1989–2001

As a result of institutional inheritance, the roundtable accord, and Polish political traditions, the new democracy found itself with a system combining parliamentary government with a president with limited but still significant powers. The major legislative body is the Sejm, elected through proportional representation; the executive is a prime-minister-led government derived from the Sejm; the constitution was quickly altered (in 1990) to provide for the popular election of the president, the head-of-state, to serve a five-year term. Thus the most important elections in Poland are parliamentary, both because it is a Sejm majority (whether based on a single party or a coalition) that will create the government and because it is the Sejm that has the power to facilitate that government's work or bring it down. New elections to the Sejm must take place within four years after the previous elections, but they may take place earlier if the government loses the support of a Sejm majority. (The elections to the less important Senate take place at the same time.) The other important election, that for president, takes on a significance greater than the president's actual powers would suggest, as a result of the prestige of this office and the symbolic power of a national mandate for a single individual.

Indeed the first completely free election held in the Third Republic, in 1990, was for the presidency. The facts that it was free and it was for the presidency already indicated the untenable nature of the roundtable agreement a bare eighteen months after it had been crafted. Lech Wałęsa was backed by much of the post-opposition camp, including various Catholic and conservative parties and led by the Center Accord (PC). His most serious rival appeared to be prime minister Tadeusz Mazowiecki, who was supported by almost all of the rest of the former opposition, largely organized in the Citizens' Movement for Democratic Action (ROAD) and the Forum of the Democratic Right. The communist successor party, the Social Democracy of the Republic of Poland (SdRP), joined with a variety of other post-communist organizations in the Alliance of the Democratic Left (SLD), and nominated Włodzimierz Cimoszewicz—a former PZPR member who had *not* joined the SdRP—as its presidential candidate. The largest party in terms of membership (about 400,000) was the Polish Peasant Party (PSL). It too sought to shake off its communist past and nominated its leader, Roman Bartoszcze.

TABLE 4.1 Presidential Election Results, 1990

Candidate and Party	Votes	Percent Votes Cast	Percent Electorate[a]
First Round (November 25)			
Lech Wałęsa (Solidarity KO)	6,569,889	40.0	23.9
Stanislaw Tymiński ("X")	3,397,605	23.1	13.8
Tadeusz Mazowiecki (ROAD)	2,973,264	18.1	11.8
Włodzimierz Cimoszewicz (SdRP)	1,514,025	9.2	5.5
Roman Barłoszcze (PSL)	1,176,175	7.2	4.3
Leszek Moczulski (KPN)	411,516	2.5	1.5
Second Round (December 9)			
Lech Wałęsa	10,622,696	74.3	38.7
Stanislaw Tymiński	3,683,098	25.7	13.3

[a] Turnout in first round was 61 percent, and 53 percent in second round.

Wałęsa topped the other candidates in the first round but was well short of the 50 percent needed to avoid a runoff (Table 4.1). The greatest shock was the second-place showing of outsider Stan Tymiński, a Polish emigrant to Canada, and the elimination of Mazowiecki. The second-round runoff produced the expected result: Wałęsa received 74 percent of votes cast to Tymiński's 26 percent. This is the one and only time that a wildcard player has made a mark in Third Republic politics.

The first completely free parliamentary elections took place more than two years after the signing of the roundtable pact, in October 1991. This parliament was the product of a complicated electoral law awarding representation to parties that won even a tiny percentage of votes. As a result, voters had a wide array of choices; parties combining different positions on economic policy, the church, the communist heritage, Europe, and nationalism sought out niche constituencies in a way that was never to recur. The election results demonstrated how the electorate took advantage of this menu for choice; twenty-nine parties were represented in parliament (Table 4.2). There was no overwhelming support for any one political orientation, though clearly right-of-center groups fared better than left-of-center ones. Parties and leaders with coalition-building skills had to forge new governments out of the fragmented parliament. The government that lasted longest (all of eighteen months) was an intricate

TABLE 4.2 Parliamentary Election Results, October 27, 1991

Party	Percent Votes Cast[a]	Sejm (N=460)	Senate (N=100)
Democratic Union (UD)	12.3	62	21
Alliance of the Democratic Left (SLD)	12.0	60	4
Catholic Electoral Action (WAK)	8.7	49	9
Center Accord (PC)	8.7	44	9
Polish Peasant Party (PSL)	8.7	48	8
Confederation for an Independent Poland (KPN)	7.5	46	4
Liberal Democratic Congress (KLD)	7.5	37	6
Peasant Accord (PL)	5.5	28	7
Solidarity (S)	5.1	27	12
Polish Beer Lovers' Party (PPPP)	3.3	16	0
Other parties	11.9	43	20

[a] Turnout was 41 percent.

seven-party coalition headed by Poland's first woman prime minister, Hanna Suchocka.

Were it not for personal rivalries and internal disputes within the Solidarity camp, the 1993 parliamentary elections would not have ended with a stunning victory for the ex-communists (Table 4.3). To be fair, the ex-communists had completed a remarkable comeback. In Warsaw, where leaders of a number of influential parties contested the election, SLD head Aleksander Kwaśniewski placed far ahead of his counterparts in votes received, for example, more than doubling the total for Bronisław Geremek, a leading light in the post-Solidarity camp. But the SLD victory was a victory more for machine politics than personality politics. And issues played an important role, too. Shock economic therapy had generated a political backlash, and the SLD got a lot of mileage from its punchy slogan: "It doesn't have to be like this." The coalition government formed by the SLD and PSL was initially headed by PSL leader Waldemar Pawlak, but after less than two years he was replaced by Józef Oleksy of the SLD, who himself was replaced by the SLD's Cimoszewicz when Oleksy was accused of spying for the Russians.

In 1995 thirteen candidates contested the first round of the presidential elections. The three-month campaign was notable for a dramatic surge in popularity for incumbent Wałęsa, whose chances looked extremely poor

TABLE 4.3 Parliamentary Election Results, September 19, 1993

Party	Percent Votes Cast[a]	Sejm (N=460)	Senate (N=100)
Alliance of the Democratic Left (SLD)	20.4	171	37
Polish Peasant Party (PSL)	15.4	131	36
Democratic Union (UD)	10.6	74	4
Union of Labor (UP)	7.3	41	2
Confederation for an Independent Poland (KPN)	5.8	21	0
Nonparty Bloc for Reform (BBWR)	5.4	16	2
German Minority	0.6	4	1
Fatherland Alliance (*Ojczyzna*)	6.4	0	0
Solidarity (S)	4.9	0	10
Center Accord (PC)	4.4	0	0
Liberal Democratic Congress (KLD)	4.0	0	1
Other parties	14.8	2	7

[a] Turnout was 51 percent.

at the start but who began to close the gap on longtime front-runner Kwaśniewski. Other than his legendary stature, the main asset that the Solidarity founder brought into the campaign was to be the only "electable" candidate of the center-right. His campaign posters succinctly depicted the choice in the election: "There are many other candidates. There is only one Wałęsa." In the first round, Kwaśniewski (35 percent) edged out Wałęsa (33 percent) with two centrist candidates following (Table 4.4). The momentum seemed to favor Wałęsa, and all he had to do was unify the Solidarity bloc in the second round to mathematically assure himself of reelection.

But television debates turned the tables on Wałęsa. Kwaśniewski's youthfulness (he was forty-one), eloquence, and good manners contrasted sharply with an exceptionally irascible and arrogant Wałęsa. Of what importance were political biographies when the clash of personalities was so stark? With a high turnout in the second round, Kwaśniewski won by a very slim margin: 51.7 percent to 48.3 percent. Wałęsa had so antagonized his former associates in Solidarity that many of their supporters refused to vote for Wałęsa in the runoff. For example, over 40 percent of ex-KOR dissident Jacek Kuroń voters turned from Wałęsa to

TABLE 4.4 Presidential Election Results, 1995

Candidate and Party	Votes	Percent Votes Cast[a]
First Round (November 5)		
Aleksander Kwaśniewski (SLD)	6,275,670	35.1
Lech Wałęsa (Ind.)	5,917,328	33.1
Jacek Kuroń (UW)	1,646,946	9.2
Jan Olszewski (RdP)	1,225,453	6.9
Waldemar Pawlak (PSL)	770,419	4.3
Tadeusz Zieliński (UP)	631,432	3.5
Hanna Gronkiewicz-Waltz (ZChN)	492,628	2.8
Janusz Korwin-Mikke (UPR)	428,969	2.4
Andrej Lepper (Samoobrona)	235,797	1.3
Jan Pietrzak (Ind.)	201,033	1.1
Tadeusz Kozluk (Ind.)	27,259	0.2
Kazimierz Piotrowicz (Ind.)	12,591	0.1
Leszek Bubel (Ind.)	6,825	0.04
Second Round (November 19)		
Aleksander Kwaśniewski (SLD)	9,704,439	51.72
Lech Wałęsa (Ind.)	9,058,176	48.28

[a] Turnout in first round was 65 percent, and 68 percent in second round.

the ex-communist. The decline in Wałęsa's fortunes was brought home by Popowie, the town in which he was born, where he was defeated by a margin of 13 percent!

But all was not lost for the Solidarity bloc. Without the drawback of having Wałęsa serve as its standard-bearer, it began to piece together a new coalition. Its efforts bore fruit when in 1997 it squeezed the former communists from power. The breakdown in voting between left and right was not much different than it had been four years earlier (in fact the SLD increased its vote-share), but running this time as an electoral coalition (Solidarity Electoral Action or AWS) made all the difference for the right (Table 4.5). In a dull campaign devoid of serious controversy, Marian Krzaklewski's AWS won nearly 7 percent more votes than the SLD. Fifty-two of the 201 AWS seats went to representatives of the Solidarity trade union, 45 to Catholic activists in it, and the remainder to various conservative and nationalist groups.

TABLE 4.5 Parliamentary Election Results, September 21, 1997

Party	Percent Votes Cast[a]	Sejm (N=460)	Senate (N=100)
Solidarity Electoral Action (AWS)	33.8	201	51
Alliance of the Democratic Left (SLD)	27.1	164	26
Freedom Union (UW)	13.4	60	5
Polish Peasant Party (PSL)	7.3	27	3
Movement for Poland's Reconstruction (ROP)	5.6	6	4
German minority	0.4	2	0
Union of Labor (UP)	4.7	0	0
Other parties	7.7	0	11

[a] Turnout was 48 percent.

As a result, Cimoszewicz's government was replaced by one led by Jerzy Buzek of the AWS, an academic and union activist. Krzaklewski, like Kwaśniewski four years earlier, decided to pass on the post of prime minister and focus instead on the 2000 presidential contest. He was subsequently criticized for weakening representative government through this choice and through his sometimes thorny relationship with Buzek.

The AWS needed a coalition partner to secure a governing majority in the Sejm, and it turned to the Union of Freedom (UW), which had won a respectable 14 percent of the vote and aspired to the role of key centrist party, such as played by Germany's Free Democrats. The UW's leadership included Leszek Balcerowicz of shock therapy fame and former prime ministers Mazowiecki and Suchocka. Aware that it held the balance of power in parliament, that it had a prestigious past, and that its leaders were popular with Western politicians, the UW was able to obtain influential ministerial posts in return for joining the AWS in a coalition. Balcerowicz returned to his former posts of deputy prime minister and finance minister; his party colleague Geremek became foreign minister; Suchocka was appointed justice minister and procurator general; and Janusz Onyszkiewicz got back the defense portfolio he had held in an earlier coalition government. The AWS–UW coalition was a conspicuous example of the tail wagging the dog.

TABLE 4.6 Presidential Election Results, 2000

Candidate and Party	Votes	Percent Votes Cast[a]
First Round (October 8)		
Aleksander Kwaśniewski (SLD)	9,485,224	53.9
Andrzej Olechowski (Ind.)	3,044,141	17.3
Marian Krzaklewski (AWS)	2,739,621	15.6
Jarosław Kalinowski (PSL)	1,047,949	6.0
Andrzej Lepper (Samoobrona)	537,570	3.1
Lech Wałęsa (ChDIIIRP)	252,499	1.4
Janusz Korwin-Mikke (UPR)	178,590	1.0
Piotr Ikonowicz (PPS)	139,682	0.8
Jan Łopuszański (PP)	89,002	0.5
Dariusz Grabowski (KdP)	39,672	0.2
Tadeusz Wilecki (Ind.)	28,805	0.2
Bogdan Pawlowski (Ind.)	17,164	0.1

[a] Turnout was 61 percent.

The 2000 presidential election held none of the suspense of the previous one. Early on the saying was that the only public figure in Poland popular enough to defeat Kwaśniewski was his wife. Even the probability of a runoff—required only if no candidate captured half the votes in the first round—was low. Nevertheless, voters were aware that giving Kwaśniewski a mandate to be head of state for a second five-year period was of great consequence. Twelve candidates contested the election but only three received double-digit support: Kwaśniewski (54 percent of votes cast), independent Andrzej Olechowski (17 percent), and Krzaklewski (16 percent). Former president Wałęsa managed just 1 percent (Table 4.6).

As inevitable as the result was, the reelection of a president was a milestone in recent Polish history. The 2000 election also exposed the congenital weakness of the Polish right. The AWS lost over one-third of the support it had received in parliamentary elections three years earlier.

The SLD defeated the right for the second time in as many years in the 2001 parliamentary elections, coming within fifteen seats of winning an absolute majority in the Sejm (Table 4.7). Perhaps just as important as the success of the left was the shake-up of the Polish electoral scene represented by these elections. Four out of the six parties or coalitions winning parliamentary seats were new to the Sejm; only the SLD–UP and

TABLE 4.7 Parliamentary Election Results, September 23, 2001

Party	Percent Votes Cast[a]	Sejm (N=460)	Senate (N=100)
Alliance of the Democratic Left (SLD) – Union of Labor (UP)	41.0	216	75
Civic Platform (PO)	12.7	65	—
Self-Defense (Samoobrona)	10.2	53	2
Truth and Justice (PiS)	9.5	44	—
Polish Peasant Party (PSL)	9.0	42	4
League of Polish Families (LPR)	7.9	38	2
German Minority	0.4	2	0
Solidarity Electoral Action—Right (AWSP)	5.6	0	—
Union of Freedom (UW)	3.1	0	—
Senate Bloc (AWSP, PiS, PO, UW)	—	—	15
Other parties	0.6	0	2

[a] Turnout was 46 percent.

the PSL would be returning to their old offices. The centrist UW failed to meet the 5 percent threshold and was replaced by the new centrist Civic Platform (PO), which was the runner-up with a less than impressive 12.7 of the vote. The PSL came in a disappointing fifth, winning fewer votes than its rival for the peasant vote, the protest party Self-Defense (SO), which was third with 10.2 percent of the vote. The right was represented by two new parties (which might more properly be described as unofficial election alliances taking the legal form of parties to avoid the higher threshold required of coalitions), Law and Justice (PiS) and the League of Polish Families (LPR). The governing AWS coalition, weakened by the defections of many of its constituent parties and individual leaders, failed to meet its threshold and found itself with no seats. Leszek Miller, one of the SLD leaders least repentant about the party's communist pedigree but also a consummate politician, became prime minister, leading a minority government.

This quick sketch of elections in the Third Republic suggests many questions. How did the left recover from its low point in 1989? Does its success suggest that Polish voters have taken a turn to the left or are evidencing nostalgia for the People's Republic? Does this pattern, in which first former oppositionists, then former communists and their allies, then former oppositionists, then former communists win majority control of the parliament, represent healthy turnover? Does this represent the development of a balanced party system, offering the voters real choices?

In order to answer these questions this chapter takes a close look at the players of the game, while the following chapters examine the society that both provides them with resources and limits their possibilities and the changing sets of rules that more or less constrain them.

Political Elites

Who are the people who lead Poland's political parties? Who are the people who run for and win seats in the Sejm and Senate, who participate in parliamentary committees, and who, when the occasion permits, form the government? Who are the people who find themselves running state agencies or ministerial departments as a result of political appointment? In what ways do they differ from or resemble the rest of Polish society?

Questions about political elites are crucial for the study of any democracy. Michael Burton, Richard Gunther, and John Higley offer a straightforward and thus useful definition of elites: "persons who are able, by virtue of their strategic positions in powerful organizations, to affect national political outcomes regularly and substantially."[1] If we amend this definition to include persons whose individual reputations suffice to make their voices on public affairs heard (former presidents such as Wałęsa and Bill Clinton come to mind), this specifies the set of people with whom we are here concerned. These elites and the organizations they lead overwhelmingly play the active roles in politics; their characteristics may thus be expected to shape political processes and outcomes.

Elites: What Characterizes Them

How then do Polish elites resemble one another and how might they differ from the rest of Polish society? Are they qualified to carry out the responsibilities of the positions in which they find themselves?

Polish political elites are overwhelmingly male.[2] In both the 1993–1997 and the 1997–2001 Sejm only 13 percent of the deputies were female. (The percentages for the corresponding Senates were nearly identical.) Female parliamentarians tended to have higher education and a longer work record in trade unions or political parties than their male colleagues. They were found much more frequently on the left than on the right; for example, in the 1997–2001 Sejm, 19 percent of SLD deputies were women, but only 10 percent of AWS deputies were women.[3]

Gender in elected local government presents a more complicated picture. The percentage of women in *voivodship* (regional) councils in 1998 was even lower—11 percent—but women played a somewhat larger role at lower levels. In the most urban of local government organs—a type of city council of county (*powiat*) status found in medium and large cities—women constituted 20 percent of councillors, whereas in more rural councils their numbers hovered around 15 percent. Women are similarly underrepresented in the politically appointed upper levels of state bureaucracy—a 1998 survey of regional prefects, their deputies, and central state officials from directors of ministerial departments up through cabinet ministers found that only 16 percent were female.[4]

Not surprisingly, Polish parliamentarians are overwhelmingly in their forties and fifties (71 percent at the start of the 1997–2001 Sejm). However, it is striking how few are over the age of fifty-nine (6 percent), as well as the fact that this number did not increase from the third (elected in 1997) to the fourth (elected in 2001) of the democratically elected parliaments. Nearly 23 percent of the 1997–2001 Sejm deputies were under forty, a share slightly lower than that in the previous Sejm.

Local politics does not appear to be a training ground for future national elites, since both local councillors and local party leaders are older on average than their national counterparts. Poles sixty and above play a relatively larger role in local and regional councils, ranging from 9 to 13 percent of councilors depending on the level, whereas under-forties play a smaller role. One Polish sociologist, observing that the average age of local party elites is older than that of the delegates at their own party's national congresses, speculates that ambitious young people joining parties immediately concentrate their activity on the national level.[5] Here the exception to prove the rule would be one of the most promising Polish politicians, Warsaw's youthful mayor, Paweł Piskorski, who took office in 1999 when barely into his thirties—Warsaw city government is hardly an obscure local position.

Degrees held and fields of specialization may tell us something about the qualifications of Polish elites, as well as about their possible cognitive biases. As might be expected, the political elites are highly educated, with over 80 percent of parliamentarians holding university degrees, as do an even higher percentage of politically appointed administrative elites. Summarizing a study of both political and business elites in Poland, sociologist Jacek Wasilewski asserts that one-sixth have doctorates;[6] in this Poland resembles Germany more closely than it does the United States or the United Kingdom, for example.

Twenty-two percent of 1997–2001 Sejm deputies and party leaders had degrees in law (a relatively small percentage by the standards of many countries), but engineering and the humanities are also well represented among the deputies, with 16 percent each. Political elites in the state bureaucracy were more likely to have law degrees (34 percent) or economics degrees (20 percent versus 9 percent for the Sejm deputies), and less likely to be trained in the humanities (7 percent), while holding almost the same percentage of engineering degrees (17 percent). Wasilewski suggests, quite plausibly, that the sizable proportion of engineering degrees in political positions that would not appear to call for such skills is a relict of the communist era.[7] The road to an elite career has changed and young Poles are increasingly training in law, economics, management, or politics for careers in state administration and/or party politics.

Although the political elites are more highly educated than Poles on average, the range and distribution of their fields of specialization is thus far not unrepresentative of that of university-educated Poles. (There are, for example, sizable percentages of scientists, doctors, and agricultural specialists sitting in the Sejm.) But to look for ways in which Polish elites may tend to form a cohesive group, as well as ways in which channels of political recruitment may be narrowing, we must ask another basic cocktail-party question: Where did they go to school? A wide variety of schools are represented among the almae matres of the current political elites—from no longer existing communist party schools to medical academies—but a clear pattern appears to be developing. Already the upper levels of the state bureaucracy are dominated by the graduates of six prestigious state universities, three in Warsaw, and one each in Cracow, Gdańsk, and Poznań; in fact, well over a third are graduates of either the University of Warsaw or the Main School of Economics.[8]

Like their counterparts elsewhere, Polish political elites tend to differ from their fellow citizens in their social origins. A 1998 survey of Sejm deputies and party leaders indicates that the fathers of 38 percent had been managers, professionals, or elites themselves. Only 18 percent had fathers who were manual workers, and 22 percent had fathers who were peasants or agricultural workers, a far cry from Polish society as a whole.[9] Though these statistics may seem hardly surprising, it is worth noting given both the ideology of the previous regime and the role of blue-collar workers, peasants, and their organizations in the transition from that regime.

Another important question about elites in any country is whether there is one set or several. That is, do elites from different sectors—especially politics, culture, the business sector, and associations—constitute a relatively homogeneous group, or are they separate and competing? As of yet there is no solid research comparing the family backgrounds, educational choices, and career trajectories of elites from various important spheres of Polish life, and indeed these patterns should still be in flux, given the recent transformation of political and economic systems.

Nevertheless, some conclusions can be drawn about the relationship between political and economic elites, based on a 1998 survey carried out by Polish sociologists Janina Frentzel-Zagórska and Wasilewski. While these elites resembled each other more closely than they do Polish society on average, some differences in the two groups may be noted. Women are even more poorly represented among business leaders in the largest Polish firms—only 8 percent. Of a similar age distribution, these business elites were even better educated, with nearly 97 percent having university degrees; the same highly respected state universities dominated on their resumes as well. Polish business at this level does not seem to be a field for humanities majors or even lawyers; 79 percent had specialized in either economics or engineering, a percentage well over twice as large as that among political elites. They are somewhat more likely than political elites to have fathers who were themselves elites, managers, and professionals, and less likely to have blue-collar workers or peasants as fathers. Strikingly, they are much less likely than political elites to have been involved in opposition to the communist regime or to have been members of the Solidarity movement. Correspondingly they are much more likely to have actively supported the regime—over half of those old enough had been members of either the communist party, one of its satellite parties, and/or a pro-regime youth organization.[10]

Finally, do the political elites support democracy? Burton, Gunther, and Higley assert that "a key to the stability and survival of democratic regimes is . . . the establishment of substantial consensus among elites concerning rules of the democratic political game and the worth of democratic institutions."[11] Has such a consensus—about both the freshly forged rules of the democratic game and the worth of the young democracy itself—been established among elites in Polish politics?

For elite commitment to the specific institutions that now constitute Polish democracy, we must look at their actual behavior. As the following chapter shows, controversies over particular institutions continue, but this is not surprising given their newness. As for a consensus on democracy itself, surveys of elites suggested that it was already present as early as 1991 or 1993.[12] Certainly as of 1998 an overwhelming majority (85 percent) of political and economic elites (including former communists) polled said that the current system was significantly better than the preceding one; another 12 percent said that the current system was somewhat better. Though survey responses to these and other general questions about democratic values cannot measure the respondents' commitment to these values, these at the very least demonstrate that there exists a norm of allegiance to the current democratic system. There are, however, limits to this loyalty. In the same survey, 21 percent of elite respondents agreed that the country's economic interest could be a reason for limiting democracy, and another 9 percent were noncommittal.[13]

Elites: What Divides Them

Even more important than the question of what characterizes political elites is the question of what divides them. We might have two concerns here. Since we want to know about the stability of Polish democracy, we might ask whether or not Poland's elites are too deeply divided to lead a consolidated democracy. But the relative elite consensus on democracy suggested by survey responses has already answered this question. This is confirmed by observation of political processes since 1989. Even though Polish politicians may be highly critical of one another, of each other's morals and pasts, as well as of their policy choices, they do not fit Burton, Gunther, and Higley's description of a "disunified elite," the members of which distrust each other deeply, view politics as a zero-sum game, and even as war, and "engage in unrestricted, often violent struggles for domination."[14]

But we are also concerned with the specific forms that this Polish democracy takes; we want to know what kinds of policy are likely to result from political processes, what kinds of interests are likely to be better represented than others, and how actual political representation will reflect and shape mass preferences. Therefore we also want to identify the specific divisions among the elites.

But, given the similarities detailed above, are there then important objective differences among Polish political elites? Referring to party congress delegates surveyed in 1993 and 1995, Mirosława Grabowska describes them as practically indistinguishable: "These relatively young men, living in cities, very well educated, with desirable professions, were surely educated at the same schools, perhaps even work at the same institutions, walk the same streets. They really could belong to a single party."[15] But in fact Grabowska and other researchers have found two important differences in the lives of these elites, two areas in which they differ dramatically from one another. The first to be discussed here is their political activity under the communist regime; the second is the role of organized religion in their lives.

Why should pre-transition political involvement serve as an important objective characteristic distinguishing political elites from one another? Because of its importance for elites themselves and because it is to a large extent a dichotomous variable, a question the answer to which is "either-or" rather than a range of possibilities in between.

The past, and particularly the communist past, is still very much present in Polish politics. Politicians, as well as the journalists and commentators who analyze them, refer frequently and without the slightest hint of pretension to their "biographies." A former communist, now turned social democrat, will state—somewhat defensively—that he has nothing to be ashamed of in his biography. A journalist, writing about a former opposition hero whose present political fortunes are in decline, might mourn the waste of such a splendid biography. When local party activists were interviewed by a team of social scientists in 1995 and 1996, they emphasized any oppositional past they had. To have actually been an opposition activist constituted valuable political capital. Almost all former communists asserted that they had been reformers within the ruling party. Those in post-Solidarity parties who had not taken part in opposition activities described their strong "internal resistance" to the regime. (Exceptions here are a small number of respondents who, in the years preceding the communist collapse, were either too young for political activity or lived abroad.)[16]

The second reason why political activity under the communist regime serves as a source of objective difference is because of its dichotomous nature. Although it was never quite as simple as that old "them versus us" perspective would make it seem, there was a big difference between supporting the communist system by participating in a pro-regime organization or being active in opposition activity.[17] True, there are a couple of possible intermediate categories, including those who switched from support to opposition (13 percent of 1998 parliamentarians and party leaders, for example) and those who simply were not politically active under the communist regime (16 percent of the same group). But, as Poland entered the new millennium, those who had been active either in support of the communist regime or in opposition to it still constituted a majority of political elites. This percentage is lower among politically appointed administrative elites (55 percent in 1998) than among parliamentarians and party leaders (70 percent), but both numbers represent higher shares than in Polish society as a whole.

Thus, for example, around 37 percent of 1997–2001 parliamentary deputies had actively supported the communist regime, and 35 percent had opposed it. Of those administrative elites who largely owed their jobs to the governing parties of the same time period, 27.5 percent had actively supported the regime and another 27.5 percent had opposed it.[18]

Religion is the other area in which there is a dramatic objective difference among political elites. It is true that in Poland—on the elite as well as on the mass level—there is only one significant religion at play: Catholicism. The difference lies in the role of that religion in one's life, which may effectively be measured in frequency of church attendance. Forty-five percent of parliamentary deputies and party leaders say that they go to church every week, and another 16 percent say they attend only a little less frequently. On the other hand, 15 percent say they never go to church, and 24 percent say they attend sporadically. This is not just a matter of busy schedules or backsliding—probably over half of political elites who do not attend church regularly consider themselves nonbelievers.[19] (In contrast, while as many as 26 percent of Poles say they attend infrequently or never go to church, only 4 percent describe themselves as nonbelievers.)[20] This then is a conspicuous difference within political elites, between those who attend mass without fail and those in whose personal life the Catholic Church plays no role and who indeed consciously identify with a more secular heritage.

Are these two objective differences related to each other, or do they form crosscutting divisions? Do they help explain why an individual is active in one party rather than another? Do they help explain the relationships between parties, including how parties see each other and which parties can work with which other parties? And do these differences thus constitute a real cleavage among political elites, whether in terms of parties or policy preferences or both?

There is a strong correlation between these two differences. Indeed Grabowska goes so far as to describe Polish political elites as coming from one social stratum but two separate worlds—on one hand a world of devout Catholics with a Solidarity past, and on the other hand a world of nonreligious people with a communist past.[21] A 1998 study indicated that 60 percent of political and business elites whose political roots were in the anti-communist opposition attended church at least once a week, whereas only 17 percent of those whose political roots were in the communist regime and its allied organizations did the same (35 percent of those who had not been politically active during the communist era were church-goers).[22] Similarly in a 1993 study of strictly political elites, 57 percent of those with Solidarity origins were weekly church-goers, and only 19 percent of those with a communist past attended weekly.[23]

These factors are also strongly associated with the political party to which a member of the political elite belongs. Former communists are to be found in the SLD. Approximately 3 percent of this party's elites attend church at least once a week. Former oppositionists are to be found in a variety of parties frequently referred to as post-Solidarity parties. The percentage of their elites who describe themselves as weekly church-goers ranges as high as 96 percent (an outlier is the center-liberal UW, with as few as 36 percent regular church-goers). Former members of the communist-regime-allied United Peasant Party (ZSL) are to be found in the Polish Peasant Party. Over 40 percent of these elites attend church on a weekly basis.

Research on local party elites carried out in 1998 confirms that an individual's pre-transition political activity, as well as that of his family, plays an important role in both the decision to get involved in democratic politics and the choice of party. Some SdRP activists referred to family traditions of leftist politics, almost all spoke proudly of their PZPR experience, and many described their involvement in the SdRP as only logical, given their past. More than one activist of the Christian National Union (ZChN), a post-opposition Christian-right party, evoked his father's or other family members' participation in the Home Army resistance to the Nazi occupation, and other members of post-opposition parties referred to their own Solidarity experience. All PSL activists interviewed referred to family traditions of peasant activism, and many mentioned their involvement in the satellite ZSL as a natural precursor. (Apparently, religion as a motive for political involvement or for joining a particular party was brought up only by ZChN activists.)[24]

The primacy of the political past also becomes evident when we examine how political elites view parties other than their own. Here the most striking feature is the antipathy that has been shown to the former communists of the SLD by elites from all post-opposition parties. This has been manifested in public and private remarks, legislative initiatives, and reporting and commentary by media allied with those parties. As a matter of course many politicians from these parties refer to their SLD counterparts as reds, post-communists, and communists. They frequently slip and use the initials PZPR rather than SdRP or SLD. The long-lasting debate over decommunization was particularly intense. Many politicians favored a legal ban—to last as long as ten years—on former communists (or former communist officials of a certain rank) holding political or administrative positions. It should not be at all surprising that when pollsters asked party elites their levels of sympathy toward various other parties, the SLD came in dead last. Whom then did SLD politicians intensely dislike, disregarding any similarity of their policy positions? It was the only political competitor at that time using the name Solidarity, that is, the Solidarity trade union's electoral list.[25]

When we look at which Polish parties will officially cooperate with which other parties, whether in electoral alliances or governing coalitions on the national or local level, we see that this antipathy also affects the parties' behavior and thus directly shapes and limits political possibilities. Until the 2001 parliamentary election there had not been any national governing coalition cutting across the divide between former communists and former oppositionists—this in spite of the fact that coalition government has been the rule, with no one party winning enough seats to govern by itself. Although a party with some post-Solidarity roots, the Union of Labor (UP), became a junior partner in government with the SLD, after forming a joint electoral alliance for the 2001 campaign, the more telling fact is that an alliance between these two officially social democratic parties did not take place in any earlier parliamentary elections. Thus every government since 1990 could be described as either post-opposition or post-communist, patched together out of a variety of parties with at least some mutually incompatible policy positions, and often with the participation of the conveniently unclassifiable PSL.

This was not just a matter of chance, of how the political dice (or rather the numbers of seats) fell each time a government was to be formed. A multinational team of political scientists, examining the responses of party elites to a survey question on possible coalition partners, could find only one pair of Polish parties willing to cooperate with each other across this fundamental divide, the SLD and the UP, and—as we shall see below—their classification of the UP as post-Solidarity is questionable.[26] Nor is this limitation only present on the level of national politics. Though there have been many instances of strange bedfellows in local government coalitions, the responses by local party activists interviewed in 1995–1996 demonstrated that—at least in Warsaw and the four small towns where the research was carried out—no parties except the PSL and the UP were willing to form an official coalition with the SLD on the local level. The one Union of Freedom respondent in any of the four towns who found a local coalition with the SLD an acceptable possibility hastened to add that he would resign from his party if it formed a national coalition with the SLD at that moment.[27] Confirming this cleavage, when asked to name the most important factors preventing political agreement in Poland, deputies from the 1993–1997 parliament listed "differing relationship to the past" most frequently; "ideological and worldview differences" were listed less than half as often.[28]

All this strongly supports the existence in Poland of a profound elite cleavage based primarily on the political past but reinforced by corresponding relationships to organized religion. This historical-cultural cleavage is characterized by, but not limited to, former communists on one side and former oppositionists on the other. But is this necessarily the most important cleavage dividing Polish elites? In spite of their many demographic similarities, there might be consistent patterns of differing policy orientations among elites that play an equal or larger role in shaping the party system (and thus the electorate's options).

Certainly there are important differences in policy preferences among Polish political elites. The two dimensions in Figure 4.1 may be used to describe most of those differences. Economic policy lies on the horizontal axis, ranging from reliance on the state to solve economic problems on the extreme left to pure market solutions on the extreme right. The vertical axis may be termed traditionalist–secular. Here one extreme is advocacy of the most traditionalist responses possible, relying on a fundamentalist interpretation of Catholic teachings, as well as specifically Polish traditions, to direct state choices. The other extreme is a knee-jerk secularism or even anti-clericalism, designing social and cultural policy to maximize individual freedom and disregard traditionalist values and sensibilities.

But do these policy dimensions themselves constitute deep divisions or cleavages, fundamentally structuring political interactions in Poland? For the time being, the answer for each one must be no, for different reasons.

It is true that most of the economic policy issues confronting Poland since 1989—such as whether to privatize slowly or quickly or whether to fight unemployment through public works programs or lower taxes—can themselves be placed on the horizontal state–market dimension. Certainly Polish elites disagree on important aspects of how to confront these challenges. In spite of near consensus on the benefits of a market econ-

Figure 4.1 Political Parties and Approximate Ideological Orientations, 2001

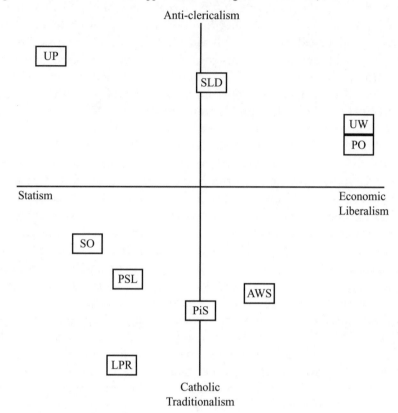

omy and capitalism, as well as on prioritizing economic growth over equi-table redistribution, individual politicians and groups of politicians can be distinguished by how large a role they see for the state in the economy, as well as on the costs that the young, the old, and the unemployed can be expected to pay for a healthy and efficient economy.

But these disagreements find only partial expression in the party sys-tem itself. As is evident from Figure 4.1 as well as in the following section on political parties, economic policy orientations do vary from one party to another—although some surprising pairs of parties have similar policy profiles. But these orientations also vary widely within parties. The 1997 election, for example, was primarily a battle between the two major elec-toral blocs, the SLD and the AWS, each of which represented a roughly similar and wide range of opinion on economic policy. Not surprisingly their campaigns were dominated by cultural and historical issues—the role of the church and decommunization. One observer asserted that "campaign debates scarcely touched upon social and economic problems."[29]

Most Polish parties can be described more easily in terms of the traditionalist versus secularist dimension, but to a very large extent this coincides with the historical-cultural cleavage. The deeply Catholic former oppositionist lives in one world and has one worldview; the former communist who attends church at most for marriages and baptisms lives in another world and has a different worldview. The former tends to advocate policy positions in line with church teachings and traditional Polish values; the latter worries about too much church influence on the state.

Not only do religion and history overlap, but it also appears that for now the historical component dominates, and it would therefore be inappropriate to view this as just another version of the authoritarian–liberal value cleavage found in, say, Western European democracies. When push comes to shove, that is, in the formation of governing coalitions, it has been history that decides. Thus, when the SLD won a plurality but not a majority of parliamentary seats in 1993, it found itself forming a coalition not with liberal parties closer to it on this policy dimension but instead with the much more traditionalist peasant party, which—as a successor to the former communist ally, the ZSL—was already tainted "pink." Likewise in 1997 the AWS (an alliance of primarily traditionalist parties) formed a coalition with the more liberal Union of Freedom. The primacy of history is confirmed by the research on local parties already cited, in which the individual's and their family's political biography was mentioned far more frequently than religion when activists were asked to explain their motives for political involvement.

As one local party activist observed with regret, the existing parties have their origins in history rather than in programs.[30] This is not to say that the differences in policy preferences among elites are not important. To some extent these are discussed below, as the parties themselves are presented; the final chapter on policy challenges examines these further. But as of yet these policy differences do not *define* the elites, nor determine the fundamental dynamics of elite politics. It is the historical-cultural cleavage that has structured the party system, shaping elite choices to form new parties or to become involved in a particular party, as well as limiting the possibilities of cooperation between parties. When 1993–1997 parliamentarians were asked to rate the deepness of various divisions on the Polish political scene, the division between the post-Solidarity camp and the post-PRL (People's Republic of Poland) camp came in first. Eighty-six percent rated this division as either essential or very deep; in dramatic contrast, only 27 percent had the same opinion of the division between proponents and opponents of integration into the European Union.[31]

The historical-cultural cleavage among political elites has shaped political possibilities and outcomes for over a decade in the life of the Third Republic. Will it endure and continue to shape Polish politics? We might intuitively expect that this cleavage, based as it is on a specific historical experience, will disappear with time, and should indeed already be fading. After all, there is a generation of twenty-somethings entering politics with no adult memories of life under communist rule. On the other hand, research on much older democracies has shown that cleavages deriving from particular societal conflicts can endure long after the experiences that gave rise to them.[32] To the extent that alignments are rooted in sociodemographic traits, that corresponding values are transmitted from generation to generation, and that patterns of association are structured around a cleavage, that cleavage can last for a very long time.

Are those conditions present here? Whether one is a nonbeliever or a religiously observant believer is most definitely a sociodemographic trait; political traditions have been passed down between generations throughout the previous century in Poland; and, as we show later in this chapter, the historical-cultural cleavage is expressed in some associational patterns. Even as new generations begin to regard the evaluation of the PRL's achievements or the culpability for communist-era crimes as topics better left to their recently completed history classes, new cultural controversies based on religious and moral values may come to take their place, with the warring sides still taking up their positions along the old fault line. The historical-cultural cleavage has at least the potential to persist. As we examine political parties in the following section we shall see more of how this cleavage shapes the party system, and of how crosscutting policy dimensions may be represented within this system, as well as possible signs that this cleavage may be growing shallower as alliances or even significant parties are forged across it.

Parties and the Party System

Out of the six nationwide political parties winning parliamentary seats in the 2001 elections, three had been formed less than a year earlier, including the second-runner, Civic Platform. It is clear that the Polish party system is still in flux, even in the second decade of post-communist democratic politics. As a result, Polish elite politics is better understood in terms of camps—that is, groupings defined not by organizational lines but by patterns of association, similar worldviews, and/or shared policy orientations—rather than in terms of specific parties.[33] The classic terms left and right apply here, although in the early 1990s many Poles wondered if these labels might already be anachronistic. By now Polish elites, as well as their fellow citizens, overwhelmingly recognize the existence of a leftist camp and a rightist camp. As we might expect, in Poland the terms left and right most frequently refer to the two sides of the historical-cultural cleavage, and less often—to the frustration of many analysts as well as many politicians themselves—to differences on economic policy.[34] For example, not only are former communists considered by all including themselves as the left, but rightist politicians will sometimes refer to former opposition colleagues who oppose strict decommunization policies as leftist.

Here we first examine a leftist camp dominated by former communists—with, however, an important exception. Then we turn to the others. This includes the divided and fractious right, as well as two important sets of groupings that persistently refuse to fit into either the leftist or the rightist camps or perhaps even onto a coherent left–right spectrum. One of these is what is called in Polish politics the center (which on an economics-based spectrum would fall to the right of other parties). The other consists of those peasant parties and other movements that aspire to represent rural interests in Poland.

The Left

The left in Poland today consists of the SLD and the UP. Other tiny leftist parties have come and gone, but none significantly affects the vote share of the now behemoth SLD.[35] Although both the SLD and the UP are officially social-democratic and although together they have formed both a successful electoral alliance and a government, in many ways the two are polar opposites—as the following analysis shows.

The most striking fact about not just the Polish left but the entire political party scene is the success of the communist successor party, the SLD. In every free parliamentary election it has increased its share of the vote—from 13 percent in 1991, to 21 percent in 1993, to 27 percent in 1997, to 41 percent in 2001.[36] The former communists have gone from humiliating defeat in the partially free elections of 1989 to democratic victories resulting in simultaneous control of both the presidency and the parliament by 2001. This outcome suggests one crucial question: Why has the SLD been so successful?

Some of the reasons for the SLD's continuing success are discussed elsewhere in this book. Winning in electoral competition depends not just on one's own virtues, but also on the mistakes and failings of one's opponents; thus the discussion of other parties, and particularly of the right, sheds light on this question. Electoral success also depends, of course, on what the voters are looking for—this is discussed in the next chapter—but since the Polish electorate has not taken a dramatic turn to the left in its values, the question remains rather how the SLD has managed to beat all challengers at presenting the image of pragmatic competence that these voters want.

Observers and political players alike agree on several characteristics of the SLD that lie at the heart of its success—the SLD is unified, nothing if not pragmatic, and rich in both tangible and intangible assets. Where disagreements arise is on the relative importance of these characteristics, as well as on their sources. Here the most important controversy is over the extent to which the SLD's victories are built on ill-gotten gains, that is, on resources that it, its members, and its friends inherited from the former ruling communist party. Our analysis of the SLD's strengths shows that there is some truth in this, but the picture is more complex than the ill-gotten gains argument suggests. Two aspects of the post-communist legacy—the material and human resources that the former communists retained after 1989 *and* the anti-communist sentiment and policy initiatives they faced—have worked together to make the SLD what it is today: the most cohesive, pragmatic, and effective party on the Polish political scene.

The unity shown by the post-communist left is impressive on any terms, but against the chaos of mutual recriminations, accusations, schisms, fractures, and defections manifested in the rest of the Polish political scene it is near miraculous. As we have observed, the Polish United Workers Party (PZPR) convened for its eleventh and final party congress on January 27, 1990. Within two days the former ruling party had dissolved itself, and this final congress was transformed into the founding congress of the Social Democracy of the Republic of Poland.[37] The SdRP became the core of the post-communist left, bringing together formerly pro-regime trade unions, smaller parties, other organizations, and independents to form a lasting coalition, the Alliance of the Democratic Left.

This coalition—open to almost anyone who wanted to join, but overwhelmingly dominated by the SdRP together with the National Trade Union Accord (OPZZ)—proved more cohesive and coherent than almost any actual Polish party, and finally in April 1999 turned itself into a political party (only five of the thirty-two organizations constituting the SLD coalition refused to join the SLD party).

The SdRP and the SLD have avoided visible and divisive struggles for leadership. There has been—by Polish standards—a remarkable degree of leadership continuity within the post-communist left. At the SdRP founding congress in January 1990 the brand-new social democrats chose as their chair Kwaśniewski, who had been a junior minister in the last PZPR governments; Kwaśniewski would remain SdRP chair until elected president in 1995. At the same congress they chose as secretary general Leszek Miller, a former Central Committee secretary considered to be supported by the PZPR apparatus, who would later lead the SLD to its 2001 victory and become prime minister.

Neither the continuity nor the lack of dramatic internal struggles, however, should be interpreted to mean that the SLD has been dominated by one or two strong personalities, or that there are no differences of opinion within its leadership. Unlike their counterparts in other parties, local SdRP activists interviewed made no mention of individual leaders as they talked about their party or their reasons for joining.[38] There have been leadership rivalries—Kwaśniewski, for example, faced a serious rival in Józef Oleksy for several years—and there have been differences about how to handle specific issues. SLD politicians, however, have managed to keep the public expression of these differences to a minimum. In the SLD, conflicts take place behind closed doors.

An excellent example—the exception that proves the rule—was a 2000 confrontation between Miller and Cimoszewicz over a Sejm vote to confirm former Deputy Prime Minister and Finance Minister Leszek Balcerowicz as president of the central bank. Cimoszewicz opposed this nomination, apparently on the grounds that it was part of a compromise between the SLD's opponents to avoid early elections that the SLD was sure to win. Miller supported this nomination, at least to the point of arguing that SLD deputies should be allowed to vote their conscience and supposedly asserting that he intended to absent himself and not vote, in order to help the nomination pass. Two aspects of this incident are important here. First, both this debate and the vote actually contested by Cimoszewicz and Miller were internal, within the SLD's parliamentary club. When Cimoszewicz's side carried the day and passed an internal resolution requiring party discipline in casting parliamentary votes against Balcerowicz's nomination, all their colleagues including Miller complied. Second, the nomination was only in question because several members of the governing AWS actually broke their own party discipline in the Sejm itself, voting against the nominee or making themselves absent. The newspaper headlines the next day were about the internal SLD quarrel rather than the AWS defectors—the one an exciting novelty, the other business as usual.[39]

If this cohesion is not a function of lack of leadership rivalries or internal tensions, might it then be a result of ideological uniformity? The evidence suggests otherwise. While SLD activists may be in relative agreement on sociocultural questions—preferring that the church and perhaps even its values be kept as far away from state policy as politically feasible—their stances on economic issues vary wildly, with the party encompassing both nostalgic socialists and neoliberals. A cross-national survey of Central and East European party elites noted this broad spread of economic policy preferences within the SLD and suggested that "the SLD might experience considerable internal strain in its efforts to maintain a common economic policy position."[40] Does it? The head of the SLD 2001 election campaign described the SLD's cohesiveness in this way: "internal discussion, external discipline." [41] Although there is no doubt whatsoever about the SLD's external discipline, there is little indication of any particularly intense or meaningful internal discussion. Alone among local party activists interviewed in 1995 and 1996, SdRP members neither mentioned any intraparty conflicts nor polemicized with central party policies. These interviews paint a picture of "an ideally coherent grouping, in which no internal divisions exist, and decisions taken at the top do not cause tensions or conflicts among those below."[42]

To understand how such unity is possible we need to examine another internal factor contributing to the SLD's success—its pragmatism. But we also can look for part of the answer in the siege mentality that developed among former communists at the start of the Third Republic. As our discussion of the historical-cultural cleavage showed, for most of the post-Solidarity political elite, former communists were pariahs. Thus they had no political home that would take them in, outside the SLD. Even the Union of Labor, which contained a mix of former oppositionists and former communist party members, looked suspiciously on former apparatchiks; nor, for those whom it might find acceptable, did that small and ideologically leftist party seem to promise any real refuge and support. And political refuge and support appeared indispensable after 1989 for any former communist intending to have a successful career in public affairs or, often, even the business world. Anti-communist rhetoric and proposals for decommunization on the personnel level (for example, banning former communists from holding important positions), together with informal decommunization (in which former PZPR members lost their previously assured jobs or sometimes simply discovered that their party credentials were no longer a guarantee of upward advancement), combined to create a strong sense of outside threat.

In part the members of the SLD have been forced together by common defensive interests, by the perceived need to protect themselves and their supporters from decommunization policies, both formal and informal, and by the fact that they have had few potential partners elsewhere in Polish politics.[43] Thus, for example, when SLD prime minister Oleksy was accused of spying for Russia in 1995, his party colleagues united around him, praising him and heaping invective on his accusers. As soon as he resigned as prime minister, they elected him chair of the SdRP, giving him 308 out of 325 votes. At least one journalist referred to this critically as reflecting an "all for one and one for all" mentality.[44]

The state of siege, however, is passing. While for several years politicians of the right were known to walk out of parliament when Miller had the floor, prominent rightist Stefan Niesiołowski of the Christian National Union is now on first-name terms with Miller, with the two addressing each other with the familiar second-person form rather than the formal third-person (but, significantly, this final tidbit was still seen as remarkable enough in 2001 to turn up as a "believe-or-not" item in a newspaper quiz on political knowledge).[45] On the level of parties and alliances, new developments indicate that the SLD is no longer a pariah—for example, the emergence of a new party, Civic Platform, which specifically rejects the historical-cultural cleavage. As for individuals, personnel decommunization policies have increasingly become moot as the years pass and former communists in administration and politics accumulate a post-1989 record on which to be judged. If SLD unity had been based entirely on threats and rejection from anti-communists, its future would be in doubt.

But another factor helping the SLD remain unified has been its political pragmatism. When ideological differences simply are not that important, when ideology itself plays a minor role, it is easier to stay together, and also easier to avoid public quarrels. Even more importantly, this pragmatism has allowed the SLD to mold itself to the wishes of the electorate, in more ways than one.

Both sociological research and political observation suggest that the SLD is remarkably pragmatic. The apt title of an article cited several times in this chapter may be translated as "The Pragmatic United Governing Party" (in a play on words that reproduces the initials of the former ruling PZPR). Sixty-eight percent of SdRP congress delegates surveyed said their party should strive for as broad electoral support as possible—the highest percentage among all the parties surveyed at their congresses in 1995 and 1996; only 28 percent of SdRP delegates said the party should instead work for the concerns of particular sectors supporting it. Fifty-eight percent asserted that the party sometimes can abandon some of its promises rather than fulfilling all its campaign pledges—again the highest percentage.[46]

This pragmatism has been most glaringly obvious in economic policy. In both propaganda and practice the SLD has been remarkably moderate, given the party's origins in a Marxist-Leninist party that had created and administered a centrally planned economy. Every time the SLD has campaigned against a post-Solidarity incumbent government, it has pledged not to abandon the ongoing economic reforms, but instead to carry them out better and to take care of those hurt worst by the reforms. When in government from 1993 to 1997, the SLD made no major changes of direction in economic policy, in spite of its coalition with the more statist PSL. Evaluating the coalition's economic performance, experts George Blazyca and Ryszard Rapacki described it as generally characterized by continuity—continuing the policies of the reformist post-Solidarity governments—with a few differences, such as more frequent yielding to sectoral pressures as well as delays in privatization (with important economic ministries firmly in the grip of the SLD during this period, these choices may be safely attributed to the post-communists, even during the tenure of the PSL's Pawlak as prime minister).[47]

This moderation was if anything even more pronounced during the 2001 parliamentary campaign. Faced with near-certain victory (given many months of dominating the public opinion polls and the absence of any serious challenger), the strategic choice for the SLD was to run a campaign designed to prepare the ground for the real choices its leaders would have to make in government. Thus when the SLD and the UP met three months before the election to ceremonially vote on their joint platform, the keynote speech was given by an economist who warned against making unrealistic promises to the electorate: "Don't promise to grow pears on willow trees!" The speakers who followed took his advice seriously. Typical was a proposal for improving the lot of retired people, cautiously prefaced with the phrase, "If the state budget allows. . . ." The few propositions likely to upset a fiscal conservative were hardly leftist, for example, a proposal for tax breaks for firms investing in areas of high unemployment.[48]

The ease with which the SdRP/SLD turned away from socialist economic ideology is not in itself surprising, given the visible bankruptcy of the command economy in its final decade—by all reports there were few, if any, true believers left in the communist party by 1989. Nevertheless, by the admission of the 2001 campaign chief himself, the broad spectrum of economic orientations present in the SLD still extends all the way from the center (some would say the center-right) to the extreme left.[49] Such breadth does not in and of itself guarantee moderation; politics would be far too easy if one could simply average out a variety of opinions and go with the arithmetic mean. Indeed, tension between the 1993–1997 SLD–PSL government and the National Trade Union Accord, which was itself part of the SLD, demonstrated the potential for problems. Clearly OPZZ activists, who represented several million dues-paying wage earners, felt an imperative to be advocates for the direct and immediate interests of those millions. By no means did this involve supporting every aspect of their government's cautious and responsible economic policies. Why then did this tension never develop into the kind of publicly embarrassing and unity-destroying schism that has characterized the right side of the Polish political spectrum?

Similar questions may be posed about the moderation and pragmatism increasingly displayed by the SLD in foreign policy. Here the most important development is the SLD turning its focus from the east to the west. In supporting Polish entry into NATO the SLD reversed not just its PZPR predecessor's position, as it had on economic policy, but its very own stance of the early 1990s, when SLD leaders and members had virulently opposed even the extension of NATO to Poland's western border, that is, the inclusion of eastern Germany in the alliance. Now the SLD takes pride in Poland's NATO membership, pointing to the positive role President Kwaśniewski played in achieving this, and hopes to be able to call itself the party that brought Poland into the European Union. How was such a dramatic turnaround possible without internal struggles tearing the party apart?

We might expect pragmatism in sociocultural issues to be even harder to achieve for the SLD. Here its activists share a more coherent set of policy preferences directly derived from their shared heritage, reinforced by their daily lives, and never discredited (as socialist economic values were discredited by the collapse of communism) nor invalidated by geopolitical changes (as was the early SLD foreign policy stance). Years of survey research on both the elite and mass levels show that SLD activists differ from the vast majority of Poles not just in their church-going habits but also in their preferences concerning such policy matters as religion in schools. Yet in 2001 these elites got over 40 percent of those same Poles to vote for them, with voters perfectly aware that each vote cast for the SLD–UP coalition would mean a stronger hold for the left on the trifecta of Polish politics—the government, the parliament, and the presidency.

This was possible because in recent years the post-communist left had moderated its stance in matters of church–state relations and religious values in policy. After playing the anti-clerical card in the 1993 campaign by warning of the dangers of theocracy and building on voter dissatisfaction with the then growing role and political ambitions of the Catholic Church, in parliament the SLD continued its attacks on the church and its influence. In coalition government with the traditionalist peasant party, however, the SLD had to prove more moderate in practice. The call to remove religious education from public schools was gradually dropped, for example, and the SLD failed to liberalize the restrictive abortion law, thus involuntarily breaking a campaign promise. As for the Concordat, discussed more fully below, although resistance from the SLD delayed ratification until after the 1997 election of a post-Solidarity-dominated parliament, it was the SLD's own President Kwaśniewski who signed it in February 1998, obviating years of post-communist attacks on this agreement regulating relations between the Polish state and the Vatican.

After the mid-1990s the SLD was gaining little from what was often called its "cold war" with the Catholic Church, and gradually found compromise to be the better part of valor. In 1996 SdRP chair Oleksy warned party elites not to accept the label of doctrinaire anti-clericalism: "The Social Democracy [SdRP], operating in an overwhelmingly religious society, must remember that millions of Catholics vote for it, and that it wants them to vote for it forever."[50] Similarly, in 2000 Miller asserted: "Poland cannot be understood without the Church, there is no Poland without the Church. The left cannot be eternally ready for a religious war."[51]

There was thus no room for anti-clericalism in either President Kwaśniewski's successful bid for reelection in 2000 nor in the SLD's 2001 election campaign. In fact, the post-communist elites now directly offend devout Catholics only by accident, when through carelessness they inadvertently remind the public of the differences in their worldviews. For example, Kwaśniewski's poll standings took a dip shortly before the presidential election upon the release of a videotape showing him privately joking with a colleague who went down on his knees and kissed the ground in mocking imitation of Pope John Paul II's habitual gesture upon disembarking from a plane. Showing remarkable yet necessary pragmatism, the SLD has effectively relegated not religious values but rather its members' own secular values to the realm of the private and sworn off anti-clerical slogans and programs in politics.

This pragmatism, visible in the early 1990s and by now pronounced in all policy spheres, has allowed the SLD to mold its image and program to the voters' wishes, as well as to make macroeconomic and foreign policy choices while in government that meet with the approval of international organizations, observers, and foreign states. Furthermore, the SLD's pragmatism itself pleases the voters. The Polish electorate has come to distrust ideology, associating it with conflict and inefficiency, and has a strong preference for practical and pragmatic politicians. The SLD is ready to meet this demand.

But what explains the extraordinary pragmatism of the SLD? Many Poles, especially those hostile to the party, see pragmatism's roots directly in the SLD's origins. In its final decades the PZPR had become the party of opportunistic careerists and power-seekers; the transformation to the SdRP and the SLD had changed nothing: "In that political season the leading role of the party and the Warsaw Pact were in fashion, in this season the fashion is democracy and NATO."[52]

But answers based on the character of individuals are not the stuff of comparative politics. Political parties elsewhere display varying mixes of pragmatism and ideology. Particularly in the post-communist democracies with rapidly changing political, economic, and even geopolitical situations and a high degree of political uncertainty, the kind of pragmatism that allows a party to adapt its program on demand to the voters' wishes is a highly desirable quality. It often ensures electoral success and political power. Yet few parties can be as simultaneously flexible and effective as the SLD.

A more interesting answer to this puzzle—one that also derives (although less directly) from the party's origins—lies in two facts. First, in 1990, when the SLD/SdRP began its activity, it was already richly endowed with necessary assets, and thus did not face the kind of start-up costs required of the post-Solidarity parties. Second, because of the stage of siege constituted by decommunization pressures and the rise to power of anti-communists, there existed a core of activists, members, and supporters who would stay loyal to the former communist party as long as it resisted decommunization policies and defended at least some elements of their common heritage.

Here is where what some call the former communist party's "ill-gotten gains" exert a major and most enduring effect. It is by means of its proclaimed *goals* that a new political party stakes its claim on support from its environment. In order to initiate the flow of necessary resources from potential activists, donors, and members, a new party must choose and commit itself to a set of well-designed goals. To keep this flow of resources coming, the new party must then maintain those goals.[53] But an existing and well-endowed organization does not have to use goals to convince potential activists and donors that it deserves support; instead it can choose and even adapt its goals to appeal to the voters rather than mobilize resources.

The PZPR-turned-SdRP was such an existing and well-endowed organization. Instead of making a clean break with the communist party and renouncing its physical assets, as some members strongly advocated, the founders of the SdRP chose "not to cut the umbilical cord" and instead made their quasi-new party the legal heir to the PZPR.[54] As a result, the SdRP began life with a valuable nationwide infrastructure of buildings, office equipment, phone lines, and cars—not to mention bank accounts and income-producing enterprises. Legal efforts were eventually made to deprive the successor party of its official endowment, largely on the grounds that the Polish state had paid for all of this and thus was the true owner. But by then most assets had been transferred into other hands in one way or another, and thus effectively shielded from legal action. Thus, by 1999, the newly formed SLD *party* did not need to be an official heir to the SdRP; conveniently, when the SdRP dissolved itself in 1999 shortly after the creation of the SLD party, the issue of the several million dollars owed to the state treasury by the SdRP was left hanging.

But even without the umbilical cord the SdRP would have stood out as an exceptionally well-endowed organization in the Poland of 1990. Because of the lack of independent formal organization in communist Poland and the monopolization of state structures by the official parties, the SdRP/SLD started off with a stock of organizational skills that far outstripped those of its potential rivals (the important exception to all of this is the PSL, to be discussed below). Furthermore, given the long history of the PZPR, together with its nationwide structure made up not just of a formal network of organizational units, but also of informal networks of patronage and exchange, the former communists were rich in the social capital of mutual acquaintance and trust.

Even the tangible assets of the SdRP/SLD are notoriously hard to measure and quantify; the effort has kept many Polish attorneys and experts profitably employed for several years. But one concrete and even quantifiable item is party membership. In 1990, when most of its rivals were trying to pull together members and resources to build organizational capacity nearly from scratch, the SdRP found itself with 22,000 members within two months of its official birth. Most observers contrasted this with the two-million-strong membership that had gone up in smoke when the PZPR dissolved itself, and shook their heads at the sad condition of the former communists. They overlooked the significance of the fact that 22,000 adult and mentally sound Poles were ready to sign on with the successor party to the recently disgraced PZPR, at a time when very few were interested at all in joining parties—even the more respectable post-opposition parties.

For the former communists who immediately joined, and especially for the activists who continued to work in the central and local structures of what was now the SdRP, this party had much of the "taken-for-granted" character of a long-standing, well-institutionalized organization. Members, activists, and supporters were already committed to the party, and the party's survival was an end in itself. Thus neither the party's purposes nor its internal distribution of power were subject to continual questioning by participants.[55] Even from the start the SdRP and the SLD coalition it founded could concentrate on crafting slogans and programs to appeal to the voters.

But simple inertia is not enough to keep activists, members, and supporters committed to the party no matter what it may do. As we have shown, the SLD has been characterized by remarkable programmatic flexibility. Though not quite a political chameleon, this party is capable of completely reversing its foreign policy position in a few short years, as well as severely playing down its most unifying and hot-button set of issues, namely, secular versus Catholic values. What keeps SLD activists loyal? Even if we do not assume that party activists are necessarily more extreme than the party electorate, we might expect both activists and supporters to balk at faithfully following this party through its programmatic twists and turns.

This question can be phrased more specifically: What makes commitment worth it to them? Parties able to keep their activists and supporters happy by ministering to their particularistic concerns tend to enjoy greater flexibility on broad questions of strategy. Herbert Kitschelt's model of internal party politics produces the concept of "lobbyists," party activists who seek selective goods to be provided to very specific constituencies.[56] If the party is seen as the best or only supplier of these goods, these "lobbyists" are ready to stomach whatever else the party's current program contains.

One possible candidate for the particularistic benefits received by those who give their time and money to the SLD is the material advantage accruing to SLD officeholders and political appointees. More valuable here than the salaries and official perks of the jobs are the enormous opportunities for political patronage. By the mid-1990s it was clear to Poles that government contracts, licenses, hiring (not just in state agencies but in the many semiprivate firms still controlled by the state), and a myriad of other types of decisions that bring profit to particular interests in the private sector are an economic bonanza to whomever controls them. Some of the payoffs may come in quasi-legal forms such as jobs or investment opportunities for officeholders' relatives, but undoubtedly a large share comes in the clearly illegal form of the notorious cash-filled envelope. While political patronage certainly took place under the 1989–1993 governments, the conventional wisdom is that this phenomenon mushroomed and became institutionalized into democratic Polish politics under the SLD–PSL governments of 1993–1997. Certainly the number of jobs subject to political appointment and filled on a partisan basis increased significantly.

But, as discussed below, the SLD's rightist rivals were fast learners, at least in this regard, and put their lessons to good use in government from 1997 to 2001. If patronage to the point of outright corruption suffices to reduce the salience of ideological differences and to keep activists loyal and committed, how can we explain the phenomenon of the AWS—simultaneously corrupt, ideologically driven, and at war with itself?

The most plausible reason for SdRP/SLD activists' tolerance of their party's policy switches lies elsewhere. What the post-communist left, and only the post-communist left, could provide for former communists has been protection from the hostility of anti-communists, and especially from both the threat and reality of decommunization. The same external pressures that keep its elite unified make the SLD the monopoly supplier of protection for former communists—from elites to rank-and-file. No other party could be looked to for defense of their jobs, their pensions (for example, from legislative changes that would have stripped former security service employees of their higher veteran-equivalent stipends), or their heritage (for example, from changes in textbooks or wording in official proclamations that would symbolically wipe out any of the achievements of the People's Republic). Not surprisingly, this is the one policy area in which the SLD has not wavered, consistently doing its best to deliver the goods.

As a result the SLD has not needed to use its economic, foreign policy, or sociocultural stances to mobilize activists or resources. Instead it has been free to tell the voters what they want to hear, and also able, for the most part, to follow moderate policies while in office. More than any other party on the Polish political scene, the SLD has succeeded in making itself into a catchall party, one appealing across the board to voters in all social categories rather than focusing on a single clientele.[57] Paradoxically, as we have shown here, this was possible precisely because the SLD has had a narrow core clientele safely in its pocket.

The public unity displayed by the SLD (while their opponents wash their own dirty linen over and over again in the evening news), the skills evident in their political campaigning and media appearances, and the nonideological pragmatism they demonstrate at every turn—all this goes to present a picture to the Polish voter of competence and professionalism. When asked before the 2001 elections which parties would do the best job of reviving the economy, taking Poland into the European Union, and lowering unemployment, Poles most frequently chose the SLD–UP coalition.[58] Social psychologist Mirosława Marody explains: "The average voter sees it like this: 'All politicians are swine, but there are amateur swine and professional swine. Of the two evils I prefer the latter.'" Especially when out of government, the SLD has been, in the eyes of the Polish voter, the professional swine—the ones whose competence if not their honesty can be trusted, the ones who will not let their ideology get in the way of governing the country and pleasing the electorate.[59] Even though it is harder to maintain that image of professionalism when actually on the job, as the difficulties of the SLD after 2001 while leading its coalition with the UP and PSL demonstrate, the SLD remains unified, relatively effective, and the most professional-appearing force on the Polish political scene.

Many of the characteristics of the SLD show up best when contrasted with its coalition partner, the Union of Labor. Tomasz Nałęcz, later to become a UP leader, described the response received when he and others tried in 1990 to persuade Kwaśniewski to join them, and not the former apparatchiks, in a more radical break with the PZPR past: The future president excused himself, explaining that Nałęcz and his colleagues were good for having a drink with, but not for doing politics together: "He said that when he asks an apparatchik for something, he knows it will be done, but with us it'll immediately turn out that there's something more important—the child got sick or the dog is starting to scratch itself."[60]

Although the UP is often referred to as a post-Solidarity party, its actual heritage is hybrid. The UP was formed in 1992 by combining two tiny post-Solidarity parties—Solidarity of Labor (SP) and the Democratic-Social Movement (RDS)—with an equally weak Polish Social-Democratic Union formed by former PZPR members who had renounced the communist party's assets. The founders were optimistic, aiming to become the major party of the left. The SdRP/SLD, they hoped, would inevitably collapse—after all, a political party could not be built solely on the basis of shared biographies.[61] In its debut in the 1993 parliamentary elections the UP won over 7 percent of the vote and 41 Sejm seats—a respectable if not necessarily promising showing; in 1997, however, it failed to make the 5-percent threshold and found itself shut out of the Sejm for four years.

To say the UP has been more ideological than the SLD would be an understatement. While local activists of both parties described themselves as leftist when interviewed, especially when giving their reasons for being active in their chosen party, there was no indication of what the SdRP activists understood by leftist—that is, they did not define the left nor did they mention any traditionally leftist economic concerns. In contrast, UP activists frequently mentioned social justice and the economic plight of the weakest.[62] As for sociocultural issues, although delegates at the 1995 UP congress were nearly three times as likely as their SdRP counterparts to describe themselves as believing and practicing Catholics, their policy preferences are similarly secular. In fact the Union of Labor has consistently taken up prominent stands on sensitive issues, for example, in 1996 introducing legislation allowing abortions for women in difficult personal situations, and women's rights have been an integral part of its agenda. In surveys of delegates at UP, SdRP, Union of Freedom, and Christian National Union party congresses, UP elites were least likely to opt for a catchall party strategy, and thus most likely to favor concentrating on winning support from certain sectors.[63] UP criticism of the SLD has, predictably, focused on its "pragmatic opportunism."

As for internal conflict, the UP has been plagued with this problem from the start, most intensely over purely political questions of cooperation, whether formal or informal, with other political parties. The first serious controversy arose over the party leadership's decision not to join the

SLD–PSL governing coalition in 1993. Many activists were seriously disappointed and even embittered by losing what they saw as the opportunity to have a real impact on policy. The official reason for UP withdrawal from coalition talks was that the SLD's economic program was not sufficiently leftist, but much of the leadership had doubts about working with the SLD's Miller and Cimoszewicz. As the decision was made, one UP leader with an impressive opposition record was heard to say, "It's not just that they're communists—they're right-wing to boot!"[64]

Another internal quarrel arose over the question of which candidate to support in the 1995 presidential elections. Many, including most of the leadership, strongly favored Kuroń of the Union of Freedom, an icon of the Solidarity era and one of the most highly respected former opposition intellectuals. But a majority of UP congress delegates instead chose human rights ombudsperson Tadeusz Zieliński; one UP vice-chair interpreted this as—at least in part—retaliation by those who were disappointed by the 1993 decision not to join the governing coalition.[65]

The party was again torn by questions of political strategy after failing to win any seats in the 1997 parliamentary elections. With political oblivion staring the UP in the face, the question of coalition with the SLD became more urgent. Before 1998 was out, many of the party's founders had left the party, citing their unwillingness to work closely with the communist successor party.

The key to all of these conflicts within the UP is the division between former communists and former opposition members. Delegates at the UP 1995 party congress were more or less equally divided between former PZPR members and former Solidarity members.[66] The former communists within the UP have consistently favored cooperation and even coalition with the SLD. The former oppositionists—many of them, including most of the big names, now having left the party—were consistently more suspicious of the SLD and ready to consider alliance with the left wing of the post-Solidarity Union of Freedom, for example, by supporting Kuroń for president.

Thus the formation of the SLD–UP coalition in 2001 did not signify the weakening of the historical-cultural cleavage; it may even be interpreted as confirmation of its continuing strength. The 1992 creation of the UP had been an attempt at ignoring the differences between former communists and former anti-communists—building a party across the historical divisions. With the departure of the UP's most prominent former oppositionists, the road to cooperation and even coalition with the SLD was open, but this would not represent a cross-cleavage alliance.

Nine prominent UP members, including Ryszard Bugaj, left-wing economist, chief architect of the Union of Labor, and expert for Solidarity in
1980–1981, gave their conclusions in an open letter announcing their resignation from the UP: "Our assumption that a noncommunist left could
be built with the participation of postcommunist circles was mistaken.
The divisions and the historical interpersonal bonds turned out to be
deeper than we thought."[67]

Given the dynamics within the left described here, there was every indication that the new SLD–UP–PSL government formed in the fall of
2001 would be as pragmatic as the 1993–1997 SLD–PSL governments.
The impact of the UP's greater radicalism was likely to be muted, given
both the power imbalance between the two parties and the fact that the
departure of many prominent post-Solidarity figures has left the UP itself
staffed more heavily by practical moderates. Therefore, even though the
leftist government is supported by a president from the same camp, we
may expect it to make no major changes in policy direction or political
practices. The implications of this continuity for the policy arena are addressed in Chapter 7. As for political practices, unfortunately more "business as usual" implies further institutionalization of political patronage
and corruption.

What are the chances that the Polish left may evolve in the future, and
perhaps develop a more pronounced leftist profile, whether in economic
or sociocultural issues? Such a development would be most probable
when the historical-cultural cleavage becomes shallower, or at least less
loaded with direct and personal threats to former PZPR members, as a
result of generational change. As the perceived threat to the interests and
heritage of former communists becomes less of an issue, the SLD may
lose its hold on this captive clientele and as a result find itself pressed to
take up more classically leftist positions in other policy spheres.

The Others

Well over 40 percent of Poles describe themselves as right or center-right
in their political preferences.[68] Nevertheless, *rightist parties* received only
23 percent of the vote in the 2001 parliamentary elections and 18 percent
of parliamentary seats. Why is the Polish right so weak?

The question of the right's weakness is not the same as that of the left's
success. The weakness of the right cannot be explained by, nor is it a mere
reflection of, the strength of the left. In fact, in liberal democratic systems
such as that in Poland today, a strong left tends to produce a strong right,

as competition forces improvements and opponents learn, even involuntarily, from one another. In the SLD the Polish right faces a strong opponent—capable and united—yet this competitive pressure has not led the right to effectively emulate the left's virtues. The successes of the left have led the right, properly, to fear marginalization, as the left wins commanding leads in public opinion polls and dominates national government posts, leaving the right shut out of government and sometimes even out of parliament as well. But even if the prospect of political marginalization has created a siege mentality in right and center-right political elites, this has not yet resulted in the kind of cohesion and dedication to a common cause that have so strengthened the left.

What then is wrong with the Polish right? The Polish press, as well as the well-informed sector of the Polish public, finds this question easy to answer. The right is several times more divided than the left, significantly more ideological, and equally corrupt. It is easy to list these three flaws, but to understand their implications and their causes—and thus the prospects for future change—we must examine each one more carefully.

First and foremost, the Polish right—whether we define it as the post-opposition camp or as those parties and political elites who emphasize traditional and religious values—has been and remains extremely divided. The right is divided to and beyond the point of being self-defeating.

The most notorious example of the Polish right's inability to unite even in the face of dire political necessity occurred in 1993. The electoral law had been revised to avoid a repeat of the 1991 Sejm with its 29 parties, and thus thresholds of 5 percent for parties and 8 percent for coalitions had been introduced. Nevertheless, the right and center-right competed in seven separate political groupings.[69] Four of these won vote shares ranging from 2.7 percent to 4.9 percent and thus received no seats; two won between 5 and 6 percent of the vote and just squeaked into the Sejm; one, an alliance of two parties, won 6.4 percent, but received no seats since it failed to meet the higher 8 percent threshold for coalitions.

The 1993 election results may be the most glaring and quantifiable example of the cost to rightist elites (and to their loyal voters!) of lack of unity, but examples abounded in the first years of democratic politics. The only reason voters found themselves going to the polls on September 19, 1993—less than two years after the previous Sejm election—was because of defections in a center–right coalition; four months earlier Solidarity deputies had voted against the Suchocka government they had previously supported. The center–right government before that had fallen as a result of a scandal around political lustration—the process of opening up secret

police files to identify communist regime collaborators in public life today. Certain rightist elites accused others of having been secret police in-
formers during the communist era, while other rightist elites accused the
accusers of misusing Interior Ministry files for private political gain.

In spite of the costly lesson of 1993, rightist political elites failed to
agree on a single candidate for the 1995 presidential election; their electorate divided its votes among four separate candidates, and it is by no
means certain that all the voters who supported other rightist candidates
turned out to vote for Wałęsa in the second round, which he narrowly lost
to the former communist Kwaśniewski.

The formation of Solidarity Electoral Action in 1996 created hope that
the self-destructive behavior of the right might be at an end. Although
one important rightist party, Jan Olszewski's Movement for Poland's Reconstruction (ROP), did not join the AWS, more than twenty other parties of the right did, uniting around the Solidarity trade union, and
around Solidarity's leader, Krzaklewski, who was credited with bringing
together the irreconcilable. Their leaders signed a common charter, attracted other parties and organizations to join them, and were soon running neck-and-neck with the governing SLD in the public opinion polls.

Largely united—at least temporarily—in the AWS, the right won the
1997 parliamentary elections, receiving 33.8 percent of the vote and becoming the numerically dominant partner in a governing coalition with
the relatively compatible Union of Freedom. Victory did not, however,
strengthen the bonds holding the AWS together. Internal disputes
plagued it for each of its four years in government.

Worse yet, these disputes intensified as the date of the next parliamentary election grew closer. Representative here is one print journalist's account of twenty-nine days spent conscientiously watching two public
television news programs. This took place in the spring of 2001, less than
six months before the parliamentary elections. In the life of the AWS she
noted the following events: a close vote in the AWS leadership not to allow a prominent member who had been accused of being an informer to
return to his previous party office, in spite of insufficient evidence having
been found for the charges; an AWS congress with the slogan "Unity, but
not at all costs," at which that member was conspicuously absent; one
constituent party leaving the AWS, joining a new centrist movement, and
being accused of betrayal by Krzaklewski; another constituent party announcing its own policy position at odds with that of its government; two
new parties being formed within the AWS; a prosecutor beginning an in-
vestigation of the financing of Krzaklewski's presidential campaign; a

constituent party considering an alliance with ROP, the rightist party that had remained outside the AWS; a financial scandal involving the daughter of an AWS activist; the AWS prime minister and Krzaklewski disagreeing over whom they should name to head the campaign for the upcoming parliamentary election; and one of the new parties conducting a demonstration to publicize its policy position.[70]

To observers' surprise, the various components of the AWS fought the actual 2001 election campaign in only two incarnations: Solidarity Electoral Action—Right (AWSP) and Law and Justice (PiS). The right was also represented by the League of Polish Families (LPR), which included at least one politician who had previously been a member of AWS. Shortly before this development, newspapers and magazines had been competing to present complicated charts trying to make sense of the various splintering fractions of the AWS, including the past political peregrinations of their leaders, and political cartoonists had been having a field day. The failure of the AWSP and the relative success of PiS and the LPR suggested that the right's future might lie with more ideologically coherent parties (the PiS was united by its law and order concerns, while the LPR was composed of devoutly Catholic Euroskeptics), but ideological coherence creates its own limits. With only 10 and 8 percent of seats, respectively, neither the PiS nor the LPR plays a major role in the current Sejm.

Empirical data together with the impressions of the Polish public all indicate that the right is much more ideological than any other part of the Polish political spectrum, including the center and peasant parties as well as the left. Given the lack of organizational continuity on the right, with new parties forming, splintering, merging, and splintering again (with emphasis on the splintering), it has been hard for social scientists to identify a particular rightist party for even medium-term research projects. The exception has been the Christian National Union (ZChN), which was founded in 1989 and has stubbornly persisted ever since (not always, of course, with the same leadership). Research on the ZChN shows its national and local elites to be consistently more ideological than those of the leftist and centrist parties also examined (although sometimes the Union of Labor comes close). Sixty-eight percent of party congress delegates surveyed asserted that the party should realize all of its promises to the voters. More than twice as many ZChN delegates as delegates to other party congresses claim that they joined the party in order to realize its goals; this striking difference suggests that the goals of the ZChN are more clearly articulated as well as more important for its activists.[71] Similarly, when interviewed about their reasons for joining, local ZChN activists emphasized national values, Christian values, and the program of their party: "As a Catholic and a patriot, the ideological program of the ZChN suited me best."[72]

Of course, it may well be, and our observations would suggest, that the ZChN is one of the most ideological *and* ideologically coherent of rightist parties in Poland, and that this is directly tied to its exceptional institutional persistence. Nevertheless, research on party leaderships both inside and outside the 1993–1997 Sejm indicates that many other rightist elites share at least some of the outlook associated with ideological dogmatism. Krzysztof Jasiecki finds a negative attitude toward political consensus and compromise among a significant proportion of rightist elites. This attitude was not shared by all rightist politicians surveyed, but it was conspicuously absent in other political groupings. Jasiecki notes the use of phrases such as "resignation from principles for offices" and "political prostitution" to define political consensus, and ascribes this attitude at least in part to negative evaluations of the 1989 roundtable and its aftermath; for some, compromise as a political tactic has been forever discredited by this historical compromise between communists and oppositionists.[73]

The final fatal flaw of the right is that it has shown itself to be just as corruptible as the left. There were already some signs of this in the post-Solidarity governments of the early 1990s; it was not without reason that critics called their political construction the "republic of buddies." But the practices of political patronage and corruption described by this term were developed much further under the 1993–1997 SLD–PSL governments, allowing the AWS to present itself in the 1997 campaign as the morally superior alternative, as the people who could clean up the Augean stables left by the former communists and their allies.

But having won control of the government in 1997, both the AWS and its centrist coalition partner continued the same practices that had been quasi-institutionalized under the SLD–PSL governments. Scandal followed scandal in the press, and though many party leaders appeared irreproachable in their conduct, they had plenty of colleagues who more or less explicitly subscribed to the "TKM" philosophy. (The initials stand for a Polish phrase that can be best translated as "f——, it's our turn now!")[74] Thus when pollsters asked, less than three months before the 2001 parliamentary elections and after nearly four years of an AWS government, which political force could be most trusted to fight corruption, both the SLD and the PSL were mentioned more frequently than either the AWS or the UW.[75] The most trusted party was the new Law and Justice, then campaigning on a program of fighting crime and not tolerating corruption; after the 2001 election it found itself the strongest party of the right, with 10 percent of Sejm seats.

The flaw of corruption is the most easily explained of the Polish right's weaknesses. Like any child on a playground, the right may claim "he did it first," referring not only to the 1993–1997 governments but also to the decades of communist-party rule that left the party itself, its allied organizations, and its individual members financially well situated for the competition of both the market and electoral arenas. Polish journalist Ryszard Holzer reports a conversation with a rightist political activist who explained his actions in this way: "The communists already did their stealing and hold the economy in their fist; now we have to put our own economic elite up against them." How can such an economic elite be created, asked Holzer. The answer he received was simple—that the means don't matter, that the only important thing was that such an elite emerge.[76]

In 1997, after four years of SLD–PSL governments, 55 percent of Poles surveyed believed that many government officials derived illegitimate benefits from their positions. In 2001, after four years of an AWS-led government, 70 percent of Poles surveyed believed this.[77] (See Chapter 7 for international surveys that indicate a high level of corruption by 2000.) Was the Polish public growing increasingly cynical, or for some reason were more and more outrageous scandals becoming known under the 1997–2001 government? Although there has been no definitive research carried out on this topic, the latter explanation appears plausible, whether we ascribe it to rightist politicians stealing more, or stealing less skillfully, or being caught more often. The lack of central authority and discipline in the AWS made it impossible to effectively rein in dishonest and abusive practices, even when these threatened to hurt the Solidarity coalition as a whole. In addition, the lack of unity within the coalition, characterized by conflicts both between constituent parties and between individual politicians, made it more likely that scandals would be revealed, as rivals made known each others' crimes.

This brings us back to the Polish right's central and defining problem—its chronic lack of unity. It is easy enough to diagnose the right's tendency to tear itself apart, over ideological battles just as often as over individual rivalries or tactical disputes. What is harder to explain is its inability to overcome this, to muster sufficient pragmatism and organizational skills to work together effectively to oppose the serious and dangerous opponent it sees in the left.

One possible explanation has been offered by Polish political scientist Tadeusz Szawiel, who finds at least part of the answer in the half-century-long repression of the right side of the political spectrum in Poland. From 1939 to 1944 all Polish elites were decimated, but rightist intellectuals and politicians never had the chance to recover that leftist elites (both communist and noncommunist) had after World War II. More elites of the right perished, and more of them emigrated. Those who remained had little or no chance to develop or teach their ideas in mass media, educational institutions, or social or political organizations. With some exceptions beginning primarily in the oppositional 1980s, individuals of rightist convictions had no chance to develop organizational skills in social and political work until 1989.[78]

A complementary explanation can be found by looking at the greatest hope and the greatest disappointment of the right thus far in the Third Republic—the AWS. The AWS was seen by many as the reverse image of the SLD. Here it appears that the right was learning from the left's example. Both movements were broad coalitions of parties, trade unions, and other organizations, each apparently united only by the political past.

There were two key differences, however. One difference might instead be defined as too close a similarity: While the SLD was united by the common biographies of its participants, the AWS also was united by the common biographies of the SLD, rather than by the biographies of the individuals and organizations that made up the AWS itself. It was opposition to and antipathy toward the SLD that brought the many component parts of the AWS together. True, former oppositionists dominated in the AWS, but for the majority their experience of working together in one united movement was limited to the sixteen months of Solidarity in 1980–1981 and perhaps a few weeks of election campaigning in 1989.

The other key difference was that while the AWS was united by and drew most of its resources from the Solidarity trade union, the SLD was anchored by two large organizations. Only one of the SLD's core components was a trade union, with its concomitant distinct goals and alternative array of tactics; the other, the SdRP, was a well-articulated and well-organized party with a nationwide organizational network. The AWS had no equivalent to the SdRP, and was therefore effectively dependent on an organization for which elections and parliament were not the primary arenas of play, and for which union members and not the voting public were the primary constituents.

In fact, in the Third Republic Polish rightist parties have *two* perennial candidates for external sponsorship, two nonparty entities that could be huge sources of support, to whom these parties keep looking for legitimation and aid. One is the Solidarity trade union, the other is the Catholic Church. The church's sponsorship helped the AWS to unite in 1996. (In an analogous way, the fundamentalist Catholic radio station Radio Maryja helped a group of previous political rivals coalesce in the League of Polish Families and come from behind to win seats in the 2001 Sejm.)

Paradoxically, the presence of these two nonparty entities, inextricably tied to the right, may be a hindrance to strong rightist parties. Angelo Panebianco's concept of political party institutionalization suggests that parties sponsored by an external organization will tend to be weakly institutionalized.[79] In this analysis, external sources of legitimation will mean that the party itself will be less of a cohesive whole. In the case of the Polish right, it may also drive further wedges between the existing parties as they compete for the support of union and church.[80]

Finally, the transition from communist rule was not itself a unifying experience for the right. In fact the serious controversies and mutual recriminations over the Polish roundtable are themselves a source of divisions. The sequence of events was so unexpected, so implausible on the surface, that many who were not part of the negotiations find a secret pact, a conspiracy more believable than the claim that experienced politicians negotiating together produced an outcome so radically different from their hopes or intentions.

As well as a left and a right, there has consistently been a *center* to the Polish political spectrum, although the vote share received by centrist parties in parliamentary elections has never surpassed 15 percent. Until 2001 the center was characterized by cohesiveness and corresponding organizational continuity. In the first years of the Third Republic it was represented by two post-Solidarity parties, the Democratic Union (UD) and the Liberal Democratic Congress (KLD); in 1994 the two came together to form the Union of Freedom (UW), a party that by itself defined the center of the political spectrum until the challenger Civic Platform (PO) emerged to deal it a possibly lethal blow in the 2001 parliamentary elections.

In spite of their limited electoral appeal, the UW and the UD and KLD before it, together with individuals who would eventually join the party's leadership, played crucial roles in governments of the first years of the Third Republic. Poland's economic transformation was begun and key stages of it carried out by politicians who were or who became leaders of these parties. Government ministers belonging to or supported by these parties crafted much of the new democracy's foreign policy, and were architects of many crucial institutional reforms. Many of the reforms and policies discussed in Chapter 7 were the work of these politicians.

The UW's position relative to the historical-cultural cleavage was always ambiguous, and this may have been part of its weakness. Although both the UW and its UD predecessor were strongly associated with the pre-1989 opposition, the roles played by its most prominent former oppositionists were criticized by many members of the anti-communist right. The UW/UD politicians had been founders of the Workers' Defense Committee (KOR) and intellectual advisers to the Solidarity opposition movement, rather than worker-leaders of Solidarity itself.[81] With this background, as well as the fact that several of them had been PZPR members at an earlier point in their careers, they were already tainted "pink" in the eyes of many rightist politicians. The role these centrists had played at the roundtable, as architects of Poland's historic compromise, condemned them further, as did the moderate and conciliatory policies of the first non-communist government, led by Tadeusz Mazowiecki, who would become head of the UD.

On both sociocultural and historical policy issues, the UW and its predecessors did tend to take moderate positions, in between those of the former communists and the right. Increasingly, especially in its UW incarnation, the center appeared to be consciously noncommittal on sociocultural issues, concentrating its attention on economic policy. Here the influence of economic reformer Leszek Balcerowicz, UW head from its creation in 1994 through 2000, was strongly evident. In the sphere of economic policy the UW's position was clear—it was the neoliberal party, the party of fiscal restraint and of rapid transformation. In a sense, the UW may be seen in this regard as the exact opposite of both the left and the right. Thus the UW was defined by a specific economic approach and remained vague on sociocultural issues, whereas both left and right contained a broad spectrum of economic views but were defined, in their own way, by their preferences on sociocultural issues.

This approach allowed these centrist parties for several years (over half the short lifetime of the young Third Republic at the time of writing) to have an impact on government policy all out of proportion to their electoral strength. It may also have been the cause of the UW's dramatic defeat in 2001—finally failing to meet the 5 percent threshold to enter the Sejm. The UW and its UD predecessor can fairly be described as policy-seekers rather than vote-seekers, making many decisions on the basis of some vision of what was best for the country rather than what was politically best for the party itself. Whether or not the policies pursued by these centrist parties were in Poland's interest is a question best left to the economists or better yet the historians; the one certain thing is that these political choices, for example, tax reforms pursued by Balcerowicz in the AWS–UW government or the decision to support rather than attack the unpopular AWS government after leaving the governing coalition, were very costly for the UW.

The effective replacement of the UW by PO in the 2001 elections— PO won almost an identical percentage of votes as that received by the UW in 1997, including a large percentage of former UW voters— brought up urgent questions about the future of the center in Polish politics. Created early in 2001 by three politicians (a UW defector, an AWS defector, and one successful private businessman and former official under both communist and noncommunist regimes, who admits to informing for Polish security services), PO is something of a paradox. It is an anti-party centrist party, a populist neoliberal party. Although it did not hide its economic orientation during the 2001 campaign, its most prominent policy position has been its opposition to state subsidies for political parties, and its strongest rhetoric has been against political parties and politicians. PO's success can be attributed to these stances, popular with a disillusioned electorate, as well as the avowed newness of this party. In spite of the party origins of its founders and many of its new members, as a brand-new party PO succeeded at presenting a fresh image and avoiding the stigma of responsibility for the failures of the Buzek government that burdened the UW.

In addition there is a subset of parties in Poland that do not fit on the classic left–right spectrum in any fashion—the *peasant parties*. In the interwar period these parties played a central role in the politics of nearly all East European states including Poland. The agrarian sector has remained sizable into the twenty-first century and we should therefore not be surprised that the Polish party system includes peasant parties that have on occasion played pivotal "bit parts" in the new democracy.

For most of the Third Republic rural interests have been represented by two competing organizations, the Polish Peasant Party (PSL) and Self-Defense, both of which aspire to represent a broader array of Polish society, based on varying combinations of appeal to traditional values, patriotism, and populism. Although the PSL contains elements of the historical peasant party (the interwar PSL), in organizational, personnel, and resource terms it is primarily a successor to the United Peasant Party (ZSL), the communist party's loyal ally for decades. This is reflected in its huge party membership (the largest of any Polish party), its nationwide organizational structure, and its resource base—the PSL gets most of its income from the highly desirable real estate it inherited from the ZSL.

Self-Defense, on the other hand, emerged in 1991 as a populist and rural movement. Its protest activities are discussed in Chapter 7; its electoral efforts met with no success until the parliamentary elections of 2001, when it not only won 10.2 percent of the vote but, even more significantly, came in ahead of the PSL, with only 9 percent. Self-Defense's 2001 success does not necessarily reflect greater discontent among Polish have-nots, but rather the increased skill of this party, and its leader, Andrzej Lepper, in presenting themselves to the public as both populist *and* responsible political players. With the entry of both the peasant Self-Defense and the rightist League of Polish Families into the Sejm, Polish Euroskeptics finally have official parliamentary representation.

Other Players on the Political Scene

Political parties and their leaderships are not the only actors who play a role in political processes and outcomes. Other organizations and entities make choices, pursue agendas, mobilize resources, and thus shape political possibilities. Here we examine a few of them: the Catholic Church, trade unions, business interests, and the mass media.

The Catholic Church

As we have seen, the Catholic Church in Poland has been in the center of the political arena for decades. One difference in the role of the church in the Third Republic is that it has been met with greater public skepticism than at any time in the recent past. New restrictions on abortion, the requirement that public schools provide religious education (though pupils do not have to take it), the principle that Christian values must permeate public broadcasting, and the general triumphalism and wealth of church leaders in the post-communist period have alienated many lay Catholics.

Intervention by the church in the democratic policy process has at times boomeranged against it. Its stand on abortion triggered a backlash. After the communist regime's liberal abortion-on-demand policy, many Poles were upset by the highly restrictive law passed under an early Solidarity government; this was arguably the first indication that the public would not reject everything done by the communists or accept everything done by Church-backed politicians. The abortion controversy gave rise to a perception of a meddling and misguided church, which it has never fully overcome.

The church has also suffered a backlash for its perceived role in helping deprive women of rights they had received under the communist system. Whereas Marxism made the economic liberation of women a high priority (which conveniently doubled the labor force and helped facilitate extensive economic development), Catholicism stressed the unique role women play as mothers and the nucleus of the family. If the communist system imposed a double burden on women, as indispensable participants in the labor market and as homemakers, the Church took a narrower view, seeing women as givers of life, raising children to be practicing Catholics, and serving as the heart of the family. Indeed, some church leaders did not conceal their satisfaction that high unemployment rates (from which women suffered disproportionately) made many women's roles conform better with Catholic teachings.

The church's role in the writing of a new constitution was equally contentious. Lawmakers were divided over the church's insistence that it receive official recognition of its special role in Polish society and, conversely, that the idea of a secular state be constitutionally rejected. Some church leaders even demanded a specific clause on the protection of human life from conception until birth and pressed for a provision making marriage only possible between members of the opposite sex. However, the tentative agreement established between the Polish state and the Vatican, termed the Concordat, has had the most far-reaching implications for the part the church will play in Poland in the future.

The term "Concordat" has rarely been used by the Vatican. The 1925 Concordat brought even Piłsudski into conflict with the church. Effectively it allowed the church to make property claims that went back to the nineteenth century. The state did not act impartially, being generous with regard to the Catholic Church and less so with regard to the Orthodox Church. The most recent Concordat was signed in late July 1993 between President Wałęsa and Pope John Paul II. Its opponents alleged that many of its provisions were in violation of the European Community treaty. The 1993 agreement consisted of twenty-nine articles and began with the assertion that "the Catholic religion is practiced by the majority of the Polish population." A similar clause in the constitution of the Second Republic was a source of particular controversy, since at the time Poland had a few sizable ethnic and religious groups. The Concordat expressed the intention "to eliminate all forms of intolerance and discrimination based on religion," but it formalized Catholic education in schools. Church marriages were to have the same legal status as civil ones, though there were no changes in divorce laws.

Probably the most controversial aspect of the agreement was Article 22, a cryptic clause dealing with restitution of church property. A special church–state commission was to be set up to make changes in legislation that would "take into account the needs of the Church given its mission and the practice hitherto of church life in Poland." Added to this was Article 27: "Matters requiring new or additional treatment will be regulated by new agreements or understandings." Sejm approval of the Concordat would thus provide a carte blanche for future changes. As one writer has put it, "Today anyone who naively believes that church–state conflict was invented by communists and that with their demise this chapter is closed forever is making a major and possibly in the future a costly mistake."[82] Further, given that the agreement was signed while the Sejm was dissolved, it appeared that the church was daring the political parties to stand up to its considerable power in the midst of an electoral campaign.

When the SLD–PSL coalition government took office, it was careful not to antagonize Pope John Paul II and Polish Primate Cardinal Józef Glemp on the question of Concordat ratification. The fact that the mainstay of the PSL constituency—the peasantry—was largely Catholic and conservative on social issues compelled the PSL, in particular, to tread carefully on the issue. During the spring of 1995, SLD head Kwaśniewski met with church leaders and appeared to hammer out a constitutional formula that would satisfy both Cardinal Glemp and the government. There would be no provision asserting the separation of church and state. Instead, the state and church were declared to be autonomous and independent in their own spheres of activity. In addition, the constitution would make no reference to the state's neutrality on religious matters.

Many Poles were disappointed in the leadership of Cardinal Glemp, who was viewed as too conservative and certainly not the equal of Cardinal Stefan Wyszyński, the Catholic Primate who had struggled valiantly against the Stalinist authorities in the 1950s. They were upset at the ineptness Glemp showed in the early 1990s, first in dealing with the controversial plan to build a Carmelite convent close to Auschwitz, which he eventually agreed to abandon. Similarly, Glemp has been consistently slow to condemn the anti-Semitic remarks or Good Friday displays produced regularly by Father Henryk Jankowski, Wałęsa's confessor.

The Episcopate has shown ambivalence toward the prospect of Poland's accession into the EU. Glemp and others are aware that EU membership would make Poland a more secular society, as its laws and regulations would have to conform to the *acquis communitaire,* a body of laws that are the same for all member-states, whether Protestant, Catholic, or Greek Orthodox. Surveys of the Polish clergy demonstrate the same ambivalence. Priests see many practical advantages for Poland in joining the EU, but worry about the negative impact of EU membership on moral and religious values and on the Polish family.[83]

Interest Groups

Of the many different interest groups present in a modern democracy, here we examine two: trade unions and business lobbies. Traditionally these interests are among the best organized in a capitalist system and possess conflicting interests, making a comparative assessment useful in determining who is empowered and how.

One Polish academic has put forward the idea of trade union dependency, a subset of path dependency (a perspective in which initial steps limit later possibilities), to explain the part played by labor in democratic Poland. From this perspective, "the initial role of trade unions in politics, and especially the role of Solidarity, leaves a permanent mark on the shape of the political system in Poland."[84] This is a thinly veiled reference to the influence exerted by the Solidarity trade union on politics in 1980–1981, and to its aspirations to continue shaping politics at the turn of the century by way of the AWS party. Union heads, such as Wałęsa and Krzaklewski of the AWS and Alfred Miodowicz and Ewa Spychalska of the OPZZ, often defended the need to conflate union and political roles as a necessity dictated by the logic of transition. Under normal circumstances, "Trade unions and their members can choose between the group interest and the interest of the whole society." But in a transition, ambitious union heads choose both.

There were thirteen trade unions in the SLD coalition of thirty-three entities; there were just two unions in the AWS coalition of thirty-seven organizations, but one of these was the successor of the legendary Solidarity union. If unions were better served organizationally than might have been expected in the transition period, the practice of linking union and party structures was dysfunctional for the emergence of a clear party system.

After its halcyon period, the Solidarity union has come to be viewed as ineffective in resolving the major problems faced by working people: unemployment, decline in living standards, and marginalization in the privatization process. The union had only 1.3 million paid-up members in 2001, down from nearly 10 million in 1981. In 1994 former union leader Wałęsa even turned down an invitation to address its annual congress, declaring "This is not my Solidarity." Under pressure after AWS head Krzaklewski's poor showing in the presidential election in 2000, Solidarity decided to decouple party and union leadership positions. In the following year's parliamentary elections, the Solidarity movement lost ground, perhaps foreshadowing a return to its primary role as labor union.

The OPZZ has done better in maintaining a large membership—about three million, down from over four million in the early 1990s—and taking a direct part in power through its central role in the SLD electoral machine; it had 44 deputies in the 1997–2001 Sejm. Created by the martial law government in 1984 as a replacement for the troublesome Solidarity, it has taken on a political life of its own and has remained left-of-center in politics even as its political sponsors—the PZPR and SLD—became more centrist and pragmatic. After having firebrand leaders like Miodowicz and Spychalska, however, it has safeguarded its organizational interests and handed leadership over to an apparatchik, Maciej Manicki.

Solidarity and OPZZ do not control Poland's entire trade union movement. For example, the Polish Teachers' Union has proved to be very militant, organizing nationwide strikes in 1999. Solidarity of Individual Farmers is an influential agrarian union, as is the Self-Defense League. In many respects their methods of influencing politics are more like the Western model since they are first and foremost interest groups, not entities within a party coalition.

How have business interests been organized in Poland's capitalist system? A number of organizations represent Poland's new entrepreneurs: the Confederation of Polish Employers, the National Economic Office, the Business Center Club, and the Polish Business Council. In 1994 the first dedicated local business lobbying group, the Polish Federation of Independent Entrepreneurs, was founded. The question arises whether Polish employers have formed a unified and centralized lobby to transmit their interests to the government, as in France and Germany, or whether they remain an individualistic, decentralized business lobby, as in Britain and the United States.

There is wide recognition of the lobbying role played by business. The majority of managers (56 percent) agree that individual lobbying by firms is a universal phenomenon in Poland, and 62 percent asserted that it was an effective method.[85] One-quarter of parliamentarians and one-third of city councillors surveyed claimed that politicians take the interests of business firms into consideration in their public service.[86] Respondents to another survey identified informal personal contacts as the most commonly used form of economic lobbying.[87] Indeed, one study (cited earlier) found that nearly one-half of the economic elite surveyed claimed to be acquaintances with a national politician, almost three-quarters claimed that in matters of basic concern to their firms they could get access to the top leaders in the country, and one-fifth claimed they were in a position to get access to someone of higher rank than a government minister.[88] As one academic studying lobbying concluded, "the absence of autonomous structures of civil society has shifted social interactions to the sphere of personal and non-institutional contacts."[89]

Foreign corporations are some of the most active lobbyists in Poland. These include Proctor and Gamble, Philip Morris, Pepsico, and United Distillers. Specialized lobbying firms in the areas of public affairs, public relations, and governmental relations have become more common. One-issue lobby organizations have also emerged; for example, an anti-pirating lobby made up of Polish and international software firms has been established.

How have business and labor groups interacted in the political arena since the establishment of a market economy? The most ambitious effort to incorporate these groups in the political process came in 1994 with the creation of the Tripartite Council, which brings together representatives of employers, employees, and the state. The Council was intended to institutionalize the looser arrangements for interest group representation envisaged in the 1992 Enterprise Pact. But this corporatist model, where political decisions are based on negotiations among organized interests, has not really taken off in Poland. The Tripartite Council has proven weak, paradoxically because the major labor confederations can best exert influence through their incorporation into political parties, whereas employers suffer from organizational weakness—both in confederating effectively and in having a party that gives priority to its interests (the SLD is, ironically, the best of a bad lot in this regard).

Have business groups been able to influence governments that, whether based on the SLD or AWS, contain union representation? Remarkably, members of the political elite more often cited business as having a great or very great influence on the Cimoszewicz-led SLD government during 1996–1997 than on the Buzek government after 1997 (by a margin of 23 compared to 13 percent). On the other hand, unions were seen as more influential under Buzek compared to Cimoszewicz (59 compared to 21 percent). Obviously AWS shaped the Buzek government in a way that the OPZZ could not hope to do with the SLD government, which apparently balanced interests better.[90]

The Mass Media

Independent mass media are essential to an open and pluralistic democracy. In Poland the free flow of political information after 1989 has made citizens more knowledgeable about their democracy, invariably leading to critical and even cynical views about their rulers.

As with other resources, the structure of the mass media was shaped by both the previous system and the transition process. Former communists have retained ownership of certain important magazines and newspapers, for example, the weekly *Polityka* and the daily *Trybuna*. Not surprisingly, media outlets owned by ex-communists cover the SLD more favorably. In a similar fashion, the Polish Peasant Party effectively controls some agrarian-oriented publications.

The transition process left its largest stamp on the Polish media scene through the 1989 establishment of *Gazeta Wyborcza* ("Election Gazette"), the daily newspaper that the opposition was allowed to start up in order to conduct an election campaign. *Wyborcza* quickly became the largest daily in Central Europe and has spawned a media empire of local editions, special supplements, and other tie-ins. Under the idiosyncratic leadership of its editor-in-chief, former dissident Adam Michnik, the newspaper has consistently supported a secular and neoliberal line, opposing draconian decommunization policies and emphasizing the importance of Poland's return to Europe. More often than not, this has meant supporting parties of the center except when, as in the case of Civic Platform, the movement challenges Michnik's sentimental favorite, the Union of Freedom. Thus as a result of the accidents of transition, the largest-circulation daily in Poland supports a relatively unpopular political orientation.

Many other newspapers and periodicals—some new, some refurbished—are either independent or sympathetic to other political perspectives. For example, the daily *Zycie* has a decided center-right orientation. The Catholic press has perhaps undergone the least change during the transition since there were already several flourishing and relatively independent titles under the communist system (for example, the opinion leader *Tygodnik Powszechny*, an intellectual weekly from Cracow). In addition, throughout the 1990s foreign ownership of newspapers and periodicals circulating in the country has increased. French, German, and Italian communications groups are active in the Polish market.

At the time that the Third Republic was created, broadcast media were dominated by state-controlled television and radio. Predictably, control over public television has sparked a number of political battles. Between 1993 and 1997 the SLD government stacked the committee overseeing the media (the National Broadcasting Council) and filled the post of director of state television with their own supporters. Yet the AWS-led Buzek government tried to do much the same between 1997 and 2001 but was frustrated by the long tenures in office of SLD and PSL appointees. Nevertheless, the significance of these tugs-of-war over top positions in public television decreased as many other TV channels became available to Poles through startup networks, cable, and satellite feeds. One important development is a new family-oriented network begun in 2000 (originally by Franciscan monks) to counter sex, violence, and sensationalism on both public television and the primary commercial networks.

Pornography in the media has been a sensitive political issue since 1990. A regular source of entertainment in the Polish press is the latest lawsuit or criminal charges against the satirical and erotic weekly *Nie* ("No"), founded and controlled by former communist government spokesperson and multimillionaire Jerzy Urban. The political impact of *Nie* comes not so much from its sympathy to the SLD as from its antipathy to and scandal-mongering about center, center-right, and rightist politicians. Generally Polish press laws on pornography are liberal. The fate of a recent church-backed law passed by the Sejm banning pornography is typical. The bill would have provided for two-year jail sentences to newsagents who sold such "soft porn" as *Playboy* and five-year sentences for stocking hard porn. The bill was vetoed in 2000 by President Kwaśniewski.

Now that we have become familiar with the actors who are playing the democratic game, we need to examine why some attract the support of Polish citizens and others do not. Regardless of how resource-endowed, flexible, and cohesive a political group may be, it needs to effectively aggregate the interests of the electorate. The following chapter examines the played upon: what divides them, as well as their political attitudes and behavior.

5

·~·

The Played Upon: Society

Where would politicians be without a society to act upon? Variously referred to as the political environment, the bottom section of a feedback loop leading into the "black box of authority," the suppliers of support for the political system, and the source of demands on the system, political science literature does not provide a flattering vocabulary for those of us who are mere members of society. As citizens we are aware that our political rights sometimes seem contingent on our performing political responsibilities. It may confirm for us that we are living in a system where *noblesse oblige* reigns.

To be sure, Polish society at the beginning of the 1980s seemed to be the exception to this rule. The rebirth of the idea of civil society had taken place precisely in the Poland that was poised to rally around a social movement called Solidarity. When martial law was imposed to crush this experiment in self-government, outside observers painted a romanticized vision of Polish society. Poles acted with grace, not recklessness, in response to the military crackdown. The very convening of the roundtable, that exercise in elite deal-making, constituted recognition of the importance of Polish society; the communists came to the table because of what they feared Polish society might do, and the anticipated reactions of that society were the ammunition of the negotiators. The roundtable brought together rival elites, but it was all about society.

For Poles those events belong to a different era, one whose passage cannot be measured in years. Poland has returned to normal politics now, and thus the salient questions are what does society provide for politicians to work with, and what does society think about being used in these ways?

Cleavages

In order to understand how society itself affects politics, to understand how societal characteristics may both limit and create political possibilities, we must look first and foremost at social cleavages. Such a cleavage is a division in society along which conflict *may* arise. Cleavages are thus both the bread and butter of democratic politics—creating differences in interests, ideologies, and identities that may translate into differing policy preferences—and the potential fault lines on which a society can tear itself apart.

How do Poles differ from one another? Which of these differences constitute the basic stuff of democratic give-and-take in the Third Republic? Are these differences overlapping or crosscutting? If two cleavages crosscut each other and thus present Poles with a choice of pertinent social grouping—say deeply devout Catholics or unemployed workers in depressed regions—which will dominate? What are the dividing lines shaping the mass political space in Poland, those divisions with which political elites must contend, whether they choose to work on one side of a particular cleavage or build an alliance across it?

Another crucial question is whether or not the particular set of cleavages in a society increases or decreases the stability and quality of its democracy. The most useful categorization of families of cleavages drawn by many political sociologists distinguishes between cleavages based on interests and those based on identities. The usual prediction is that the former, usually socioeconomic in nature, will be more favorable for democratic politics, whereas cleavages based on identity are more likely to destabilize a democracy.

In their study of politics in four post-communist democracies, Jon Elster, Claus Offe, and Ulrich K. Preuss distinguish between socioeconomic cleavages, political-ideological cleavages (based on preferences for different types of regimes), and cleavages based on cultural identities, whether ethnic, linguistic, or religious.[1] They assert that socioeconomic conflicts are most amenable to compromise: "While this type of conflict is often intense, stable solutions in the form of *quantitative* compromise are, as a matter of principle, easy to achieve through demands, threats, bargaining, and concessions that are being made in terms of income, social security, or co-determination."[2] Managers and workers, for example, are not only mutually dependent, but face a divisible pie of economic costs and benefits. Ideological and cultural cleavages, on the other hand, center on possibly irreconcilable conflicts, in which compromise may well be logically impossible or passionately condemned. One example is the different worldviews that lead one set of people to support abortion rights and another to oppose legalized abortion. Here there may be no talk either of mutual dependence or of a divisible pie.

Ominously, Elster, Offe, and Preuss, among others, suggest that post-communist societies will—at least in their initial stages—be characterized by a relative lack of socioeconomic cleavages. They derive this not just from the relative social equality and the lack of real collective actors representing economic interests under the communist regimes, but also from the uncertainty as to where any individual's economic interest might lie in an economy undergoing radical transformation. They suggest, then, that the more dangerous ideological and cultural cleavages will dominate in the initial stages of post-communist democracy. They must therefore be carefully examined.

Class and Occupational Differences

If Poland was proclaimed to be a classless society during the communist period, it was expected to be an explicitly class-based society under capitalism. It is a paradox, then, that class differences had a profound impact on politics in the communist period but have been of only marginal importance under the democratic system so far.

One of the explanations for this is that the class structure has dramatically changed together with the economic system. The working class is both ideologically and economically less important today. It has shrunk in size as smokestack industries have fallen into decline and the service sector expanded in their place. Entrepreneurship, management, financial services, and other white-collar employment are the defining features of an advanced capitalist system. Though Poland does not yet have the kind of late capitalist social structure that characterizes the United States or Western Europe, structural shifts have already begun. By 2000 the service sector employed 46 percent of the workforce, less than the two-thirds share found in Britain, France, and Germany, but much more than ten years earlier. The expansion of the middle class is seen as reducing class conflicts; growth in the service and other middle-class sectors may have such an effect in Poland.

Meanwhile one in four Poles still works in industry and manufacturing. Economic changes have threatened the interests of traditional proletarian "elites" such as coal miners, while bringing jobs and higher wages to sectors such as construction, which is witnessing a building boom. Such changes shake the internal stability and social solidarity of this class. Both reformed communist and Solidarity labor unions have tapped into the discontent of previously advantaged workers, as well as other sectors, to establish politically influential working-class movements. Admittedly these trade unions have not been able to defend the interests of workers—indeed, even their jobs—as in the past, but they can be pivotal at election time.

There is more to the decline of the traditional working class than ineffective union structures. Sociologist Włodzimierz Wesołowski contended that "systemic transformation disintegrates older interest structures and creates new ones." Although the "transgressive interest"—that is, one common to all society—reflects a general desire for a private, market economy, it is not easily compatible with the particularist interests of various groups. Capitalist transformation has "decomposed" workers' interests into specific occupations (textile worker, miner) and, further, into particular firms. For Wesołowski, then, it is difficult to speak any more about the interests and values of workers as a class; the new interest structures differentiate categories of workers from each other.[3]

One of every four Poles is still employed in agriculture, a huge percentage given the share of agriculture in the Polish economy. Polish agriculture was primarily based on the family farm even under the communist regime, so dismantling the communist economic system brought fewer changes to agriculture than to other sectors of the economy. The majority of farms continue to be small and inefficient, and the people working them are largely deprived of anything beyond a basic education. The lot of former employees of state agricultural cooperatives has been no better. Both groups are still considered to be peasants. The peasant movement has traditionally had a voice in Polish politics and that has not changed with democracy. It is the group most opposed to Polish membership in the EU, it is the most conservative Catholic section of society, and it has engaged in extraparliamentary protests more often than other social groups. The strongest class-based political cleavage today in Poland divides peasants from those with urban occupations, whether worker or intellectual.

Let us examine the prestige of different occupations in order to explore the connection between class and status. In the view of Poles in 1999, the most prestigious occupations were university professor, doctor, teacher, and judge; each was listed by two-thirds or more of respondents. The jobs with least prestige were unskilled worker and political party functionary, cited by under one-quarter of respondents.[4] Following a decline in the prestige of nearly all occupations between 1987 and 1995—a period of economic uncertainty—this socio-occupational hierarchy became relatively stable. The transition from communism to capitalism was reflected in the prestige scale that emerged: working-class jobs (for example, coal miner) declined in status, and professional categories gained status. In this respect there was greater congruence between class and status than there had been under communism. On the other hand, by comparison to the West the evaluation of intellectuals and professionals still seems inflated and that of people in business underestimated.

Gender and Age

Men's politics differ from women's in familiar ways. First and foremost, men are more involved and interested in politics than are women; this is no different in Poland than it is in Western democracies. Part of the explanation, sociologist Renata Siemieńska argues, is that women "often do not have a sense of group community or identity. Many women have a stronger feeling of being members of other groups not based on gender."[5] This may help explain why a unified feminist movement has not emerged in Poland even though many feminist organizations were set up in the 1990s. In addition, since 1990 women in Poland have faced renewed pressure applied, among other forces, by the church, the media, the government, and the labor market to return to the traditional role of homemaker.[6] The very struggle to resist this stereotypical image has required feminists to divert effort and attention away from the political arena.

Differences between Polish men and women in participation in public life do not themselves constitute a political cleavage; neither, on the other hand, does the lower rate of female participation prove that no potential cleavage exists. One decided difference between men and women can be found in their relationship to religion. Twice as many women as men (14 percent versus 7 percent) declare themselves to be deeply religious; at least twice as many women as men attend church more than once a week. Women are more likely to attend church regularly and less likely to describe themselves as nonbelievers.[7] To see whether this or other differences in the daily lives or life chances of men and women currently have political significance, we must look at differences in voting patterns, discussed later in this chapter.

Is there a generation gap that divides Poles politically? One impact of political, economic, and/or social transformations is that they freeze certain generation gaps into place, leaving certain groups forever (or rather for their lifetimes) defined by what life stage they were at when the transition took place.

On one end of this spectrum are the one out of every five Poles who in 2000 were under fifteen years of age and so could not remember anything of the communist period. Forty-four percent of the population was under thirty and therefore had spent their entire adult life under a democracy. Could this age breakdown and the absence of experience of communism in their lives that went with it serve as a political fault line sometime in the future? Conversely, could we suggest that those who were in the workforce during the communist era (making them over thirty now) have different politics today than those who were still college aged or even younger?

It goes without saying that younger Poles were more supportive of systemic change than older ones. At the same time, "the socialization process within the family plays a pivotal role in shaping the value system of a new generation."[8] An intergenerational transfer of values within the family unit (that is, from both mother to child and father to child) has effects on the psychological functioning of younger people. Parents who occupy higher socio-occupational positions and are therefore more likely to be open-minded and less distressed by systemic change pass this sense of well-being on to their children. Accordingly, while the younger generation is generally more in favor of the new system, variations in this attitude can be explained by parents' background.

A surprising finding from surveys carried out in the mid-1990s was that younger people were less enthusiastic about democracy than older people. Young respondents were evenly split between declaring democracy to have advantages over other systems and declaring that nondemocratic governments were at times more desirable than democratic ones (adults favored democracy by a two-to-one margin). More tellingly, 43 percent of young respondents said it was hard to say which system was better. On the other hand, if writing graffiti in defense of democracy was a sign of commitment to it, young people admitted to defacing public places for this purpose twice as often as older people.[9] Indeed, as we report later, the first part of this decade was punctuated by regular anarchist protests by young people who seemed to be expressing their cynicism about the new system that was supposed to save Poland.

The New Democracies Barometer found that by 1998 the group most positively evaluating "the current political system of free elections and governing with many parties" was those under nineteen; over three-quarters expressed favorable opinions of the system whereas only two-thirds of other age categories did. Young people were also more trusting of and less cynical about such institutions as political parties. Even though they possessed no real comparative experience of this, under-nineteens believed that ordinary people could influence the government much more in the current system than under the communist regime. Their sense of political efficacy (57 percent thought the new system was more open to their influence) was especially great compared to the over-sixties age group (only one-third of whom agreed with this). In keeping with their upbeat view of the democratic system they grew up with and, conversely, their critical approach to the system their parents had earlier lived under, young Poles were more inclined than all other age groups to say that it would take years for the government to deal with the problems inherited from the communists. Those in their forties, that is, the generation best represented in the new system, were more convinced than any other group that the problems would definitely be resolved soon.[10]

Students often offered harsh assessments about the effectiveness with which the new system actually embodied the political values it proclaimed. In a survey of one higher education center, students listed which basic values were actually present and which should be present in Polish society. The largest discrepancies were between patriotism (21 and 71 percent, respectively), truth (8 and 84 percent), social justice (11 and 80 percent), social equality (18 and 63 percent), human dignity (18 and 77 percent), human rights (34 and 60 percent), and solidarity (19 and 58 percent). By contrast, values that students more often claimed were already present as opposed to proposing they should exist included religion (55 and 35 percent), freedom (62 and 36 percent), and democracy (54 and 42 percent).[11] Generally, then, students embraced these basic values but were critical that a number of them had not taken root in society.

One potential age-based cleavage—currently perhaps the most important—is that between those who were too old at the time of economic transition to make any kind of effective adjustment to new conditions and those who have a fighting chance to adapt. Those most dramatically affected are of course retired people living on fixed incomes. This group, already at least teenagers when communism was imposed on Poland after World War II, has suffered the most of any group from the democratic opening of the 1990s, the second major regime change of their lives. They are experiencing high levels of poverty, are dependent on a less efficient health care system, and are seeing their incomes and life savings undercut by inflation. It is interesting that this group tends more than any other to identify themselves as politically right wing.[12]

Religion

At least 96 percent of Poles say they are Catholic. The next most cited religion is Eastern Orthodox, with 1.4 percent self-declared adherents. Protestant religions are mentioned by 0.3 percent of those surveyed,[13] and Muslims and Jews are not statistically numerous enough to be recorded. Another 1.6 percent of Poles claim no religious affiliation.[14]

Looking at these raw numbers, one might think that there was no place for a deep and politically significant religious cleavage in Polish society, yet elites and masses alike identify religion as a factor dividing Poles, and—as we see later in this chapter—religion has been identified as a major influence on electoral behavior in the Third Republic. What then is the nature of the religious cleavage in Poland today?

The fundamental religious cleavage in Poland lies somewhere between devout and regularly practicing Catholics and those in whose lives the church and religious practice do not play such a large role. The latter group includes both those who had a specific family heritage of intentional secularism (derived from nineteenth- and twentieth-century leftist traditions) and those for whom and for whose families religion came to play a smaller role, whether as the result of incentives and sanctions under the communist regime or in response to the temptations and pressures of advanced capitalism. A useful statistic indicating the sizes of these groups comes from a 2000 CBOS survey, which shows 58 percent of Poles declaring they attend church at least once a week and 26 percent attending not at all or only a few times per year; another 16 percent—harder to classify—assert that they make it to church once or twice a month. Women, the elderly, rural dwellers, and inhabitants of Poland's southern provinces are characterized by high levels of religiosity.[15]

Do church attendance statistics reflect a politically significant division? Attitudes toward the Catholic Church itself as an institution would suggest so. Before communism's fall, Polish society appeared to be near unanimous in its trust in the Catholic Church, with at least 90 percent of survey respondents expressing confidence in the church, making it the most trusted institution in Poland. But only about 50 percent of respondents continued to trust it by 1994, placing it behind both the army and the police. In a survey of Poles' assessment of public institutions carried out in 2000, only 57 percent gave a favorable evaluation of the church and 26 percent a negative one. That put the church behind institutions such as firefighters, the postal service, the media, and even the national sports lottery (see Table 6.2).[16]

The correlation is not perfect, however. By the mid-1990s there was growing consensus that the church had misplayed its hand. In an attitudinal survey carried out in 1994, 71 percent of respondents asserted that the church had too much influence in public life. In 1999 that figure had dropped only slightly, to 61 percent. Nonreligious Poles most often accused the church of having too much political influence. Conversely, "three-quarters of fervent believers and over one-half of regularly practicing Catholics have no reservations about the presence of religion and the Church in public life."[17] Nevertheless, when the question was asked if the church should have a say in political affairs, the responses were even more categorical: If already in 1985 a clear majority (62 percent) of respondents was opposed, this increased to an overwhelming 87 percent in 1999. Yet these results need to be placed in context. Three-quarters of respondents acknowledged that the church's influence on state policy had increased since 1989.[18] Thus the perception was that the church had overreached rather than unjustifiably interfered in politics.

There is plenty of evidence to suggest strong correlations between church attendance and attitudes on sociocultural issues, from abortion to crucifixes in classrooms and religious teaching in schools.[19] Certainly not all regular church-goers adhere strictly to church teachings in sociocultural areas, but there is a very strong relationship between religious practice and belief, on the one hand, and the desire to see state policy reflect religious values. This is reflected in left–right political identification. Sociologists Tadeusz Szawiel and Mirosława Grabowska have consistently found a powerful relationship between religion and left–right self-identification: In Poland, religion appears to play a much larger role in determining whether people identify themselves as right-wing or left-wing than any socioeconomic factors.

Examination of the survey research on which this conclusion is based shows an interesting and potentially significant pattern of clustering along the left–right spectrum. Poles who attend church at least once a week tend to describe themselves as relatively right-wing in their beliefs. But there is a pronounced difference between those who attend regularly and describe themselves as "deeply believing" and those who attend regularly but describe themselves simply as "believing": on a 10-point scale of left–right identification (with 10 indicating the far right), the average selected by the former group is 7.34, whereas the average selected by the latter group is 6.33. On the other hand, the average self-placement for those who attend less than once a week and yet describe themselves as believers is 5.79, and the average for those who do not attend church at

all is 5.28. Thus the largest single gap in left–right self-identification is
between those who describe themselves as deeply believing and the rest.
This suggests the possibility that the politically pertinent line of cleavage
sometimes lies not between the majority constituted by regular church-
goers and the rest of society, but between a deeply devout 10 to 14 percent and all the others.[20]

Former Communists versus Anti-Communists

In their seminal analysis of political cleavages and party systems, Seymour M. Lipset and Stein Rokkan trace twentieth-century cleavage
structures in Western Europe to major conflicts that occurred centuries
earlier in those countries.[21] This would suggest that to identify the cleavages potentially present in any country outside the set considered by
Lipset and Rokkan, we must examine that country's history, searching for
conflicts deep and broad enough to generate enduring cleavages. The history described in Chapter 2 presents a new type of candidate conflict: the
conflict between those who benefited from and supported the communist
system and those who opposed it. With varying intensity this conflict
lasted for several decades, shaping the lives, careers, and associations of
countless Poles. In its early years the conflict manifested itself in a bloody
civil war in which thousands lost their lives. With Solidarity's emergence
in 1980 this conflict became broader than ever, involving a huge proportion of Polish society. Even during years in which there were no visible
expressions of this conflict, it still constrained the associational networks
and career possibilities of many Poles.

Has this communist–anti-communist conflict resulted in a cleavage
anywhere near as significant as that presented in Lipset and Rokkan's
analysis by the Industrial Revolution? Does this cleavage have the potential to last? The previous chapter delineated just such a cleavage among
Polish elites as the primary pattern shaping the dynamics of elite politics.
Is there a matching cleavage among average Poles, or is this just the peculiar obsession of an isolated political class?

Whether it matters to themselves or not, there are objective differences
in the biographies of today's Polish citizens. A small percentage belonged
to the former communist party; the vast majority did not. An increasing
number of Poles have had no experience of the communist past. The
number of communist party supporters should take into consideration
the family of each party-card holder; family members participated in the
system through the benefits accrued by the officially communist head of

household. In addition we must factor in members of the satellite parties and other regime-allied organizations, as well as their family members.

One indication of how Poles view their own individual pasts may be found in their answers to surveyors asking if they would like to see their own secret police files. This question began to be asked in December 1997 as elites debated whether citizens should be able to examine the information collected about them by the communist-era security forces. In an early flush of prurient interest—"I wonder what they could have written about me"–43 percent of respondents said they wanted to see their files; 42 percent thought that no files had been kept on them. By May 1999 only 28 percent said that they would like to examine their own files and 7 percent said they would not. On the other hand, the proportion stating that they did not think that the secret police would have bothered collecting any data on them had increased markedly to 60 percent. This new result seemed to reflect a more realistic assessment by citizens of their political insignificance to the communist regime. Effectively, the majority was acknowledging that they had played no role in the communist years and therefore would have been of no interest to the secret police.[22]

On the other hand, at least for those who did belong to either the communist party or the Solidarity trade union, the past has a major effect on political identification today. The survey results examined by Szawiel show a strong correlation between those memberships and self-placement on the 10-point left–right scale. The average selection by former PZPR members was 4.65; the average selection by former Solidarity opposition members was 6.47.

Furthermore, even those who never belonged to either organization may still be divided by their attitudes toward Poland's recent past. Based on survey respondents' answers to questions ranging from their evaluations of the communist system to their preferred policies toward former communist leaders, Szawiel concludes that there is a strong connection between left–right identification and Poles' feelings about communism: "Opponents of communism and socialism as forms of government as well as people who feel that the collapse of communism was good for Poland declare a more right-wing identity, similar to those who never were PZPR members or who belonged to Solidarity in 1980–1981."[23] Given the relative lack of correlation of classic left–right economic attitudes (such as egalitarianism) with left–right political identification, this correlation is striking.

Will this cleavage endure with generational change? As with the corresponding cleavage among elites, this will depend on the extent to which it is reinforced by a cleavage based on lasting values—such as the religious cleavage—and reproduced by intrafamily transmission as well as social patterns of association.

Political Geography

Regional political differences have existed in Poland under a variety of regimes. As with the case of France, militancy is a distinguishing mark of the country's capital whereas apathy or even reaction characterizes the countryside. Under the partitions, uprisings in Warsaw against tsarist rule left a permanent imprint on the nation's consciousness. In Austrian-controlled Galicia, where Cracow is situated, a combination of the ingrained conservatism of the social elite, peasant passivity, and greater autonomy provided by the Habsburg empire produced a less politicized region. In Prussian-governed lands such as around Poznań, greater adherence to a work ethic and the idea that economic prosperity could compensate for political weakness took hold.

Such at least is the image many Poles have when discussing their political geography. Much changed in the twentieth century as a result of wars. The rural inhabitants of eastern lands were transplanted to Poznań and other territories such as Pomerania and Silesia obtained from Germany in 1945. Communist social engineers decided to combat Cracow's conservatism and Catholicism by building a suburb around a gigantic steel mill, thereby bringing in tens of thousands of hardhat workers to the area. Łódź, the "Polish Manchester," was displayed as a model of how state ownership of industry put an end to the exploitation of workers—especially of women employed in the textile industry—by foreign capitalists, as had occurred in the interwar period. Warsaw's militant history had to be in the minds of successive communist rulers when they undertook grandiose projects like reconstructing the Royal Palace destroyed in the war, building a huge National Library that took over a decade to complete, and constructing an underground metro that took even longer to extend into the city center.

But communist leaders overlooked the potential political danger lurking in the seaport cities, above all, Gdańsk, whose status before 1939 as an international city to which Poland had a corridor through German lands was a spark for Hitler's attack on Poland. It was in Gdańsk that shipyard workers revolted in 1970 when food price increases were announced at Christmastime. And it was in Gdańsk that better organized workers in 1980 put forward political demands that would require the system to become more pluralist.

Worker militancy along the seacoast from Gdańsk to Szczecin proved to be the communist regime's undoing. The area provided a fertile ground for nurturing important opposition leaders including Wałęsa himself. When a multiparty system emerged after 1989, arguably the most pro–free-market grouping was the Liberal Democratic Congress (KLD), led by a number of Gdańsk-area business people. Significantly there was virtually no overlap in leadership between the older trade unionist group from Gdańsk and the younger entrepreneurs. Yet one other politician also got his start in Gdańsk. Kwaśniewski had studied at the university and became head of the communist youth movement there. The historic city had indeed become a center in Poland's political geography.

One other region merits attention for its distinct political culture and economic development—Silesia. The most industrialized part of Poland, it was home to a massive coal-mining sector whose expansion was the pride and joy of the communist regime. Under the old system it was said that the most important political position in the country, after the first secretary of the PZPR, was the head of the Katowice party organization in Silesia. Gierek's career was made on the strength of his performance in Silesia, and subsequent communist leaders from the region were very powerful in national politics through their virtual ex officio membership in the Politburo. The feast day on December 8 of St. Barbara, the patron saint of miners, was practically a "national" holiday in Silesia under the communists. An attempt to weaken the power base of Katowice in order to check his rivals was supposedly one of the major reasons why Gierek subdivided Poland from 17 to 49 provinces. This reform was later reversed in 1999 by another Silesian, Prime Minister Jerzy Buzek, whose government united various parts of the region into a single Silesian province.

The importance of Silesia in national politics was reaffirmed in 1993 when the ex-communist SLD tapped worker discontent in the sprawling industrial region to win huge electoral majorities and catapult to power in parliamentary and then presidential elections. A few years later, Solidarity union strongholds in Silesia were used to underpin the AWS alliance headed by a local trade union militant, Krzaklewski, who had been educated in the region. When the AWS won the 1997 election, Krzaklewski asked Katowice University professor Buzek to head the government. He was the first prime minister to serve a full four-year term, symbolizing perhaps the enduring importance of Silesia in Polish political life. The "autochtone" character of many Silesians—partly Polish, partly German in linguistic and cultural terms—had another political effect. Two-thirds of Silesian respondents believed that their region would enjoy better prospects for economic development if it was more independent from the central authorities in Warsaw.[24] If there is any part of Poland that has a basis for breaking away from central control, it is Silesia.

Of course political geography is constructed on more than just politics. Hubert Tworzecki described some of the overlapping cleavages found in Poland's regional politics: "The strength of anti-communist sentiments in the south-east of the country is clearly visible, as is their weakness in the north-west. This suggests that the Anti-communism/Old System cleavage is to some extent a consequence of differences in the historical experiences and current social and economic makeup of Poland's regions." But there is more: Differences might also stem from "dissimilar economic profiles of the regions: large-scale commercial agriculture, both private and collective in the west, versus small, almost entirely private farming in central, eastern, and southern regions." Tworzecki acknowledged that the relative importance of all of these factors was hard to measure, but he concluded that "It is clear, however, that anti-communist sentiments are stronger in places upon which the more than forty years of communist rule had less of an impact, places in which the social structure and the socioeconomic character did not change dramatically in the recent past."[25]

Electoral Behavior

Turnout and factors shaping turnout are issues that must be addressed prior to looking at the factors that influence voters' choices. Poles have shown more interest in presidential than in parliamentary elections. Turnout for the former has ranged from a low of 53 percent in the 1990 second round (when the only question was by what margin Wałęsa would beat Tymiński) to a high of 68 percent in the 1995 Wałęsa–Kwaśniewski runoff (decided by a narrow margin). The 2000 election had been a foregone conclusion for some time and the turnout of 61 percent was not surprising. With the exception of the June 1989 semi-free parliamentary election—few people realized at the time that it would prove so historic—when 63 percent of voters cast ballots, successive parliamentary elections have generally drawn about one-half of the electorate to the polling stations. As elsewhere in electoral democracies, voting in local elections in Poland seldom wavers from the 10 to 25 percent range.

Many explanations have been advanced for why so many citizens fail to vote, or to vote regularly. For one, the new political parties have not offered clear and consistent programs, making partisan identification difficult—at least for those voters who do not identify with either of the two historically and religiously defined camps. The near consensus among parties on the major issues—market reform, less government, membership in NATO and the EU—has apparently reduced voters' interest. Political leaders—with the exception of some presidential candidates—have generally been uncharismatic and lacking in personal appeal. Exhaustion with and cynicism about politics after the Manichean struggle of the communist period has produced greater citizen indifference and apathy.

Some studies indicate that nonvoting patterns conform to a political geography. The highest rates of participation are usually recorded in Galicia (the area near Cracow that was once under the Habsburgs) and the industrial region of Pomerania (Poznań and its vicinity, once Prussian); the lowest occur in the former Russian-administered Congress Poland (the provinces east of Warsaw) and, next-lowest, the recovered territories (formerly German) in Silesia, where massive postwar resettlement had created social problems such as crime and alcoholism.[26]

Yet another explanation offered for low turnout is that during the first eight years of the Third Republic, too many elections were held to maintain voter interest. To be sure, there was no surge in turnout in 2000 and 2001 after a three-year lull, but this might be explained by the predictability of the outcome. Everyone knew that the post-communists were bound to win both the presidential and the parliamentary elections—reducing or increasing their margin of victory was a weak motivator for half-hearted voters.

Groups ranking lower on the socioeconomic scale have higher rates of abstention and more volatile voting patterns, but the question remains whether differences in voters' economic situations have significant influence on voting preferences. The answer for Poland, for the time being at least, appears to be that they have limited impact. Krzysztof Jasiewicz, for one, contended that "The electoral behavior of Poles is determined not by socio-economic but axiological divisions."[27] He claimed that factors such as age, sex, income, education, unemployment, and place of residence accounted for only a small degree of variance in the popularity of different parties.[28] As further evidence of the weak role played by economics in determining voting, he pointed to how the economic views of supporters of the two major parties in 1997 in reality did not differ much. Jasiewicz argued, instead, that differences in values differentiated the two blocs of supporters, which together represented two-thirds of the electorate. More specifically, the preferences of the two-thirds of the electorate that voted for the SLD or the AWS followed patterns posited by the party self-identification model, in which voters select candidates and parties by the camp to which they belong rather than by issue stances or policy agenda.[29] Since in Poland, as we have seen, the major political camps are determined by the historical-cultural cleavage among elites, this indicates a major role—even when indirect—for religion and for attitudes toward the communist past, but a minor one for economic factors.

The most distinctive feature of Poles' electoral behavior derives directly from the cleavages discussed in a previous section: Religiosity is of the "greatest relevance to voting choices," whereas cleavages based on socio-economic class are only a "weak source of partisanship."[30] Practicing Catholics had higher rates of participation in national and especially local elections than the less religious.[31] They also voted for the nationalist right more than secular-oriented voters. Tworzecki's analysis of electoral behavior drew him to the conclusion that "religiosity (operationalized as the frequency of Church attendance) is of major importance as a predictor of support for the rightist tendency." This was true not just at the individual but also at the collective level. Thus a region's religiosity was a strong predictor of AWS support in 1997.[32] Writing about that election, Jasiewicz put it best: "If at the end of the twentieth century in Poland we want to guess how someone voted in recent elections or will vote in the next ones, we have to ask him not about his occupation, education level, or paycheck, but how often he recites the rosary."[33]

Do past party or opposition memberships or attitudes toward the communist system still affect voting? The tendency of Polish voters to base their choices on the major political camps, that is, choosing a post-communist or a post-Solidarity candidate or party with apparently little consideration of economic programs, would suggest that the answer is yes. This is confirmed by the role played in Polish elections by left–right identification, which we already have seen is closely linked both with religiosity and with relationship to the communist past. SLD voters in 1997 identified themselves as left-wing and AWS voters considered themselves right-wing. Interestingly, SLD supporters perceived their party to be more leftist than it actually was, just as AWS voters thought of their alliance as more right-wing than it really was. The author of this study concluded: "Left–right self-identification was unambiguous and clearly discernible in regard both to the electorates of the parties (sharply distinguishing them) and to political parties as organizations (clear left–right profiles of parties found in social perceptions)."[34] The past does help explain present political outlooks.

What types of orientations do supporters of particular parties have? How distinctive are they? One provocative study involving psychological profiling of party supporters finds, for instance, that the politically best informed and most interested vote for the SLD and UW. Supporters of these two parties also have less authoritarian dispositions. Paranoic personalities and those most politically alienated favor the AWS, PSL, and ROP. Finally, the most depressed individuals vote for the PSL and the Pensioners' Party.[35] Such results of course raise more questions than answers.

Evaluations of the performance of capitalist and democratic Poland were also linked with voter choices. Even after four years of SLD–PSL governments, PSL voters were most critical of current political and economic conditions whereas UW voters were most satisfied and optimistic. SLD and AWS constituencies were somewhere in between, with the first group somewhat more satisfied with the system than the second. As this study concludes, "The SLD is on the one hand a party of successful people and on the other one for channeling nostalgia for People's Poland and the discontent of the losers."[36]

Presidential elections reflect some of the same voting patterns as parliamentary elections, but there are significant differences because the weight of individuals and their characteristics intrudes on that of parties and their programs. Jasiewicz's observation of the October 2000 presidential election pointed to the salience of religiosity as a variable affecting voting,[37] but other factors also gained weight. Fifty-four percent of Krzaklewski voters were women and 46 percent men (Table 5.1). That would seem to indicate that women, who were generally more religious than men, were predictably supporting the most Catholic candidate available. Yet 53 percent of Kwaśniewski supporters were also female, indicating that the religious–secular divide was not overriding. Moreover, the two peasant movement candidates, Andrzej Lepper and Jarosław Kalinowski, received the bulk of their votes from men.

Two-thirds of Kwaśniewski voters were aged twenty-five to sixty, that is, a mix of those remembering the communist system well and those with little memory of it. Two-thirds of Krzaklewski supporters were forty and older, that is, they were of working age during the communist period. Was there some connection, then, to the communist versus anticommunist cleavage? The top two vote-getters in 2000 were communist-era officials, and in a postelection television interview Kwaśniewski

TABLE 5.1 Share of Support for Presidential Candidates from Different
Demographic Categories in the 2000 Election (in percent)

	Kwaśniewski	Olechowski	Krzaklewski	Kalinowski	Lepper
Age					
18–24	16	19	10	11	14
25–39	27	31	23	31	28
40–59	41	39	39	43	41
60+	17	11	28	15	17
Sex					
Women	53	52	54	45	34
Men	47	48	46	56	66
Place of Residence					
Cities (above 200,000)	23	35	27	5	9
Towns (50,000–200,000)	20	19	17	5	10
Towns (under 50,000)	26	24	24	13	17
Rural	30	22	32	78	65
Education					
Primary	13	7	16	23	25
Vocational	27	17	24	34	40
Secondary	45	47	40	34	30
University	15	30	20	9	4
Occupation					
Manager	11	20	12	6	3
Entrepreneur	8	13	8	4	5
Farmer	5	2	6	37	31
Blue-collar worker	17	11	13	13	19
Clerical	13	15	10	8	4
Housewife	4	3	4	4	3
Retired	26	16	35	18	22
Student	9	15	8	6	5
Unemployed	7	5	5	5	8

Source: Polish Television (TP SA), "Election Studio" program (October 8, 2000); see
http://157.25.180.53/wybory2000.

emphasized that "the historical baggage of the past had no significance."[38] Indeed he added ironically that those who were slaves of ideology—the anti-communist variant, not Marxism—were the biggest losers in this election. Perhaps Kwaśniewski had developed into such a skilled and popular incumbent that more traditional voting patterns were skewed. On the other hand, the majority of Poles' reluctance to be drawn into anti-communist campaigns, discernible earlier in their skeptical attitudes about political lustration, seemed to be growing as a stable feature of electoral behavior.

The rural–urban cleavage did not show up in patterns of support for Kwaśniewski and Krzaklewski; each of them drew support in similar proportions from rural and urban areas. There was talk of "two Polands" when the regional breakdown of the electorate was carried out. Kwaśniewski won over 60 percent of the vote in the western provinces of the country but he was below 50 percent in the eastern and southern provinces. The educational level of voters was not a predictor of support for either of these two candidates. By contrast, Olechowski voters were more urban and better educated, as might be expected for a candidate who was supported by many Freedom Union leaders. One important cleavage that did affect levels of support for the candidates was socio-occupational background. Blue-collar and clerical workers favored the former communist, managers and entrepreneurs preferred Olechowski, and pensioners liked Krzaklewski best. Finally, joining the Kwaśniewski bandwagon in 2000 were 25 percent of both UW and PSL voters and one-half of UP voters from 1997. By contrast, Krzaklewski barely held onto one-half of 1997 AWS supporters. Clearly the presidential election transcended many of the cleavages found in legislative contests.

Let us now focus on the issue of electoral volatility. What is the extent of volatility in Polish elections? Have a great number of voters switched their party preferences regularly? Or has electoral stability increased as the party system has become more bipolar?

Given a rapidly evolving party system, it is not surprising that some experts point to great electoral volatility in the 1990s. One study comparing the 1993 and 1997 parliamentary elections, for example, found that 58 percent of voters switched their support and only 23 percent cast ballots for the same party or its successor. Women were more electorally volatile than men, as were those with less education, less income, and rural residence. In addition, people with lower socio-occupational status less often expressed definite and enduring party preferences.[39] Farmers, blue-collar workers, and the unemployed were good examples of this. Not surprisingly, those who expressed satisfaction with the functioning of democracy and believed the present system to be better than the previous one comprised the most stable group in the electorate. Conversely, those who considered the new system worse than the communist one were the group most likely not to vote.

But a different view of electoral preferences is taken by Mirosława Grabowska. She highlights the tendency of voters to increasingly remain loyal to one party:

> What becomes more important from election to election is how someone voted before: if in 1989 someone had voted for Solidarity, then he did not vote for the SLD in either 1993 or 1997, but if he had voted for the [communist] government side, then he did not vote for Solidarity in 1993 nor for Wałęsa but Aleksander Kwaśniewski in 1995. If in 1993 someone had voted for Solidarity, then in 1995 she voted for Wałęsa and not Kwaśniewski, but if someone had voted for the SLD, then in 1995 she did not vote for Wałęsa but Kwaśniewski and in 1997 again voted for the SLD.[40]

Of course exceptions can be found to this pattern. For example, a bandwagon effect facilitated Kwaśniewski's victory in the 2000 presidential election. Many voters (as we discuss below) crossed over to support him. Similarly, the SLD handily won the 2001 parliamentary elections, drawing support from many voters who had chosen the AWS in 1997. If there was one clear tendency, it was the exponential growth of the SLD electorate from election to election—even in 1997 when the government was formed by a coalition of AWS and UW. But that was also attributed to the weakness of the right and the perception of voters that a ballot cast for a conservative splinter party was a wasted ballot. Grabowska's proposition about more stable voting patterns does apply, then, to a majority of the electorate.

Mass Political Attitudes

Political culture consists of deeply embedded political values, attitudes, knowledge, and behavior shared by a particular nation. It is defined by the more enduring political orientations of a country rather than by short-term trends. Poles' nineteenth-century insurrectionary history and their cyclical assaults on the communist system in the second half of the twentieth century provide strong evidence for the proposition that Poland's political culture has been revolutionary when it has been under foreign rule.

Findings of attitudinal surveys conducted since 1989 reveal the emergence of a value system that differs from the one in existence a decade or so ago. On the basis of such short-term trends, can we speak of a culture shift, for example, toward democratic values in Poland? Is a new political culture in the making? Or has an irreversible cultural break with the past yet to occur?

It is unquestionable that most Poles—however slowly or reluctantly—have embraced the core values of the new system and discarded those of the previous regime. The ways in which political elites and average citizens have changed their respective attitudes are, however, a fuzzier subject. In her study of Poland, Frances Millard asserted that "if the state institutions and political elites were quite successful in adapting themselves to the procedural requirements of liberal democracy, they were less successful in forging links with society."[41] The same Polish society that toppled communism may today be estranged from its elected representatives in terms of values held. Have Poles internalized a value system distinct from their leaders? Keeping in mind the elite attitudes examined in Chapter 4, an examination of mass political attitudes can provide answers to these questions.

Norms about the community in which a citizen lives take on great significance in a postmodern world dominated by fragmentation and transience. With the rising exposure to global cultural influences, and with the rapid turn in the region from a political identity imposed by Russia to one shaped by the values of the West, Poles nevertheless do not seem anxious about the society they live in. The continued religious and ethnic homogeneity of Polish society anchors community identity. But also noteworthy is the inclusive rather than exclusionary understanding of citizenship that Polish respondents hold. In a 1994 survey, respondents were asked who in their view was Polish. The leading answers were someone who speaks Polish (cited by 96 percent of respondents), whose citizenship is Polish (92 percent), whose parents were Polish (82 percent), or who lives in Poland (80 percent). Surprisingly, not much more than one-half of the sample (57 percent) said that a Pole was someone who was Catholic.[42] These answers on national identity indicate a liberal orientation at odds with sharply drawn ethnic boundaries and their enforcement, such as the goal of Germany's radical right in the 1990s. If political culture reflects the types of relationships that prevail among members of different groups, then we can say that tolerance, a core concept of Western liberalism, has grown in Poland since the 1990s.

Citizens' Evaluations of Political Change

An integral feature of political culture is citizen attitudes toward the system of government. One Polish political scientist claimed that a democratic transition posits no specific normative model.[43] A consolidated democracy does, however; for a democratic culture to take root in Poland, liberal values need to appear and authoritarian ones must fade. A more participant culture in which citizens are informed about politics and make political demands is a further sign of a modern democratic system.

Whether Poland had a head start in developing a participant culture has been a subject of considerable debate. Some studies have highlighted the deferential, subject culture of many Slavic societies where citizens passively obey rulers, a tendency that was reinforced by Soviet-style authoritarianism.[44] As a result, both the pre-communist and communist pasts in Eastern Europe were characterized by lack of elite responsiveness to the public will.[45] Other studies have stressed the distinctiveness of national cultures—in the case of Poland, the experience of insurrectionism and anti-authoritarianism—and their general incompatibility with the communist normative system.[46] Still others point to the more recent experience of building a civil society—a private sphere of life for citizens free of governmental interference—undertaken in Poland in the mid-1970s, much earlier than in other states in the region. Learning how to organize outside of the structures of power facilitated the transition to democratic procedures and laid the groundwork for the spread of liberal values.

When Polish society was freed from the imposed model of communist political culture, it was unclear which legacy would reemerge to shape citizens' political values. Early in the transition, Poles expressed comparatively little confidence in the emergent system. In a 1995 survey, one-half of respondents agreed that Poland had come out well after the collapse of communism, but 42 percent also claimed that political authorities were now less concerned with the citizenry.[47] That same survey also found that about 40 percent of Poles associated the concept of democracy with negative attributes (Table 5.2). In 2000 the results were somewhat more encouraging for the new system. One-third of respondents answered that given the choice they would like to return to the life they had in the last decade or two of socialism. Those who considered themselves left-wing and, especially, were worse off economically expressed this preference most. By contrast, a substantial majority (57 percent) was happy to continue to live under the present system.[48]

A decade after the democratic breakthrough, then, some Poles still expressed ambiguous feelings about the new and old systems. On the one hand, they were more critical than others in the region about the functioning of their democracy. In seven surveys carried out from 1993 to

TABLE 5.2 What Poles Associate the Concept of Democracy With, October 1995 (in percent)

A system of civil liberties	20
A system of social justice	17
Chaos	16
Rule by the majority	14
Empty words	12
A system providing prosperity	8
A government of party cliques	7
Bureaucracy	4
Hard to say	2

Source: Mirosława Grabowska and Tadeusz Szawiel, *Budowanie demokracji*. Warsaw: PWN, 2001, p.99, Table 7.

1999, the public opinion research center CBOS not once found more respondents satisfied with the functioning of democracy than dissatisfied; in fact in 1999 over 60 percent expressed unhappiness and less than 30 percent satisfaction.[49] On the other hand, Poles were more satisfied than others that communism had been laid to rest. When asked in 1999 to reflect on whether the collapse of communism was a good thing, 80 percent of Poles (a figure similar to that of West Europeans) said yes and only 6 percent said no. Other Central Europeans gave an approval rate nearer 70 percent.[50]

Many of the factors that determine whether individuals welcomed or opposed the transition to a market democracy are unsurprising. According to sociologist Maciej Słomczyński and others: "Generally, those who are younger, self-directed, have a sense of well being, occupy higher stratification positions, are economically successful, and live in modernized regions tend to be supportive of systemic change. Those who are older, rigid, distressed, occupy lower stratification positions, are economically unsuccessful, and live in underdeveloped areas tend to be averse to systemic change."[51] It is worth considering the often overlooked factor of psychological functioning in this context. They concluded that "support for systemic change is related to two dimensions of psychological functioning: self-directedness of orientation and distress. Those individuals who are open-minded in their psychological outlook tend to be supportive of systemic change, while those who are distressed tend to be averse to systemic change."[52]

Perhaps an unusual feature of a society that had organized the Solidarity movement to break free from authoritarianism was the evidence indicating that Poles had become politically apathetic after the democratic breakthrough. In 1992 fewer than half of Poles expressed an interest in politics—a rate considerably lower than in the United States or most other Western countries. In a democracy it is assumed that a variety of institutions represent citizen interests, yet in 1992 only 26 percent of respondents agreed with the statement that "there are now organizations, associations, or unions in Poland that serve the interest of people like you," whereas 53 percent disagreed. One Polish scholar offered an ominous interpretation of these results: "Frustration leads to attitudes more compatible with authoritarianism than with democracy."[53] But several convincing explanations were advanced for the decline in political participation. One was that citizens were choosing not to participate "based on their increasing distrust of current political leaders and institutions and high levels of political apathy rather than on alienation or a learned sense of helplessness from the communist system."[54] In 1993 individuals' economic problems also adversely affected political participation.

The link between public alienation from politics and distrust of political leaders was still in evidence in December 1999. CBOS reported that "the majority of Poles do not feel that politicians currently in charge of the country sufficiently represent their interests. The institutions charged with a lack of sufficient care for public needs are the central authorities, the government, and also, to a lesser degree, the provincial authorities."[55] Between 1992 and 1999 never less than three-quarters of Poles gave a negative assessment of the statement, "people like me have influence on national affairs." In May 1999 only 10 percent claimed they had such influence.[56] The sense of political efficacy remained low in Poland, then, though in many other countries citizens also felt that they had little control over their decisionmakers.

The early 1990s World Values Survey pointed to another aspect of Polish political culture. It was described as a "hyper-Catholic society . . . manifesting relatively traditional cultural values across a wide range of areas. Not only in religion, but also in politics, gender roles, sexual norms and family values, their values are far more traditional than those generally found in industrial societies."[57] The role of religion in Polish political choices and self-identification partially confirms this, although we have also seen that a sizable sector of society does not fit this description.

Another indication of public attitudes toward political change concerns citizens' ideas about which were the most significant political develop-

TABLE 5.3 Events of the Past Ten Years That Were Most Significant and Pivotal for
Poland's History, June 1999 (in percent)

Signing the round table agreement in April 1989	45
Withdrawal of the Russian military from Poland in September 1993	44
Poland's entry into NATO in March 1999	43
Ratification of a new constitution in April 1997	26
The first direct presidential elections in November 1990	20
The elimination of censorship in April 1990	17
Introduction of the agreement on association with the European Union	14
The first completely free parliamentary elections in October 1991	14
The parliamentary elections of June 4, 1989	13
The Sejm's enactment of the Balcerowicz plan in December 1989	8
The formation of the government of Tadeusz Mazowiecki in September 1989	7

Source: Krzysztof Pankowski and Beata Roguska, "Oceny zmian po roku '89," in
Krzysztof Zagórski and Michał Strzeszewski (eds.), *Nowa rzeczywiś tość: Oceny i opinie
1989–1999.* Warsaw: DIALOG, 2000, p. 35. Respondents could choose three events from
the list given.

ments of the years 1989 to 1999. By far the three events identified by respondents that overshadowed all others were the 1989 roundtable agreement, the withdrawal of Russian forces from the country in 1993, and
joining NATO in 1999 (Table 5.3). The authors of the study speculate
that what these three caesurae had in common for respondents was the
fact that they brought Poles together rather than divided them, as happened, for example, in the case of elections or the Balcerowicz plan.[58]
Nevertheless, it is startling that the creation of the first noncommunist
government under Mazowiecki in September 1989 should evoke little
sense of being a historic breakthrough. In one sense, the agreements concluded by elites that had the least input from citizens were those perceived as the most important. This may be connected to the public's sense
of political inefficacy; citizens' self-loathing leads them to undervalue the
events that they have shaped.

Finally, public attitudes toward decommunization might suggest
whether citizens desired a total break from the past—a thick line (*gruba
kreska*) to be drawn between the communist and democratic regimes. In
one study, decommunization, which entailed purging the communist
legacy from political life, was ranked last of eleven priorities listed by

respondents. Surveys between 1989 and 1992 revealed that it was consistently perceived as a minor issue, and even where there was consensus that higher-ranking party leaders should be punished, over time opinion shifted toward a more forgiving approach—for example, from 64 percent backing prosecution of Politburo members in February 1991 to just 36 percent in July 1992 in one survey.[59] Rather than viewing Polish public opinion as "soft on communists," it may be more accurate to underscore its concern with defending the principle of equality under the law for all citizens.

Social and Economic Values

One of the questions dominating Polish sociological research since 1989 has been the extent to which the prescriptive communist value system had taken hold among citizens and how easy or hard it was going to be to dislodge it. If we assume that the two core values in the communist prescriptive political culture were social justice and egalitarianism, then large sections of Polish society internalized these ideals during the communist period.[60] But communist values also prescribed deference to authority, the centrality of the common good, and, officially at least, a nonmaterialist (more accurately, nonconsumerist) way of life. In these areas, Polish political culture proved resistant to the regime's indoctrination efforts.

At the outset of the 1990s, Poland ranked twenty-eighth out of forty-three societies in terms of espousing postmaterialist values. Let us recall the meaning of this term and of its opposite, materialism: "Materialist priorities are tapped by emphasis on such goals as economic growth, fighting rising prices, maintaining order and fighting crime; while *Postmaterialist values* are reflected when top priority is given to such goals as giving people more say on the job or in government decisions, or protecting freedom of speech or moving toward a less impersonal, more humane society."[61] The shock therapy that was administered to Polish society in the early 1990s would have forced citizens to shift to materialist priorities even if they had not previously held them. This was essential to a survival strategy. This materialism nevertheless stood in contrast to the more idealistic project of building a civil society undertaken by democratic dissidents in the 1970s.

Early in the 1990s the uncertain consequences of the transition to a market economy were reflected in a body of public opinion that revealed considerable anxiety. Egalitarianism, the core value of the socialist normative order, largely carried over to the democratic system—for the first few years. Comparison of survey data for 1988 and 1993 showed no decline in egalitarian attitudes. Furthermore, "for both 1988 and 1993, structural blame, that is, an attribution of one's failures to conditions outside of one's control, proved to be associated with pro-egalitarian orientation."[62] Another study carried out in the first years of the transition discovered that the issues considered important by the public were egalitarian in character: unemployment, inflation, agriculture, poverty, crime, and housing.[63]

Etatist attitudes holding that the state's responsibility was to safeguard minimum living standards for everybody also survived the early years of regime change. When asked what type of society was preferable—one in which individual interests dominated or where the state provided citizens with guarantees—Polish respondents displayed a slight preference for the latter (36 percent to 30 percent, with 29 percent attracted to a middle road).[64] But comparative attitudinal data for 1988 and 1993 already began to point to a decline in support for state paternalism. To be sure, some groups, notably the elderly, the poorly educated, laborers, and rural residents, actually expressed greater support for welfare policies during this transitional period. A more nuanced conclusion was that "while the 'myth of the market' had been destroyed for many by 1993, the majority of individuals in Poland did not want to see a return to . . . welfare state policies."[65]

One Polish research team concluded that there were "'path dependent' trends in people's adjustment to the initial phase of the post-communist transition."[66] By the second half of the decade, the egalitarian mind-set characteristic of the communist era weakened as large numbers of Poles found employment in the more remunerative, opportunity-filled private sector. A February 2000 CBOS report made the categorical assertion that Poles would now put freedom before equality in social life if they were faced with such a choice (57 percent compared to 35 percent).[67]

Today's political culture has been modified by over a decade of democratic experience. Some statist values remain, but among young people in particular they have given way to individualist ones. Political behavior, a central aspect of political culture, is now channeled through the ballot box, though public demonstrations (against abortion and EU agricultural products, for health care reform and farm subsidies) also reflect the more participatory culture. Some skeptics have detected a lag between the precocious growth of democratic institutions and a slower transformation of societal values in Poland. By the turn of the new century this seemed to be an exaggerated concern.

Popular Protests

In September 1999 about 30,000 demonstrators took part in a protest in Warsaw. Although protests by individual occupational or social groups have been a regular feature of public life in the Third Republic, this was possibly the nearest Poles had come to a public act of social solidarity since a noncommunist government was installed exactly a decade earlier. As it was, the number of participants was disappointing; organizers had been hoping for at least 100,000 demonstrators.

Who the protesters are in democratic Poland and what they want are questions that no longer have the straightforward answers as under the communist regime. The socio-occupational diversity of protesters and their different agendas were already discernible in the early 1990s when public employees, industrial workers, and farmers took strike action, demonstrated, blocked roads, and destroyed produce to vent their anger at what were seen as insensitive political authorities. Coordinated action involving several groups was a rarity. Perhaps symbolic of the disarray of this period were the regular, disruptive protests staged by young people supporting anarchist causes, asserting alternative lifestyles, and scorning establishment politics and society. But anarchist demonstrations waned, it seemed, in tandem with the consolidation of the new political system.

The most common form of protest action in Poland is the strike. By far the worst year for strikes was 1993, when 7,443 strikes were staged, encompassing 383,000 workers. From 1995 on there were never more than 42 strikes in any given year and never more than 44,000 workers were involved.[68] Those totals showed that Poland by the end of the decade had relatively more labor peace than a number of Western European democracies.

Let us consider the Third Republic's protest years—the early 1990s—and what was unique about them. Grzegorz Ekiert and Jan Kubik described the all-encompassing nature of these protests:

> Protest actions ranged from single, isolated strikes and local demonstrations organized by small groups of activists to nationwide protest campaigns that would last for weeks and involve hundreds of public institutions and enterprises as well as thousands of workers and public sector employees. Small protests usually centered around a variety of local issues. They were spawned by grievances concerning housing, transportation, and various decisions and permits issued by local governments. . . . Large protests usually addressed larger economic and political issues and centered on government

economic policies. During these protest campaigns, entire regions of the country and branches of industry and the public sector were the scene of escalating protest actions.[69]

Protests took many different forms: "strike alerts, one-hour-long warning strikes, symbolic solidarity strikes (displaying flags, signs, and banners), publication of statements criticizing government policies and demanding policy changes, and rallies and demonstrations, as well as protracted and desperate strike campaigns that lasted for months." [70] Ekiert and Kubik also referred to blockades of roads and occupation of public buildings, such as the three-week-long sit-in at the Ministry of Agriculture in April 1992 that brought the peasant-based Self-Defense League its first taste of notoriety. Issue-based protests took second place to economic interest-based actions. Less than 5 percent of demands concerned ecological-, abortion-, and AIDS-related subjects. An interesting point was that "structurally, the principal cleave of protest politics after 1989 was very similar to the one driving anticommunist politics; in both cases it was 'the state' versus 'the people dependent on it.'"[71]

Did protests have any impact? The authors of this study were of two minds. Their most important claim about protests is clear and substantiated by political developments: "If protest does not involve violence and if protesters do not promulgate antidemocratic programs, unconventional but institutionalized political participation . . . is a sign of democratic vitality or successful democratic consolidation."[72] So these protests indicate the presence of a healthy democracy. But do they make for good public policy? Ekiert and Kubik insist that "protest did not have any substantial impact on macroeconomic policies" and its impact on privatization policies was "limited."[73] Nevertheless, they also state that "protests contributed to many policy changes and reversals of specific decisions of local and national authorities."

If many individual state economic decisions are being made on the basis of which group protested when (particularly at what stage in the electoral cycle) and how conspicuous or difficult their protest was, there is necessarily going to be an impact on the quality of economic policy. Sometimes these protests may draw valuable attention to short-sighted policies, but sometimes they may result in resources being directed toward the most vocal group and thus away from others. Possibly the most dramatic case of allocation of resources to the most organized and vocal groups at the cost of other more deserving sectors has been successive governments' capitulation to workers' demands for the preservation of the

privileged position of inefficient state industries. Ekiert and Kubik acknowledged that this was one area in which protests proved effective.

If Poles were just as likely to strike as to protest in the first years of
transition, this changed from the mid-1990s on. For a start, the most
consistently militant group in Polish society became farmers. Their
demonstrations and radical actions peaked in 1999, and though economic
deprivation was one of the main sources for discontent, there were other
reasons as well. A sense of political marginalization lay behind farmers'
protests. This sense had two interrelated causes: (1) the insubstantial role
played by the rural sector in planning the political and economic transition in Poland, which alienated farmers not only from the ruling elite but
also from their supposedly own peasant elite;[74] and (2) the inevitable by-
product of the government's agrarian policies that limited subsidies to the
countryside while providing no resources for rural economic reform and
restructuring. Peasant protests were not endorsed, of course, by any parliamentary party. At best the "establishment" PSL took a wait-and-see
attitude. Self-Defense, which was behind many of the actions, had no
representation in the Sejm. Not surprisingly, rural respondents had more
positive evaluations of the benefits brought by the League's actions in defense of farmers than of the PSL.[75]

This new agrarian radicalism was starting to resemble that of the capitalist interwar period when Wincenty Witos became a champion of the
cause of peasants. But an interesting coincidence was that farmers in EU
countries also took protest actions at this time. The fact that relations between government and farmers were affected by more general conditions
prevailing in countries with different levels of economic development and
civil society persuaded one scholar to comment that "the Polish farmer is
well prepared for entry into the European Union."[76]

The best-known agrarian leader in Poland is Andrzej Lepper. A member of the former communist party until 1980, he graduated from an agricultural school and worked as a private farmer until emerging as leader of
a hunger strike of farmers who could not pay off loans in 1991. The following year he became head of the newly organized Self-Defense agrarian trade union. From then on he organized controversial farmer protests,
including occupation of town halls, the march on parliament in 1993, the
farmers' national demonstration in Warsaw in 1998, and a blockade of a
border crossing that same year. Dozens of times he was charged with organizing illegal occupations of buildings and blockades, using force, incit-
ing others to commit criminal acts, and defaming state authorities. Lepper was jailed several times, but he began to defy court summons and

missed court appearances. Surprisingly, many of the charges against him were dropped, giving rise to rumors that he had been let off by local authorities in return for a pledge that he would not organize protest actions in the locality. Funds in his organization's bank accounts sometimes went missing and some of his associates resigned because of a perception of wrongdoing by their leader.

Many observers have condemned him as Poland's most anti-democratic politician, but Lepper was a presidential candidate in both 1995 and 2000. Running as the Self-Defense candidate in the first election, he finished ninth of thirteen candidates with 1.3 percent of the popular vote. The next time he ran as an independent and finished fifth, more than doubling his support. His share of 3 percent of votes cast was about as much as Wałęsa and slightly ahead of his PSL rival Kalinowski. Ironically, then, the recourse to extraparliamentary means of protest brought Lepper a notoriety that has paid dividends: Despite the image he has cultivated as an anti-establishment leader, he now must be considered part of the political elite. In 2001 he was elected a deputy of the Polish Sejm.

As radical as some of the actions taken by farmers in the 1990s were, other groups (for example, public service workers) also took up forceful protests, whether by strikes or demonstrations, such as occupation of government ministries. Paradoxically, industrial strife had lessened as a result of economic and labor reforms. In particular, the 1991 law governing collective bargaining had provided guidelines for negotiation, mediation, and arbitration, cutting down strike action. By the mid-1990s what industrial strikes there were tended to be legal rather than wildcat; they were also less "emotional" than in the past.[77] These conflicts were generally about salary issues and were cyclical in that the same issue came up as a source of dispute several times. The greatest change, however, was in the sectors striking. Protests by health care workers and teachers showed the breadth of protest action. Increasingly strike action was taken up by white-collar workers in the service sector, perhaps a strong indication that Poland was on its way to becoming a postindustrial society. Summing up the different sectors and occupations, agendas, and methods involved in protests, one Polish industrial sociologist labeled the 1990s the "decade of transformed conflicts."[78]

Economic Interests versus Religion and the Past

In examining political protests in this chapter we have found—finally—a pattern of political interaction in the Third Republic focusing around the

economic self-interest of social groups (as opposed to corruption, patronage, and economic lobbying, which focus on the economic self-
interest of individuals and organizations). It stands in contrast to the political cleavages based on relationships with religion and with the communist past that characterize elites and the voting public.

In spite of the fact that for over a decade Poland has been going
through massive economic transformation that involves countless state
decisions directly affecting the lives of various sections of Polish society,
the major political games taking place within the official arenas of the
new democratic political system have not been structured on the basis of
economic interest. Instead the economic interests of many sectors adversely affected by state policies find their primary expression in strikes,
road blockades, marches, and sit-in occupations of government buildings.
For many of these social groups, the abstract "economic interest" could be
better and more concretely characterized as the ability to feed, clothe, and
properly educate themselves and their families.

Here we might follow Sherlock Holmes and ponder the significance of
"the dog that didn't bark in the night," in this relative absence of economic interest from official democratic processes. How do we explain
this? It seems likely that the cleavage pattern on the elite level—specifically, the dominating historical-cultural cleavage—limits the possibilities
on the mass level. The existence of two major camps, one composed of
former communists (usually called left-wing) and the other made up of
former oppositionists (usually called right-wing), presents Polish voters
with a particular set of choices. Voters cannot vote for nonexistent parties,
nor will many of them vote for marginal parties that lack the resources to
communicate their messages on the national media stage.

On the other hand, perhaps not all of this pattern is attributable to the
deep cleavage dividing elites. Poland does face a limited set of economic
policy possibilities given the imperatives of market-aimed transformation
and the constraints set by the need to participate in an increasingly glob-
alized international economy. For parties that hope to govern Poland, certain policy agendas may simply be untenable. Another explanation might
be that of the Elster, Offe, and Preuss thesis, that the uncertainty accom-
panying economic transition discourages the articulation of economic interests. But this appears to be invalidated by the nature of political
protests in the Third Republic. Protesting nurses, coal miners, and private
farmers seem to have no difficulty in identifying where their economic
interests lie.

But we have still not accounted for the implications of this relative absence of economic interest. What does it mean for democracy and, specifically, for the building of strong links between society and its political representatives? An answer may be found in the data on values discussed earlier. Lack of representation of their fundamental interests does frustrate Poles, although it has not reached the point of undermining Polish democracy. Contrary to Elster, Offe, and Preuss's suggestion of the dangers of identity- and culture-based cleavages, in Poland the larger role played by these divisions has not resulted in destabilizing and irreconcilable conflicts, perhaps because of the pragmatism of the major party representing the minority side of these cleavages, that is, the SLD, the Alliance of the Democratic Left.

How does the fact that conflicting economic interests are rarely articulated in the democratic games of elections, parliaments, and governments affect policy itself? In particular, how does it influence the construction and revision of economic policies? To explore this question we must examine the actual arenas in which policymakers are chosen and policies are made and implemented; to address this, Polish political institutions are the topic of the following chapter. We must also examine the key policy challenges, in economics as well as in other spheres, that confront Poland; this will be considered in the seventh and concluding chapter.

6

Political and Economic Arenas: The Institutions of the Third Republic

One of the defining characteristics of democracy is that political outcomes are determined by rules of the game, which—in a consolidated democracy—are designed and accepted by all major political actors. These rules are written into a country's constitution, they can be found in laws passed by an elected assembly or approved in a general referendum, and they can also originate in conventions and traditions recognized over time. Rules identify the jurisdiction and powers of various governmental institutions—president, prime minister, cabinet, parliament, judiciary. Rules also determine how the officeholders of these institutions are to be selected.

In Poland, constructing democratic institutions appeared to be difficult, tedious, and even anticlimactic after the Herculean struggles to topple the ossified and authoritarian communist system. In some areas, the nature of institutional change was sweeping, immediate, and palpable. For instance, the country was almost immediately renamed from the Polish People's Republic to simply the Polish Republic, as it had been in 1918. If the interwar system constituted the Polish Second Republic, then the new democracy is called the Third Republic. The forty-odd-year existence of the People's Republic was thus treated as an anomaly—as not really having been a Polish state. It is sometimes facetiously referred to as the Second-and-a-Half Republic.

Almost as soon as the Third Republic was proclaimed, new political structures as well as economic ones (discussed later in this chapter) were created. But in other spheres change was slow in coming and ambiguity was to prevail for many years. There were strong disagreements among political actors and within society over which institution should be paramount in the Third Republic—the president or parliament. As a result, constitutional reform had to be carried out piecemeal and in a way unsatisfactory to those who wanted to eliminate the vestiges of communism as quickly as possible. Transitional institutional arrangements exasperated many political players, and became a new source of conflict that for a time superceded the communist versus anti-communist divide.

The early years of the democratic transition in Poland were both exhilarating and frustrating. The achievements of this period were significant yet were overshadowed by the bickering of aspiring new leaders. In particular, the seemingly blind and conflictual ambitions of a host of new actors quickly exposed the absence of even minimal solidarity in a movement that had just a short time earlier been unified under the Solidarity banner. Institutional disorder provided some political outsiders, like a Pole returning from business ventures in the Peruvian Amazon (Stan Tymiński), with an opportunity to exert influence and gain credibility. A political system does not thrive in an institutional vacuum, and that appeared to be the main failing of the emergent post-communist regime. Now, with over a decade of hindsight, let us examine whether the largely unplanned regime change described in Chapter 3 was accompanied by largely unplanned institutional change, and if so whether this had any enduring dysfunctional effects on the new system.

Political Structures

To democratize the Polish political system, a whole set of new institutions and legal provisions had to be introduced to replace those inherited from the communist period. A partial list would include:

1. removing all the official symbols and terms of the previous system (the country's name, its coat of arms, flag, and anthem);
2. creating the political institutions of democracy, including the presidency, the Senate, and an overhauled system of local government;
3. replacing the Polish constitution of July 22, 1952, which was drafted during the Stalin era, and—to enhance constitutional rule—giving real autonomy to the Constitutional Tribunal, an appellate body;

4. enacting electoral laws that would govern multiparty competition;
5. creating a new institutional framework for economic activity, in particular, passing legislation to expand private ownership rights while delimiting state ownership rights;
6. enshrining principles incorporating civil rights and ensuring appropriate institutional safeguards for them, such as an office of the Commissioner for Civil Rights (originally created in 1987); and
7. strengthening the independence of the judicial branch of government.

This list of changes is not exhaustive, though it does identify the key areas for which the architects of the post-communist system had to draft blueprints. To a certain degree the interwar experience served as a model in the crafting of a democracy, for it was natural in the flush of triumph after the 1989 democratic breakthrough for the major political players to look to Poland's prior experiment with democracy for guidance. At the same time, the structure of the new political system had to incorporate compromises with its communist predecessor. Let us review some of the blueprints for institutional reform, then, that were advanced in the first decade in the life of the new republic.

The Logic of Institutional Reform

Establishing a constitutional framework that sets out the political rules of the game and the institutions that allocate values in society is the most daunting challenge encountered by a new regime. The political science literature on institutionalism suggests which designs for democratic construction seem most appropriate to a country at a particular stage of development and with a particular kind of social and ethnic makeup. Yet possibly the best place to begin the analysis of institutional change is with the writings of an economic historian, Douglass North.

For this Nobel Prize–winning economist, "institutions exist to reduce the uncertainties involved in human interaction. These uncertainties arise as a consequence of both the complexity of the problems to be solved and the problem-solving software (to use a computer analogy) possessed by the individual. There is nothing in the above statement that implies that the institutions are efficient."[1] North's concern was to understand why some societies develop efficient, adaptive, growth-promoting institutions and others do not. The answer lay in a society's willingness to abandon institutions that do not work: "It is essential to have rules that eliminate not only failed economic organization but failed political organization as well. The effective structure of rules, therefore, not only rewards successes, but also vetoes the survival of maladapted parts of the organizational structure."[2] North contended that "the society that permits the maximum generation of trials will be most likely to solve problems through time."[3]

This trial-and-error approach works only under conditions of continuity and stability. In less modern societies, informal constraints imposed primarily by traditional codes of behavior ensured stability even as institutions underwent incremental change. By contrast, modern political systems can provide the stable conditions required for institutions to adapt to new exigencies by creating and enforcing formal constraints. According to North, "stability is accomplished by a complex set of constraints that include formal rules nested in a hierarchy, where each level is more costly to change than the previous one."[4] It is here that efficiency-promoting constitutional provisions and institutional designs become so important to the success of a new regime.

The emergence of many new democracies in the 1980s called political scientists' attention to the connection between an array of institutional variables and democratic consolidation. As two writers already stressed in 1984, "political democracy depends not only on economic and social conditions but also on the design of political institutions."[5] The subsequent literature on democracy therefore concentrated on the part played by such institutional factors as presidential and parliamentary systems of government, and party and electoral systems. Constitution making was crucial in mapping out a system based on the rule of law while acknowledging the specific political realities, for example, the role of the Catholic Church, prevailing in a country. In general, the consensus among specialists was that the rules that placed constraints on political actors had to be devised in such a way that actors found it in their interest to maintain rather than to subvert democracy. When it came to institutional design, then, a mix of high principles and political pragmatism seemed the best combination to keep a young democracy afloat.

Constitutional Change

After the 1989 roundtable agreement had been concluded, drafting a new constitution to reflect the proposed political changes in Poland became an urgent task. At the same time, writing an entirely new constitutional document could clearly not be done overnight. Between 1989 and 1992 only piecemeal change was possible, which produced a much-amended version of Stalin's 1952 constitution. The so-called "Little Constitution" of October 1992 represented a more sweeping attempt at change, but even its title (similar to Poland's earlier provisional constitutions) implied its transitional nature.[6] The constitutional stalemate followed from disagreements over very basic philosophical questions. For example, should the new constitution's preamble refer only to "the Polish nation" or to "all citizens of Poland"? Should the special role of Catholicism in the country be explicitly recognized (as had been the case in the Irish constitution) or should it not enjoy constitutional status?

It took eight years to resolve most of these issues. When a new constitution was submitted for public approval in a referendum in May 1997, only 43 percent of the electorate turned out at the polls. Just 53 percent voted in favor of its adoption. Constitutional burnout and its anticlimactic arrival had resulted in little enthusiasm for such a potentially historic document.

Let us review the incremental approach to constitution making in Poland.[7] To make good on the promises given by the communist delegation at the roundtable negotiations, the 1952 constitution had immediately been amended to provide for the establishment of a revamped presidency, a resurrected Senate, and new electoral laws. These quick-fix changes enacted on April 7, 1989, did not in themselves signal the end of the ancien régime. But the fast-paced events of the summer did, and on December 29, 1989, the parliament passed legislation formally changing the country's name from the Polish People's Republic to the Polish Republic. The first two chapters of the 1952 constitution were replaced with a new section entitled "Foundations of the Political and Economic System." Constitutional specialist Stanisław Gebethner contended that it was this new chapter that provided a "radical—even revolutionary—change of the concept of both the political system and the economic system."[8]

The revolutionary changes started with the very first article, which had previously defined Poland as a socialist state. Now it stated that "the Polish Republic is a democratic legal state implementing the principles of social justice."[9] The very character of the Polish state was being redefined, then. In addition, the previous language of Article 1 saying that power was vested in the hands of working people in town and country was deleted. New Article 2 asserted that "supreme power is vested in the nation." Gone was the class nature of communist society. So, too, was former Article 3, which had identified the leading role of the Polish United Workers Party (PZPR) in Polish society. A new Article 4 outlined instead the bases of a multiparty system: "Founded on the principles of free will and equality, political parties organize citizens of the Polish Republic with the objective of influencing the policies of the state in a democratic manner."[10]

The December 1989 changes also encompassed the economic system. All references to the special status of socialist forms of ownership—state and cooperative—and to a centrally planned economy were removed. Article 6 now read: "The Polish Republic guarantees freedom of economic activities regardless of the form of ownership." Article 7 followed with "The Polish Republic protects ownership and the right to inheritance and guarantees full protection of personal ownership."[11]

On March 8, 1990, parliament approved a constitutional change that reorganized the structure of local government in the country. Instead of democratic centralism (control by higher party-state bodies over local authorities), French-style communal assemblies and regional prefects were introduced as the basis of the new system. Central budgetary allocations were to be slashed and self-government was more closely tied in with self-financing.

Another major constitutional revision was enacted on September 27, 1990, setting out the procedure for electing the president. Article 32 made the election direct, the term of office five years, and the powers of the office separate from those of the parliament. In general terms, the president was "the supreme representative of the Polish state in internal and external affairs." This represented a band-aid approach, and the ambiguous character of executive power hamstrung Polish politics until the 1995 presidential election.

Until 1997 the most comprehensive constitutional overhaul came with the passage of the Little Constitution, signed into law on November 17, 1992. The title was a reference to Poland's earlier little constitutions, such as the February 20, 1919, act investing Józef Piłsudski with the powers of chief executive. As one constitutional specialist explained: "This description is reserved for an act that regulates the fundamental principles and institutions of the political system, above all, the organization and method of functioning of state authority, for a transitional period."[12]

The 1992 Little Constitution addressed the pressing problem of distinguishing between the powers of the president and those of other branches of government. Even though it dropped wording describing the Sejm as the supreme authority in the country, the act formalized the gridlock in Polish politics by declaring that the country had "a presidential–parliamentary system of government." The distribution of power between branches of government called for by the 1992 Little Constitution resembled that of the interwar republic to 1926. The power of the executive branch—defined as including both president and prime minister—was circumscribed. A form of Sejmocracy emerged in the first years of the new system and little could get done without legislative approval. Because some important issues were not resolved by the Little Constitution, and because technically some parts of the 1952 Stalin constitution remained in force, agreement on a completely new constitution was highly desirable.[13]

In the fall of 1994 the Sejm began debate on seven different versions of a new constitution proposed by Lech Wałęsa and the main political parties. Only Wałęsa's draft advocated a strong presidency. His failure to get reelected in December 1995 was, in large measure, a popular vote against establishing a strong executive branch. The new president, Aleksander Kwaśniewski, went out of his way to stress that he was a "parliamentarian" and was content to preside over rather than dominate Polish politics. Wałęsa's defeat signified not only a shift in power from Solidarity to ex-communist forces, but also a change from an active to a passive presidency.[14]

The constitution finally adopted in May 1997 incorporated references to both the Polish nation and its citizens, and to both Catholicism and other faiths.

Checks and Balances

The institutional choices available for new democracies are actually very limited. Essentially, the question is, as Juan Linz and Arturo Valenzuela asked starkly: "Presidential or parliamentary democracy: Does it make a difference?"[15] Seeking to answer this question, Matthew Shugart and John Carey reported that the breakdown rate for new democracies was 50 percent for presidential and 44 percent for parliamentary systems. But when less developed countries experiencing chronic instability were excluded, it was parliamentary systems that proved more prone to democratic reversal than presidential ones.[16] There was therefore no conclusive answer as to which system consolidated democracy best.

So another problematic had to be considered: identifying the source of threats to young democracies in order to infer which institutional arrangements prove more stabilizing. Some time ago Seymour M. Lipset discovered that citizens of newly democratic regimes evaluated these regimes to a very high degree by their current performance. This made the new democracies more vulnerable to collapse when an economic or social crisis arose. The reason for this was that these citizens often failed to distinguish between the source of political authority (such as the constitution) and the agent of authority (the current government). The failures of a particular government became equated with flaws in the political system. New democracies could not contradict this presumption because they were by definition unable to invoke a record of past successes.[17] To make matters worse, ineffective or simply underachieving governments in new democracies can break down because of a sudden expansion in citizen rights, such as the free flow of information in a society and newly acquired rights of association and speech.[18]

The separation of powers is the most obvious way of deflecting public criticism of a particular government. Citizens can single out the less competent branch of government and attack it without bringing into question the entire political system. Nonetheless, tensions between executive and legislative branches can impede overall efficacy, thereby exacerbating public discontent. Separation of powers between the two branches, together with the simultaneous legitimacy of the president and the legislature, contribute to stalemate when agendas and policies of the two conflict. Stalemate or, worse, confrontation is exacerbated when the president and the legislative majority belong to different political parties. Building safeguards against overconcentration of power in one branch (as through a checks-and-balances arrangement or a semipresidential system in which institutional power sharing is formalized) is important. But such arrangements can also act as an obstacle to coherent policy formulation.

The key to ensuring both effective and responsible government is attaining an equilibrium state. Adam Przeworski described what this involves:

> To be stable and effective, democratic institutions must not generate governments unresponsive to the changing relations of political forces, governments free from the obligation to consult and concert when they formulate policy, governments unconstrained to obey rules when they implement them. Yet they also must not paralyze decisions and their implementation. All interests must be represented in the making of policy, but none should be able unilaterally to block its formulation and implementation.[19]

Pacts among democratic actors, such as between those in control of different branches of government, to suppress excessive political competition can be especially functional for democratic consolidation. But are pacts between politicians the only way to reach this objective? Can we really not tell whether one institutional configuration is superior to another in achieving this objective?

Shugart and Carey listed the potential benefits of presidential systems of government. First and foremost they provide for accountability. Popular election of the president for a fixed term cannot be overridden by shifts in coalitions, as in parliamentary systems, and the president's performance is transparent to voters. Such systems ensure identifiability. Voters have a clearer idea of what alternative governments would do, and therefore they can vote prospectively, in anticipation of contenders' future performances. These systems lock in mutual checks between president and legislature since each has an independent popular mandate. In parliamentary systems, by contrast, the prime minister, his or her cabinet, and parliament all have a stake in surviving for as long as possible and avoiding premature elections. This can lead to mutual collusion rather than mutual checks. Finally, by virtue of being above partisan politics, the executive in a presidential system can serve as an arbiter of political conflict and mediator of legislative disputes.

At the same time, the presidential system, in which the chief executive has an independent mandate from the people, has its disadvantages. The president may be intolerant of legislative opposition to his policies. In attempting to break down immobilism, he or she may try to bypass the legislature and rule by decree or to force constitutional reform favoring his office; both options have been tried in Poland. But if an "immobilized" president accepts his or her fate while remaining committed to democracy, the ensuing political stalemate and the inability to handle crisis and instability may eventually incline the military to intervene in politics, as in Chile in 1973.[20] Again, evidence of political turmoil in Poland in 1992 indicated that this scenario was not as far-fetched as it appeared.

The threat of stalemate seems to be more benign in a parliamentary system. A prime minister usually belongs to the same party as the majority in parliament. Should the prime minister lose the support of the legislative majority, institutional measures such as dissolution of parliament, a vote of no confidence in the government, or asking another leader to form a new government minimize the danger of prolonged deadlock. Above all, parliamentary systems ensure wide representation for various groups. Even if a single party wins a parliamentary majority, the largest losing party can assume the role of official opposition while all the other parties begin to work toward increasing their representation next time around. Representation is particularly important for new democracies, since all significant political actors learn to have a stake in continuing with the democratic game. Presidentialism is more of a zero-sum game: One group's victory is the other group's loss, and this for the duration of the president's term in office. Juan Linz concluded, therefore, that "parliamentarism provides a more flexible and adaptable institutional context for the establishment and consolidation of democracy."[21]

However, a parliament characterized by a fragmented party system and shaky coalition governments can engender political instability on its own.[22] The resulting political chaos can mimic the problems of stalemate between president and legislature and may even provoke an antidemocratic coup.[23] The threat of breakdown in this case leads to the inescapable conclusion that a strong party system enhances the prospects for political stability. In particular, a two-party system in which each of the contenders must appeal to a broad section of the citizenry is, in theory anyway, likely to produce moderation, accommodation, and aggregation of diverse interests.[24] In turn, the number of parties in a political system is in part a function of the electoral system, that is, whether elections are decided by simple majority in single-member constituencies, by proportional representation in multiple-member districts, or by a combination of the two. As we see in the case of Poland, as the probability of a parliamentary rather than a presidential system increased, manipulating electoral rules so as to produce a strong party system became very important in ensuring political stability.

A presidential system characterized by a strong executive is an unlikely outcome of a democratic transition from communist rule. Indeed, the raison d'être for extrication from authoritarianism is the creation of institutional pluralism, wherein many parties and many bodies share power and check one another. Keeping political actors committed to democracy requires dispersing power widely. But political leadership remains pivotal during the transition. The behavior of political elites can stabilize or undermine democratic government in a pluralist society. Especially where social cleavages are deep and easily converted into political cleavages, adversarial politics within the elite may deepen political fragmentation. By contrast, consensual elite behavior can counterbalance these cleavages and produce a consociational type of democracy.[25]

Popular perceptions of leadership in early 1990s Poland focused on adversarial relations. Yet the difficult task of putting together coalitions to form governments hinged far more on consensual, pragmatic politics. For example, the intricate multiparty governments that ruled Poland up to 1993 were a testament to the value of coalition building. The right, at least, was never able to replicate these alliances as successfully in subsequent years, but the legacy of those first years was significant in, first, stabilizing the system in its nascent phase and, second, holding out hope to leaders and parties that they could one day hold power as part of a broad coalition. By contrast, the paradoxical legacy left by Wałęsa entailed a consensus reached among most politicians and much of society that his adversarial politics had to be avoided at all costs in the future.

The Presidency

The constitutional role of the presidency in the Third Republic is circumscribed. The Little Constitution had called Poland "a presidential–parliamentary system of government," but the constitution of 1997 abandoned this concept, although ironically it may have reinforced it through the measures that were enacted. Article 10.1 of Chapter 1 declares that "the system of the Polish Republic is based on the separation and balance of legislative authority, executive authority, and judicial authority."[26] The presidency makes up just one part of the executive branch; the government, or Council of Ministers, makes up the other (Article 10.2)(Figure 6.1).

The Polish president is elected directly by the voters and needs to obtain a majority of votes cast. If no candidate obtains a majority on the initial ballot, a runoff is held two weeks later between the top two vote-getters from the first round. The winner of the runoff becomes president. The term of office is five years (as in France now), and a two-term limit (as in the United States) is in force. The constitution makes no provision for a vice president. In the event of the president's incapacity or death, the marshal of the Sejm (similar to Speaker of the House) assumes the office until new elections are held (in contrast to Russia, where the prime minister succeeds the president).

The 1997 constitution designates the president as head of state and commander-in-chief of the armed forces. Article 126.1 declares that the president is "the supreme representative of the Polish Republic and guarantees the continuity of state authority." Chapter 5 enumerates the specific powers of the office. They include the right to designate the prime

Figure 6.1 Structure of Poland's Political System

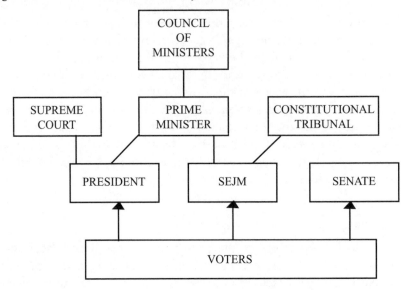

minister (though not cabinet ministers), initiate legislation, veto bills (which the Sejm can override by a three-fifths majority), refer bills to the Constitutional Court for a ruling as to their constitutionality, under certain conditions dissolve parliament and call early elections, call a referendum, oversee defense (indirectly through the defense ministry and through appointing the Chief of the General Staff of the armed forces) and national security matters (together with the National Security Council), declare martial law if the Sejm is unable to meet quickly, and represent the state in foreign relations. The president can issue decrees and administrative acts, the latter requiring the prime minister's countersignature.

The officeholder has a constitutionally recognized administration, called the presidential chancellery (Article 142.2b), to help carry out duties and provide advice. Having full-time advisors can reinforce a political convention that has emerged in the Third Republic that the president should not officially belong to a political party. This, of course, does not erase an incumbent's previous party membership and bonds of association and loyalty (for example, Kwaśniewski and the Alliance of the Democratic Left, the SLD) nor does it prevent the setting up of a presidential party (as Wałęsa did with the Nonparty Bloc for Reform, BBWR). But it does make the incumbent independent of a party apparatus when trying to draft policies.

An institutional modification enacted in April 2000 concerned campaign financing of presidential elections. Article 11, paragraph 2 of the 1997 constitution had adopted the principle of the transparency of political party finances; the 2000 law extended this principle to presidential candidates. An institutional prerequisite to achieve this objective was the establishment of electoral committees for candidates. One thousand voters had to support the setting up of such a committee before it would be registered with the State Electoral Commission. The electoral committee would then need 100,000 signatures to submit the name of a presidential candidate for the Commission's approval. Only then could it conduct an election campaign. A limit of 12 million *złoty* ($3 million) was placed on a candidate's campaign expenses, with registered political parties allowed to contribute markedly more than private donors. In this way future presidential elections were likely to involve contests between candidates from different political parties. The convention established by Wałęsa and Kwaśniewski that a president should be above party politics was likely to be undermined since an independent candidate with no party affiliation would in future be at a disadvantage in terms of campaign financing. One bizarre change made to the presidential election ordinance was dropping the threat of sanctions against an electoral committee that did not follow the rules on campaign revenues and expenses.[27] In that respect campaign financing was becoming as confusing in Poland as in the United States.

Despite the powers and functions assigned to the office, Poland's president does not really stand at the top of a semipresidential system of government, as his counterpart in France does. When political problems arise, it is parliament and the prime minister that have to address them; it is the prime minister and his government that formulate policy and direct the executive apparatus.

The Legislative Branch

Whereas the communist system had only one legislative body, the Sejm, the Third Republic—emulating both Western and interwar Polish models—established two legislative chambers. The lower house, the Sejm, consists of 460 deputies, and the upper house, the Senate, is made up of 100 members (as laid out in Chapter 4 of the constitution). On the few occasions when the two meet together in joint session, they are jointly referred to as the National Assembly.

Direct elections to both houses must be held no more than four years apart. Early elections can be held if (1) a government cannot be formed; (2) a vote of no-confidence in an existing government is passed (however, a "constructive" no-confidence vote, which is not mentioned in the constitution but has been used in Poland and resembles that found in Germany, would only mean that the present government should resign or reconstitute itself—not that elections should follow); or (3) the president decides, under certain conditions, to dissolve the legislature. As in most parliamentary systems, the prime minister, or head of the government, seeks whenever possible to influence the timing of elections so as to coincide with an upswing in his or her party's fortunes.

The Sejm enacts legislation through three readings of a bill, after which it is sent to the Senate for approval. The Senate can make changes to the bill or even vote it down, but the Sejm can have its way by enacting the bill again with a simple majority vote. The bill becomes law when the president signs it. The power of the Senate is limited, and calls for its elimination have increased. We should recall how it was little more than a bargaining chip at the 1989 roundtable used to forge a compromise between the political actors. But as in Canada, even a purposeless Senate has developed institutional interests that make its abolition near impossible.

The Sejm, then, is the locus of Polish politics. It is where the competitive party system plays out for most of the year (the Sejm recesses briefly in summer). The extended, often-heated debates on legislative bills give the lower house the constant visibility that the presidency does not possess. The most controversial issues of Polish politics after 1989 have been debated in extenso in the Sejm: enacting a new constitution, defining the official place of the Catholic Church in society, determining women's access to abortion, drafting legislation on the privatization of state-owned industry, clarifying the public role that former communist officials could play in a democratic Poland (through the so-called lustration law that required a "background check" of candidates for high office to determine whether they had worked secretly with the former security apparatus), reorganizing local government, ratifying membership in NATO, and, of course, the passing of government budgets.

If the Sejm has the power to make or break prime ministers and their cabinets, it also serves as the stage where the performance of a backbench parliamentarian is noticed, leading to her or his promotion to a ministerial post. Deftness as chair of a Sejm committee is also a path to political advancement. Each of the major parties has a parliamentary caucus that in great measure determines who will hold positions of leadership, and it looks to a deputy's Sejm record (attendance, speeches, bills proposed, voting) for guidance. One of the most overlooked factors in smoothing the process of democratic transition was the shift in power in 1989 within the communist party from its own bureaucratic apparatus (Politburo and Central Committee) to its representatives in the Sejm. The PZPR caucus was the forum that allowed future president Kwaśniewski and future prime minister Józef Oleksy to rise to prominence. It is no exaggeration to claim, then, that in addition to its all-important legislative function, the Sejm can be a kingmaker. On the other hand, if Poland was to develop into a two-party system under which parliamentary whips for each party reined in their members to vote in disciplined blocs, the Sejm's role would diminish. Much of the crucial preparatory work of politics would then take place in a different arena, that of the majority party caucus.

The composition and functioning of the Sejm has been affected by the prevailing electoral laws that determine how deputies are elected to parliament. The 1989 contract Sejm was chosen on the basis of an agreement between communists and the opposition about how they would split seats. Clearly this was a flawed system of representation and so for the October 1991 elections a new electoral ordinance was required. The method of electing a Senate of 100 was simple: In each of the 47 provinces voters would choose 2 senators by plurality; 3 each would be chosen in the densely populated metropolitan areas of Warsaw and Katowice. The complicated formula for the Sejm identified 37 constituencies that would provide anywhere from 7 to 17 members each, depending on their size, for a total of 391 seats.[28] Sixty-nine other deputies would be elected indirectly: Parties would provide national lists of candidates and any which received more than 7 percent of the national vote would be apportioned seats based on a mathematical formula.[29]

The 1991 electoral law was hypersensitive to the support accorded small parties. No minimum threshold was required to obtain Sejm representation. As a result, the ordinance institutionalized party fragmentation in the Sejm, thereby directly affecting government stability. Yet it should come as no surprise that such a law was adopted. At least initially, the architects of the new system wanted to ensure that no political force went unrepresented and that each could expect greater gains from participating in the electoral process than from pursuing any form of political activity outside of it. Groups quickly realized that they had more to lose from opting out of democracy than from staying in. If they fared poorly in one election, they could also hope that they would perform better the next time. The electoral law accomplished the desired effect in the first phase of the democratic transition and was scrapped as soon as it had outlived its usefulness.

President Wałęsa had opposed the 1991 law and had asked that minimal thresholds be set for Sejm representation, thereby limiting representation for minor parties.[30] Ironically, when a majority in the Sejm finally agreed with him that the proliferation of small parties in the legislature had become dysfunctional, it produced a victory for his opponents. The 1993 revision to the electoral law incorporated a formula that rewarded the major vote-getting parties by allocating them a disproportionate number of seats in parliament. By contrast, it deprived weak electoral parties—those obtaining less than 5 percent of the popular vote—of any representation in the Sejm; an exception was made for parties representing minorities, which were exempt from the 5 percent requirement.[31] In turn, electoral alliances that brought several parties together on the same ticket now had to reach an 8 percent threshold to obtain seats. In October 1993 only one electoral alliance—Wałęsa's nemesis, the SLD—cleared the 8 percent threshold needed to send deputies to parliament and went on to form a government. The socialist alliance's victory was not what Wałęsa had in mind when he suggested designing an electoral law that would produce strong parties.

The Prime Minister and the Cabinet

As in continental European states like France and Italy, the government in Poland is called the Council of Ministers. Article 146.1 of the constitution states that "The Council of Ministers carries out the domestic and foreign policies of the Polish Republic." Article 146.2 also gives it residual powers, that is, powers not assigned to other bodies. Another key function of the government, or cabinet, is drafting the annual budget. In theory, the government carries out all of these functions subject to the approval of the legislature. Article 157 introduces the doctrine of the collective responsibility of the government to the Sejm, but also of the individual responsibility of each minister to the Sejm for the functioning of his or her department. According to the 1997 constitution, there are areas of jurisdiction in which the government and the prime minister can issue decrees on their own and which do not need Sejm approval.

Officially the prime minister is nominated by the president (just as the British prime minister is appointed by the Queen). In practice, it is usually the leader of the largest party in parliament who enjoys the right of first refusal of the position. In Poland, however, it has happened that the candidate for prime minister was not drawn from the ranks of the strongest party. Thus, ironically, both the Solidarity camp in 1992 and the SLD in 1993 nominated the pivotal Polish Peasant Party (PSL) leader, Waldemar Pawlak, to be prime minister. Significantly, in each case he did not last long.

Although the new political system is just over a decade old, it appears that the office with the greatest power (if not prestige) is that of prime minister. President Wałęsa's power was neutralized between 1993 and 1995 when the parliament and prime minister were controlled by the opposing camp (the SLD). Similarly, President Kwaśniewski was potentially at a disadvantage when parliament and prime minister were in the hands of the opposing Solidarity Electoral Action (AWS) following the 1997 elections. The right's disunity and Kwaśniewski's personal popularity in great part made up for whatever institutional disadvantage he had.

Throughout the 1990s no single party or even electoral alliance was able to obtain an absolute majority of parliamentary seats, so prime ministerial turnover and cabinet reshuffles were commonplace (Table 6.1). Between 1989 and the end of 1997, ten persons were nominated to be prime minister and form a cabinet: Czesław Kiszczak as the last communist party nominee; Mazowiecki as the first noncommunist prime minister; the first economic neoliberal, Jan Krzysztof Bielecki; the first prime minister to be ousted by the president, Jan Olszewski; Pawlak, who could not form a government the first time he was asked; the country's first woman prime minister, Hanna Suchocka; Pawlak again, this time as successful nominee of the resurgent ex-communist coalition; Oleksy, the first prime minister who came from the ex-communist party (SLD) but also the first to fall victim to charges (never proved) that he worked with Soviet and Russian intelligence agents; Włodzimierz Cimoszewicz, the first to fail in a presidential bid (in 1990) but return as prime minister; and Jerzy Buzek, chosen to form a new government following the victory of Solidarity Electoral Action in the September 1997 Sejm elections. Only Buzek, who, ironically, was not even head of the AWS, managed to keep the job of prime minister for more than a year and a half; indeed he served out a full four-year term. With a comfortable majority coalition in the Sejm, his successor, the SLD's Miller, also had the chance to complete a full term. From an Italian variant of constantly changing governments

TABLE 6.1 Presidents and Prime Ministers in the Third Republic

Presidents	Took Office	Supported by	Left Office
Wojciech Jaruzelski	August 1989 [a]	PZPR	Dec. 1990
Lech Wałęsa	December 1990	Solidarity	Dec. 1995
Aleksander Kwaśniewski	December 1995	SLD	Dec. 2005 [b]

Prime Ministers	Took Office	Supported by	Left Office
Tadeusz Mazowiecki	August 1989	Solidarity, ZSL, SD	Dec. 1990
Jan Krzysztof Bielecki	December 1990	Solidarity, KLD, PC	Dec. 1991
Jan Olszewski	December 1991	PC, ZChN, PL, PSL	June 1992
Waldemar Pawlak	June 1992 [c]	PSL	July 1992
Hanna Suchocka	July 1992	UD, KLD, ZChN, etc.	May 1993 [d]
Waldemar Pawlak	September 1993	PSL, SLD	March 1995
Józef Oleksy	March 1995	SLD, PSL	Jan. 1996
Włodzimierz Cimoszewicz	February 1996	SLD, PSL	Oct. 1997
Jerzy Buzek	November 1997	AWS,UW; AWS	Oct. 2001
Leszek Miller	October 2001	SLD – UP, PSL	—

[a] Jaruzelski was elected indirectly, by the National Assembly.

[b] Scheduled date for leaving office.

[c] Pawlak was nominated as prime minister but could not form a government.

[d] Suchocka lost a vote of confidence in May but remained in office until September.

and prime ministers, Poland seemed to be heading for a more stable German or French system of longer-serving cabinets.

In any case it is unclear whether the turnover of governments in the first years of the Third Republic produced real political instability. The complex six- and seven-party coalition governments of the early 1990s with their carousels of incoming and outgoing ministers had a logic of their own, primarily that of loyalty to one's own political camp. The Sejm's insistence on the accountability of governments to it also promoted responsive government. It could force changes in prime ministers and their cabinets when they were out of touch with the political consensus in the Sejm. Following the 1993 electoral law that awarded parties winning the most votes a disproportionately large number of parliamentary seats, governments had a stronger support base in parliament and so fell less often even if they were now less representative of voters' preferences.

Conflict and Cooperation in a
Hybrid Parliamentary–Presidential System

Examining the formal rules does not give us a true picture of how a political system works. To understand how Poland's executive and legislative institutions have functioned, we need to look at how presidents, prime ministers, governing coalition partners, and parliamentary parties have interacted with one another.

At the outset it should be said that it is a tribute to Polish democracy that the balance of power between the executive and legislative branches of government is no longer a controversial issue. But it took years of political uncertainty, frustration, and even crisis before this most fundamental of institutional issues to a democracy was resolved. Ironically, it was the same leader who had engineered the democratic breakthrough who became one of its most destabilizing figures. In early 1990s Poland the strong personality and messianic drive of President Wałęsa had become a cause for alarm about unchecked executive power. Pundits attributed to Wałęsa a desire to establish a dictatorship of the proletariat that the communists had failed to do—in this case the ruling proletariat was not be the working class as a whole but rather a single former shipyard electrician.[32]

Of course there was more to the institutional disequilibrium than the president's behavior. A sequence of largely ineffectual and unstable government coalitions, together with bickering among the many parties represented in the Sejm and the fact that it was virtually in continuous session, aggravated the problem of executive–legislative relations. But when politics are characterized by instability, inevitably attention focuses on the executive leader. Wałęsa, who had become president in December 1990 after direct elections, liked to refer to the interwar experience. The chaos and paralysis that a powerful legislature had engendered then had convinced Piłsudski that a strong executive was a prerequisite of political efficacy and stability; that was why he carried out the 1926 coup. There is no evidence that Wałęsa was plotting a coup to wrest power from the legislature in the early 1990s, but he clearly favored a strong presidency and was contemptuous of parliamentary government. Accordingly, during his five-year term he undermined the authority of a succession of prime ministers, in the process heightening the very political instability he condemned.

In May 1992 Wałęsa described the three-cornered conflict involving the Sejm, the government, and himself as a "Bermuda triangle." If Poland evolved into a mixed presidential–parliamentary system, it owed much to this "war at the top" (as Wałęsa also referred to it).[33] The Little Constitution institutionalized this imperfect system, and one writer summed up conflict-ing interpretations of that act this way: "Some articles in the Polish press denounced the document as creating a 'Sejmocracy,' while others com-plained that it gives the president too much power." Probably the most tren-chant comment about the enactment of the Little Constitution came from a Sejm member who stated: "This bill's greatest advantage is that it can be passed at all."[34]

The reality was, then, that in the first half of the 1990s the personal re-lationships between president and prime ministers were crucial to deter-mining institutional stability. Wałęsa originally selected Mazowiecki as prime minister in 1989 because he saw him as less of a threat to Wałęsa himself than the alternative choices. Mazowiecki soon proved to be inde-pendent-minded and decided to run for president against Wałęsa, thereby deepening the rift within Solidarity ranks. Wałęsa trumpeted his victory in presidential elections in December 1990 as a direct mandate to govern from the people. By contrast, the Solidarity government became a lame duck, an offspring after all of the tainted contract Sejm.

To replace the defeated Mazowiecki as prime minister, Wałęsa settled on Jan Krzysztof Bielecki, a leader of the free market Liberal Democratic Congress (KLD). But the Sejm decided to hold elections in October 1991, and the KLD's poor showing led to the appointment of former Solidarity lawyer Jan Olszewski as prime minister. He headed a center–right coalition government in the fragmented 29-party Sejm. Ol-szewski was determined to increase the power of the prime minister, and his confrontations with the president brought Poland's democracy to the brink of collapse. For starters, Olszewski replaced Wałęsa's appointee as defense minister even though the still-operative though much-amended 1952 constitution gave the president broad authority over security and defense policies. The showdown between Olszewski's defense ministry and Wałęsa's national security bureau represented more than a clash of personalities; it brought into question the fundamental question of execu-tive–legislative relations and who was responsible for what policy.

In February 1992, frustrated by what he saw as an obstructionist parlia-ment and a meddling president, Olszewski asked the Sejm for emergency decree powers. The Sejm did not provide them, but his defense minister carried out a purge of senior military officers supposedly compromised by previous service to the communist regime. Tension between prime minis-ter and president was heightened, and charges and countercharges of coup plotting brought unprecedented drama to Third Republic politics. As if this were not enough, in the spring of 1992 several sealed envelopes were presented to Wałęsa by Olszewski's interior minister. They contained the names of some sixty persons who, it was alleged, had been collaborators and agents of the communist regime. The "revelations" contained in these documents included copies of Wałęsa's purported loyalty pledges to the communist secret police after the December 1970 political unrest. Olszewski was clearly behind the disclosure of secret police dossiers on prominent officials, though he may have been unaware that some files contained forged documents. In any case, the disclosure of confidential files on political leaders was a strategy to sweep away established political actors.

The inability of prime minister and president to achieve any type of modus vivendi, Olszewski's effort to obtain decree powers, a tug-of-war over who was in charge of the armed forces, charges of a coup attempt, and efforts to embarrass Wałęsa with the collaboration issue, all led to Olszewski's removal in June 1992. An intriguing interpretation of these intriguing events is that the dismissal of Poland's most anti-communist prime minister was itself the result of a conspiracy by the political elites of the former communist regime.[35]

Wałęsa again had difficulty in getting the Sejm to approve his choice of successor to Olszewski. He threatened "extraordinary measures" that would likely have involved the dissolution of parliament and the holding of new elections. Yet, paradoxically, the choice of Waldemar Pawlak, leader of the PSL (a party whose origins, we recall, lay in the communist-era ZSL), represented an attempt by Wałęsa to build bridges between the communist and Solidarity blocs. With the toppling of the virulently anti-communist Olszewski government, it appeared that the time was right to pressure the rival blocs to learn to cooperate. Pawlak's failure to secure the support of post-Solidarity groups ranging from peasants to liberals doomed his efforts at forming a government. This was to be as close as his party was to come to forging a coalition with the post-Solidarity camp; in 1993 and again in 2001 the PSL joined the SLD to form coalition governments. As for Wałęsa, his bridge-building exercise—admittedly on his own idiosyncratic terms—proved premature. Seven of the parties that had refused to cooperate with Pawlak quickly joined a new post-Solidarity coalition; Hanna Suchocka of the Democratic Union (UD) received parliamentary approval for her government one day after Pawlak's resignation.

Suchocka and the UD inevitably became the targets of charges of "recommunization" leveled by right-wing groups, though Wałęsa refrained from joining in. Indeed, after stormy relations between the president and three preceding prime ministers, the relationship between Wałęsa and Suchocka became a model of coexistence. Pundits reported that Poland's first woman prime minister brought elegance, tact, and articulateness to political leadership—qualities all missing in the president. The complementarity of the two leaders ended only in September 1993, when Suchocka's party suffered electoral defeat. It was during her term that the Little Constitution, regulating the relationship between president and prime minister, was adopted.

In 1993 the SLD swept to power in parliamentary elections and Wałęsa had little choice but to accept the SLD–PSL coalition's successive candidates for prime minister. Their first selection was PSL head Pawlak, who was replaced less than two years later by an SdRP leader, Józef Oleksy, then marshal of the Sejm. SdRP chief Kwaśniewski agreed to his deputy's selection as prime minister, preferring to wait and run for the presidency in 1995.

Wałęsa believed that forcing the ex-communists to govern directly would pay political dividends: They would become entrapped in a political morass during the crucial months before his reelection bid. Thus he taunted Oleksy for planning to travel to Moscow (as U.S. President Clinton did as well) to attend celebrations commemorating the fiftieth anniversary of the Allies' victory in Europe during World War II. Wałęsa said that he would remain at home on this important occasion for Poles. He added that the constitution gave the president the responsibility for directing foreign policy and therefore Oleksy could not represent the Polish state during his Moscow visit. His gamble in confirming a former communist as prime minister and then limiting his autonomy backfired, however. The SLD skillfully exploited its new power and visibility and was able to elect its leader to the presidency in place of Wałęsa, who had finally outsmarted himself.

With the presidency and prime ministership in the hands of the ex-communists, the road was clear to enacting a new constitution in 1997. The clear rules governing relations between the two executive branches thus established reduced the likelihood of personality conflicts between a president and his prime minister ever again having the destabilizing ramifications that they had earlier. In any case, Kwaśniewski's style was consensual, not conflictual, which earned him widespread popularity and reelection in 2000. In a March 2000 opinion poll of respondents' views of various institutions, Kwaśniewski's presidency received a considerably higher positive evaluation (67 percent) than the government and parlia-

TABLE 6.2 Public Opinion on Selected Institutions in Poland, March 2000 (in percent)

Institution	Positive Evaluation	Negative Evaluation	Hard to Say
Firefighters	85	5	9
State radio	82	6	12
State television	76	13	12
Postal service	73	16	12
President	67	18	15
National sports lottery	57	9	34
Roman Catholic Church	57	26	18
Local government	41	37	22
Ombudsperson	41	19	41
Tax agency	35	33	33
State security agency	34	17	49
Police	29	57	13
Courts	20	57	23
Senate	18	55	28
Solidarity trade union	16	57	27
National Trade Union Accord	15	42	43
Public health service	14	78	8
Parliament	13	65	22
Government	13	68	19
National football team	10	60	30

Source: Pracownia Badań Społecznych, "Instytucje i urzędy w Polsce, czerwiec 2000"; see http://www.pbssopot.com.pl/wyniki_instytucje062000.html.

ment (13 percent each), and even enjoyed a comfortable margin over the Catholic Church (57 percent)(Table 6.2). Even as the popularity of the SLD-led government dropped at the start of 2002, as it confronted serious economic difficulties, Kwaśniewski's held firm.

A test of how the two offices would work together came in 1997 when a Solidarity coalition returned to power in the Sejm. But relations between Kwaśniewski and prime minister Buzek were never acrimonious over the next four years. Nor did the president find the Miller-led SLD–UP–PSL government formed after the 2001 elections uncongenial. Ultimately, though, rules now shape political processes more than personalities.

The Judicial Branch

A branch of government in as much disuse and disrepute in the communist period as parliament was the judiciary. Its function had been to apply "class law," that is, to favor (in an affirmative action type of way) working people rather than hand down impartial judgments. Working people inevitably became synonymous with the PZPR, the party of workers, and so the judicial branch served the interests of the *nomenklatura* and not of society. Legal experts involved in the transition to democracy in Eastern Europe stressed that regime change would be measured by the degree to which there was a return to the rule of law and the construction of a *Rechtsstaat*, or a state based on laws. As with other branches of government, judicial change involved preparatory work that took the first half of the 1990s to complete.

Chapter 8 of the 1997 constitution identifies the system of courts and tribunals as a separate branch of authority independent of the others. The judicial system is made up of the Supreme Court, general courts, administrative courts (including the Supreme Administrative Court), and military courts. Supreme Court judges are appointed by the president on the advice of the National Judicial Council. They have life terms, cannot be removed, are dependent on no one, and cannot belong to a political party or trade union. An additional body is the Constitutional Tribunal, which, as in France or Germany, rules on the constitutionality and offers binding interpretations of laws, delimits the jurisdiction of different branches of government, and undertakes other kinds of judicial review. The Constitutional Tribunal consists of fifteen judges elected by the Sejm for one term lasting nine years. In its first decade in existence it saw its mission as laying the foundation for a democratic law-based state and, for the most part, succeeded in gaining widespread credibility.

Another important judicial body is the Tribunal of State, to which leaders of national institutions—the president and the prime minister, individual ministers, heads of the National Bank, members of the National Radio and Television Council, the head of the Chief Inspectorate (or NIK, which inspects and audits the work of the state administration and other state institutions), and the head of the armed forces—must answer for the constitutionality of their acts. During the 1990s both the Supreme Court and the Constitutional Tribunal issued rulings that upset both the executive branch of government and lawmakers. For example, in 1997 the Constitutional Tribunal concluded that the previous year's law easing restrictions on abortion did not fully comply with Poland's constitutional framework. The ruling could only be overridden by a two-thirds majority in the Sejm, but the new conservative AWS government preferred not to pursue the matter.

Poland's Third Republic also has a Civil Rights Ombudsperson. The official is chosen by the Sejm for a five-year term and is responsible for determining whether citizens' rights and freedoms are promoted or infringed upon by state bodies. The first three ombudspersons (one was a woman) were legal scholars who won much praise for their work. About 50,000 letters from citizens per year were received by the office. The majority dealt with issues such as housing, pensions, taxes, and workers' rights. The 1997 constitution also established an Ombudsperson for Children's Rights. In these ways the new judicial system has dramatized the break with the previous one by providing a panoply of institutional mechanisms for protecting civil rights.

Other Public Institutions

We have been focusing mostly on the institutions of the presidency and the legislature, but many other government institutions were overhauled in the early 1990s. Some were eliminated altogether and replaced by new structures. Functional ministries such as defense, foreign affairs, and internal affairs were revamped and restaffed. A completely new State Security Agency (UOP) was set up to replace the communist security apparatus. Unfortunately it soon found itself in the middle of a political controversy and its impartiality came under attack. In 1995 and 1996 several UOP officials supported the claim of the internal affairs minister that then Prime Minister Oleksy had worked for Soviet intelligence. The charges were not proved and the security apparatus was condemned for playing dirty politics.

Other ancillary institutions inherited from the communist regime were, sometimes surprisingly, kept largely intact, even if they were reorganized. These included the Central Office of Planning, the Central Office of Statistics, the National Bank, the Main Control Office, and the Office of the Council of Ministers.

Over the course of the 1990s regional and local government was completely restructured and subnational authorities were granted new responsibilities and revenue bases. The most comprehensive legislative act in this area came in 1999 and separated territorial administration into provincial (*wojewódz two*), county (*powiat*), and village (*gmina*) levels. The financial autonomy of provinces was enhanced, but most of the revenue of districts and villages came from allocations out of the central government budget. Most importantly, the internal administrative boundaries of Poland were drastically redrawn. The forty-nine provincial authorities were compressed into sixteen, marking a return to historic regional names that had disappeared during the late communist period. Power in the provinces rested in a provincial self-government headed by the leader of the most influential party in the province. A government-appointed administrative prefect (*wojewoda*) was to be responsible for ensuring the legality of the self-government's work and public safety in the province. Predictably the selection of prefects became a politicized contest between the major parties in parliament.

In addition, 308 rural counties and 65 towns having the powers of counties were established. Alongside reform of territorial administration, public services (such as health care) were reorganized on a corresponding territorial principle. The rationale for administrative restructuring was that many European states had been decentralizing power for many years. Yet it was not clear that regional and local government reform really transferred significant power from the center. These changes to the political and administrative structures were intended to accelerate the processes of democratization, decentralization, and de-etatization.

One other body established by the Sejm that had an impact on political life in the formative years of the Third Republic was the Commission on Constitutional Responsibility. Its purview included looking at charges that former communist leaders had acted unconstitutionally. Thus in 1993 it considered whether legal proceedings should be launched against Jaruzelski and Kiszczak for having destroyed public documents—minutes of Politburo meetings held between 1982 and 1989. Jaruzelski contended that the documents had to be destroyed because they recorded sensitive negotiations between communists and church and opposition figures who could otherwise be harmed by revelation of their bargaining positions. By a majority the commission recommended that the National Assembly drop legal proceedings against Jaruzelski and Kiszczak. Showing its evenhandedness, the commission also determined that charges of economic wrongdoing by members of Suchocka's Solidarity-based government were unfounded. Because this commission was chaired by a former communist party member, its claim that early in the life of the Third Republic it was judging both communists and noncommunists impartially may have contributed to the legitimacy of both new public institutions and the overhauled communist party. In addition, it put to rest the notion that a special tribunal should be set up to prosecute former high-ranking communist officials.

Economic Structures

Designing the economic institutions of a free economy was as great a challenge as crafting a political democracy. What institutions were needed in Poland depended on what general model of an economic system was chosen. There were a number of realistic alternatives open to a country emerging from communist rule.[36] One typology developed to apply to postcommand economies is that proposed by Oxford professor John Gray.[37] Let us consider his four Western and three non-Western models.

The first Western model is the German social-market economy, often perceived in Eastern Europe as the postwar success story par excellence. The principal theoretical assumption distinguishing this model is that the institutions of the free market are not the inexorable product of spontaneous economic activity but, rather, the result of institutional design and constitutional construction—very much as North argued. Key ideas flowing from this assumption are, following Gray:

- Market freedoms are not guaranteed by a policy of nonintervention, or laissez-faire; they are created and protected by a competition policy that requires the constant monitoring, and recurrent reform, of the legal framework within which market exchange occurs.
- Market institutions are justified not by their embodiment of any supposed structure of fundamental rights, but by their contribution to individual and collective well-being. They are therefore perpetually open to revision and reform by reference to this undergirding process.
- Market institutions are not free-standing, but come embedded in other institutions, including those in which government acts to protect citizens from forms of insecurity that market institutions by themselves may create, or are powerless to prevent.[38]

Given the German influence in Central Europe over the centuries and the recent East European experience of etatism linked to communist rule, the German social-market model seemed potentially to be the most attractive option for East European states after 1989.

A second model is that of Swedish egalitarian social democracy. In its early phase, up to 1932, when the Social Democrats came to power, Sweden was characterized by limited government of a classical liberal kind. After 1932 and the expansion of welfarism, Gray stresses, "even at its most interventionist, Sweden was never as corporatist as the UK in the seventies; and for most of its recent history it has been more thoroughly capitalist in its productive institutions than most other Western countries."[39] The egalitarian model may have been well adapted to an ethnically and culturally homogeneous society that had never experienced full feudalism, in all of these respects different from Eastern Europe. In addition, the high costs of welfarism made this option less viable in a capital-starved state like Poland.

The problem with the third model identified by Gray—Anglo-American capitalism—is that because it "is the result of a long, unplanned evolutionary development in which the common law played a large part, it is not readily exportable—especially to countries with very different cultural, legal, and political traditions."[40] The unplanned emergence of industrial capitalism in England followed centuries of agrarian capitalism. In turn the large corporation at the heart of modern American capitalism is both difficult to reproduce elsewhere and possibly at odds with cultures in which municipal and cooperative sectors have flourished in the past. Anglo-American capitalism prospered under conditions of limited government, something Eastern Europe had little experience with.

One other Western model noted by Gray is the Chilean one of capitalist development under authoritarian dictatorship. This model was unsuitable not only because of the natural revulsion that many East European societies felt for renewed dictatorship but by the fact that it was built on a preexisting legal infrastructure of market institutions—precisely what East European states needed to construct.

For Gray, the three non-Western models have less applicability to the specific conditions in which Eastern Europe finds itself. The East Asian model posits strategic governmental intervention in the economy. In Japan, the Ministry of Trade and Industry played a pivotal role in research and development strategy; in Taiwan, tariffs and subsidies promoted industrial development; in South Korea, banks were key instruments of government policy; in Singapore and Malaysia, governments played interventionist roles in many different ways. The East Asian model, then, requires the state to create successful market institutions and to remain engaged in regulating capitalist development, something to which the right-leaning Polish governments of the early transition period were opposed.

The Chinese model is based on even greater degrees of interventionism and authoritarianism. For Gray, in China "market institutions are most likely to be stable and successful if they do not replicate those of the West, but are instead molded so as to reflect the distinctive values and surviving traditions of native cultures."[41] By contrast, Poland desperately wanted to copy the Western institutions.

Finally, Gray identifies Atatürkist Turkey as a much-neglected non-Western model. Less for reasons of its distinctive economic policy than because of the efforts made by an authoritarian state to modernize and secularize society and to create the legal individual, this model is applicable only to the less-developed regions of the post-communist world.

This typology points out that models of economic development depend on what role the state plays. Should it be expansive, regulatory, or nominal? On the one hand it is clear that enhanced state capacity is a requirement for effective economic policy and "reconstructing the state is an amorphous and frustrating task, a project of decades if not generations." On the other, "transforming the state from problem to solution" has been the key challenge facing a nation like Poland that is seeking to promote economic development.[42]

New Institutions

A set of new public economic institutions was created to speed up the transition from a state-managed economy to a free market one. Many different laws had to be enacted to change the legal structure shaping economic activity. These included revision of the civil code, the laws establishing a new personal income tax and corporate income tax, a new employment law, the law on state enterprises, the securities market and mutual funds act, the law on financial restructuring of enterprises and banks, the law on pension revalorization, various privatization bills, a customs law, a foreign investment law, anti-monopoly legislation, and legislation on land use.[43]

Some of the innovative bodies set up included an Economic (as well as Social) Committee of the Council of Ministers (that is, government advisory bodies), the Ministry of Ownership Transformation (or Privatization), the Ministry of Foreign Economic Cooperation, and the Antimonopoly Office. Early in the transition the Warsaw Stock Exchange resumed trading, half a century after it had been closed by the outbreak of World War II. Its first home, the former PZPR Central Committee building in Warsaw, symbolized like nothing else the drama of the economic transition. Just as important in streamlining the economic system was elimination of institutions when they were not needed. A good example here was the scrapping of the privatization ministry in 1996 to reflect the fact that the state was no longer central to the growth of market relations.

A 1990 law on privatization had initially set up the privatization ministry to take charge of the sell-off of public companies to private buyers. Headed twice by Janusz Lewandowski, it also managed the distribution of free shares in companies to the public. In time, the argument that such a program was impractical led to a shift in policy toward "pre-privatization restructuring," aimed at making state enterprises more attractive to purchasers in the medium term. The ministry's program of "quick privatization" of small- and medium-sized firms, launched in July 1991, was its major success.

In 1992 the State Agency for Foreign Investment (PAIZ) was established to stimulate investment in Poland by bringing together potential Western investors with Polish enterprises that were on the selling block. Financial backing for the agency's operations was provided by the West, specifically by the European Union's PHARE program—initially designed to provide technical assistance but by 1994 also involved in direct investment projects. Foreign investment began to flood into Poland in the later 1990s, largely due to the Polish economy's strong growth. But PAIZ was, like the privatization ministry, an important institution that kickstarted the transformation in a less auspicious period.

One other institutional arrangement dating from the early 1990s that was crucial to the success of economic transformation was the Enterprise Pact. Concluded in 1992 after a summer of industrial unrest, it brought together Polish business confederations, the trade union sector, and the government within a set of procedures designed to secure both labor peace for the country and greater policy input for business and labor. Many privatized enterprises were required to set aside up to 20 percent of their shares for their workforce: Up to 10 percent was to be given outright to employees, and another 10 percent was available for purchase by them at half their market value. In this way the pact drew both the Solidarity and post-communist trade union structures into the new market system and provided them with a platform for articulating their views through membership of management boards. Paradoxically, the former communist-allied trade union OPZZ was more supportive of the Enterprise Pact than Solidarity. It also tended to push wage claims less often than did the Solidarity union. In 1994 the pact was replaced by a new body, the Tripartite Council, discussed in the previous chapter.

The Economic Infrastructure and Privatization

Privatization was the centerpiece of a strategy aimed at creating a market economy in Poland. But what does privatization really mean? First and foremost it is about the transfer of ownership from the public to the private sector, that is, a shift from one type of economic system to another. According to United Nations economist Jozef van Brabant, private ownership is neither an end nor even a means in itself: "The key variable in bolstering economic efficiency in the PETs [planned economies in transition] through some form of privatization in a reliable, predictable, and sustainable manner is not ownership *per se*, but rather the market structures through which the assets will henceforth be allocated; ensuring that proper market structures come about is, therefore, a critical task."[44]

There are various objectives to privatizing a state economy. Purely economic goals include improving economic efficiency, separating the role of government as producer from its other functions, strengthening a shareholding culture with private monitoring of enterprise performance, slashing the government's budget deficit by the sell-off of loss-producing enterprises, developing financial markets, promoting competition, and eliminating inflation-producing monetary "overhang," that is, the situation of too much money chasing after too few goods.[45] Three important political goals of privatization are expanding liberties by restricting the role of government in the economy primarily to the enforcement of property rights; pursuing private property rights, thus supporting social stability and democratic consolidation; and getting rid of politically shaped management structures and, conversely, generating a "break-through of competent managers."[46]

Economists agree that privatization involves a fundamental change in the ownership structure. The state can divest itself of ownership through a profit-oriented *custodian model*. This entails setting up holding institutions run by state officials that assume custody of public assets. Variously referred to as corporatization and commercialization, this model proposes the creation of large-scale investment funds that gradually transfer ownership to the private sector. This model was adopted in Poland, and it met with limited success because investment fund management turned out to be a difficult structure to bring to life.

As outlined in the April 1993 mass privatization bill, management of 200 selected state-owned enterprises was to be handed over to twenty national investment funds that, in turn, would distribute shares to the population. Citizens could activate their shares by paying a registration fee (about $20). After that share prices would be listed on the Warsaw Stock Exchange and shares would be traded over the counter. The success of the investment funds depended on the skills of the fund managers, whose job was to convert the enterprises in their portfolios into profitable investments. A state selection committee was set up to appoint fund managers, and, surprisingly, even post-communist groups agreed that the expertise of foreign fund managers and management consultants was highly desirable. But it was some time before the national investment fund program got off the ground.

Other forms of privatization were also tried out in Poland. An *institutional-ownership model* gives control of state enterprises to financial institutions such as banks, insurance companies, and retirement plans. These institutions are driven by the profit motive and initially serve as proprietary agents of state enterprises. Under the *labor-management model*, capital assets are transferred to employees. The corruption-prone *political-market model* transfers the majority of assets to communist officials. Sometimes referred to as *spontaneous privatization*, the *nomenklatura* begins to capture all property rights to the assets under their control, and retains those rights even when out of office. As its name implies, the *foreign-agent variant* allows for extensive ownership by financial interests from outside the country. The *universal-market model*, in which all citizens with adequate funds can buy shares of state enterprises being sold off, is another method that was used in the early years of economic transformation.[47] The Buzek government reintroduced this model in a much revised form when it adopted the mass enfranchisement program. This allowed up to 7 percent of stocks in privatized companies to be distributed to average Poles.

But the most common forms of privatization in Poland, as elsewhere, have involved the *sale of state-owned assets*: through capital-market operations (such as a stock market); through a public offering of a block of shares at fixed prices; through auction markets, in which assets are sold as a unit to a buyer; through worker and management buyouts; and through debt equity swaps with banks, creditors, and foreign companies.[48]

Was privatization, then, successfully carried out? A milestone was reached in 1993 when private companies accounted for just over 50 percent of the gross domestic product and slightly more of overall employment. The most successful program proved to be the "small privatization" of approximately 125,000 retail outlets and small businesses operating as part of the state sector in 1989. The least successful aspect of privatization was, inevitably, selling off the juggernaut state enterprises. Five years into the transition, only one-quarter of the 8,500 large state enterprises had been privatized. By contrast, over 95 percent of the approximately 2,000 large companies in existence in 1994 were new firms started up with foreign capital, or with foreign capital and a Polish partner.

Ironically, then, the huge economic structures set up by the former communist command economy were of little value in a free market economy. Conversely, the large corporations that help support a capitalist system had to be created from scratch. To the extent that privatization engendered a new economic culture and institutions, it could provide conditions stimulating the development of corporate structures. But the communist economic legacy, especially in the industrial sector, could not be legislated away with privatization decrees. It will only disappear as efficiency-oriented institutions take hold and undermine the legacy.

This chapter has described how a wide variety of institutions have shaped Poland's political and economic life after 1989. They have anchored a system that has engineered a social transformation of massive proportions—indeed one that some observers say is unprecedented in its suddenness and scope. Rules and institutions have generated outcomes that actors and the acted upon could not by themselves produce. Political and economic structures are both more robust *and* supple today than when the transition began in Poland. They are still not as powerful and "taken-for-granted" as those in, say, Germany, which are over fifty years old, not to speak of the United States or Britain. What is important is that for a country that spent four decades in the amorphous institutional fog of a communist system, institutions now matter.

7

—∽∾∿—

Policy Challenges
Shaping Poland's Future

As remarkable as the Polish road to democracy has been, the journey is not complete. Many challenges remain, some as fundamental as what Poland's future identity is to be. If the post–Cold War international environment has largely served as a facilitator of democratic consolidation, it has also placed constraints on the ability of a nation to shape its own future. No clearer example of this exists than the European Union's conditions for admitting new members. Poland's legal, economic, and social infrastructures are being transformed to conform to EU standards, but is the country's identity being remade in the process? A related question is how Poland is to deal with economic inequalities that have grown under capitalism. Its recent past, as a communist welfare state, shaped a paternalist culture that has not disappeared. But its plausible future, as a productive link in the global economy, requires the nation to confront a harsh reality of private-sector utilitarianism and governmental noninvolvement. What choices will Polish leaders make over the next few years?

Poland's state and society are products of domestic as well as international conditions. A different challenge facing lawmakers is to construct more effective and transparent institutions. We have examined the functioning of key political institutions like the presidency and parliament, but others in need of reform include public and local administration, the educational system, and the judiciary. Some of these sectors have been plagued by shady or corrupt practices. The effort to hold them more accountable by making their dealings transparent to the interested publics is a major project, which can affect Poland's credibility both at home and abroad.

Finally, Poland is confronting the challenge of building a secular state for a Catholic nation. Catholicism has defined the Polish nation for over a thousand years, including long periods in which no Polish state existed. How can Poland today construct institutions and make policy that reflect this heritage and incorporate its values, and yet meet the expectations of the majority of citizens, who—whether or not they attend mass regularly—want a secular state?

European or Polish?
The European Union, NATO, and Neighbors

Many nations in Europe are concerned with losing their national identity as the European Union pushes forward with a plan for greater political and cultural integration. In the 1990s the goals of developing a European passport, a European currency, and a European anthem were attained. The idea of a set of core European values and the notion of a transnational European identity have been vigorously promoted. Admittedly, voters in smaller European states like Denmark and Ireland were squeamish about having their sense of nationhood overwhelmed by these processes. In 2000 Danes voted against joining the European currency union and the following year the Irish rejected the Nice agreement that laid the groundwork for adding new members to the EU. In Britain, Sweden, and even France, more and more people expressed fears about the vision of a political union of Europe sketched by German Chancellor Gerhard Schroeder in 2001. Many Euroskeptics wondered whether this vision was to serve as a Trojan horse for the emerging dominance of Germany within Europe.

In turn, joining NATO brought new responsibilities as well as security advantages to former communist countries such as Poland. Among the dilemmas that troubled the new NATO members was the need to ensure civilian control over the military, to spend more on defense, to purchase state-of-the-art weapons systems, and to provide political and logistical support for American-led military initiatives such as the bombing of Serbia in 1999 and the war on terrorism in 2001 to be waged jointly under the Treaty's Article 5.

Furthermore, the regional politics of Central Europe were not as harmonious as might be expected given continentwide processes of unification. To the east of Poland lay chaos and instability. Belarus and Ukraine had encountered even greater problems in their transitions to democracy and the free market than had Russia. Poland's southern neighbors, the

Czech and Slovak Republics, had been more successful and were aspiring to EU membership too. But prospects for regional cooperation were paradoxically undermined as all EU aspirants looked westward for direction. Finally, there was Putin's Russia casting a shadow over the entire region. Directly or indirectly, Russia's politics continued to influence developments in Eastern Europe. Let us look in turn at how these institutional and national actors will shape Poland's future.

The European Union

One study of Poland's debate on Europe begins with the controversial assertion that "For Poland integration with the European Union means more that just adopting a certain direction in foreign policy. It represents a choice of civilization."[1] In the run-up to the 2001 parliamentary election, SLD leader Miller expressed confidence that he would be at the head of a government that would preside over the most momentous event in the country's politics since Mieszko converted to Christianity in 966: Poland's accession to the European Union. Clearly, from the Polish perspective joining the EU would be as historic as breaking away from the Soviet bloc.[2]

When Poland's communist system toppled in 1989, political optimists predicted that the country would be a member of the EU before the 1990s were out. Few anticipated how complicated the process of accession would be and how it was going to involve more than political considerations; goodwill alone would not suffice. As part of the process of integration into European political structures, Poland joined the Council of Europe in November 1991 and signed the European Convention on Human Rights and Fundamental Freedoms that came into effect in January 1993. The Convention provides recourse to the Council of Europe's legally binding mediation whenever violations of civil rights are alleged. Successive Polish governments have made clear their willingness to be bound by the decisions of the Council and also of the European Court of Justice.

After receiving associate membership status in the EU in 1993, Poland formally applied for full membership in April 1994. During the mid-1990s the twelve EU members adopted a wait-and-see attitude to the rapid changes taking place in Eastern Europe. In January 1995, Austria, Finland, and Sweden were admitted under a fast-track process and the enlarged EU then hesitated about whether to expand further quickly. In March 1998 it finally opened accession negotiations with Poland and

TABLE 7.1 Public Opinion on Advantages for Particular Social Groups from Poland's Integration into the European Union, May 1998 (in percent)

Group	Will Gain	Will Lose	No Change	Hard to Say
Foreign business people	72	5	9	14
Educated people	67	6	13	14
Polish business people	64	14	9	13
Political elites	61	9	14	16
Workers	23	40	18	19
Conmen and swindlers	41	22	16	21
Ex-communist *nomenklatura*	23	22	25	30
Unemployed	33	27	21	19
Clergy	18	18	38	26
Peasants	16	54	12	18

Source: Maria Gerszewska and Jacek Kucharczyk, "Oczekiwania Polaków wobec negocjacji z Unią Europejską," in Lena Kolarska-Bobińska (ed.), *Polska Eurodebata.* Warsaw: Instytut Spraw Publicznych, 1999, p. 36, Table 7.

four other Central European candidates. The Treaty on the European Union signed in Nice in December 2000 opened the road for expansion, but the Irish referendum result rejecting the terms of the treaty made it unclear how quickly expansion would occur.

The issues identified by Poles as most important in negotiating with the EU differed from those that the European Commission considered most important. The topic identified by the greatest proportion of Polish respondents in 1998 was the future of Poland's farming sector (66 percent), followed by Poles' right to work in EU states (54 percent) and their right to reside in EU states (37 percent). The buying of real estate in Poland by foreigners ranked much lower (10 percent),[3] even though the Miller government had to make a concession to its coalition partner, the PSL, to seek restrictions on land sales to foreigners in negotiations with the EU. This was not surprising given considerable agreement among survey respondents that foreign businessmen would do best by Poland's integration into the EU and Polish farmers would do worst (Table 7.1). A longitudinal study of attitudes revealed that Polish respondents increasingly believed that existing EU states would gain more from expansion (from 41 percent in 1993 to 54 percent in 2001) than Poland (5 and 6 percent, respectively); in both these years one-quarter thought that both sides would gain equally.[4]

Throughout Central Europe hopes for EU entry raised by the start of formal negotiations were set back when European Commission President Romano Prodi presented progress reports on the candidates in October 1999. They had recorded little improvement, he said, since the Commission had issued initial evaluations in 1997 (which had been very encouraging for Poland). He announced that from now on the Commission would monitor applicants' claims about progress more closely, implying less trust in their self-reporting. Prodi also emphasized that the accession timetable would be based on merit rather than politics. Although Poland claimed it had done much to adapt its laws and structures to EU criteria, the 1999 Commission report contended that it had "not progressed significantly." Moreover it observed "a notable lack of progress" in reforming such areas of contention as state aid for ailing industries, steel restructuring, agriculture, and fisheries. Poland missed the December 1999 EU deadline for enacting a law on government assistance that would define when the state could help companies and when it could not. This was the result of a split in Buzek's coalition government between state interventionists (primarily found in the AWS) and neoliberals believing that the government should keep out of the economy (primarily in the UW).

The EU identified other serious problems in Poland's application. Infrastructure was well below EU standards. For example, the country had one of the lowest levels of interstate highways per land area in all Europe. In 1994 the government approved a program to construct 1,500 miles of privately financed turnpikes, but by 2000 only 65 miles had been finished. In the end the government realized that the state had to take part in infrastructural projects and a new law establishing a National Motorway Fund authorized public money to be used to build highways.

What proved most frustrating for Poland's Europhiles about these criticisms was how far the country had already traveled to meet European standards. In mid-2000 it submitted a detailed timetable to the EU on enacting 150 laws needed to prepare for membership. The Polish government's target for admission into the EU was 2004, but the EU Enlargement Commissioner stated that 2006 was more realistic. The exact criteria for assessing candidates' records had not been finalized and negotiations on the thorniest issues had not begun. Wealth levels, environmental standards, legal harmonization, unrestricted movement of workers, development of more backward regions, and agricultural policy were the crucial problems affecting accession. Disagreements on how much funding Poland and other applicants could tap from the EU's agricultural and structural funds had also to be resolved.

One of Western Europe's greatest fears was large-scale westward migration from Central and Eastern Europe. This was an emotional issue in many EU states and was most dramatically illustrated by the success of Jorg Haider's far-right Freedom Party in Austria in 2000. The question for many in the West was whether Polish workers would migrate in search of jobs should the country enter the EU. In 1992 Portuguese workers, who had roughly one-half the income of their German counterparts at that time, migrated in great numbers to the richer EU states when their country became a member. In 2000, Poles' incomes were only one-sixth of those in Germany. If, as one German think tank contended, a direct relationship exists between income gaps and migration, then a forecast of 500,000 Central Europeans moving to Western Europe per year if borders were fully opened could not be ruled out. Especially in Germany, which was wrestling with new laws on citizenship and immigration to normalize the status of its 9 million foreign nationals, a backlash against further labor migrants was likely. As a result, it seemed likely that a two-year minimum transition period on migration of labor would be set as part of the EU plan on enlarging into Eastern Europe.

The main policy challenge for Poland in this area seems to be to decide what restrictions required by the EU on migration of people are acceptable. This raises the more general question about whether Poland will be incorporated into the so-called Schengen agreement even after EU membership. It is one of the most sensitive issues in the accession talks. Negotiators have tried to weigh the costs of excluding East European states against the benefits of maintaining high standards of public security for the current fifteen members. The Schengen agreement, signed at a village in Luxembourg in 1985, established an open border regime among countries and allows people to cross frontiers without passport and border controls. Conversely, strict and secure border controls along the "external borders" with nonmember states have to be maintained.

If Poland was admitted into the Schengen area, it would, for example, have to build a restrictive Schengen curtain on its borders with Belarus, Russia, Ukraine, Lithuania, and even Slovakia (if it was not admitted to the EU at the same time). Such "enforced borders" would be costly to construct and, perhaps more significantly, politically expensive, creating rifts between Poland and its restless eastern neighbors. Yet that seemed to be the only alternative. At a conference held at the Center of European

Political Studies in Brussels in July 2001 and organized by the Batory Foundation, experts discussed the likelihood that Poland might only be ready for Schengen membership ten years after joining the EU. That would be bad news for Germany, which would have to enforce its eastern border more strictly. It would also instill in average Poles a feeling that EU membership had brought no benefits at the grassroots level.

One other obstacle for Polish admission into the Schengen regime is the need for cooperation among members' police forces and justice systems. This requires shared databases and computer systems, which Poland presently cannot provide for. Paradoxically, then, accession into the EU but not into the Schengen area might compound some of Poland's foreign policy problems.

A majority of Poles has been convinced for some time that their entry into the EU would be as a second-class member. Fifty-five percent of respondents to a 1998 national survey indicated this status, whereas only 29 percent believed that Poland would be a member of equal rank with the existing fifteen.[5] Support for entry between 1999 and 2001 remained constant: About 55 percent of respondents said they would vote in favor of membership in a referendum and slightly over one-quarter would vote against. But these figures were down from the high point in May 1996, when 80 percent were for and only 7 percent against. Moreover, on the practical question of whether Poland was ready to become a full EU member, opinions in March 2001 differed little from those of June 1994: In each case 45–47 percent thought that Poland was only halfway there.[6] By 2002 the Polish government was faced with the conundrum, then, of preventing public morale on the EU from slipping, maintaining elite consensus in favor of membership (which had been shaken by the electoral breakthrough of two Euroskeptic parties—Samoobrona and the League of Polish Families, or LPR—in the fall 2001 elections), negotiating a good deal for Poland, and, probably most importantly, keeping the EU interested in the value of eastern enlargement. The change in political climate was exemplified in late 2001 by the willingness of over a hundred Sejm deputies (from LPR, PiS, and Self-Defense) to introduce a motion of no confidence in Foreign Minister Cimoszewicz for his handling of negotiations with the EU.

NATO

In Chapter 1 we discussed how at some critical junctures in their history Poles may have felt abandoned by the West. Some indeed have made the argument that the West's indifference to their country continued well into the twentieth century. Pleas directed toward France, England, and other Western powers to send troops to defend and even die for Gdańsk in 1939, for Wilno and Lwów in 1944–1945, and for a truly independent Poland in 1944–1947 went unheeded. Early assistance to Poland might have reduced the numbers of Western soldiers who subsequently had to die fighting for their own countries against the same enemies—Hitler and Stalin. Not without irony, one Polish historian remarked that no matter how well Poles speak French or English, they never seem to be able to make themselves understood by these nations' leaders.[7]

The weakness of Poland's strategic position is self-evident. It is situated in the central lowlands of Europe with no natural borders in the east or west. During his visit to Warsaw in June 1995, then U.S. Defense Secretary William Perry called Poland "the key to European security." For Poland the key to European security was membership in NATO. After the Cold War, NATO's role was revised not only to provide a security umbrella for member states but also to promote democratic values in Eastern Europe. Advocates of Poland's membership in the alliance stressed this idea, as well as how NATO enlargement would signify the disappearance of the division of Europe agreed upon at the Yalta conference in 1945.

Successive Polish governments cautioned against creating a new division of Europe running along either the Oder (Poland's western border) or Bug (its eastern border) Rivers. They disclaimed interest in becoming an *antemurale occidentalis,* and already in the early 1990s signed bilateral treaties with all neighboring states including Belarus and Ukraine. These treaties were designed to guarantee a framework for cooperation while affirming the principle of the inviolability of state borders as they currently existed. More recently Poland has given a high priority to promoting the security interests of its eastern neighbors Lithuania and Ukraine.

In January 1994 a summit of NATO members decided to offer former Soviet-bloc countries admission into a newly created Partnership for Peace (PFP) program. At first some Central European leaders felt that the creation of the PFP was a ruse to drag out the process of extending a Western security umbrella over the region. More cynical observers believed that the unintended (or perhaps intended) consequence of delaying tactics was to allow a resurgent but pro-Western Russia to regain influence over the region. From its inception, Poland was one of the leading critics of what was seen as this halfway house for Eastern Europe. In mid-1994 the Polish defense minister attacked the PFP plan for not making clear how a state was to move from partnership to NATO membership. President Wałęsa expressed frustration with the West's step-by-step approach: From its perspective Poland had first to join the EU, then integrate economically with the West, then accept PFP, and only later receive firm Western security guarantees. Polish leaders felt that economic and military integration with the West should be simultaneous.

In July 1994 President Bill Clinton visited Poland and announced a $100 million fund for carrying out joint military programs with democratic partners in Central Europe. Small-scale but highly publicized NATO exercises were held shortly after in Poland. In September of that year an amendment put forward by U.S. Senator Hank Brown to a bill in Congress offered Poland, Hungary, and the Czech Republic preferential terms for purchasing U.S. arms. These terms were modeled on those extended to strategic U.S. allies such as Israel, Saudi Arabia, and South Korea.

The decision whether to press ahead with NATO enlargement involved a diplomatic contest between the Cold War superpowers—the United States and Russia. In April 1995 the Republican majority in the U.S. House of Representatives passed a resolution supporting NATO expansion into Central Europe. Russia's reaction was to threaten to scrap both the START–2 (Strategic Arms Reduction Talks) and the Conventional Forces in Europe (CFE) treaties should Poland, the Czech Republic, Hungary, or Slovakia be admitted into the Western military alliance. President Yeltsin recommended instead that Poland should return to its interwar foreign policy of maintaining equidistance between Russia and the West. Russia also threatened to reevaluate the bilateral treaty it had signed with Poland in 1992 and its agreement to cancel each country's reciprocal debt.

Russia's weakness was never more clearly demonstrated than when NATO pressed ahead with enlargement. In 1997 Poland was officially invited to become a member of the alliance, and in the spring of 1998 the U.S. Senate approved the inclusion of Poland (together with the Czech Republic and Hungary) in the NATO treaty. But only a year later NATO undertook a bombing campaign against Serbia following Yugoslav president Milosevic's intransigence on guaranteeing minority rights for Kosovo Albanians. The military offensive began barely twelve days after Poland formally joined NATO.

Of the three new members, Poland gave the strongest support to the air attacks. Foreign Minister Bronisław Geremek acknowledged that NATO's actions might not conform to international law, but he stressed that the alliance had to do whatever was necessary to halt genocide. Yugoslavia under Slobodan Milosevic posed "a serious menace to the fundamental values on which international order is based," he asserted. Opinion polls showed that 60 percent of the Polish public backed the air strikes. But President Kwaśniewski told the nation on March 24, just before the air campaign began, that "This is a very sad evening." And on May 14, Defense Minister Janusz Onyszkiewicz sought to calm fears about what Poland's share of NATO's costs were by claiming that it was set very low at 2.38 percent and took into consideration the timing of Poland's entry to NATO.

NATO membership significantly affected Poland's relations with Russia. The military campaign against Yugoslavia put Poland and Russia squarely on opposite sides. In January 2000, not long after an agreement on Kosovo was reached and United Nations peacekeepers were deployed in the province, Warsaw expelled nine Russian diplomats for spying. In March of that year pro-Chechen demonstrators vandalized the Russian consulate in Poznań, infuriating the Kremlin and leading to the temporary recall of Russia's ambassador. In April, in a report that was supposed to be secret, Poland's security service warned that Russian intelligence was stepping up activity in the country. Were Poland's security services orchestrating, or at least not discouraging, anti-Russian sentiments? It is of course difficult to say, but what was entirely predictable was the response of public opinion. A CBOS public opinion survey published that month found that only 2 percent of Poles considered relations with Russia to be good; 40 percent claimed they were bad.[8] Since then relations with Russia have improved, especially after President Putin's well-received visit to Poland in early 2002, but any minor disagreement between the two countries has the potential to arouse deeply held mutual suspicions.

Poland's Neighbors

The shakeup in Eastern Europe's state system that occurred in the early 1990s had a significant impact on Poland's security. The number of neighbors increased from three (the USSR, Czechoslovakia, and East Germany) to seven (Russia, Lithuania, Belarus, Ukraine, Slovakia, the Czech Republic, and Germany). In the west the neighboring state is a pivotal member of NATO and the EU—the reunified Federal Republic of Germany. By contrast, in the east and north Poland's borders are shared with states suffering from varying degrees of political and economic instability. Belarus has not made much effort to desovietize and

TABLE 7.2 Attitudes of Poles, Czechs, Hungarians, and Lithuanians Toward Selected Nations, October 2000 (on a scale from 1= dislike to 7 = like)

Attitude Toward	Poles	Czechs	Hungarians	Lithuanians
Americans	5.4 (1)	4.6 (7)	4.8 (3)	5.0 (6)
French	5.3 (2)	5.3 (2)	4.6 (6)	5.3 (2)
Italians	5.2 (3)	4.5 (8)	4.8 (4)	5.3 (4)
English	5.2 (4)	4.9 (4)	4.9 (2)	5.0 (6)
Swedes	5.0 (5)	5.2 (3)	5.1 (1)	5.5 (1)
Hungarians	5.0 (6)	4.1 (10)	—	4.6 (12)
Czechs	4.9 (7)	—	3.8 (12)	4.8 (10)
Slovaks	4.7 (9)	5.3 (1)	3.6 (16)	4.2 (15)
Japanese	4.7 (10)	4.6 (6)	4.5 (8)	5.3 (3)
Lithuanians	4.5 (11)	3.8 (14)	3.7 (13)	—
Germans	4.3 (13)	3.7 (15)	4.6 (5)	5.3 (5)
Israelis (Jews)	4.2 (18)	4.0 (13)	3.9 (10)	3.4 (23)
Russians	3.8 (21)	2.9 (22)	3.2 (19)	4.9 (8)
Ukrainians	3.7 (22)	3.1 (20)	3.1 (20)	4.7 (11)
Romanians	3.3 (23)	2.7 (23)	2.8 (21)	3.9 (18)
Gypsies	3.3 (24)	2.2 (24)	2.6 (24)	2.5 (24)
Poles	—	4.1 (12)	4.5 (7)	4.4 (13)

Source: "Stosunek polaków, czechów, węgrów i litwinów do innych narodów," CBOS, no. 165 (listopad 2000). See http://www.cbos.com.pl.

has lurched from one political crisis to another. Ukraine has had little success with economic reform, is very corrupt, and remains dependent on Russia. Lithuania has made much progress in consolidating democracy but its interest in becoming a part of NATO threatens to transform it into a political battleground between Europe and Russia. In the north, Poland shares a border with Kaliningrad, a region of the Russia Federation. But it remains unclear whether Kaliningrad will serve as a free market model for all of Russia or at some point as a front line for Russian revanchism. Given these conditions, it is not surprising that Poles are suspicious of their eastern neighbors (Table 7.2) but full of admiration for Americans who live far away.

Attitudes of Poles toward other nations have remained relatively constant since the fall of communism. Together with Czechs and Hungarians,

Poles are favorably disposed toward nations thought to be part of the advanced Western world. Thus respondents in these three countries (as well as in Lithuania) expressed a strong liking for the Japanese but not for Chinese or Vietnamese (not included in Table 7.2). In comparative terms, the most-liked nation in 2000 was Sweden, which enjoyed the dual advantage of being seen as a capitalist and a compassionate people. For historical reasons, neither Poles nor Czechs, the two Slav nations in the study, ranked Germans high on their list of favorite peoples.

Poles, Czechs, and Hungarians tended to be indifferent to (defined as a 4 on the scale) or even show dislike of (below 4) nations to their east, in particular Russians and Ukrainians. We might note that the idea that civilization ends on the eastern border is a phenomenon found not just in Poland but in Western Europe as well.

Poles were fonder of Americans than were any other respondents. They especially differed from Czechs in this regard. To observers of Poland the pro-American bias has always stood out. In general the nations Poles liked most did not share borders with the country. Poles were no different from their counterparts in the survey in most disliking Roma (Gypsies) and Romanians (a nation in which Gypsies are numerous). Poles ranked "Israelis (Jews)"—as the questionnaire framed this nation—eighteenth of 24 on the list. Even so, the location on the scale that Poles placed Israelis was one of indifference rather than dislike, an attitude shared by Czechs and Hungarians.

Generally, we can say that the historical attitudes of peoples living in Central and Eastern Europe toward each other are accurately reflected in the attitudinal data compiled at the turn of the twenty-first century. They corroborate results obtained from earlier surveys. One sociologist offered a simple explanation for the pattern of likes and dislikes: "the wealth of a nation, Catholicism, and wartime allies exerted the strongest relative influence on Poles' likes."

There were four types of ethnic groups toward whom Poles exhibited consistent attitudes: (1) advanced capitalist economies and liberal democracies (such as the United States, England, and France), which received the highest scores; (2) those most ethnically different from Poles (Chinese, Gypsies, Arabs, and, to a lesser degree, Jews), which received mixed evaluations; (3) post-communist countries (such as Russia, Belarus, Lithuania, and Slovakia), which were generally negatively assessed; and (4) two neighbors with which historical conflict remained imprinted in people's minds (Germany and Ukraine), which were very negatively assessed.[9] The inescapable conclusion deriving from these data was that

Poles wanted very much to be like Americans and wanted to avoid re-sembling Russians, Ukrainians, Gypsies, and, in varying measures, other Slavic and East European nations. This was a bizarre, self-deprecating self-image that being part of the Soviet bloc had fostered.

Whatever their likes or dislikes, for Poland, accords with Germany have always carried special significance. In 1990 a border treaty formal-ized bilaterally what had been concluded at the two-plus-two (West Ger-many, East Germany, the United States, the Soviet Union) negotiations: The Oder and Neisse Rivers officially became the post–World War II border between Germany and Poland. In June 1991 the two countries agreed on a treaty on good-neighbor relations. Quickly Germany became Poland's largest trading partner and a major aid donor. In 1993 it ac-counted for 28 percent of Poland's imports and 36 percent of its exports. In the five-year period 1990–1994, Germany provided Poland with $12.1 billion in aid.[10]

In the early 1990s Poland concluded other pan-European, regional, and transnational agreements. The country joined the Organization for Security and Cooperation in Europe (OSCE), which promotes East–West relations and peaceful resolution of conflicts. Its membership of fifty-five states in the year 2000 gives it considerable leverage as the most all-inclusive pan-European institution. On the regional level, in February 1991 Poland's president attended a summit with his Czechoslo-vak and Hungarian counterparts in Visegrad, Hungary. The main objec-tive was to forge trading relations among the countries on the basis of their new free market economies. As one scholar wrote, the summit "was hailed at the time as a major breakthrough in Central European coopera-tion." But the Visegrad group soon confused means with goals: "Instead of becoming an organization promoting intraregional cooperation as well as integration at the European level, the Visegrad process became fixated almost exclusively on the latter—in effect, it became a vehicle for coordi-nating Central Europe's 'road to Europe' while development of closer ties within the region languished on the back burner."[11]

The absence of a common vision turned the four-member Visegrad group (after Czechoslovakia's split into two nations in 1993) into largely a political consultative body. By 2001, its chief goal was to coordinate the efforts of its members to join the EU, but it was failing at that, too. Refer-ring to Poland, which was falling behind in accession talks, Czech and Hungarian leaders emphasized how it was not possible to wait for any country to catch up in seeking integration with the EU. The Visegrad group did set less ambitious goals for itself, such as fostering nongovernmental regional cooperation through the Visegrad Fund—money contributed by the four governments plus private donors to support projects in culture, education, and science. The group also complemented another multilateral structure, the Central European Free Trade Agreement (CEFTA), which was signed in March 1993. When CEFTA expanded into Slovenia and Romania, a common market of 90 million people had been created. Though not the EU, it was an opportunity for the six members to demonstrate that they were committed to regional cooperation. From the perspective of Brussels, however, it is striking how unenthusiastic Central Europeans have been about regional cooperation plans.

Addressing Economic Inequalities: Globalization or Paternalism?

For many Polish citizens, Westernization more than anything meant converting the economy from a command model to a free market. Related to this was the conviction by many that only a capitalist system could promote economic development beyond the early stages of industrialization. The bottom line has therefore been whether Westernization has improved general socioeconomic performance and individual well-being.

Since 1989 many Poles have become skeptical about such "Western" values as individualism, freedom, and democracy as their living standards have declined. Uneven economic growth across sectors—services, manufacturing, mining, agriculture—and across class lines—management personnel, office workers, blue-collar workers, farmers—has produced both satisfaction and disaffection with capitalism. Depending on which groups flourish or languish under the new system, democracy can be reinforced or weakened. It is said that a prospering middle class can consolidate democracy, but a battered but militant working class can weaken it.[12] Has Poland's conversion to a capitalist economy, then, legitimated the new system through its results and has it paid off for most of its citizens?

In a capitalist system, *government performance* and *economic performance* are not the same thing. In describing communist regime performance in Chapter 2, the two categories could be treated as one: The performance of a public-owned and state-managed economy could be equated with regime economic performance. But since 1989 economic growth has occurred precisely outside the public sector. That makes it difficult for the democratic regime to be given credit for this since it is the private sector that is seen as dynamic and successful. Yet the fiscal, monetary, and price-and-income policies that stimulate growth of the private sector should be regarded as indicators of the government's positive economic performance. The extent to which the state has privatized, made more efficient, or closed down public-sector firms can also indicate regime performance.

Since 1989 Polish citizens have not always taken into account the more indirect role played by the government when assessing its economic performance. Many were socialized into communist notions of rationality and efficiency and are still unfamiliar with the logic of Western capitalist democracy. As a result, they may have harsh views of their government for its macroeconomic policies while simultaneously blaming it for the shortcomings of the private sector. Obviously different self-interested economic actors employ different performance criteria. Those actors adversely affected by the transition are usually hypercritical of incumbent governments and vote against them in elections. For example, the two parties that made up the Buzek government together received less than 10 percent of the total vote in the September 2001 legislative elections. Yet to be fair to that government and others operating under a free market, it could hardly be held responsible for all the vagaries of Poland's economic performance between 1997 and 2001, which was not all bad anyway.

The Western Model of Reform

Much was written in the early 1990s about the interconnectedness between political and economic reforms. Conventional wisdom has it that to be effective, economic reform must be accompanied by democratization so as to confer legitimacy on the incumbents carrying out change. But an academic literature emerged that criticized efforts at simultaneous economic and political transition. As one article summed up this literature, "There are two versions of this 'transitional incompatibility' thesis, one focusing on democratization's potential to undermine economic reform, and the other contending that the heavy cost of economic reform can turn crucial social actors against democratization."[13] Let us review the arguments for and against the "big bang" (or shock therapy) approach to economic transformation that informed policy discussions in Poland in the early 1990s.

Two American economists, Stephan Haggard and Robert Kaufman, explored the relationship between economic and political *crises*:

> Despite the fact that economic crisis overlapped a new wave of democratization in the developing world, recent literature on the transition to democracy

has largely eschewed economic variables. Emphasizing the autonomy of the political realm, this analysis has focused rather on factors such as pact-making among political elites, institutional relations between civilian and military authorities, and the way electoral and constitutional rules structured opportunities for the democratic opposition under authoritarian rule.[14]

Haggard and Kaufman examined the connection between economic shocks and regime change in the 1980s in Latin America, Africa, and Asia, and found little. Instead, "regime survival appeared to depend on the existence of mechanisms of interest representation that channeled, and therefore controlled, group conflict."[15] The implication for Poland was that intermediary structures between government and the public had to be established in order for the transition to be consolidated. Yet the Polish experience has suggested something different, if still obvious: Strong economic performance (such as high annual GDP growth) can make the need for new interest structures superfluous. On the other hand, without such mechanisms incumbent governments—not the capitalist system—become the target of voters frustrated by transition costs.

The two economists also investigated the sequencing of economic and political liberalization. When economic reform is instituted before a political opening occurs, the paramount idea is to suppress opposition to reform for a given period, and once economic successes have been recorded to open up the political sphere. This was the strategy adopted by Southern Cone bureaucratic-authoritarian regimes in the 1960s and 1970s, of East Asian states in the 1970s, and of China in the 1980s. In some respects it was also the strategy employed in the 1980s by Jaruzelski in Poland. Because of its complexity, simultaneous economic and political liberalization is carried out less often; Mexico in the second half of the 1980s is a rare example of this.

The final sequence involves instituting democracy first and structural adjustment later. Obtaining political legitimacy for a reformist government is treated as the top priority in the transition. Argentina, Brazil, and Peru in the late 1980s and, for Haggard and Kaufman, much of Eastern Europe are examples here. The advantage of democracy-first sequencing is that new governments can fully exploit the ineptitude of their predecessors. The disadvantage is that the new democratic government has to adopt stringent structural adjustment measures that can create short-term hardship.

Haggard and Kaufman concluded that, regardless of sequencing, consolidation of democratic rule ultimately depends on "the extent to which adjustment policies actually result in economic recovery."[16] Poor economic performance can result directly in a collapse of elected governments, but an alternative outcome is a "stylized process of political decay" that "while stopping short of formal regime change would nonetheless drain constitutional institutions of their democratic content."[17] Economic deterioration can lead to an increase in crime, industrial unrest, riots, civil violence, downward social mobility, and social polarization. Fortunately for Poland, solid economic growth has allowed the country to escape most of these pathologies.

The author of the economic plan for Poland's rapid capitalist conversion acted on the belief that political change alone would likely bring the country limited or no economic gains. As economist Leszek Balcerowicz put it: "Economic progress cannot be achieved by democratic policies alone. . . . There is no correlation whatsoever between democracy and economic progress, i.e., economic growth. However, there is a marked correlation between the type of economic institutions, such as property rights or whether the economy is open or closed to the outside world, etc., and economic growth."[18] Balcerowicz was attentive to the opportunities for radical change available in the short period of "extraordinary politics" that followed a great political breakthrough and that was what the timing of his shock therapy sought to exploit. He recognized that when the inevitable return to normal politics occurred, the menu for economic choice would be narrowed.[19]

To be sure, limited experimentation with a Western market economy model predated the Balcerowicz plan by a few years. Shortly after the United States in February 1987 lifted the last of the economic sanctions leveled at Poland as punishment for martial law in 1981, a leading Polish official traveled to Washington to discuss debt rescheduling and to request new credits. Later that year Poland, with U.S. support, was admitted to the World Bank. The communist government held a referendum on whether the public favored rapid economic changes. Two-thirds of voters (though only 44 percent of eligible ones) backed the proposal. In 1988, price liberalization, enabling the market to respond to supply and demand, led to increases in food prices of 40 percent and energy of 100 percent. In November 1987 parliament passed a law sanctioning private enterprises, and many of the first to be set up were run by members of the communist *nomenklatura*. The ruling elite was being converted to the advantages of the Western market economy.

The Solidarity-led governments of 1989–1993 accelerated economic transformation. Their economic policies included restricting the money supply, freeing the prices of nearly all goods from state controls, limiting the budget deficit (International Monetary Fund aid was made contingent on keeping the deficit close to 5 percent of GDP), and promoting currency convertibility (helped by the creation by Western institutions of a *złoty* stabilization fund). Recommended by the IMF, these policies became the basis for the plan developed by Balcerowicz, who was appointed minister of finance and economic reform in September 1989. The crash stabilization package was forced through at the end of December using the authority of the IMF and of Western economists like Jeffrey Sachs, an adviser to the Polish government at the time. But even Sachs recognized the paradox inherent in the "big bang" approach to reform: "Why should something 'so good' feel 'so bad'?"[20]

The Balcerowicz plan had many critics. As one of them put it, "The architects of reform were persuaded that their blueprint was sound—no, more: the only one possible."[21] Reform was unresponsive to public preferences: "Radical reform was a project initiated from above and launched by surprise, independently of public opinion and without the participation of organized political forces" and, accordingly, "had the effect of weakening democratic institutions."[22] The passage of the Balcerowicz plan itself was considered an example. The Sejm was "given sixteen pieces of legislation and told that it must approve the nine most important before the end of the month to meet the IMF conditions."[23]

Following consideration of seventeen different drafts of a privatization bill, in July 1990 a law was finally passed. It was followed by another law transforming 40 percent of state firms into public corporations. Privatization of state-owned industrial juggernauts was poorly conceived but, fortunately, it was not critical to the success of economic reform. For one economist Poland's remarkable recovery owed most to "creating conditions for virtually unrestricted entry of private firms into all sectors of the economy and fields of activity."[24] As we see below, however, the government still had a lot of work to do to ensure a successful transition.

Macroeconomic Successes, Societal Setbacks

The success of the reform program is irrefutable. Exhibit A is GDP growth, which ranged between 4 and 6 percent annually from 1994 to 2000. For all their criticism while out of power, SLD governments did not tamper with the essentials of the free market reforms that Balcerowicz had introduced. Admittedly the short impact of shock therapy was high unemployment, double-digit inflation, a decline in industrial production (transport and construction sectors were an exception), and a drop in real income. Thus over the period 1989–1992, the cumulative GDP fell by 17 percent, cumulative inflation was 175 percent, and unemployment rose by 13 percent.[25]

But the Balcerowicz plan did achieve its most important objectives: stabilizing the currency, restricting budget deficits and hyperinflation, creating a domestic capital market, increasing trade with the West, and spurring foreign investment. Profitability, even in the public sector, was stimulated and a 1993 World Bank report found that many state-owned enterprises had turned the corner: Better management, a sleeker and less overpaid labor force, and better product quality and assortment were important factors in generating earnings. Growth in the construction sector was particularly buoyant as infrastructural changes became a top priority. But the chemical, petrochemical, and electrical industries also recorded unprecedented growth. By contrast, heavy industry—the mainstay of the socialist economy—flagged. Coal output was down to just 60 percent of that recorded in the peak years of the 1980s and steel output was halved. In short, structural adjustment had the effect of shifting investment from energy- and labor-intensive industries to capital-intensive ones.

If foreign investment was only a trickle up to 1993, the expectations of Western-style consumption patterns for a 40-million-strong market, low labor costs, and the country's location as springboard for the enormous Russian and Ukrainian markets helped propel Western investment higher. Already in 1993 Poland's was the world's best-performing stock market (though only twenty firms were listed at that time). Investors became even more bullish on Poland in subsequent years. In one survey conducted in early 2000, chief executives at the world's largest companies ranked Poland as the fifth most attractive location for foreign investment after the United States, Britain, China, and Brazil.

The main lure was a relatively efficient private sector comprising small businesses, privatized companies that used to be state-owned, and foreign-owned firms. The Polish government cashed in on privatization with revenues from sell-offs totaling $8.3 billion in 1999 alone. By 2000, foreign direct investment inflows had reached nearly $10 billion, the highest in Eastern Europe and over three times the Russian total. That represented approximately $230 per person—about $100 less than the Czech total but $80 more than the Hungarian one.

It is a cliché that capitalism produces losers as well as winners. While some business people, especially those with political connections, became millionaires overnight, millions of Poles who had enjoyed guaranteed incomes, housing, and health care in the communist period lost them. The problem of persistent unemployment marred Poland's economic success. An unemployment rate of 15–20 percent may be understandable during the early years of structural adjustment, but it was hard to fathom why in 2001 about 3 million Poles, or 16 percent of the labor force (after Slovakia the highest rate of any OECD country), had no jobs. The rate was likely to rise further as industries had to restructure in preparation for joining a single European market and as a worldwide recession grew in 2001.

Among the sectors hit hardest by unemployment were those employing female labor: light industry, the educational system, the health service, and state administration. In the early 1990s nearly two-thirds of the non-manual unemployed were women. Regional variations in the proportion of unemployed women were also significant: In Warsaw 5 percent of women in the labor force were without work, whereas in rural Suwalki, Olsztyn, and Koszalin Provinces the proportion was over 20 percent. To make matters worse, women's prospects for returning to the labor force were dramatically poorer than men's; at one point the number of openings listed for women was one-seventh of what it was for men.[26]

In agriculture, farm incomes were halved between 1988 and 1992. Indeed, some of the greatest losers in the economic transition were peasants running small-sized, inefficient family farms. Demand for many of their products, including meat, fell as state contracts were voided and private consumption declined. In the first years after its introduction the market economy achieved something that the centrally planned economy had never accomplished—a reduction in the consumption of meat. In 1997 annual per capita meat consumption was about 125 pounds, the lowest figure since the 1970s and about 15 percent below that of 1980 when shortages of meat at subsidized prices led to protests and the birth of Solidarity. Eating well and the other benefits of capitalism—home ownership, family trips, durable goods—were out of the reach of ordinary people throughout the 1990s.

The socioeconomic standing of the family was dramatically changed with the transition to a market economy. The authors of one study drew the following, perhaps overdramatic contrast:

> The average Polish family in the era of real socialism accepted as certainty that employment might be poorly paid but it was there; that housing could be obtained through state allocation; that a mother who wanted to have a child could count on an entire system of benefits during pregnancy and up-bringing of the child; that free medical care was guaranteed . . . , that the

child could be left in a nursery or preschool; that the only school fees were voluntary contributions to the parents' association, that every interested young person who was at all intelligent could continue her studies.[27]

The capitalist economy changed this picture:

Today the average Polish family has to recognize that it might find itself without any means of subsistence if its only provider were dismissed from work; that saving to buy a flat is almost impossible; that with a doctor under the threat of imprisonment for performing an abortion, a mother may have to give birth to a fifth or sixth child for whom, in the event of illness or disability, she could not afford to buy medicine or pay for an operation; whom she will never be able to take on a holiday or send to college; and it goes on.[28]

Another issue was whether the best and the brightest had already emigrated from Poland before the communist collapse. In a seven-year period ending in 1992, some 1.7 million Poles moved to another country. Nearly half were between twenty-five and forty-nine, and many were well educated and in the professions. A decade later, emigration still offers many Poles the best hope for socioeconomic advancement, a possibility that the EU fears.

Because so many Poles have been out of work, spending on public services has had to remain higher than what is economically efficient. In 2001 it raised the budget deficit beyond the government target of 2.6 percent of GDP. That in turn fueled inflation, which stood at 12 percent in mid-2000 (but declined to 7 percent a year later). Interest rates had been kept very high to control inflation, but when Balcerowicz took over as central bank governor in 2000 they were cut from 23 to as low as 17 percent in 2001. High interest rates made the *złoty* appreciate in value, by up to 15 percent against the euro in 2001. That in turn made Polish exports expensive abroad, limited output, and discouraged firms from expanding. There was concern, however, that allowing the *złoty* to depreciate to a new equilibrium point could produce the type of currency crash that had happened in Hungary in 1995, the Czech Republic in 1997, and Russia in 1994 and 1998.

Other economic statistics were equally alarming to those who had not benefited from the boom of the second half of the 1990s. Annual GDP growth fell to around 2 percent in 2001. Compounded by a global slowdown, consumer spending declined and the stock market lost one-third of its value that year. High short-term interest rates offered few prospects for a reversal of this trend. The current account balance dropped from a

4 percent surplus of GDP in 1995 to a 7 percent deficit by 2001. Part of the reason lay in falling exports, especially the crash of the Russian market, but a larger issue was how competitive Polish-made goods really were. Another problem was that the public sector remained bloated and inefficient and still had to be streamlined. Large state enterprises in the energy, steel, and chemicals sectors had not made a full conversion to free market principles, including on labor policies.

Poland's labor costs were among Eastern Europe's highest. A relatively high minimum wage, high payroll taxes that employers paid, and a strict labor code restricting employees' ability to change jobs undermined the competitiveness of the labor market. Despite this, in March 2001 the Sejm shortened the work week from 42 to 40 hours, feeding worries that companies would get even less from their employees for the same wages. The Buzek government that was closely linked to the Solidarity trade union had been constrained in undertaking major labor market reforms. The SLD government that succeeded it was also cautious about proposing labor market deregulation since many of its core supporters were employed in public enterprises. Ironically, then, state paternalism had been rejected as a policy by the major parties yet it continued to shape the problemsolving ability of successive governments.

Regional economic disparities in Poland remain significant. Urban areas have pulled further ahead of rural ones in all important economic indicators. Differences between regions as well as within regions are marked. For a time the Buzek government created special economic zones that enjoyed tax breaks so as to draw investment, create jobs, and ensure more robust development. As an example, Wrocław had one of the lowest unemployment rates in the country, but the region surrounding it, Lower Silesia, cradle of the obsolete coal industry, had one of the highest. So a special economic zone was created around the former coal boomtown, Walbrzych, which had become a depressed district. But in January 2001 the EU ordered that these zones be eliminated on the grounds that they were given unfair advantages. The rationale was that inequalities should not be legislated away.

Poland's economy faces the same challenge from globalization as that of many other countries today. World trade produces benefits to all participants, but not in equal proportions. Furthermore, those in Poland gaining from the global economy overshadow the many who obtain nothing or even suffer because of loss of employment, reduced benefits from a scaled-down state, or inability to organize their interests effectively. Poland has not witnessed the massive anti-globalization demonstrations seen in recent years in cities of the advanced Western economies: Seattle, Québec City, Genoa. But that does not mean that problems similar to those sparking the protests in the West are not present in Poland.

Forging Effective and Transparent Institutions

Poland's future will be shaped not only by the degree to which it integrates into European structures or how it resolves its economic problems, but also by the nature of institutional development that occurs in its political and economic life. Effective institutions are not fixed once and for all but adapt to meet changing circumstances and different goals. Whether they involve relations between executive and legislative branches of government (a conflictual subject that only reached an equilibrium point with the adoption of the 1997 constitution), regulative bodies overseeing the functioning of the private sector, or local administration implementing policies most directly affecting citizens' lives, a democracy requires institutions to be adaptive, responsive, and accountable. One of the most serious problems that Poland faces at this stage of its development is rampant corruption. Transparent institutions that inhibit corrupt practices and reward honest ones are key to addressing this problem, which has tarnished the country's otherwise impressive transition to democracy and a free market.

Effective Institutions

We became familiar with some of the views of economist Douglass North in the previous chapter. Let us return to a few of his ideas. A prerequisite for economic growth, North has argued, is the establishment of institutions that create an incentive structure. Institutions need to be both sufficiently stable and powerful to enforce rules. The reason is that "the overall stability of an institutional framework makes complex exchange possible across both time and space."[29] Informal constraints matter as well. These include modification of formal rules, socially sanctioned norms of behavior, and internally enforced standards of conduct. More specifically, a pervasive work ethic, honesty, and integrity lower transaction costs (which include rule enforcement) and facilitate complex productive exchanges. What applies to economic growth can also apply to political development. Effective institutions are those that facilitate and regulate political bidding and bargaining.

The importance of a country's experience with institutional adaptation and informal constraint patterns led North to speak of path dependence. Path-dependent growth signifies "an adaptively efficient path [that] allows for a maximum of choices under uncertainty, for the pursuit of various trial methods of undertaking activities, and for an efficient feedback mechanism to identify choices that are relatively inefficient and to eliminate them."[30] Prospects for economic success improve under capitalism, then, since its incentive and constraint structures promote experimentation and allow decisionmakers to identify and establish the right set of institutions. A country's ability to effect discretionary, corrective institutional modification to any inefficient path development is thus a crucial factor in promoting progress.

The question remains, however, of what is required for efficient institutions to exist at a given time. North tells us that "one gets *efficient* institutions by a polity that has built-in incentives to create and enforce efficient property rights."[31] In its many variants, this was the logic underlying regime change in Poland after 1989; we examined the rationale employed by the actors of change in previous chapters. Here let us look at the "second wave" of Polish reforms begun in 1999.[32] The Buzek government undertook an ambitious package of four reforms: public administration, social security, health care, and education. The first reform required the greatest amount of institutional restructuring. As we saw in the previous chapter, it collapsed forty-nine *provincial governments* into just sixteen while also reformulating the functions of county and village councils.

Like territorial reorganization, reform of *social security* was designed to lead Poland irreversibly away from the communist past. It was intended to halt the spiraling deficit of the pension system in particular and make it pay for itself. The extent of the problem was seen in the fact that state pensions accounted for 16 percent of GDP, the highest ratio of any European country (including Scandinavia). Instead of pension benefits being based on such "social" considerations as being a war veteran, having worked as a coal miner, or suffering from a disability (usually loosely defined), they were now to reflect work-related contributions to pension funds based on length of employment plus level of income. Instead of all retirement funds being managed by one organization, the notoriously incompetent Social Insurance Program (ZUS), three types of pension programs were established.

The first is a basic fund, to be administered by a restructured ZUS, that disposes of a certain percentage of the contributions almost equally paid in by employers and employees. The World Bank suggested that Poland adopt a flat rate contribution for this program, but Polish reformers chose an income-based contribution. The second program created involves general pension associations (PTE), which invest the remaining part of paid-in contributions in bonds and securities. Finally, a third program allows employees to make voluntary contributions into mutual and savings funds, depending on the type of program elected by the employer. In 1999, twenty-one new private pension funds were running that had amassed close to $1 billion in assets within a year. That sum exceeded the total amount that mutual funds had raised over the preceding nine-year period.

Another part of pension reform was to eliminate the difference in the retirement age for women and men. Adopted by the communist authorities supposedly to equalize for the additional work over their lifetime that women performed at home, the female retirement age was 55. Under the new system women who continued to retire at age 55 would simply receive fewer pension benefits. But in the end the age difference was maintained in the new legislation, and one economics professor interpreted this as "the victory of family interests, not of the individual interest of a woman."[33] To ensure institutional oversight of the pension funds, the reform set up an Office for Supervision of Pension Funds, which reported directly to the prime minister. One of the first major problems it faced was the admission by ZUS in 1999 that it did not have a reliable database for those participating in the program. The Buzek government had to acknowledge that control over the system's financing had been lost.

The third of the four reforms involved changes to the *health care* system. How successful this overhaul was is debatable. In April 2000, a year after reforms had been introduced, health care was still identified as the worst-functioning institution in Poland.[34] Reform legislation never made clear what Poland's health care model was to be or the objectives it was to meet. The major thrust of reform involved financing of health care rather than meeting patients' and medical professionals' needs. Financing was now to come not out of the government budget but from employee and employer contributions. The stated rationale for this was that health care would thereby be freed from political meddling. But this proved to be an impossible task. Determining the amount of health care contributions that would be deductible from income tax was a quintessentially political decision. Moreover, since the government was prepared to pay the contributions of those citizens who could not do so themselves, like farmers or the unemployed (who pay no income tax), the reform was always politically charged. A practical problem was that weak central supervision, together with ZUS's database problem, allowed many employers to evade making contributions for their workers altogether.

The cornerstone of the new system of financing health care was the regionally administered Health Funds (*kasy chorych*), set up in the sixteen provinces to purchase medical services for their subscribers. Patients were supposed to be able to choose their health care provider and receive reimbursement from the Health Fund. Supply and demand were to determine the amount that individuals contributed to it. The assumption was that as personal incomes grew, contributions would increase and private for-profit health care providers would be set up to meet demand. That equation did not hold up. Many people chose to go without services (like elective surgery) that they did not desperately need. These included different kinds of preventive medicine, psychological counseling, rehabilitation, and care for disabled children. Soon the Health Funds were asking for government guarantees that their deficits would be covered out of its budget.

Financing was not the only issue that hamstrung health care reform. A newly created Office of Supervision of Health Care took its mission seriously and insisted that quality standards and rates for medical services had to be set independently of market forces. This was a view that had the support of the National Chamber of Physicians, the professional association representing Poland's doctors.

Finally, a conflict of interest arose for provincial governments, which were simultaneously responsible for overseeing both the Health Funds and the health care providers that contracted with them. Predictably, political interference in health care did not decrease even though that was the stated intention behind the new system. In the case of this reform, then, the combination of new institutions, imperfect markets, and persistent state paternalism plagued the new system from early on.

The first measures in the long-awaited overhaul of the *educational system* were implemented in September 1999 and were to be completed by 2005. Universities and colleges were not affected by this reform. Education was to become the responsibility of local authorities at county and village levels. The existing eight-grade primary school system was to be superceded by a six-year program. The next level was to be a three-year middle school (*gymnazjum*) after which students could go on to a specialized grammar school (*liceum profilowane*) for a further three years, or to a two-year vocational college. Schools were to enjoy considerable curricular autonomy and could even set their own exams. In the first few years of the new system the vast majority of teachers still clung to the curriculum recommended by the Ministry of Education, and it was unclear whether the autonomy offered by the new system was really a benefit.

To ensure that schools were preparing pupils effectively and that comparative standards were maintained, exams graded by external examiners would be given in the final year of each of the three school levels. Many parents worried, of course, that by that stage it would be far too late to do something for a child attending a poor school. Testing would be supervised by eight specially created district examination commissions, while a Central Examination Commission (CKE) would work out the standards to be applied. Under the Buzek reforms, the high school diploma exam (*matura*) written in the last year of the *liceum* was to test analytic and expressive skills more than knowledge of a classical curriculum as hitherto. But the Miller government weakened this reform in 2001 by giving schools the choice of whether to use the old or new *matura*.

The Buzek government stressed the populist origins of its package of reforms. In contrast to the communist period when adopting reforms was the privilege of the political elite, recent reforms had supposedly been the product of citizens' preferences. The free press was seen as playing a central part in the public debate about changes. Yet, as we have suggested, the public was critical of the process of reform and even more critical of the effects of reform. In late 1999 three-quarters of respondents believed that implementing four reforms in one year was a bad decision—and it was particularly negative about changes to the health care system.[35] The legacy of Buzek's prime ministership also proved to be the basis for his ouster.

We can agree that what this second wave of institutional reforms has in common with the early 1990s reforms is the desire to forge efficiency-maximizing institutional arrangements. Unfortunately the political process through which these reforms had to pass eroded some of the incentives for efficiency. Whether they involved the more explicitly political reforms affecting local government, or the more social reforms dealing with social security, health care, and education, institutional change had more of a satisficing than optimizing character. Much remains to be done in these areas to meet citizens' expectations and to maximize institutional efficiency.

Transparency

For critics of capitalism, the free market system generates a variety of pathologies. Writing in the early 1990s, one Polish social scientist claimed that "a Darwinian model of social development has come to the fore in post-Communist Europe and seems to serve as a more or less explicit philosophy of the new political class. . . . The problem is that, however important the spirit of entrepreneurship is, the Darwinian model of capitalism applies neither to the realities of modern capitalism, nor to the Polish ethos."[36] What were the dysfunctions that were produced by the so-called Darwinian transformation of the Polish economy?

Violent crime increased dramatically after the fall of communism, though it did not reach the proportions in Poland that it had in Russia. In 1980 there were 589 reported homicides throughout the country; in 1995 the number had risen to 1,134. Contract killings of business rivals and even of the national police chief shocked the nation. Nearly all kinds of violent crime increased: armed robbery, assault, rape. After peaking in the mid-1990s, however, figures were down by the end of the 1990s.

White-collar crime also increased dramatically and, in this case, continued to rise throughout the decade. For example, in 1990 there were 6,042 commercial crimes but by 1999 over 27,000. The new capitalist system was rocked by financial scandals involving tax evasion, avoiding import duties, exploiting loopholes in the banking system through kiting operations, defaulting on exorbitant loans obtained through forged documents or personal connections, and outright fraud, including the setting up of bogus companies that robbed people of their savings. Six supposedly self-made Polish millionaires were arrested between June 1992 and June 1993.[37] In this first period of a free market economy many laws and regulations were unclear and encouraged abuse. Subsequent legislation made these early forms of corruption (especially tax evasion, which decreased dramatically) more difficult. But new techniques of appropriating public resources for private benefit were quickly found.

Former communist *apparatchiks* were among the first to become capitalist *entrepreneurchiks*.[38] Many were able to appropriate state-owned property during the process of privatization. They had the inside track in bidding for firms to be privatized, either through insider information or because they had accumulated capital under communist rule. In late 1994 President Wałęsa seemed to condone such activities when he claimed that efficiency overrode other considerations in the transition process.

Poland's best-known *entrepreneurchik* became Jerzy Urban, the government spokesman in the martial law years and now owner of a large publishing house and editor of the satirical weekly *Nie*. The specter of communists enriching themselves came to haunt capitalist Poland in the first years of the new system.

But the largest financial scam that occurred in 1990–1991 had little to do with the old elites. It involved two unlikely thirty-year-old businessmen, by training a doctor and a pianist.[39] Accused of conducting a kiting scheme (or *oscylator*) that robbed the banking system of over $4 billion of illegally obtained interest, they fled to Israel with $35 million before they could be arrested. Another scam pioneer was head of a savings association before suddenly leaving Poland with millions of dollars of client deposits.

For many citizens suffering from a sense of economic inefficacy at a time of supposedly great economic opportunities, such financial scandals were traumatic. The financial dealings of government ministers and parliamentary deputies in cornering shares that were purportedly on offer to the public, purchasing state-owned companies for rock-bottom prices, and receiving kickbacks on government contracts evoked outrage and a demand for anti-corruption measures. In addition, if Poles' egalitarian attitudes had not quickly disappeared with construction of the new system, it had a lot to do with perceiving the new inequalities to be the result of widespread corruption.[40]

Unfortunately for Poland, corrupt practices continued long after the democratic breakthrough, and the "republic of buddies" (see Chapter 4) was a feature of governments run both by Solidarity and by reformed communists. Based on interviews with government officials and the national audit office, the 1999 World Economic Forum survey ranked Poland fifty-second out of fifty-nine countries in terms of governmental favoritism, and forty-third in terms of insider trading (not that different from other Central and Eastern European states). A 2000 World Bank report identified "corruption at the highest levels" as Poland's most serious problem. That same year a European Bank for Reconstruction and Development (EBRD) report on the legal systems of Central European states found that perceptions of the effectiveness of laws was largely negative. In the case of the law on bankruptcy, for example, only 40 percent of Polish lawyers surveyed thought it was sound, placing Poland at thirteenth of the sixteen Central and East European states studied. The European Commission identified persisting corruption as a problem affecting Poland's application for EU membership. Finally, in its report for

TABLE 7.3 Corruption Perceptions Index, 2001 (for selected countries)

Rank	Country	CPI Score
1	Finland	9.9
2	Denmark	9.5
3	New Zealand	9.4
4	Iceland	9.2
	Singapore	9.2
6	Sweden	9.0
7	Canada	8.9
8	Netherlands	8.8
9	Luxembourg	8.7
10	Norway	8.6
13	United Kingdom	8.3
16	Israel	7.6
	United States	7.6
20	Germany	7.4
21	Japan	7.1
23	France	6.7
28	Estonia	5.6
31	Hungary	5.3
34	Slovenia	5.2
38	Lithuania	4.8
	South Africa	4.8
44	Peru	4.1
	Poland	4.1
47	Bulgaria	3.9
	Croatia	3.9
	Czech Republic	3.9
51	Slovakia	3.7
69	Romania	2.8
79	Ecuador	2.3
	Pakistan	2.3
	Russia	2.3
83	Ukraine	2.1
91	Bangladesh	0.4

Source: Transparency International 2001. See http://www.transparency.de. The 2001 CPI Score relates to perceptions of the degree of corruption in a country as seen by business people, academics and risk analysts, and ranges from 10 (highly clean) to 0 (highly corrupt).

2001, the German-based anti-corruption organization Transparency International ranked Poland only forty-fourth of ninety-one states in its Corruption Perceptions Index (Table 7.3).

The realization that the government had to tackle the culture of corruption and bribery was most forcefully driven home by accession talks with EU negotiators. In 2000 Buzek set up an anti-corruption committee with broad purview. The thinking was that public servants in Warsaw were an especially vulnerable group whose favors were sought by business people intent on greasing deals, obtaining tax breaks, and gaining legal advantages. One of the committee's first, if modest, achievements was to crack down on crooked traffic police.

In late 2000 a voluntary program called *Manus Puris* ("Clean Hands") was launched in the Polish business community to curb the taking of bribes and kickbacks. The argument was that corrupt practices erode a company's profits, lower labor productivity and quality standards of goods and services, and deter new investment. Businesses that sign on can display a sticker with the organization's logo, much like Better Business Bureau affiliates exhibit in the United States. At first many of Poland's new businesses, which had no model of civic action to emulate, were skeptical about *Manus Puris* and wondered whether it would itself be a target of bribes and favors from corrupt firms intent on "laundering" their image. Few of the leading companies listed on the Warsaw Stock Exchange or multinational subsidiaries subscribed to the program. Indeed, foreign-owned companies located in Poland also sometimes expect kickbacks for contracts or accounts opened on behalf of Polish firms.

The program requires its members to adopt work statutes that explicitly forbid bribe-taking and that protect whistle-blowers from dismissal. It was funded partly by the U.S. Agency for International Development (AID) and partly by the private, philanthropic Batory Foundation. Both the Polish-based British and American Chambers of Commerce supported the initiative, as did the World Bank and the Polish Office of Transparency International. The European Commission was, of course, committed to cleaning up corruption in prospective member states, even if it had itself been tainted by outrageous corruption among commission members and had also proved unsuccessful in reining in its most corrupt member-state, Greece. The funding agencies of *Manus Puris* reveal the principal deficiency in the anti-corruption drive: It is more of an externally driven campaign than one spontaneously created and embraced by the Polish business community.

According to Transparency International, a history of democracy plus being wealthy are the two factors that inhibit corrupt practices in a country. Poland has had neither. Credible political institutions also help: Poland's are just over a decade old. A tradition of investigative journalism is important: Only recently have Poland's largest newspapers and news weeklies realized that they had a part to play in exposing scandals. Most have now expanded their investigative reporting staffs. Forging transparent institutions may be the most difficult challenge facing Poland's structural transformation.

A Secular State for a Catholic Nation: Social, Cultural, and Ethnic Policies

To the surprise of some and to the relief of others, the Third Republic has not become a theocratic state. Catholicism in power was most closely embodied by the Wałęsa presidency of the first half of the 1990s, and a case (though not a very strong one) could be made for viewing the AWS-led coalition from 1997 to 2001 as anchored in Catholic values. The 1997 constitution was categorical that Poland was a state for both Catholics and other religious groups, for ethnic Poles and minority peoples. The Catholic Church was not given a privileged position in the country's political and cultural life, though of course that did not prevent it from shaping the values of individual Poles.

Will the Third Republic remain a state characterized by *laicité*—where, like Fifth Republic France, the separation of state and church does not prevent public funding for Catholic schools, and where Catholicism can cohabit with secularism? Or are fundamentalist Catholic groups still intent on making the Polish state serve their religious purposes? Is the popularity of Father Tadeusz Rydzyk, the voice of Radio Maryja (a radio station for devout Catholics) and a man described by the Polish press as "the most influential religious fundamentalist in Europe," an indication that Catholics are regrouping (reflected in the electoral success of the League of Polish Families in September 2001)? Or does the political dominance of the secular-oriented Alliance of the Democratic left suggest that the Third Republic is in the safe hands of anti-clericals?

Given such countervailing tendencies, the more realistic question to pose may be the following: Should Poland's Catholicism be reflected in the state's policies on a number of select issues, and if so which ones (education?) and in what ways (restricting abortions?)? We described the extraordinary influence that the church has exerted in the country in Chapter 4.

Today a consensus exists among Polish elites, at least, that church and state have to be separated. In a 1998 survey, elite respondents were asked to evaluate the statement: "The Church should be completely separate from the state, and religion should be treated exclusively as the private matter of a citizen." Of total elite members, 47 percent definitely agreed, 21 percent agreed somewhat, 10 percent said "neither yes or no," another 10 percent disagreed somewhat, and 13 percent definitely did not agree. Business elites felt most strongly (4.3 on a 5-point scale) that church–state separation was desirable, while the average answer among political elites was 3.5 and among administrative elites 3.6.[41] Further evidence of elite support for consolidation of a nonreligious polity came from the Polish business community's negative reaction to the success of the LPR in the fall 2001 parliamentary elections. Its concern was that foreign investors would be scared off by the perception of a fundamentalist revival in the country.

Poland's traditional values are marked by Catholicism, but there are cultural practices that have evolved largely independent of religious influences. A related question is: How can such embedded practices be used to meet the country's upcoming challenges? For not just institutional choices but also cultural makeup affects the success of political and economic change. Values deeply internalized by society can either promote or fetter development.[42] How those values get there is an important question. Are they the product of a country's history, the result of intense political socialization by a particular regime, the spontaneous by-product of creating a civil society, or the result of some other process? Can a given set of characteristics—in Poland's case, Catholicism, its experience of authoritarianism, and its ethnic homogeneity—be utilized in such a way that the society will respond effectively to future developmental challenges? What, in short, is the ideal-type culture for advancing political and economic development from the stage that Poland has reached at the turn of the new century?

A pathbreaking study of the link between culture and development was Robert Putnam's research explaining the different levels of development found in southern and northern Italy. This internal division has parallels with those between Eastern and Western Europe and so is worth considering here. Islamic rule was imposed on the Italian south a millennium ago, and it fostered vertical ties of dependence and exploitation. Correspondingly, an ethos of mutual distrust and conflict evolved that undermined any sense of solidarity. The north's heritage, in contrast, was of communal republicanism, itself a result of long experience of civic involvement, social responsibility, and mutual assistance. Horizontal ties of solidarity were cemented, thus laying the basis for social capital. Trust, along with norms, reciprocity, and networks, make up social capital, a public good. As we indicated earlier in this chapter, conventional capital is a private good.

Putnam contended that "a region's chances of achieving socioeconomic development during this century have depended less on its initial socio-economic endowments than on its civic endowments." In causal terms, "economics does not predict civics, but civics does predict economics, better indeed than economics itself."[43] For states having little conventional capital like Poland after communism, the fostering and marshaling of social capital became an important developmental task.

> For political stability, for government effectiveness, and even for economic progress social capital may be even more important than physical or human capital. Many of the formerly Communist societies had weak civic traditions before the advent of Communism, and totalitarian rule abused even that limited stock of social capital. Without norms of reciprocity and networks of civic engagement, the Hobbesian outcome of the Mezzogiorno—amoral familism, clientelism, lawlessness, ineffective government, and economic stagnation—seems likelier than successful democratization and economic development.[44]

The alternative to reciprocity/trust was, for Putnam, dependence/exploitation and what followed from this, underdevelopment. While accepting the importance that should be attached to social capital, Giuseppe di Palma, another specialist on democracy, interpreted the East European case in an almost diametrically opposite way. Instead of retracing history to discover where civic virtue had become rooted and where it was absent, he put a premium on the very recent East European experience of organizing against communism. If we share in di Palma's optimism, then there is a way of overcoming the dictum that capitalism punishes latecomers. The richness of the culture of dissent may compensate for the fact that democratic Poland and its neighbors were starting out at an earlier stage of economic development:

> Though East European societies suffer from relative backwardness, the legacy of dissent may help them escape the dire prophecies of the theorists of backwardness. By deciding to make civil society, rather than the state, the force behind Eastern Europe's regeneration, the dissidents have made an explicitly anti-Leninist choice. It is above all a cultural and indeed a moral choice.[45]

Such a normative structure could promote progress not by traditional developmental policies but by reconstituting citizens' relations with one another, that is, by building networks of trust and cooperation. Di Palma held out the possibility, therefore, that collective action could produce efficiency on the basis of a shorter but more recent and profound experience with solidarity and trust. The problem is that, as some of the data on cleavages and attitudinal differences regarding egalitarianism suggest, the horizontal networks so important to the rise of Solidarity may not have survived the transition process in Poland.

But are not Putnam and di Palma determinists for arguing that the sequence of development must entail a long- or even short-term experience with cooperation and solidarity that produces social capital and with it development? Tailoring a political system so that it harnesses society's present cultural makeup toward specific developmental tasks should be a way to arrive at the same result. Put another way, certain policies can be adopted that make optimum use of the fact that Polish society is overwhelmingly Catholic but largely secular oriented, that it contains attitudinal legacies of the paternalist communist past but is eager to demonstrate an entrepreneurial spirit in the new reality, and that it is ethnically homogeneous (as few other countries are today) but is very impressionable and sensitive to what other nations do.

Given these conditions, then, it is important to reflect upon what policy course could be charted that would most effectively nurture a culture of cooperation and trust in Poland, and would therefore multiply social capital—something that has been lacking in the Third Republic. Clearly one of the paramount tasks of any government in power is to meet future challenges by efficiently harnessing the most valuable cultural resources that Polish society has to offer.

In spite of the importance of cultural and related issues for Poland's future, it is nevertheless in the economy that Poland's most pressing and urgent problems are to be found. With unemployment at politically unacceptable levels and the life prospects of many Poles dismal—whether retired people, recent graduates, peasants, unskilled workers, or inhabitants of underdeveloped regions—it would seem that economic issues should be at the forefront of politics for Polish governments in the new millennium. Thus it is paradoxical that economic interests are *not* at the foundation of Poland's political divisions *nor* at the center of the elite's political (rather than policy) debates.

The situation faced by Miller's SLD after the 2001 parliamentary elections exemplified this crucial and continuing Third Republic dilemma. Here was a party leaning toward the center (or even center-right) in its economic and foreign policies. But it led a government in coalition with a more leftist party and an unabashedly agrarian party, neither of which were fully committed to the SLD leaders' vision of a free-market, European Poland. Policy compromises were necessary to maintain this fragile coalition, the only one apparently possible. In this respect, the situation of this government was not that different from that of the previous post-Solidarity government. Both were divided on economic policies, although dominated by a liberal mind-set; outside the parliament both faced the threat of popular action from well-organized protest organizations.

Our analysis of elites, society, institutions, and policy suggests a partial explanation for this paradox, that Poland's history has resulted in a cleavage pattern that has obscured the expression of economic interests. As long as elite politics remain shaped most powerfully by a historical-cultural cleavage based on individual biographies and religion, it has been hard for economic interests to be represented effectively within political institutions. The result has been a sharp disjuncture between the politics of governments and parliaments and the politics of the street—the popular protests. What was new after the 2001 elections was the rise of radical populist opposition within the parliament itself, as parties of various historical-cultural orientations attacked the government's economic and foreign policies. Rarely had economic interests found so vocal a representation within the political institutions of the Third Republic. Even though the virulent rhetoric produced in this debate spurred fears for Poland's hard-won democratic culture, if it signified a decline of the historical-cultural cleavage and a rise in the importance of the economic cleavage this could make Poland's democracy more robust, as the material interests of the less fortunate find more effective representation.

Notes

Introduction

1. Although Poland should be viewed as part of *Central Europe,* in this book the term is employed interchangeably with *Eastern Europe.* To refer to Poland exclusively as part of Central Europe would be to abandon retroactively the conventional terminology used for decades to describe the Soviet bloc. See Timothy Garton Ash, "Does Central Europe Exist?" in T. Garton Ash, *The Uses of Adversity: Essays on the Fate of Central Europe.* New York: Vintage, 1990, pp. 179–213. See also Adam Michnik, "The Two Faces of Europe," *The New York Review of Books,* July 19, 1990.

2. Data are taken from Główny Urząd Statystyczny, *Rocznik Statystyczny Rzeczypospolitej Polskiej 2000.* Warsaw: GUS, 2000, passim.

3. For an excellent summary of the recent literature on democratization, see Doh Chull Shin, "On the Third Wave of Democratization: A Synthesis and Evaluation of Recent Theory and Research," *World Politics,* 47, no. 1 (October 1994), 135–170.

4. Samuel P. Huntington, *The Third Wave: Democratization in the Late Twentieth Century.* Norman: University of Oklahoma Press, 1991, pp. 38–39.

5. For a succinct exposition of Adam Smith's general theory, see Donald Winch, *Adam Smith's Politics: An Essay in Historiographic Revision.* Cambridge: Cambridge University Press, 1978.

6. Max Weber, "Socialism," in *Weber: Selections in Translation.* Edited by W. G. Runciman. Cambridge: Cambridge University Press, 1978, pp. 251–262.

7. Barrington Moore, *Social Origins of Dictatorship and Democracy.* Boston: Beacon Press, 1966, Chap. 7.

8. Adam Przeworski, *Democracy and the Market: Political and Economic Reforms in Eastern Europe and Latin America.* Cambridge: Cambridge University Press, 1991, p. 26.

9. See, for instance, Ralf Dahrendorf, *Reflections on the Revolution in Europe.* New York: Times Books, 1990. Giuseppe di Palma, *To Craft Democracies: An Essay on Democratic Transitions.* Berkeley: University of California Press, 1990. Scott Mainwaring, Guillermo O'Donnell, and J. Samuel Valenzuela (eds.), *Issues in Democratic Consolidation.* South Bend, Ind.: University of Notre Dame Press, 1992.

10. Philippe C. Schmitter with Terry Lynn Karl, "The Conceptual Travels of Transitologists and Consolidologists: How Far to the East Should They Attempt to Go?" *Slavic Review,* 53, no. 1 (Spring 1994), 184, n. 21.

11. Alexis de Tocqueville, *Democracy in America*. Edited by J. P. Mayer. Garden City, N.Y.: Anchor Books, 1969, p. 277.

12. Herbert Kitschelt, "The Formation of Party Systems in East Central Europe," *Politics and Society*, 20 (1992), pp. 9–10.

Chapter 1

1. Oskar Halecki, *A History of Poland*. New York: Barnes and Noble, 1993, p. 5.

2. Tadeusz Manteuffel, *The Formation of the Polish State: The Period of Ducal Rule, 963–1194*. Detroit: Wayne State University Press, 1982, pp. 75–76.

3. Andrzej Wyczański, "The Problem of Authority in Sixteenth Century Poland: An Essay in Reinterpretation," in J. K. Fedorowicz (ed.), *A Republic of Nobles*. Cambridge: Cambridge University Press, 1982, p. 91.

4. Antoni Mączak, "The Structure of Power in the Commonwealth in the Sixteenth and Seventeenth Centuries," in J. K. Fedorowicz (ed.), *A Republic of Nobles*. Cambridge: Cambridge University Press, 1982, pp. 111–112.

5. Andrzej Walicki, "Polish Nationalism in Comparative Perspective," paper presented at the Conference on European Nationalisms, Tulane University, New Orleans, La., March 25–27, 1994, p. 17.

6. Janusz Tazbir, "Serce z zachodniej strony," *Gazeta Wyborcza*, January 22–23, 1994.

7. José Casanova, "Church, State, Nation, and Civil Society in Spain and Poland," in Said Amir Arjomand (ed.), *The Political Dimensions of Religion*. Albany: State University of New York Press, 1993, p. 119.

8. Norman Davies, *God's Playground*, vol. 1. New York: Columbia University Press, 1984, p. 340.

9. W. F. Reddaway et al. (eds.), *The Cambridge History of Poland*, vol. 1. Cambridge: Cambridge University Press, 1950, p. 439.

10. Jerzy Lukowski, *Liberty's Folly: The Polish–Lithuanian Commonwealth in the Eighteenth Century, 1697–1795*. London: Routledge, 1991, p. 25.

11. Davies, *God's Playground*, vol. 1, p. 487.

12. Aleksander Gieysztor et al., *History of Poland*. Warsaw: Polish Scientific Publishers, 1968, p. 323.

13. Jean-Jacques Rousseau, *The Government of Poland*. New York: Bobbs-Merrill, 1972, pp. 2, 10.

14. Quoted in Davies, *God's Playground*, vol. 1, pp. 521, 523.

15. For an incisive history, see Piotr S. Wandycz, *The Lands of Partitioned Poland, 1795–1918*. Seattle: University of Washington Press, 1974.

16. Aleksander Gella, *Development of Class Structure in Eastern Europe: Poland and Her Southern Neighbors*. Albany: State University of New York Press, 1989, p. 20. The six insurrections included the 1794 Kościuszko uprising, the 1806 rebellion in Poznań province, the 1830 November uprising, the 1846 revolt in western Galicia, the 1848 rebellion in western Poland (Wielkopolska), and the 1863 January insurrection. The 1794, 1830, and 1863 cases involved nationwide revolt.

17. Quoted in Reddaway et al. *The Cambridge History of Poland*, vol. 2, p. 338.

18. Casanova, "Church, State, Nation, and Civil Society," p. 120.

19. Adam B. Seligman, *The Idea of Civil Society*. New York: Free Press, 1992, p. 5.

20. Seligman, *The Idea of Civil Society*, p. 8.

21. For an illuminating biography, see Wacław Jędrzejewicz, *Piłsudski: A Life for Poland.* New York: Hippocrene Books, 1982.

22. Davies, *God's Playground,* vol. 2, p. 378.

23. Gella, *Development of Class Structure,* pp. 23–24.

24. E. Garrison Walters, *The Other Europe: Eastern Europe to 1945.* New York: Dorset Press, 1990, p. 180.

25. Gella, *Development of Class Structure,* p. 21.

26. The best English-language history of the period is Edward D. Wynot Jr., *Polish Politics in Transition: The Camp of National Unity and the Struggle for Power 1935–1939.* Athens: University of Georgia Press, 1974.

27. On foreign policy in this period, see Anna M. Cienciala, *Poland and the Western Powers 1938–1939: A Study in the Interdependence of Eastern and Western Europe.* London: Routledge and Kegan Paul, 1968.

28. See Jan Tomasz Gross, *Neighbors: The Destruction of the Jewish Community in Jedwabne, Poland.* Princeton: Princeton University Press, 2001.

29. The classic study of Katyn is Janusz Zawodny, *Death in the Forest: The Story of the Katyn Forest Massacre.* South Bend, Ind.: University of Notre Dame Press, 1962.

30. Jan T. Gross, *Revolution from Abroad: The Soviet Conquest of Poland's Western Ukraine and Western Belorussia.* Princeton: Princeton University Press, 1988, p. 226.

31. Gross, *Revolution from Abroad,* p. 225.

32. R. F. Leslie (ed.), *The History of Poland Since 1863.* Cambridge: Cambridge University Press, 1983, p. 221.

33. One classic study is Stefan Korboński, *Fighting Warsaw: The Story of the Polish Underground State 1939–1945.* New York: Minerva Press, 1968.

34. Quoted in John Coutouvidis and Jaime Reynolds, *Poland 1939–1947.* Leicester: Leicester University Press, 1986, p. 92.

35. Winston S. Churchill, *Closing the Ring: The Second World War,* vol. 5. Boston: Houghton Mifflin, 1951, pp. 450–451. The other zones were British, French, Soviet, and U.S.

36. *Documents on Polish–Soviet Relations, 1939–1945,* vol. 2 (1967), no. 239, pp. 416–422. Quoted in Coutouvidis and Reynolds, *Poland 1939–1947,* p. 106.

37. On Mikołajczyk and the London Poles' disputes with the PKWN, see Winston S. Churchill, *Triumph and Tragedy: The Second World War,* vol. 6. Boston: Houghton Mifflin, 1953, pp. 331–337, 365–387, 418–439.

Chapter 2

1. Joseph Rothschild, *Return to Diversity: A Political History of East Central Europe Since World War II.* New York: Oxford University Press, 1993, p. 84.

2. Hélène Carrère d'Encausse, *Big Brother: The Soviet Union and Soviet Europe.* New York: Holmes and Meier, 1987, p. 268.

3. John Rensenbrink, *Poland Challenges a Divided World.* Baton Rouge: Louisiana State University Press, 1988, p. 1.

4. Francis Fukuyama, *The End of History and the Last Man.* New York: Avon Books, 1993, pp. 45, 48.

5. Samuel P. Huntington, *The Third Wave: Democratization in the Late Twentieth Century.* Norman: University of Oklahoma Press, 1991, p. 105.

6. Huntington, *The Third Wave,* p. 86.

7. Huntington, *The Third Wave,* p. 72.

8. Andrew Janos, "Continuity and Change in Eastern Europe: Strategies of Post-Communist Politics," *East European Politics and Societies,* 8, no. 1 (Winter 1994), 3–4.

9. Janos, "Continuity and Change in Eastern Europe," p. 5.

10. F. A. Hayek, *The Fatal Conceit: The Errors of Socialism.* Edited by W. W. Bartley III. Chicago: University of Chicago Press, 1991, p. 6.

11. Hayek, *The Fatal Conceit,* p. 19.

12. Hayek, *The Fatal Conceit,* p. 87.

13. Hayek, *The Fatal Conceit,* p. 99.

14. See N. Scott Arnold, *Marx's Radical Critique of Capitalist Society.* New York: Oxford University Press, 1990, chap. 10.

15. Główny Urząd Statystyczny, *Rocznik statystyczny 1991.* Warsaw: GUS, 1991, pp. xxiv–xxvi, xxxvi–xxxviii.

16. Główny Urząd Statystyczny, *Rocznik statystyczny 1984.* Warsaw: GUS, 1984, pp. 156–163.

17. Włodzimierz Wesołowski, *Class, Strata, and Power.* London: Routledge and Kegan Paul, 1979, p. 118.

18. George Steiner, *Proofs.* London: Granta Books, 1992, p. 51.

19. Random sampling was, of course, impossible. One interesting point is that temporary visitors to the West were usually those who enjoyed the party's confidence and would, accordingly, have been more inclined to support the party. Yet the former prime minister and last party first secretary Mieczysław Rakowski noted that the first shocking results the party received in the 1989 parliamentary elections were from Poland's embassies and offices abroad. Though largely party appointees, the majority of these officials nonetheless cast their votes against the ruling communists. See Mieczysław Rakowski, *Jak to się stało.* Warsaw: BGW, 1991. The most informative single work on opinion polling in Poland is David S. Mason, *Public Opinion and Political Change in Poland, 1980–1982.* Cambridge: Cambridge University Press, 1985.

20. Krzysztof Jasiewicz, "Kultura polityczna Polaków: Między jednością a podziałem," *Aneks,* 48 (1988), 70.

21. David S. Mason, "Public Opinion in Poland's Transition to Market Democracy," in Walter D. Connor and Piotr Płoszajski (eds.), *The Polish Road from Socialism: The Economics, Sociology, and Politics of Transition.* Armonk, N.Y.: M. E. Sharpe, 1992, p. 158. He cited research examining seven Warsaw enterprises carried out by Bogdan Cichomski and Witold Morawski, "The Perception of Justice in Poland," paper presented at the Annual Meeting of the International Studies Association, London, March 1989.

22. Edmund Mokrzycki, "The Legacy of Real Socialism, Group Interests, and the Search for a New Utopia," in Connor and Płoszajski, *The Polish Road from Socialism,* p. 277.

23. Krzysztof Jasiewicz and Władysław Adamski, "Evolution of the Oppositional Consciousness," in Władysław Adamski (ed.), *Societal Conflict and Systemic Change: The Case of Poland, 1980–1992.* Warsaw: IFiS, 1993, p. 50.

24. Andrzej Rychard and Jacek Szymanderski, "Crisis and Conflict with Respect to Legitimacy," in Adamski, *Societal Conflict and Systemic Change,* p. 199.

25. Rychard and Szymanderski, "Crisis and Conflict," p. 205.

26. Rychard and Szymanderski, "Crisis and Conflict," p. 206.

27. Janusz Reykowski, "Psychological Dimensions of a Sociopolitical Change," in Connor and Płoszajski, *The Polish Road from Socialism,* p. 218.

28. Reykowski, "Psychological Dimensions," pp. 225–226.

29. Mason, "Public Opinion in Poland's Transition," p. 159.

30. Krzysztof Jasiewicz, "From Protest and Repression to the Free Elections," in Adamski, *Societal Conflict and Systemic Change,* p. 129.

31. Lena Kolarska-Bobińska, "Social Interests, Egalitarian Attitudes, and the Change of Economic Order," *Social Research,* 55, nos. 1–2 (Spring/Summer 1988), 122.

32. Lena Kolarska-Bobińska, "Economic System and Group Interests," in Adamski, *Societal Conflict and Systemic Change,* pp. 93–114.

33. Renata Siemieńska, "Zaufanie Polaków do innych narodów w okresie politycznych i ekonomicznych przemian," in Aleksandra Jasińska-Kania (ed.), *Bliscy i dalecy,* vol. 2. Warsaw: Uniwersytet Warszawski, Instytut Socjologii, 1992, pp. 208–209.

34. Aleksandra Jasińska-Kania, "Zmiany postaw Polaków wobec różnych narodów i państw," in Jasińska-Kania, *Bliscy i dalecy,* vol. 2, pp. 220, 231–232.

35. Władysław Adamski, "Poles Between East and West," in Adamski, *Societal Conflict and Systemic Change,* pp. 160, 164.

36. Jacek Kurczewski, *The Resurrection of Rights in Poland.* Oxford: Clarendon Press, 1993, p. 46.

37. Stefan Wyszyński, *Zapiski więzienne.* Paris: Editions du Dialogue, 1982.

38. Norbert A. Zmijewski, *The Catholic–Marxist Ideological Dialogue in Poland, 1945–1980.* Aldershot, England: Dartmouth, 1991, p. 138.

39. Zmijewski, *The Catholic–Marxist Ideological Dialogue,* pp. 141–142.

40. On the inability of the communist rulers to stir up rivalry between Cardinals Wyszyński and Wojtyła, see Andrzej Micewski, *Cardinal Wyszyński.* San Diego: Harcourt Brace Jovanovich, 1984.

41. John Clark and Aaron Wildavsky, *The Moral Collapse of Communism: Poland as a Cautionary Tale.* San Francisco: Institute for Contemporary Studies Press, 1990, p. 345.

42. José Casanova, "Church, State, Nation, and Civil Society in Spain and Poland," in Said Amir Arjomand (ed.), *The Political Dimensions of Religion.* Albany: State University of New York Press, 1993, p. 135.

43. Andrzej Rychard, "Participation and Interests: Dilemmas of the Emerging Social and Political Structure in Poland," in Connor and Płoszajski, *The Polish Road from Socialism,* p. 176.

44. Neil Ascherson, *The Polish August.* Harmondsworth, England: Penguin, 1983; Abraham Brumberg (ed.), *Poland: Genesis of a Revolution.* New York: Vintage Books, 1983; George Sanford, *Polish Communism in Crisis.* New York: St. Martin's, 1983.

45. David J. Ost, "Indispensable Ambiguity: Solidarity's Internal Authority Structure," *Studies in Comparative Communism,* 21, no. 2 (Summer 1988), 197. See also his *Solidarity and the Politics of Anti-Politics.* Philadelphia: Temple University Press, 1990.

46. Transcript of the founding conference of national Solidarity, September 17, 1980, p. 66. The English translation of the transcript was made available by David Ost. The Polish version was first published in *Krytyka,* no. 18 (1984).

47. Transcript of the founding conference of national Solidarity, p. 12.

48. Transcript of the founding conference of national Solidarity, p. 48.

49. Ost, "Indispensable Ambiguity," p. 191.

50. Ost, "Indispensable Ambiguity," p. 199.

51. Jack Bielasiak and Barbara Hicks, "Solidarity's Self-Organization: The Crisis of Rationality and Legitimacy in Poland, 1980–81," *East European Politics and Society,* 4, no. 3 (Fall 1990), 489.

52. Bielasiak and Hicks, "Solidarity's Self-Organization," pp. 511–512.

53. Jadwiga Staniszkis, *Poland's Self-Limiting Revolution.* Princeton: Princeton University Press, 1984.

54. Jacek Kurczewski, *The Resurrection of Rights in Poland,* pp. 212–215.

55. Roman Laba, "Worker Roots of Solidarity," *Problems of Communism,* 35 (July-August 1986), 47–67.

56. The best account is Jan Józef Lipski, *KOR: A History of the Workers' Defense Committee in Poland.* Berkeley: University of California Press, 1985.

57. Neal Ascherson, "1989 in Eastern Europe: Constitutional Representative Democracy as a 'Return to Normality'?" in John Dunn (ed.), *Democracy: The Unfinished Journey, 508 BC to AD 1993.* New York: Oxford University Press, 1992, pp. 225–226.

58. Ascherson, "1989 in Eastern Europe," p. 224.

Chapter 3

1. Jadwiga Staniszkis, *The Dynamics of the Breakthrough in Eastern Europe: The Polish Experience.* Berkeley: University of California Press, 1991, p. 98.

2. Jacek Żakowski, *Rok 1989: Geremek opowiada, Żakowski pyta.* Warsaw: Plejada, 1990, p. 29.

3. Żakowski, *Rok 1989,* p. 131.

4. Interview with Janusz Reykowski, Stanford, Calif., May 22, 1991.

5. Jacek Kurczewski, *The Resurrection of Rights in Poland.* Oxford: Clarendon Press, 1993, p. 349.

6. See Miodowicz's speech at the Eighth Plenum, reported in *Trybuna Ludu,* August 29, 1988.

7. Piotr Kwiatkowski, "Opinion Research and the Fall of Communism: Poland 1981–1990," *International Journal of Public Opinion Research,* 4, no. 4 (Winter 1992), 364.

8. *Życie Warszawy,* August 27–28, 1988. Kiszczak added that those who rejected the constitutional order of the Polish People's Republic could not participate.

9. X Plenum KC PZPR. *Podstawowe dokumenty i materiały: 20–21 grudnia 1988 r., 16–18 stycznia 1989 r.* Warsaw: Książka i Wiedza, 1989, pp. 16, 21, 24.

10. "The Geoffrey Stern Interview: Mieczysław Rakowski," *LSE Magazine* (Summer 1991), 14.

11. Karol B. Janowski, "PZPR—od monolitu i monopolu do agonii (analiza przypadku)," unpublished paper, Warsaw, April 1990, p. 21.

12. This calculation is based on interviews conducted by one of the authors, as well as PZPR documents.

13. On the political regression that occurred at the Tenth Congress, see Karol B. Janowski, *Demokracja socjalistyczna w koncepcjach polityczno-programowych PZPR.* Warsaw: Państwowe Wydawnictwo Naukowe, 1989, p. 390.

14. *Trybuna Ludu,* May 8, 1989.

15. Cited in Mieczysław Rakowski, *Jak to się stało.* Warsaw: BGW, 1991, pp. 214, 224.

16. Janusz Reykowski, "Resolving of the Large Scale Political Conflict: The Case of the Round Table Negotiations in Poland," paper presented at the Symposium of Group

Conflict, Texas A & M University, College Station, 1990, p. 11. Cited by Steven Saxonberg, *The Fall: A Comparative Study of the End of Communism in Czechoslovakia, East Germany, Hungary and Poland.* Amsterdam: Harwood, 2001, p. 272.

17. Żakowski, *Rok 1989*, p. 14.

18. Żakowski, *Rok 1989*, p. 16.

19. Żakowski, *Rok 1989*, p. 214.

20. See, for example, notes taken by Krzysztof Dubiński and published as *Magdalenka: Transakcja epoki.* Warsaw: Sylwa, 1990, pp. 88–92.

21. "Mały słownik III Rzeczypospolitej," *Wprost*, no. 27 (July 4, 1993), 38.

22. Żakowski, *Rok 1989*, p. 113.

23. Żakowski, *Rok 1989*, p. 131.

24. Żakowski, *Rok 1989*, p. 114.

25. Żakowski, *Rok 1989*, p. 71.

26. Żakowski, *Rok 1989*, pp. 71, 74, 78.

27. Żakowski, *Rok 1989*, p. 112.

28. Quoted in Dubiński, *Magdalenka*, pp. 129, 131.

29. Quoted in Dubiński, *Magdalenka*, p. 53.

30. The parliamentary scholar Stanisław Gebethner provided the political reform subtable on February 10 with data showing that 88 percent of Poles in 1988 wanted free elections.

31. See Saxonberg, *The Fall*, pp. 282–283.

32. A senate so conceived—as an institution for patronage by the political leader—is not as extraordinary as Kiszczak's proposal appeared. Appointment to the Canadian Senate is used to reward longtime friends of the prime minister's party.

33. Rakowski, *Jak to się stało*, p. 203, and one author's interviews with several participants.

34. *Porozumienie okrągłego stołu.* Warsaw: NSZZ Solidarność, Region Warmińsko-Mazurski, 1989, p. 7.

35. Other than the appointment of judges and the status of the procuracy, a third legal issue left unresolved by the roundtable was capital punishment, which Solidarity sought to end. See Kurczewski, *The Resurrection of Rights*, pp. 88–92.

36. CBOS, "Okrągły stół: Opinie o przebiegu i politycznych rezultatach rozmów," BD/95/16/89 (April 1989).

37. Kwiatkowski, "Opinion Research and the Fall of Communism," p. 369.

38. See the section "Przewidywania" in Lena Kolarska-Bobińska, Piotr Łukasiewicz, and Zbigniew Rykowski (eds.), *Wyniki badań, wyniki wyborów: 4 czerwca 1989.* Warsaw: Ośrodek Badań Społecznych, 1990, pp. 13–74.

39. Paweł Kuczyński, "Sondaż przedwyborczy dla 'Le Journal des Elections,'" in Kolarska-Bobińska et al., *Wyniki badań, wyniki wyborów*, pp. 13–25. The French organizer of the poll was Georges Mink.

40. Staniszkis, *Dynamics of the Breakthrough*, p. 199.

41. Krzysztof Jasiewicz, "Zachowania wyborcze w świetle badań z serii 'Polacy,'" in Kolarska-Bobińska et al., *Wyniki badań, wyniki wyborów*, p. 181.

42. Stanisław Gebethner, "Wybory do Sejmu i Senatu 1989 r. (wstępne refleksje)," *Państwo i Prawo*, 44, no. 8 (August 1989), 3–14.

43. Krzysztof Kosela, "Rola kościoła katolickiego w kampanii przed wyborami czerwcowymi," in Kolarska-Bobińska et al., *Wyniki badań, wyniki wyborów*, pp. 129–135.

44. Żakowski, *Rok 1989*, p. 234.

45. "Stanowisko w sprawie powołanie rządu i aktualnej sytuacji politycznej przyjęte przez XIV Plenum KC PZPR, 19 sierpnia 1989 r.," *Trybuna Ludu,* August 21, 1989.

46. Żakowski, *Rok 1989*, pp. 252–253.

47. "Stanowisko XV Plenum KC PZPR w sprawie głównych zadań partii w okresie poprzedzającym XI Zjazdu," *Trybuna Ludu,* October 5, 1989.

48. "Referat Biura Politycznego KC PZPR wygłoszony przez L. Millera," *Trybuna Ludu,* October 4, 1989.

49. Żakowski, *Rok 1989*, p. 255.

50. Żakowski, *Rok 1989*, pp. 124–125. The hard-liner was Kazimierz Cypryniak.

51. Kazimierz Barcikowski, quoted by Maksymilian Berezowski, *Koniec epoki.* Warsaw: Novum, 1991, p. 61.

52. Żakowski, *Rok 1989*, p. 276.

53. Carl Linden, "Opposition and Faction in Communist Party Leaderships," in Frank P. Belloni and Dennis C. Beller (eds.), *Faction Politics: Political Parties and Factionalism in Comparative Perspective.* Santa Barbara, Calif.: ABC-Clio, 1978, p. 379.

54. Stenogram z zebrania klubu poselskiego PZPR odbytego dnia 30 czerwca 1989 r. w sali nr 561 gmachu KC PZPR (wspólne z członkami KC PZPR), "Wystąpienie Wojciecha Jaruzelskiego," p. 4.

55. Stenogram z zebrania klubu poselskiego, 30 czerwca 1989 r., "Wystąpienie Wojciecha Jaruzelskiego," p. 8.

56. Stenogram z zebrania klubu poselskiego, 30 czerwca 1989 r., "Wystąpienie Wojciecha Jaruzelskiego," p. 6.

57. Stenogram z zebrania klubu poselskiego, 30 czerwca 1989 r., "Głos z sali," p. 13.

58. A documentary film, *Ostatki* ("Remainders"), captures the poignant but more often comic scenes of the PZPR's last congress in January 1990.

59. "Wystąpienie tow. Józefa Oleksego na wspólnym posiedzeniu Biura Politycznego KC PZPR i Prezydium Klubu Poselskiego PZPR w dniu 16 września b.r.," Informacja Nr II/175/89 (September 27, 1989), p. 1.

60. Informacja II/175/89, "Wystąpienie Józefa Oleksego," p. 2.

61. Informacja II/175/89, "Wystąpienie Józefa Oleksego," p. 14.

62. "Zasady współdziałania Komitetu Centralnego i instancji partyjnych z partyjnymi posłami i Klubem Poselskim PZPR," Zatwierdzone przez Biuro Polityczne KC PZPR, October 24, 1989 r.

63. Klub Poselski PZPR, "Wezwanie Klubu poselskiego PZPR do członków partii," January 1990.

64. "Stanowisko klubu poselskiego PZPR przed XI Zjazdem PZPR i Kongresem nowej partii," January 19, 1990.

65. *Trybuna Ludu,* January 25, 1990.

Chapter 4

1. Michael Burton, Richard Gunther, and John Higley, "Introduction: Elite Transformations and Democratic Regimes," in John Higley and Richard Gunther (eds.), *Elites and Democratic Consolidation in Latin America and Southern Europe.* Cambridge: Cambridge University Press, 1992, p. 8.

2. Unless otherwise attributed, data in this section are from Główny Urząd Statystyczny, *Rocznik Statystyczny Rzeczypospolitej Polskiej 2000*. Warsaw: GUS, 2000, passim.

3. Information on education, work record, and party affiliation of female Sejm deputies is drawn from Renata Siemieńska, *Nie moga, nie chcą czy nie potrafią?: O postawach i uczestnictwie politycznym kobiet w Polsce*. Warsaw: Wydawnictwo Naukowe "Scholar," 2000.

4. Jacek Wasilewski, "Polish Post-Transitional Elites," in Janina Frentzel-Zagórska and Jacek Wasilewski (eds.), *The Second Generation of Democratic Elites in Central and Eastern Europe*. Warsaw: Institute of Political Studies, Polish Academy of Sciences, 2000, pp. 197–198.

5. Agnieszka Jasiewicz-Betkiewicz, "Biografie—motywacje," in Mirosława Grabowska and Tadeusz Szawiel (eds.), *Korzenie demokracji: Partie polityczne w środowisku lokalnym*. Warsaw: Instytut Studiów Politycznych Polskiej Akademii Nauk, 2000, pp. 79–80.

6. Wasilewski, "Polish Post-Transitional Elites," p. 199.

7. Wasilewski, "Polish Post-Transitional Elites," p. 200.

8. Wasilewski, "Polish Post-Transitional Elites," pp. 201–202.

9. Wasilewski, "Polish Post-Transitional Elites," p. 203.

10. Wasilewski, "Polish Post-Transitional Elites," pp. 197–215.

11. Burton et al., "Introduction: Elite Transformations," p. 3.

12. Jacek Wasilewski, "Orientacje wartościujące elity," in Jacek Wasilewski (ed.), *Zbiorowi aktorzy polskiej polityki*. Warsaw: Instytut Studiów Politycznych Polskiej Akademii Nauk, 1997, pp. 274–302.

13. Jacek Wasilewski, "Normatywna integracja polskiej elity potransformacyjnej," in Henryk Domański, Antonina Ostrowska, and Andrzej Rychard (eds.), *Jak żyją Polacy*. Warsaw: Wydawnictwo IFiS PAN, 2000, p. 94.

14. Burton et al., "Introduction: Elite Transformations," p. 10.

15. Mirosława Grabowska, "Partie polityczne jako działające aktorzy: Partyjne organizacje—programy—elity," in Mirosława Grabowska and Tadeusz Szawiel (eds.), *Budowanie demokracji: Podziały społeczne, partie polityczne i społeczeństwo obywatelskie w postkomunistyczne Polsce*. Warsaw: Wydawnictwo Naukowe PAN, 2001, p. 363.

16. Joanna Kuszlik, "Pragmatyczna Zjednoczona Partia Rządząca?" and Agnieszka Jasiewicz-Betkiewicz, "Biografie—motywacje," in Grabowska and Szawiel (eds.), *Korzenie demokracji*, pp. 49–76 and 77–115.

17. An excellent fictional illustration of this is in Krzysztof Kieslowski's film *Blind Chance*, which portrays three different directions a medical student's life might have taken, depending on what happens when he runs to catch a departing train. In one life he becomes a promising young communist; in another he becomes an opposition activist; in yet another he becomes an apolitical doctor.

18. Wasilewski, "Polish Post-Transitional Elites," pp. 205–206. Most Poles would count the 13 percent of parliamentarians and 5 percent of administrative elites who had switched from active support to active opposition as part of the post-oppositional elites. Wasilewski bases his classification on a variety of activities, including membership in pro-regime student organizations or in the Solidarity trade union.

19. Wasilewski provides the numbers on elite church attendance in "Polish Post-Transitional Elites," p. 198. Grabowska and Szawiel's research on party congress delegates suggests that the majority of the attendees describe themselves as nonbelievers. See Grabowska, "Partie polityczne jako działający aktorzy," pp. 303–365; and Grabowska and

Szawiel, *Anatomia elit politycznych: Partie polityczne w postkomunistycznej Polsce 1991–1993*. Warsaw: Instytut Socjologii Uniwersystetu Warszawskiego, 1993.

20. Bogna Wciórka, "Religijność Polaków na przełomie wieków," CBOS Komunikat no. 53 (2001). See http://www.cbos.com/pl/spiskom.pol/2001/kom053.

21. Grabowska, "Partie polityczne jako działający aktorzy," p. 363.

22. Wasilewski, "Normatywna Integracja Polskiej Elity Potransformacyjnej," p. 79.

23. Jacek Wasilewski, "The Crystallization of the Post-Communist and Post-Solidarity Political Elite," in Edward Wnuk-Lipiński (ed.), *After Communism: A Multidisciplinary Approach to Radical Social Change*. Warsaw: Institute of Political Studies, Polish Academy of Sciences, 1995, p. 127.

24. Jasiewicz-Betkiewicz, "Biografie—motywacje," pp. 77–138.

25. Herbert Kitschelt, Zdenka Mansfeldova, Radosław Markowski, and Gábor Tóka, *Post-Communist Party Systems: Competition, Representation, and Inter-Party Cooperation*. Cambridge: Cambridge University Press, 1999, pp. 353–358.

26. Kitschelt et al., *Post-Communist Party Systems*, pp. 363–374.

27. Joanna Kuszlik, "Pragmatyczna Zjednoczona Partia Rządząca?" in Grabowska and Szawiel (eds.), *Korzenie demokracji*, pp. 49–76.

28. Krzysztof Jasiecki, "Konsens i konflikt w poglądach elity politycznej," in Włodzimierz Wesołowski and Barbara Post (eds.), *Polityka i Sejm: Formowanie się elity politycznej*. Warsaw: Wydawnictwo Sejmowe, 1998, p. 79.

29. Aleksander Smolar, "Poland's Emerging Party System," *Journal of Democracy*, 9, no. 2 (1998), 129.

30. Kuszlik, "Pragmatyczna Zjednoczona Partia Rządząca?" p. 54.

31. Jasiecki, "Konsens i konflikt," pp. 74–75.

32. Seymour M. Lipset and Stein Rokkan, "Cleavage Structures, Party Systems, and Voter Alignments: An Introduction," in Lipset and Rokkan (eds.), *Party Systems and Voter Alignments: Cross-National Perspectives*. London: Collier-Macmillan, 1967.

33. Janina Frentzel-Zagórska makes a convincing argument for this approach in her "Structure of the Polish Political Scene as Seen by the Elite," in Frentzel-Zagórska and Jacek Wasilewski, (eds.), *The Second Generation of Democratic Elites in Central and Eastern Europe*. Warsaw: Institute of Political Studies, Polish Academy of Sciences, 2000, pp. 217–231.

34. See, for example, Wasilewski, "Normatywna integracja polskiej elity potransformacyjnej," p. 98, as well as Tadeusz Szawiel, "Podział lewica-prawica w polityce oraz w szerszym kontekście kulturowym," in Grabowska and Szawiel, *Budowanie demokracji*.

35. The 2001 SLD–UP coalition also included three very small parties: the National Party of Retired People and Pensioners, the Democratic Party, and the Peasant-Democratic Party.

36. While that final percentage represents votes for the SLD–UP electoral coalition, the SLD can easily take the lion's share of the credit; in a CBOS poll taken in February 2001, one month before the SLD and the UP formed their coalition, 38 percent of voters supported the SLD and 4 percent the UP. *Gazeta Wyborcza*, March 10–11, 2001.

37. At least two additional post-communist leftist parties emerged from the ashes of the PZPR—the Polish Social Democratic Union (PUS), committed to a sharper break with the communist past, and the Union of Communists of the Polish Republic "Proletariat," but neither party would play a significant role. Many of the PUS founders later joined the Union of Labor. See Barbara Rogowska, "SdRP we wczesnym okresie transfor-

macji ustrojowej w latach 1989–1990. Ciągłość czy zmiana?," and Zbigniew Wiktor, "Zmierzch PZPR i odbudowa partii komunistycznej w Polsce w 1990 r.," in Stanisław Dąbrowski and Barbara Rogowska (eds.), *Z badań nad przemianami politycznymi w Polsce po 1989 roku*. Wrocław: Wydawnictwo Uniwersytetu Wrocławskiego, 1998.

38. Kuszlik, "Pragmatyczna Zjednoczona Partia Rządząca?" and Jasiewicz-Betkiewicz, "Biografie—motywacje," pp. 49–76 and 77–115.

39. *Gazeta Wyborcza*, December 23–26, 2000. For examples of conflicts within the Warsaw and Łódź SLD organizations being resolved decisively by the central leadership (by Miller in particular), see "Partia daje, partia odbiera," *Gazeta Wyborcza*, February 21, 2001, and "Wieteska non amour," *Gazeta Wyborcza*, May 17, 2001.

40. Kitschelt et al., *Post-Communist Party Systems*, p. 231.

41. Krzysztof Janik, interviewed by Agata Nowakowska, *Gazeta Wyborcza*, April 25, 2001.

42. Kuszlik, "Pragmatyczna Zjednoczona Partia Rządząca?" p. 59.

43. We are indebted to Jane Curry for much of this analysis. Also see Marjorie Castle, "The Post-Communist Identity and East European Politics," in Victoria E. Bonnell (ed.), *Identities in Transition: Eastern Europe and Russia After the Collapse of Communism*. Berkeley: Center for Slavic and East European Studies, 1996, p. 160.

44. Andrzej Chojnacki, in *Slowo-Dziennik Katolicki*, quoted in *Gazeta Wyborcza*, January 30, 1996.

45. *Gazeta Wyborcza*, January 12, 2001.

46. Grabowska, "Partie polityczne jako działające aktorzy," p. 347.

47. George Blazyca and Ryszard Rapacki, "Continuity and Change in Polish Economic Policy: The Impact of the 1993 Election," *Europe-Asia Studies*, January, 1996.

48. *Gazeta Wyborcza*, June 25, 2001.

49. Krzysztof Janik, interviewed by Agata Nowakowska, *Gazeta Wyborcza*, April 25, 2001.

50. *Gazeta Wyborcza*, December 11, 1996.

51. Interviewed by Adam Michnik and Paweł Smoleński, *Gazeta Wyborcza*, January 15–16, 2000.

52. Ryszard Bugaj, former head of the Union of Labor, writing in *Gazeta Wyborcza*, January 27, 2000.

53. See Michael T. Hannan and John Freeman, *Organizational Ecology*. Cambridge: Harvard University Press, 1989; and Angelo Panebianco, *Political Parties: Organization and Power*. Oxford: Oxford University Press, 1988, for analyses of the role that goals or ideology play in a newly formed organization.

54. This metaphor is used by Tomasz Nałęcz of Unia Pracy in an interview with Agata Nowakowska and Wojciech Załuska, *Gazeta Wyborcza*, October 30-November 1, 1993.

55. Hannan and Freeman, *Organizational Ecology*.

56. Herbert Kitschelt, *The Logics of Party Formation: Ecological Politics in Belgium and West Germany*. Ithaca: Cornell University Press, 1989.

57. For this concept, see Otto Kirchheimer, "The Transformation of the Western European Party System," in Joseph LaPalombara and Myron Weiner (eds.), *Political Parties and Political Development*. Princeton: Princeton University Press, 1966, pp. 177–200.

58. CBOS, reported in *Gazeta Wyborcza*, July 20, 2001.

59. Interviewed by Agata Nowakowska, *Gazeta Wyborcza*, April 4, 2001.

60. Interviewed by Agata Nowakowska and Wojciech Załuska, *Gazeta Wyborca*, March 30-April 1, 1993.

61. See *Gazeta Wyborcza*, June 7, 1995, for this reconstruction of the UP founders' thinking.

62. Reported in Jasiewicz-Betkiewicz, "Biografie-motywacje," pp. 77–115.

63. For party congress delegate data, see Grabowska, "Partie polityczne jako działający aktorzy," pp. 303–365.

64. Aleksander Małachowski, quoted in *Gazeta Wyborcza*, October 15, 1993.

65. *Gazeta Wyborcza*, June 7, 1995.

66. Grabowska, "Partie polityczne jako działający aktorzy," p. 362.

67. *Gazeta Wyborcza*, December 15, 1998.

68. See, for example, the results cited by Tadeusz Szawiel, "Zróżnicowanie lewicowo-prawicowe i jego korelaty," in Radosław Markowski (ed.), *Wybory parlamentarne 1997: System partyjny, postawy polityczne, zachowanie wyborcze*. Warsaw: Instytut Studiów Politycznych Polskiej Akademii Nauk, 1999, pp. 111–148.

69. The Confederation for an Independent Poland (KPN), the Nonparty Bloc for Reform (BBWR), Fatherland, Solidarity, the Center Democratic Alliance, the Coalition for the Republic, and the Union of Political Realism. We classify the Liberal Democratic Congress (KLD) as a centrist party.

70. Teresa Bogucka, "Telekreacja," *Gazeta Wyborcza*, April 11, 2001.

71. Grabowska, "Partie polityczne jako działający aktorzy," pp. 347–348.

72. Quoted in Jasiewicz-Betkiewicz, "Biografie—motywacje," p. 106.

73. Jasiecki, "Konsens i konflikt," pp. 63–64.

74. See Carolyn M. Warner, "Political Parties and the Opportunity Costs of Patronage," *Party Politics*, 3, no.4, pp. 533–548, for an analysis of how patronage can hurt a party on the electoral market.

75. *Gazeta Wyborcza*, July 20, 2001.

76. *Gazeta Wyborcza*, August 6, 2001.

77. "Korupcja i afery korupcyjne w Polsce," CBOS komunikat, July 2001.

78. Tadeusz Szawiel, "Prawica a kultura: Dlaczego prawica w Polsce po 1989 r. jest słaba i skłócona?" in Mirosława Grabowska and Stanisław Mocek (eds.), *Pierwsza sześciolatka 1989–1995: Próba bilansu polityki*. Warsaw: Instytut Studiów Politycznych Polskiej Akademii Nauk, 1997, pp. 129–149.

79. Panebianco, *Political Parties*.

80. Smolar, "Poland's Emerging Party System," pp. 122–133.

81. There were of course exceptions to this generalization, most prominently Władysław Frasyniuk, but they tended to be overlooked when this criticism was made.

82. Stanisław Podemski, "Zadowoleni i niespokojni," *Polityka*, no. 27 (July 3, 1993).

83. Lena Kolarska-Bobińska, Jacek Kucharczyk, Beata Roguska, and Elżbieta Firlit, "Duchowieństwo polskie wobec perspektywy integracji europejskiej," in Lena Kolarska-Bobińska (ed.), *Polska eurodebata*. Warsaw: Instytut Spraw Publicznych, 1999, p. 108.

84. Irena Panków, "Trade Unions and Politics," in Frentzel-Zagórska and Wasilewski (eds.), *The Second Generation of Democratic Elites*, p. 250. Much of this account on unions is based on Panków's analysis.

85. Ewa Barlik, "Kryzys wartości," *Rzeczpospolita*, July 17, 1999.

86. Mieczysław Bąk and Przemysław Kulawczuk, *Kultura polityczna polskiej demokracji*. Warsaw: Instytut Badań nad Demokracją i Przedsiębiorstwem Prywatnym, 1998.

87. OBOP, "Opinie o wpływie polskich przedsiębiorców na rząd," 1995. This result is confirmed by Marek Mlicki, "Lobbying w polskim Sejmie," in Włodzimierz Wesołowski and Barbara Post (eds.), *Polityka i Sejm: Formowanie się elity politycznej.* Warsaw: Wydawnictwo Sejmowe, 1998.

88. Zbigniew Drąg, "Elita biznesu: Autonomiczny segment elity politycznej?" in Jacek Wasilewski (ed.), *Elita polityczna 1998.* Warsaw: ISP, 1999, p. 78.

89. Krzysztof Jasiecki, "Lobbing gospodarczy w Polsce," *Studia Socjologiczne*, 4, no. 159 (2000), p. 56.

90. Cited by Panków, "Trade Unions and Politics," p. 253.

Chapter 5

1. "Consolidation and the Cleavages of Ideology and Identity," in Jon Elster, Claus Offe, and Ulrich K. Preuss, *Institutional Design in Post-Communist Societies: Rebuilding the Ship at Sea.* Cambridge: Cambridge University Press, 1998, pp. 247–270.

2. Elster et al., *Institutional Design*, pp. 249–250.

3. Włodzimierz Wesołowski, "Transformacja charakteru i struktury interesów: Aktualne procesy, szanse i zagrożenia," in Andrzej Rychard and Michał Federowicz (eds.), *Społeczeństwo w transformacji: Ekspertyzy i studia.* Warsaw: IFiS PAN, 1993, pp. 133, 138.

4. Macieja Fałkowska, "Hierarchia zawodów i czynniki życiowego sukcesu," in Krzysztof Zagórski and Michał Strzeszewski (eds.), *Nowa rzeczywistość: Oceny i opinie 1989–1999.* Warsaw: DIALOG, 2000, p. 159.

5. Renata Siemieńska, *Nie mogą, nie chcą czy nie potrafią: O postawach i uczestnictwie politycznym kobiet w Polsce.* Warsaw: Wydawnictwo Naukowe "Scholar," 2000, p. 9. See also her "Women's Political Participation in Central and Eastern Europe: A Cross-Cultural Perspective," in Barbara Wejnert, Metta Spencer, and Slobodan Drakulic (eds.), *Women in Post-Communism.* London: JAI Press, 1996.

6. For an illuminating study of how Polish women are depicted in television advertising today, in ways similar to the West, see Paulina Sekuła, "Kobieta w reklamie telewizyjnej a konflikty ról płci we współczesnym społeczeństwie polskim," in Marian Malinowski and Zygmunt Seręga, *Konflikty społeczne w Polsce w okresie zmian systemowych*, vol. 2. Rzeszów: Wydawnictwo Wyższej Szkoły Pedagogicznej, 2000, pp. 277–287.

7. Centrum Badania Opinii Społecznej, "Religijność Polaków w III RP" (March 1999). See http://www.cbos.pl/cbos_pl.htm.

8. Kazimierz M. Słomczyński with Krystyna Janicka, Bogdan W. Mach, and Wojciech Zaborowski, *Mental Adjustment to the Post-Communist System in Poland.* Warsaw: IFiS Publishers, 1999, p. 186.

9. Mirosława Grabowska and Tadeusz Szawiel, *Budowanie demokracji: Podziały społeczne, partie polityczne i społeczeństwo obywatelskie w postkomunistycznej Polsce.* Warsaw: PWN, 2001, pp. 10, 104n. The survey was carried out in 1995.

10. "New Democracies Barometer," Centre for the Study of Public Policy, University of Strathclyde, Glasgow, Scotland. See www.cspp.strath.ac.uk.

11. Artur Grzesik, "Konflikty wartości podstawowych w społeczeństwie polskim w opinii młodzieży akademickiej," in Malinowski and Seręga (eds.), *Konflikty społeczne w Polsce w okresie zmian systemowych*, vol. 2, p. 302. The survey was carried out in the 1995–1996 academic year at the teachers' college in Rzeszów.

12. Grabowska and Szawiel, *Budowanie demokracji*, p. 229.

13. The relative lack of significance of the cleavage between Catholics and the minuscule Protestant minority may be measured in the fact that the longest-serving prime minister in the Third Republic was Protestant Jerzy Buzek, at the head of a conservative coalition backed by the Catholic Church.

14. Bogna Wciórka, "Religijność Polaków na przełomie wieków," CBOS Komunikat no. 53 (2001). See http://www.cbos.com/pl/spiskom.pol/2001/kom053.

15. Centrum Badania Opinii Społecznej, "Religyjność Polaków w III RP" (March 1999). See http://www.cbos.pl/cbos_pl.htm.

16. Pracownia Badań Społecznych, "Instytucje i urzędy w Polsce, czerwiec 2000." The survey was carried out in March 2000. See http://www.pbssopot.com.pl/wyniki_instytucje062000.html.

17. Mirosława Grabowska, "Boskie i cesarskie: Religijność oraz stosunki między państwem a Kościołem a postawy i zachowania polityczne," in Radosław Markowski (ed.), *Wybory parlamentarne 1997: System partyjny, postawy polityczne, zachowania wyborcze.* Warsaw: Friedrich Ebert Stiftung, 1999, p. 181.

18. Beata Roguska and Bogna Wciórka, "Religijność i stosunek do kościoła," in Zagórski and Strzeszewski (eds.), *Nowa rzeczywistość,* pp. 193–194.

19. See, for example, Grabowska, "Boskie i cesarskie," pp. 167–202.

20. Tadeusz Szawiel, "Podział lewica-prawica w polityce oraz w szerszym kontekście kulturowym," in Grabowska and Szawiel, *Budowanie demokracji,* pp. 247–248. (This interpretation of the distances in average self-placement is ours.) Relying on different survey data, Herbert Kitschelt, Zdenka Mansfeldova, Radosław Markowski, and Gábor Tóka similarly identify positions on religious issues to have the greatest effect on left–right self-placement in Poland, in *Post-Communist Party Systems: Competition, Representation, and Inter-Party Cooperation.* Cambridge: Cambridge University Press, 1999, pp. 287–288.

21. Seymour M. Lipset and Stein Rokkan, "Cleavage Structures, Party Systems, and Voter Alignments: An Introduction," in Lipset and Rokkan (eds.), *Party Systems and Voter Alignments: Cross-National Perspectives.* New York: The Free Press, 1967, pp. 1–64.

22. Agnieszka Cybulska, Arkadiusz Sęk, Michał Wenzel, and Mariusz Wójcik, "Demokracja w praktyce," in Zagórski and Strzeszewski (eds.), *Nowa rzeczywistość,* p. 87.

23. Szawiel, "Podział lewica-prawica," p. 252.

24. Krystyna Faliszek, "Polska po roku 1989 w oczach mieszkańcow dawnego województwa katowickiego," in Malinowski and Seręga (eds.), *Konflikty społeczne w Polsce w okresie zmian systemowych,* vol. 1, p. 193.

25. Hubert Tworzecki, *Parties and Politics in Post–1989 Poland.* Boulder: Westview Press, 1996, p. 99.

26. Hubert Tworzecki, "The Political Consequences of the Cleavage Structure: The Bases of Party Support in Post–1989 Poland," doctoral dissertation, University of Toronto, Toronto, Canada, 1994, pp. 104–114.

27. Krzysztof Jasiewicz, "Portfel czy różaniec? Ekonomiczne i aksjologiczne determinanty zachowań wyborczych," in Markowski (ed.), *Wybory parlamentarne 1997,* p. 154.

28. Jasiewicz, "Portfel czy różaniec?" p. 161. Mirosława Grabowska also asserts that demographic and social attributes only weakly and selectively affect voting preferences; see her "Boskie i cesarskie," p. 199.

29. Jasiewicz, "Portfel czy różaniec?" p. 166.

30. Stephen Whitefield and Geoffrey Evans, "Electoral Politics in Eastern Europe: Social and Ideological Influences on Partisanship in Post-Communist Societies," in John

Higley, Jacek Pakulski, and Włodzimierz Wesołowski (eds.), *PostCommunist Elites and Democracy in Eastern Europe*. London: Macmillan, 1998, pp. 238–239.

31. "Religijność Polaków na przełomie wieków," CBOS Komunikat no. 53 (2001). See http://www.cbos.com/pl/spiskom.pol/2001/kom053.

32. Hubert Tworzecki, "Learning to Choose: Electoral Politics in East-Central Europe," unpublished manuscript (July 2000), pp. 173, 305.

33. Jasiewicz, "Portfel czy różaniec?" p. 167.

34. Tadeusz Szawiel, "Zróżnicowanie lewicowo-prawicowe i jego korelaty," in Markowski (ed.), *Wybory parlamentarne 1997*, p. 147. Data on self-identification are taken from this chapter. These patterns were also confirmed in an earlier study by Tworzecki, *Parties and Politics in Post–1989 Poland*, pp. 151–153.

35. Krzysztof Korzeniowski, "Profile psychologiczne electoratów najsilniejszych partii w wyborach w roku 1997," in Markowski (ed.), *Wybory parlamentarne 1997*, p. 218.

36. Jacek Wasilewski, Maciej Kopczyński, and Sławomir Szczur, "Stabilność zachowań wyborczych," in Markowski (ed.), *Wybory parlamentarne 1997*, p. 107.

37. During the electoral campaign the most damaging attack on Kwaśniewski was the film clip showing him laughing at an aide mocking the Pope. Poles were offended by Kwaśniewski's religious irreverence and his support in public opinion polls fell by up to 10 percent shortly afterward.

38. Reported in *Gazeta Wyborcza*, October 10, 2000, p. 4.

39. Wasilewski et al., "Stabilność zachowań wyborczych," p. 96. The data in this section, compiled in September–October 1997 by the Polish General Electoral Survey, are taken from this article. See especially Tables 1, 3, and 5.

40. Grabowska, "Boskie i cesarskie," p. 199.

41. Frances Millard, *Polish Politics and Society*. London: Routledge, 1999, p. 177.

42. Centrum Badania Opinii Społecznej (CBOS) as reported in *Gazeta Wyborcza* (October 3, 1994).

43. Andrzej Rychard, "Społeczeństwo w transformacji: Koncepcja i próba syntezy analiz," in Rychard and Federowicz (eds.), *Społeczeństwo w transformacji*, p. 7.

44. For a discussion of the congruence between a country's history of authoritarianism and communist totalitarianism, see Stephen White, John Gardner, and George Schopflin, *Communist Political Systems: An Introduction*. New York: St. Martin's, 1987, chap. 2.

45. See Hugh Seton-Watson, *The East European Revolution*. Boulder: Westview Press, 1983.

46. See Janina Frentzel-Zagórska, "Civil Society in Poland and Hungary," *Soviet Studies*, 42, no. 4 (October 1990), 759–777.

47. Grabowska and Szawiel, *Budowanie demokracji*, p. 91.

48. "Kto wolałby życ w PRL?" CBOS, komunikat no. 82 (May 2000). See http://www.cbos.com.pl.

49. Michal Strzeszewski and Michał Wenzel, "Postawy wobec demokracji," in Zagórski and Strzeszewski (eds.), *Nowa rzeczywistość*, p. 55.

50. Reported in *Business Central Europe* (December 1999/January 2000), p. 59.

51. Słomczyński et al., *Mental Adjustment to the Post-Communist System in Poland*, p. 188.

52. Słomczyński et al., *Mental Adjustment to the Post-Communist System in Poland*, p. 181.

53. CBOS survey. Cited by Jerzy J. Wiatr, "Social Conflicts and Democratic Stability: Poland in Comparative Perspective," in Jerzy J. Wiatr (ed.), *The Politics of Democratic Transformation: Poland After 1989.* Warsaw: Scholar Agency, 1993, pp. 14–15.

54. Robert M. Kunovich, "The 'Morning After': Political Participation During Systemic Transformation," in Kazimierz M. Słomczyński (ed.), *Social Patterns of Being Political.* Warsaw: IFiS Publishers, 2000, p. 141.

55. Centrum Badania Opinii Spolecznej, "Sense of Representation of Interests and Control of Public Affairs" (January 2000). See http://www.cbos.pl.

56. Strzeszewski and Wenzel, "Postawy wobec demokracji," p. 58.

57. Ronald Inglehart, Miguel Basanez, and Alejandro Moreno, *Human Values and Beliefs: A Cross-Cultural Sourcebook.* Ann Arbor: University of Michigan Press, 1998, pp. 30–31.

58. Krzysztof Pankowski and Beata Roguska, "Oceny zmian po roku '89," in Zagórski and Strzeszewski (eds.), *Nowa rzeczywistość*, p. 34.

59. Jerzy Bartkowski, "Public Opinion and 'Decommunization' in Poland," in Wiatr, *The Politics of Democratic Transformation,* pp. 80–107.

60. George Kolankiewicz and Ray Taras, "Poland: Socialism for Everyman?" in Archie Brown and Jack Gray (eds.), *Political Culture and Political Change in Communist States.* New York: Holmes and Meier, 1979, pp. 101–130. See also James R. Kluegel, David S. Mason, and Bernd Wegener (eds.), *Social Justice and Political Change: Public Opinion in Capitalist and Post Communist States.* Dordrecht: Aldine DeGruyter, 1995.

61. Inglehart et al., *Human Values and Beliefs*, p. 19. See Table V405 for country rankings.

62. Wojciech Zaborowski, "Social Structure, Political Affiliation, and Anti-Egalitarianism," in Słomczyński (ed.), *Social Patterns of Being Political*, p. 90.

63. Ireneusz Białecki and Bogdan W. Mach, "Orientacje spoleczno-ekonomiczne posłów na tle poglądów społeczeństwa," in Jacek Wasilewski and Włodzimierz Wesołowski (eds.), *Początek parlamentarnej elity: Posłowie kontraktowego Sejmu.* Warsaw: IFIS PAN, 1992, pp. 129–131.

64. Mary E. McIntosh and Martha Abele MacIver, "Coping with Freedom and Uncertainty: Public Opinion in Hungary, Poland, and Czechoslovakia 1989–1992," *International Journal of Public Opinion Research*, 4, no. 4 (Winter 1992), 381–385.

65. Sheri Kunovich, "Explaining Decline in Approval of Welfare State Policies," in Słomczyński (ed.), *Social Patterns of Being Political*, p. 110.

66. Słomczyński et al., *Mental Adjustment to the Post-Communist System in Poland*, p. 193.

67. Centrum Badania Opinii Społecznej, "Freedom and Equality in Social Life" (February 2000). See http://www.cbos.pl.

68. Główny Urząd Statystyczny, *Rocznik statystyczny rzeczypospolitej polskiej.* Warsaw: GUS, 2000, pp. XXXVIII–XXXIX, 142. In 1999 the Yearbook reported a total of 920 strikes involving 27,000 workers. However, 881 of them were by school workers that accounted for two-thirds of striking employees. A more accurate number of strikes in 1999, then, is 40—the strike action undertaken by employees in the educational sector plus 39 in other sectors (above all, manufacturing).

69. Grzegorz Ekiert and Jan Kubik, *Rebellious Civil Society: Popular Protest and Democratic Consolidation in Poland, 1989–1993.* Ann Arbor: University of Michigan Press, 1999, p. 109.

70. Ekiert and Kubik, *Rebellious Civil Society*, pp. 110–111.

71. Ekiert and Kubik, *Rebellious Civil Society*, p. 124.

72. Ekiert and Kubik, *Rebellious Civil Society*, pp. 194–195.

73. Ekiert and Kubik, *Rebellious Civil Society*, pp. 138–139.

74. Janusz Piegza, "Płaszczyzny podziałów społecznych lat dziewięćdziesiątych a wizje konfliktu w środowisku wiejskim," in Malinowski and Seręga (eds.), *Konflikty społeczne w Polsce w okresie zmian systemowych*, vol. 2, p. 54.

75. In 1999, 48 percent of respondents agreed that the Self-Defense League had brought the countryside more net benefits than losses; 41 percent said that of the PSL. Conversely, 27 percent said the League's actions were a net loss to the countryside; 34 percent said that of the PSL. Beata Roguska, "Opinie o polskim rolnictwie na tle ostatnich protestów," CBOS komunikat (March 1999), p. 7.

76. Zygmunt Seręga, "Rolnicy i rząd: Konflikt w społeczeństwie obywatelskim," in Malinowski and Seręga (eds.), *Konflikty społeczne w Polsce w okresie zmian systemowych*, vol. 1, p. 250.

77. Anna Stankiewicz-Mróz, "Miejsce strajku w sytuacji zbiorowych konfliktów pracy," in Malinowski and Seręga (eds), *Konflikty społeczne w Polsce w okresie zmian systemowych*, vol. 1, p. 284.

78. Kazimierz Doktór, "Od robotniczych do urzędniczych konfliktów—grupy interesów i kultura negocjacji," in Malinowski and Seręga (eds.), *Konflikty społeczne w Polsce w okresie zmian systemowych*, vol. 1, p. 253.

Chapter 6

1. Douglass C. North, *Institutions, Institutional Change, and Economic Performance.* Cambridge: Cambridge University Press, 1992, p. 25.

2. North, *Institutions*, p. 81.

3. North, *Institutions*, p. 81.

4. North, *Institutions*, p. 83.

5. James March and Johan Olsen, "The New Institutionalism: Organizational Factors in Political Life," *American Political Science Review*, 78, no. 3 (September 1984), 734–749.

6. See Richard F. Staar (ed.), *Transition to Democracy in Poland*, 2nd ed. New York: St. Martin's, 1997, chaps. 3, 5.

7. See Andrzej Rapaczyński, "Constitutional Politics in Poland: A Report on the Constitutional Committee of the Polish Parliament," in A. E. Dick Howard (ed.), *Constitution Making in Eastern Europe*. Washington, D.C.: Woodrow Wilson Center Press, 1993, pp. 93–131. Also published in *University of Chicago Law Review*, 58 (1991).

8. Stanisław Gebethner, "Political Institutions in the Process of Transition to a Postsocialist Formation," in Walter D. Connor and Piotr Płoszajski (eds.), *The Polish Road from Socialism.* Armonk, N.Y.: M. E. Sharpe, 1992, p. 241.

9. Mała konstytucja z komentarzem, czyli Ustawa Konstytucyjna z dnia 17 października 1992 r. Warsaw: Wydawnictwo AWA, 1992, p. 38.

10. Mała konstytucja, p. 38. We translate *zreszają* as "organize," though a more literal translation would employ "associate."

11. Mała konstytucja, pp. 38–39. Although the word "private" (*prywatne*) is not found in Articles 6 and 7, it can be inferred from use of the term "property" (*własność*).

12. Maria Kruk, "Co to znaczy 'Mała' konstytucja?" in Mała konstytucja, p. 4.

13. Three English-language sources for the constitutional debate in Poland are *East European Constitutional Review, East European Case Reporter,* and *Journal of Constitutional Law in Eastern and Central Europe.*

14. For an analysis of the role of the presidency, see Krzysztof Jasiewicz, "Poland: Walesa's Legacy to the Presidency," in Ray Taras (ed.), *Postcommunist Presidents.* Cambridge: Cambridge University Press, 1997, pp. 130–167.

15. Juan Linz and Arturo Valenzuela, *Presidential or Parliamentary Democracy: Does It Make a Difference?* Baltimore: Johns Hopkins University Press, 1992. For a review of choices available for institutionalizing democracy, see Larry Diamond and Marc F. Plattner (eds.), *The Global Resurgence of Democracy.* Baltimore: Johns Hopkins University Press, 1993, chaps. 8–17.

16. Matthew Shugart and John M. Carey, *Presidents and Assemblies.* Cambridge: Cambridge University Press, 1992.

17. Seymour Martin Lipset, *Political Man: The Social Bases of Politics.* Baltimore: Johns Hopkins University Press, 1981.

18. Juan J. Linz, "Crisis, Breakdown, and Reequilibration," in Juan J. Linz and Alfred Stepan (eds.), *The Breakdown of Democratic Regimes,* vol. 1. Baltimore: Johns Hopkins University Press, 1978, pp. 20–22.

19. Adam Przeworski, *Democracy and the Market.* Cambridge: Cambridge University Press, 1992, p. 37.

20. Alfred Stepan and Cindy Skach, "Constitutional Frameworks and Democratic Consolidation," *World Politics,* 46, no. 4 (1993), 19.

21. Juan Linz, "The Perils of Presidentialism," in Arend Lijphart (ed.), *Parliamentary Versus Presidential Government.* New York: Oxford University Press, 1992, p. 126.

22. Peter Taylor and Arend Lijphart, "Proportional Tenure Versus Proportional Representation," *European Journal of Political Research,* 13 (1985).

23. André Blais and Stéphane Dion, "Electoral Systems and the Consolidation of New Democracies," in Diane Ethier (ed.), *Democratic Transition and Consolidation in Southern Europe, Latin America, and Southeast Asia.* Basingstoke, England: Macmillan, 1990, p. 259.

24. Larry Diamond, Seymour Martin Lipset, and Juan Linz, "Building and Sustaining Democratic Government in Developing Countries: Some Tentative Findings," *World Affairs,* 50, no. 1 (Summer 1987), 5–19.

25. Arend Lijphart, *Democracy in Plural Societies.* New Haven: Yale University Press, 1977. In a later work, the same writer avers that electoral systems that promote two or three strong parties within a parliamentary—as opposed to presidential—democracy make for political stability; Lijphart, *Electoral Systems and Party Systems.* Oxford: Oxford University Press, 1994.

26. For the text of the 1997 constitution, see "Konstytucja Rzeczypospolitej Polskiej," *Rzeczpospolita* (April 3, 1997).

27. See Stanisław Gebethner, "Zasady jawności I publicznej kontroli finansowania prezydenckiej kampanii wyborczej w świetle znowelizowanej ustawy o wyborze Prezydenta Rzeczypospolitej," in Marcin Walecki (ed.), *Finansowanie polityki: Wybory, pieniądze, partie polityczne.* Warsaw: Wydawnictwo Sejmowe, 2000, pp. 179–186.

28. Each party would receive a certain number of seats for a constituency based on (1) the number of seats available multiplied by votes received and (2) the product divided by total votes cast. Remainders were used to distribute the balance of the seats.

29. *Ordynacja wyborcza do Sejmu i Senatu Rzeczypospolitej Polskiej.* Gdańsk: Temida, 1993. To be eligible for national seats, a party had to win seats in at least five separate constituencies or have polled 5 percent of the national vote. Alliances between party lists were permitted.

30. On the law, see Frances Millard, "The Polish Parliamentary Elections of October 1991," *Soviet Studies,* 44, no. 5 (1992), 838–840.

31. Curiously, no such affirmative action provision for minorities obtained in the ordinance for local elections where it might have even greater significance.

32. See Jarosław Kurski, *Lech Wałęsa: Democrat or Dictator?* Boulder: Westview Press, 1993.

33. Andrew Michta, "The Presidential–Parliamentary System," in Staar (ed.), *Transition to Democracy in Poland,* p. 58.

34. A. E. Dick Howard, "Constitutional Reform," in Staar (ed.), *Transition to Democracy in Poland,* pp. 102–103.

35. See Jacek Kurski and Piotr Semka, *Lewy czerwcowy.* Warsaw: Editions Spotkania, 1992.

36. An excellent source for both theoretical and empirical studies of the various forms of capitalist transformation is the journal *Post-Communist Economies* (previously known as *Communist Economies*).

37. In another typology, John E. Elliot distinguishes between market and managed capitalism and between socialism and communism. See his *Comparative Economic Systems.* Belmont, Calif.: Wadsworth, 1985. Martin C. Schnitzer focuses on modified market economies, mixed ones, and centrally planned ones. See his *Comparative Economic Systems.* Cincinnati: South-Western, 1987.

38. John Gray, "From Post-Communism to Civil Society: The Reemergence of History and the Decline of the Western Model," in Ellen Frankel Paul, Fred D. Miller Jr., and Jeffrey Paul (eds.), *Liberalism and the Economic Order.* Cambridge: Cambridge University Press, 1993, p. 37.

39. Gray, "From Post-Communism to Civil Society," p. 41.

40. Gray, "From Post-Communism to Civil Society," p. 42.

41. Gray, "From Post-Communism to Civil Society," p. 46.

42. Peter Evans, "The State as Problem and Solution: Predation, Embedded Autonomy, and Structural Change," in Stephan Haggard and Robert R. Kaufman (eds.), *The Politics of Economic Adjustment: International Constraints, Distributive Conflicts, and the State.* Princeton: Princeton University Press, 1992, p. 181.

43. For an excellent overview, see Leszek Balcerowicz, Barbara Błaszczyk, and Marek Dąbrowski, "The Polish Way to the Market Economy 1989–1995," in Wing Thye Woo, Stephen Parker, and Jeffrey D. Sachs (eds.), *Economies in Transition: Comparing Asia and Eastern Europe.* Cambridge: MIT Press, 1997, pp. 144–145.

44. Jozef M. van Brabant, *Privatizing Eastern Europe: The Role of Markets and Ownership in the Transition.* Dordrecht: Kluwer Academic Publishers, 1992, p. 148.

45. Van Brabant, *Privatizing Eastern Europe,* pp. 156–157. See his bibliography for a comprehensive list of works on the subject.

46. Van Brabant, *Privatizing Eastern Europe,* p. 158. The citation is from Anders Aslund, "Principles of Privatization," in Laszlo Csaba (ed.), *Systemic Change and Stabilization in Eastern Europe.* Aldershot, England: Dartmouth, 1991, p. 22.

47. Kazimierz Z. Poznański, "Property Rights Perspective on Evolution of Communist-Type Economies," in Kazimierz Z. Poznański (ed.), *Constructing Capitalism: The Reemergence of Civil Society and Liberal Economy in the Post-Communist World.* Boulder: Westview Press, 1992, pp. 76–77.

48. Van Brabant, *Privatizing Eastern Europe*, pp. 211–213.

Chapter 7

1. Lena Kolarska-Bobińska, "Wstęp," in Kolarska-Bobińska (ed.), *Polska Eurodebata.* Warsaw: Instytut Spraw Publicznych, 1999, p. 7.

2. For an informative collection of essays on this, see Karl Cordell (ed.), *Poland and the European Union.* London: Routledge, 2000.

3. Maria Gerszewska and Jacek Kucharczyk, "Oczekiwania Polaków wobec negocjacji z Unią Europejską," in Kolarska-Bobińska (ed.), *Polska Eurodebata*, p. 30. Respondents could identify two issues.

4. CBOS, "Opinie o integracji Polski z Unią Europejską," March 2001. See http://www.cbos.com.pl/spiskom.pol/2001/KOM036/kom036.HTM.

5. Lena Kolarska-Bobińska and Jacek Kucharczyk, "Negocjacje z Unią Europejską— opinie Polaków," in Kolarska-Bobińska (ed.), *Polska Eurodebata*, p. 16, Table 1. Eighteen percent of respondents answered that it was hard to say.

6. CBOS, "Opinie o integracji Polski z Unia Europejska," March 2001. See http://www.cbos.com.pl/spiskom.pol/2001/kom036/kom036.HTM.

7. Janusz Tazbir, "Serce z zachodniej strony," *Gazeta Wyborcza*, January 22–23, 1994.

8. Centrum Badania Opinii Publicznej, "Poles on the Relations Between Poland and Russia and the Political Situation in Russia" (April 2000). See http://www.cbos.pl.

9. Aleksandra Jasińska-Kania, "Zmiany postaw Polaków wobec róznych narodów i państw," in Jasińska-Kania, *Bliscy i dalecy*, vol. 2. Warsaw: Instytut Socjologii, Uniwersytet Warszawski, 1992, pp. 220, 231–232.

10. German Information Center, "German Support for the Reform Process in the Former Soviet Union and the Countries of Central, Southeastern and Eastern Europe," *Focus On . . .* , March 1995, p. 4. The remaining aid was to cover the transfer ruble balance, or repayment of Poland's debt to the former German Democratic Republic. The exchange rate used in all calculations was DM 1.40 to US$1.

11. Sarah Meiklejohn Terry, "Prospects for Regional Cooperation," in Richard F. Staar, *Transition to Democracy in Poland*, 2nd ed. New York: St. Martin's, 1997, pp. 215–216.

12. On the interaction between democratization and economic change, see Adam Przeworski, "Economic Reforms, Public Opinion, and Political Institutions: Poland in the Eastern European Perspective," in Luis Carlos Bresser Pereira, José Maria Maravall, and Adam Przeworski (eds.), *Economic Reforms in New Democracies: A Social-Democratic Approach.* Cambridge: Cambridge University Press, 1993, pp. 132–198. On the relationship between democracy and the capitalist state, see Graeme Duncan (ed.), *Democracy and the Capitalist State.* Cambridge: Cambridge University Press, 1989.

13. Leslie Elliot Armijo, Thomas J. Biersteker, and Abraham F. Lowenthal, "The Problems of Simultaneous Transitions," *Journal of Democracy*, 5, no. 4 (October 1994), 162. On the situation when social change is factored in, see Claus Offe, "Capitalism by Democratic Design? Democratic Theory Facing the Triple Transition in East Central Europe," *Social Research*, 58 (Winter 1991), 865–892.

14. Stephan Haggard and Robert R. Kaufman, "Economic Adjustment and the Prospects for Democracy," in Haggard and Kaufman (eds.), *The Politics of Economic Adjustment: International Constraints, Distributive Conflicts, and the State*. Princeton: Princeton University Press, 1992, pp. 319–320.

15. Haggard and Kaufman, "Economic Adjustment and the Prospects for Democracy," p. 324.

16. Haggard and Kaufman, "Economic Adjustment and the Prospects for Democracy," p. 341. See also their *The Political Economy of Democratic Transitions*. Princeton: Princeton University Press, 1995, and "The Challenges of Consolidation," *Journal of Democracy*, 5, no. 4 (October 1994), 5–16.

17. Haggard and Kaufman, "Economic Adjustment and the Prospects for Democracy," p. 349.

18. Leszek Balcerowicz, "Democracy Is No Substitute for Capitalism," *Eastern European Economies*, 32, no. 2 (March-April 1994), 42.

19. Leszek Balcerowicz, "Understanding Postcommunist Transitions," *Journal of Democracy*, 5, no. 4 (October 1994), 75–89.

20. Jeffrey Sachs, "Western Financial Assistance and Russia's Reforms," in Shafiqul Islam and Michael Mandelbaum (eds.), *Making Markets: Economic Transformation in Eastern Europe and the Post-Soviet States*. New York: Council on Foreign Relations Press, 1993, p. 146.

21. Adam Przeworski, "Economic Reforms, Public Opinion, and Political Institutions: Poland in the Eastern European Perspective," in Pereira et al. (eds.), *Economic Reforms in New Democracies*, p. 183.

22. Przeworski, "Economic Reforms," p. 180.

23. Przeworski, "Economic Reforms," p. 176.

24. Jan Winiecki, "The Sources of Economic Success: Eliminating Barriers to Human Entrepreneurship—A Hayekian Lesson in Spontaneous Development," in Winiecki (ed.), *Five Years After June: The Polish Transformation 1989–1994*. London: Centre for Research into Post-Communist Economics, 1996, p. 41.

25. Jean-Joseph Boillot, *Situation économique des pays d'Europe centrale et orientale en 1993 et perspectives 1994*. Paris: Centre français du commerce extérieur, 1994.

26. Henryk Domański, Krystyna Janicka, Anna Firkowska-Mankiewicz, and Anna Titkow, "Społeczeństwo bez reguł," in Andrzej Rychard and Michał Federowicz (eds.), *Społeczeństwo w transformacji: Ekspertyzy i studia*. Warsaw: IFiS PAN, 1993, p. 164.

27. Domański et al., "Społeczeństwo bez reguł," p. 155.

28. Domański et al., "Społeczeństwo bez reguł," pp. 156–157.

29. Douglass C. North, *Institutions, Institutional Change, and Economic Performance*. Cambridge: Cambridge University Press, 1992, p. 83.

30. North, *Institutions*, p. 99.

31. North, *Institutions*, p. 140.

32. See Lena Kolarska-Bobińska (ed.), *Druga fala polskich reform*. Warsaw: Instytut Spraw Publicznych, 1999.

33. Stanisława Golinowska, "Wdrażanie nowego systemu emerytalnego," in Lena Kolarska-Bobińska (ed.), *Cztery reformy: Od koncepcji do realizacji*. Warsaw: Instytut Spraw Publicznych, 2000, p. 82.

34. Elżbieta Cichocka, "Reforma systemu opieki zdrowotnej: Główne założenia," in Kolarska-Bobińska, *Cztery reformy*, p. 139.

35. For an uncritical account of the supposedly public-serving nature of reforms under Buzek, see Krzysztof Konarzewski, "Uwagi o polskiej reformie systemu oswiaty," in Kolarska-Bobińska, *Cztery reformy*, pp. 211–220. For public opinion data critical of reforms, see Macieja Fałkowska, "Polacy o reformach społecznych: Akceptacja, przyzwolenie czy odrzuczenie," in the same volume, pp. 285–313.

36. Jacek Kurczewski, *The Resurrection of Rights in Poland.* Oxford: Clarendon Press, 1993, p. 449.

37. In addition, several other millionaires "temporarily" left the country. This information is based on the annual survey "100 Najbogatszych Polaków" ("The 100 Richest Poles") conducted by the weekly newsmagazine *Wprost.* See *Wprost,* supplement, June 20, 1993.

38. See Jacek Tarkowski, "Old and New Patterns of Corruption in Poland and the USSR," *Telos,* 80 (1989), 51–63.

39. For an account of the twenty biggest scandals, see Wojciech Markiewicz and Piotr Sarżyński, "Wielcy podejrzani," *Polityka,* no. 31 (July 31, 1993).

40. For a comparative study of corruption in postcommunist states, see Leslie T. Holmes and Wojciech Roszkowski (eds.), *Changing Rules: Polish Political and Economic Transformation in Comparative Perspective.* Warsaw: Institute of Political Studies, 1997, Part II.

41. Jacek Wasilewski, "Normatywna integracja polskiej elity transformacyjnej," in Henryk Domański, Antonina Ostrowska, and Andrzej Rychard (eds.), *Jak żyją Polacy.* Warsaw: Wydawnictwo IFiS PAN, 2000, pp. 83–84.

42. Introductions to this subject include Michael Thompson, Richard Ellis, and Aaron Wildavsky, *Cultural Theory.* Boulder: Westview Press, 1990. Also, Peter L. Berger, *The Capitalist Revolution: Fifty Propositions About Prosperity, Equality, and Liberty.* New York: Basic Books, 1986. Of course, Max Weber was among the first to describe the cultural context of capitalism.

43. Robert D. Putnam, *Making Democracy Work: Civic Traditions in Modern Italy.* Princeton: Princeton University Press, 1993, p. 157.

44. Putnam, *Making Democracy Work,* p. 183.

45. Giuseppe di Palma, "Why Democracy Can Work in Eastern Europe," in Larry Diamond and Marc F. Plattner (eds.), *The Global Resurgence of Democracy.* Baltimore: Johns Hopkins University Press, 1993, p. 266.

Selected Bibliography
(English works only)

Adamski, Wladyslaw, ed. *Societal Conflict and Systemic Change.* Warsaw: IFiS, 1993.

Ascherson, Neil. *The Polish August.* Harmondsworth, Middlesex: Penguin, 1983.

Bell, Janice M., *Political Economy of Reform in Post-Communist Poland.* Northhampton, England: Edward Elgar, 2001.

Connor, Walter D., and Piotr Płoszajski, eds. *The Polish Road from Socialism.* Armonk, N.Y.: M. E. Sharpe, 1992.

Cordell, Karl, ed. *Poland and the European Union.* London: Routledge, 2000.

Ekiert, Grzegorz, and Jan Kubik. *Rebellious Civil Society: Popular Protest and Democratic Control in Poland, 1989–1993.* Ann Arbor: University of Michigan Press, 1999.

Frentzel-Zagórska, Janina, and Jacek Wasilewski, eds. *The Second Generation of Democratic Elites in Central and Eastern Europe.* Warsaw: INP, 2000.

Hicks, Barbara. *Environmental Politics: A Social Movement Between Regime and Politics.* New York: Columbia University Press, 1996.

Holmes, Leslie, and Wojciech Roszkowski, eds. *Changing Rules: Polish Political and Economic Transformation in Comparative Perspective.* Warsaw: INP, 1997.

Kamiński, Bartłomiej. *The Collapse of State Socialism: The Case of Poland.* Princeton: Princeton University Press, 1991.

Kloczowski, Jerzy. *A History of Polish Christianity.* Cambridge: Cambridge University Press, 2000.

Kołodko, Grzegorz. *From Shock to Therapy.* Oxford: Oxford University Press, 2000.

Markowski, Radosław, and Edmund Wnuk-Lipiński, eds. *Transformative Paths in Central and Eastern Europe.* Warsaw: INS, 2001.

Michnik, Adam. *Letters from Freedom: Post–Cold War Realities and Perspectives.* Berkeley: University of California Press, 1998.

Millard, Frances. *Polish Politics and Society.* London: Routledge, 1999.

Podgórecki, Adam. *Polish Society.* New York: Praeger, 1994.

Sachs, Jeffrey. *Poland's Jump to the Market Economy.* Cambridge: MIT Press, 1994.

Sanford, George. *Poland: The Conquest of History*. Reading, Berkshire: Gordon & Breach, 1999.

Słomczyński, Kazimierz M. *Social Patterns of Being Political*. Warsaw: IFiS, 2000.

Staar, Richard F., ed. *Transition to Democracy in Poland*, 2nd ed. New York: St. Martin's, 1998.

Staniszkis, Jadwiga. *Post-communism: The Emerging Enigma*. Warsaw: INS, 1999.

Tworzecki, Hubert. *Parties and Politics in Post-1989 Poland*. Boulder: Westview Press, 1996.

Wnuk-Lipiński, Edmund, ed. *After Communism: A Multidisciplinary Approach to Radical Social Change*. Warsaw: ISP PAN, 1995.

Wydra, Harald. *Continuities in Poland's Permanent Transition*. Houndmills, Hertfordshire: Palgrave, 2000.

Index

1989 election, *see* June 1989 elections
1990 elections, presidential, 96–97
1991 elections, parliamentary, 97–98, 133
1993 elections, parliamentary, 133–134
1995 elections, presidential, 98–100
1997 elections, parliamentary, 100–101,
    114–115
2000 elections, presidential, 102
2001 elections, parliamentary, 102–103

abortion
    ideology of UP on, 130
    image of Catholic Church and,
        142–143
age
    business elites and, 107
    political elites and, 105
    political generation gap, 155–157
    presidential vote and, 167–168
    support for systemic change and, 173
AK (Home Army), 27
Alliance of the Democratic Left. *see* SLD
    (Alliance of the Democratic Left)
ancestry, Polish, 2
anti-Semitism
    genocide in W. W. II, 25–26
    interwar Poland and, 22
Armia Krajowa (AK), 27
Ascherson, Neil, 61–62
AWS (Solidarity Electoral Action)
    1997 parliamentary election, 100–101,
        134
    2000 presidential election, 102
    2001 parliamentary election, 103, 135

coalition with UW, 101
corruptibility of, 136
formation of, 134
lack of unity in, 134–135, 138
voter turnout and, 165–170

Balcerowicz, Leszek
    achievements of, 237
    AWS – UW coalition and, 101
    economic plan development, 235–236
Bartoszcze, Roman, 96–97
Batory, Stefan, 8
BBWR (Nonparty Bloc for Cooperation
    with the Government), 24
Belarus, Polish relations with, 228–229
Bielecki, Jan Krzysztof, 201–202
broadcast media, 149
business lobbies, political influence of,
    145–148
Buzek, Jerzy, 101, 201–202

Camp of National Unity, 24
campaign financing, presidential elections,
    197
capitalist system, *see* economic inequality,
    Third Republic
Catholic Church, pre-transition
    communist era pluralism, 32
    democratic policy intervention, 36
    eighteenth century influence, 6–7
    nineteenth century messianism, 17–18
    public attitudes towards, 46–47
    resistance to communism, 53–54
    roundtable talks, 73

279